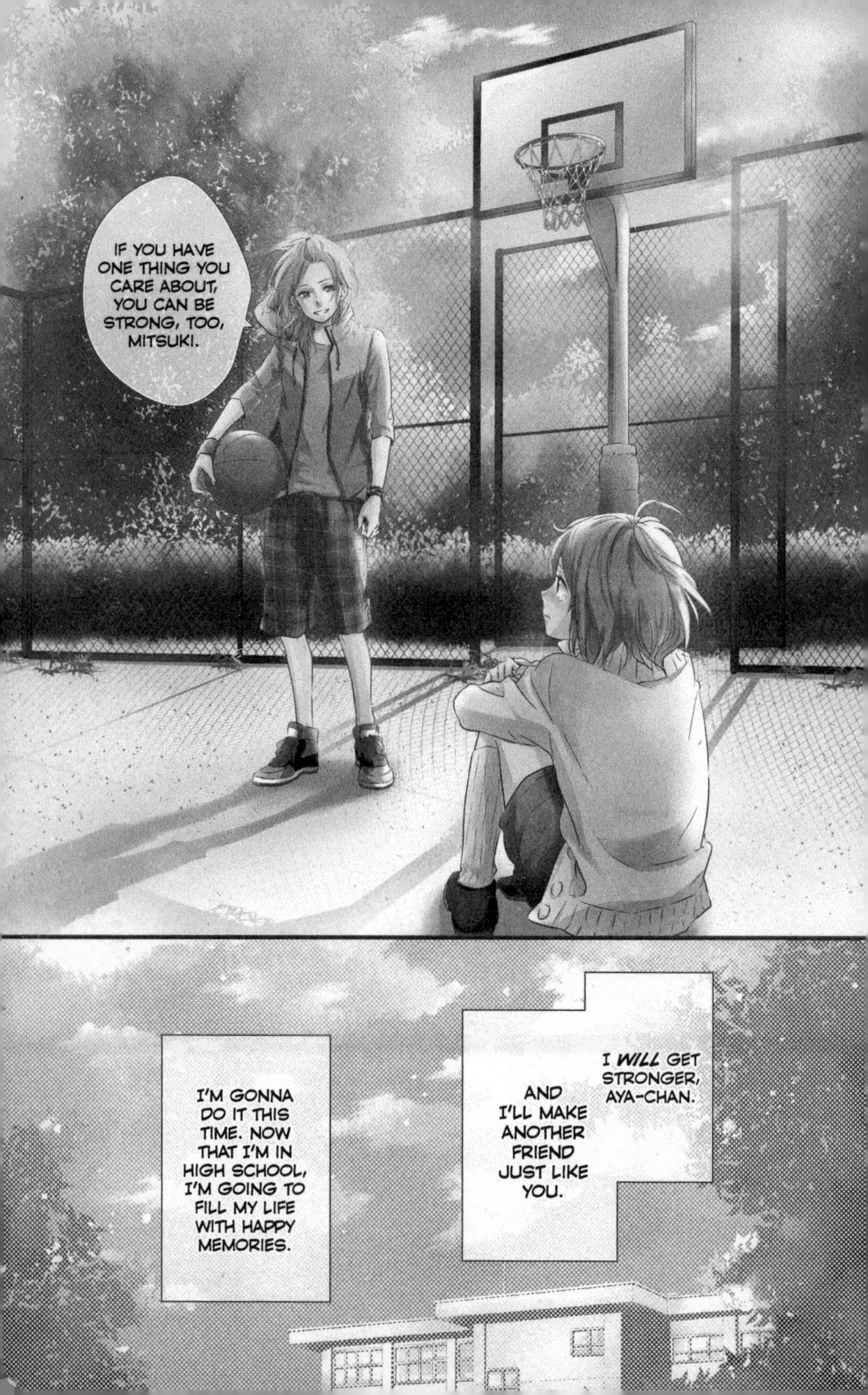
IF YOU HAVE ONE THING YOU CARE ABOUT, YOU CAN BE STRONG, TOO, MITSUKI.
I *WILL* GET STRONGER, AYA-CHAN.
AND I'LL MAKE ANOTHER FRIEND JUST LIKE YOU.
I'M GONNA DO IT THIS TIME. NOW THAT I'M IN HIGH SCHOOL, I'M GOING TO FILL MY LIFE WITH HAPPY MEMORIES.

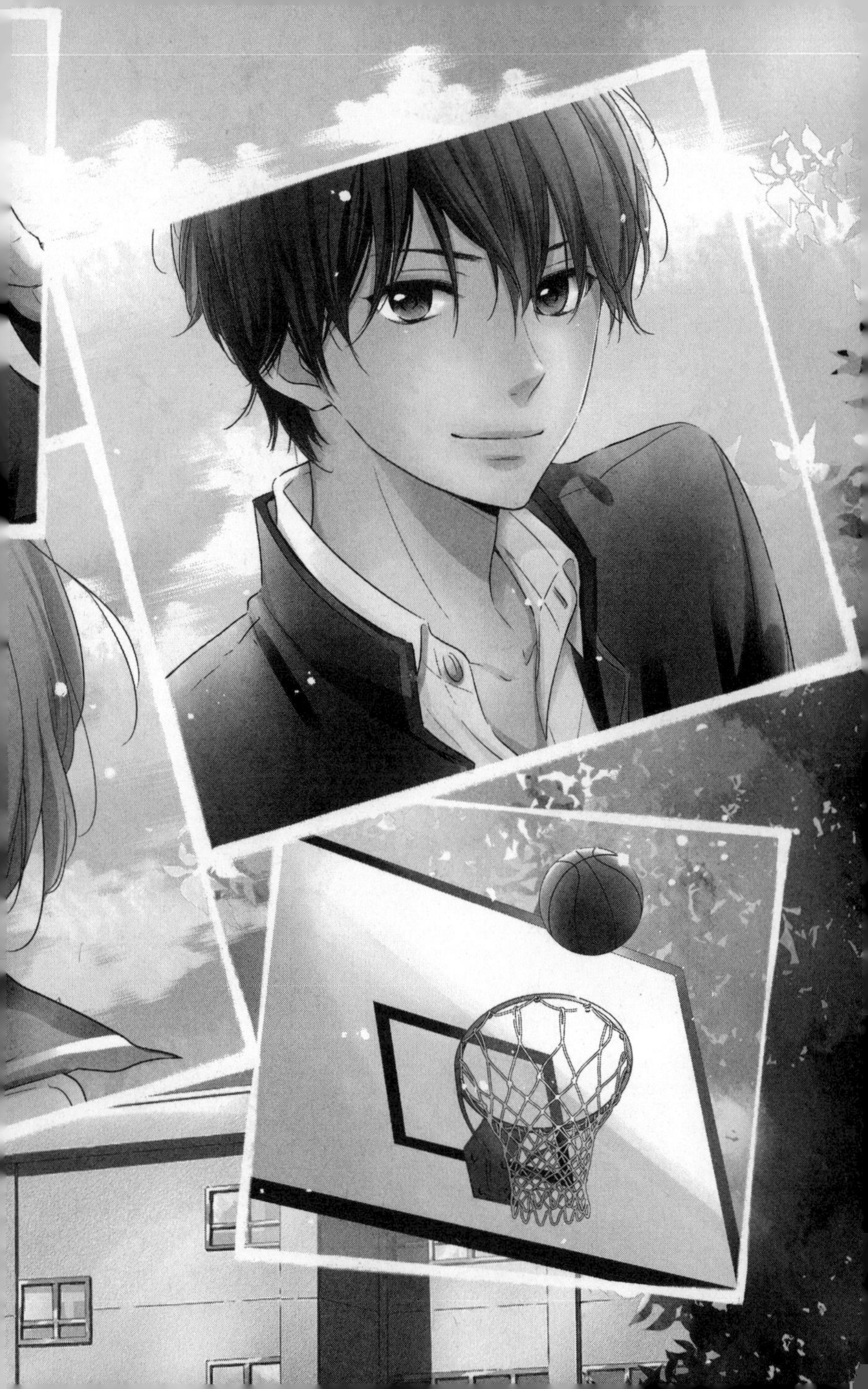

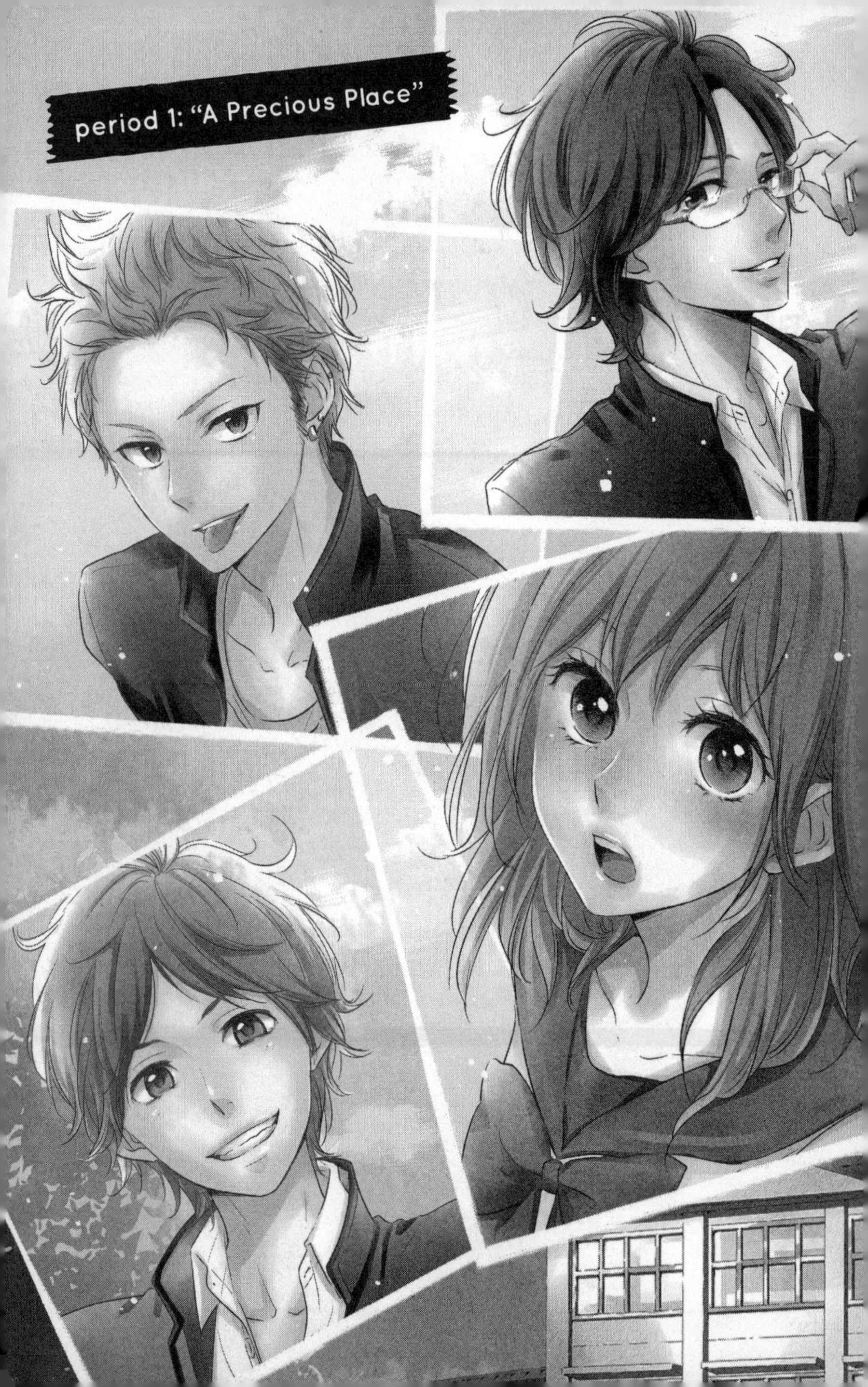
period 1: "A Precious Place"

Hello! Anashin here.
Thank you so much for picking up Volume 1 of *Waiting for Spring*. There are a lot of characters in this story, so I would be very happy if you can find at least one that you like. And if you can have fun reading the series, nothing would fill my life with more joy...
Now then, the story is about to begin. I hope you enjoy it.

But before that, time for a...
Silhouette Pop Quiz!!

Who and
who could they be?

Answer on
page 52.

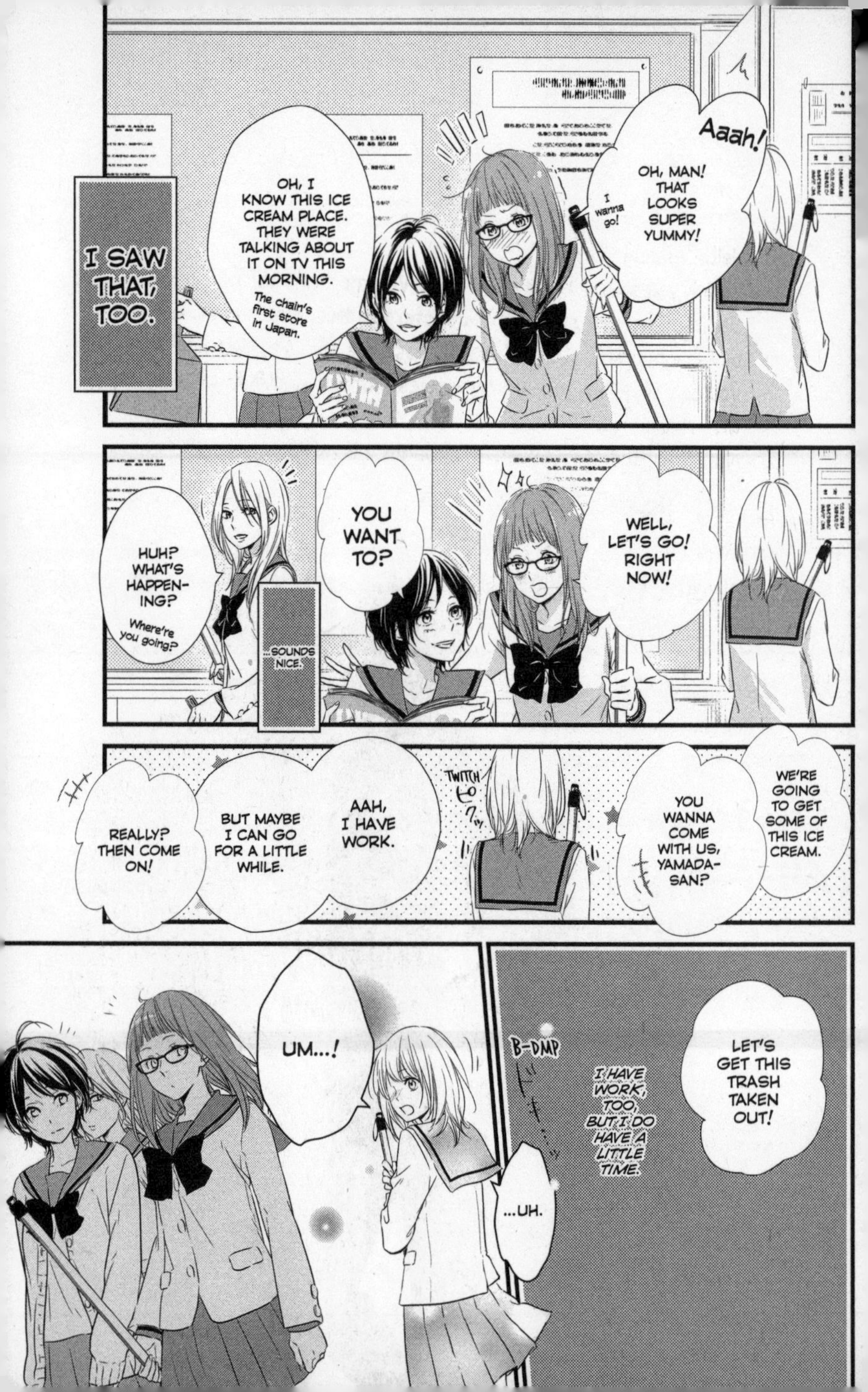
Aaah!
OH, MAN! THAT LOOKS SUPER YUMMY!
I wanna go!
OH, I KNOW THIS ICE CREAM PLACE. THEY WERE TALKING ABOUT IT ON TV THIS MORNING.
The chain's first store in Japan.
I SAW THAT, TOO.
WELL, LET'S GO! RIGHT NOW!
YOU WANT TO?
...SOUNDS NICE.
HUH? WHAT'S HAPPEN-ING?
Where're you going?
WE'RE GOING TO GET SOME OF THIS ICE CREAM.
YOU WANNA COME WITH US, YAMADA-SAN?
TWITCH
AAH, I HAVE WORK.
BUT MAYBE I CAN GO FOR A LITTLE WHILE.
REALLY? THEN COME ON!
LET'S GET THIS TRASH TAKEN OUT!
B-DMP
I HAVE WORK, TOO, BUT I DO HAVE A LITTLE TIME.
UM...!
...UH.

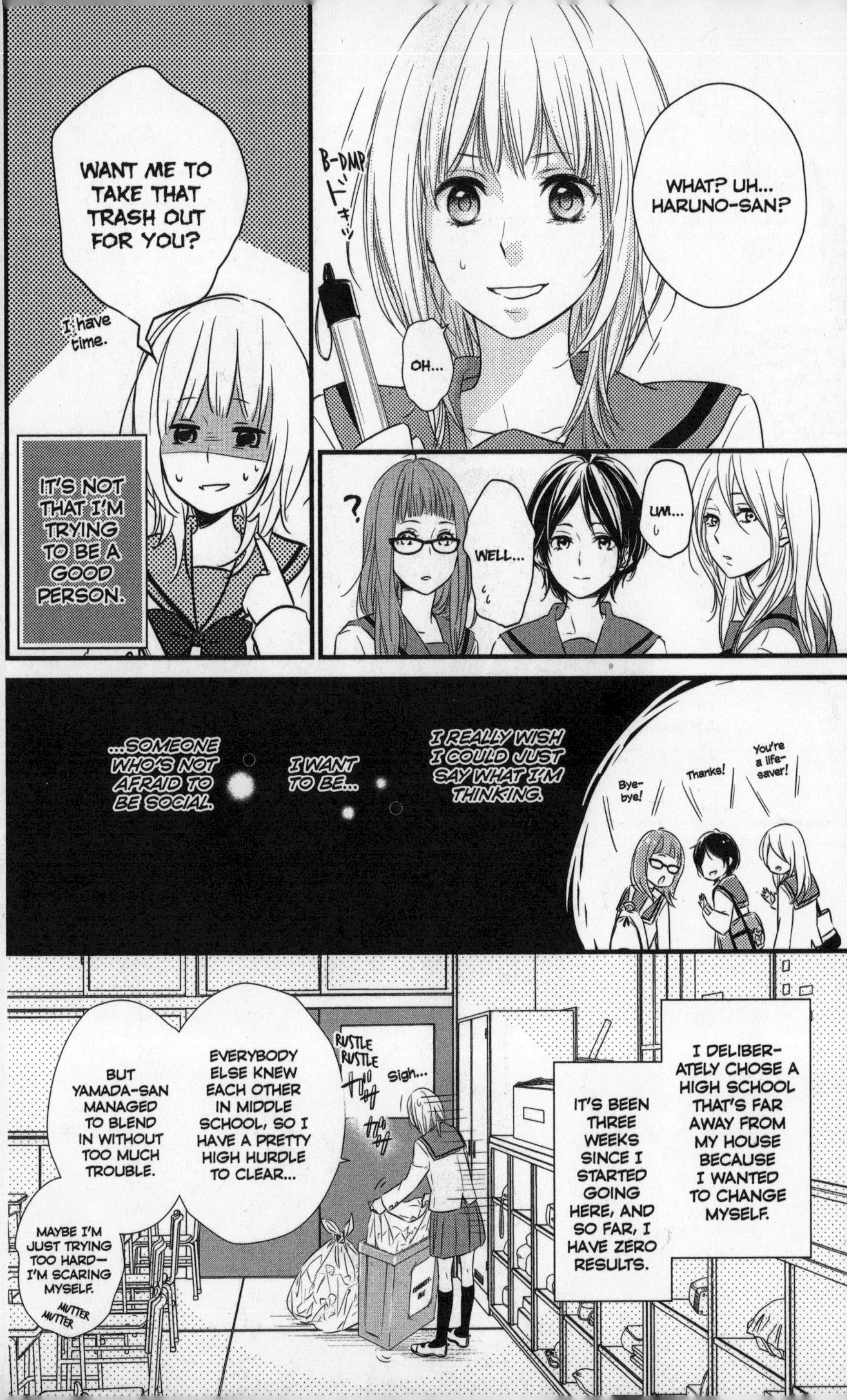
WHAT? UH... HARUNO-SAN?
B-DMP
ドキッ
OH...
UM...
WELL...
?
WANT ME TO TAKE THAT TRASH OUT FOR YOU?
I have time.
IT'S NOT THAT I'M TRYING TO BE A GOOD PERSON.
You're a life-saver!
Thanks!
Bye-bye!
I REALLY WISH I COULD JUST SAY WHAT I'M THINKING.
I WANT TO BE...
...SOMEONE WHO'S NOT AFRAID TO BE SOCIAL.
I DELIBER-ATELY CHOSE A HIGH SCHOOL THAT'S FAR AWAY FROM MY HOUSE BECAUSE I WANTED TO CHANGE MYSELF.
IT'S BEEN THREE WEEKS SINCE I STARTED GOING HERE, AND SO FAR, I HAVE ZERO RESULTS.
RUSTLE RUSTLE
Sigh...
EVERYBODY ELSE KNEW EACH OTHER IN MIDDLE SCHOOL, SO I HAVE A PRETTY HIGH HURDLE TO CLEAR...
BUT YAMADA-SAN MANAGED TO BLEND IN WITHOUT TOO MUCH TROUBLE.
MAYBE I'M JUST TRYING TOO HARD—I'M SCARING MYSELF.
MUTTER MUTTER

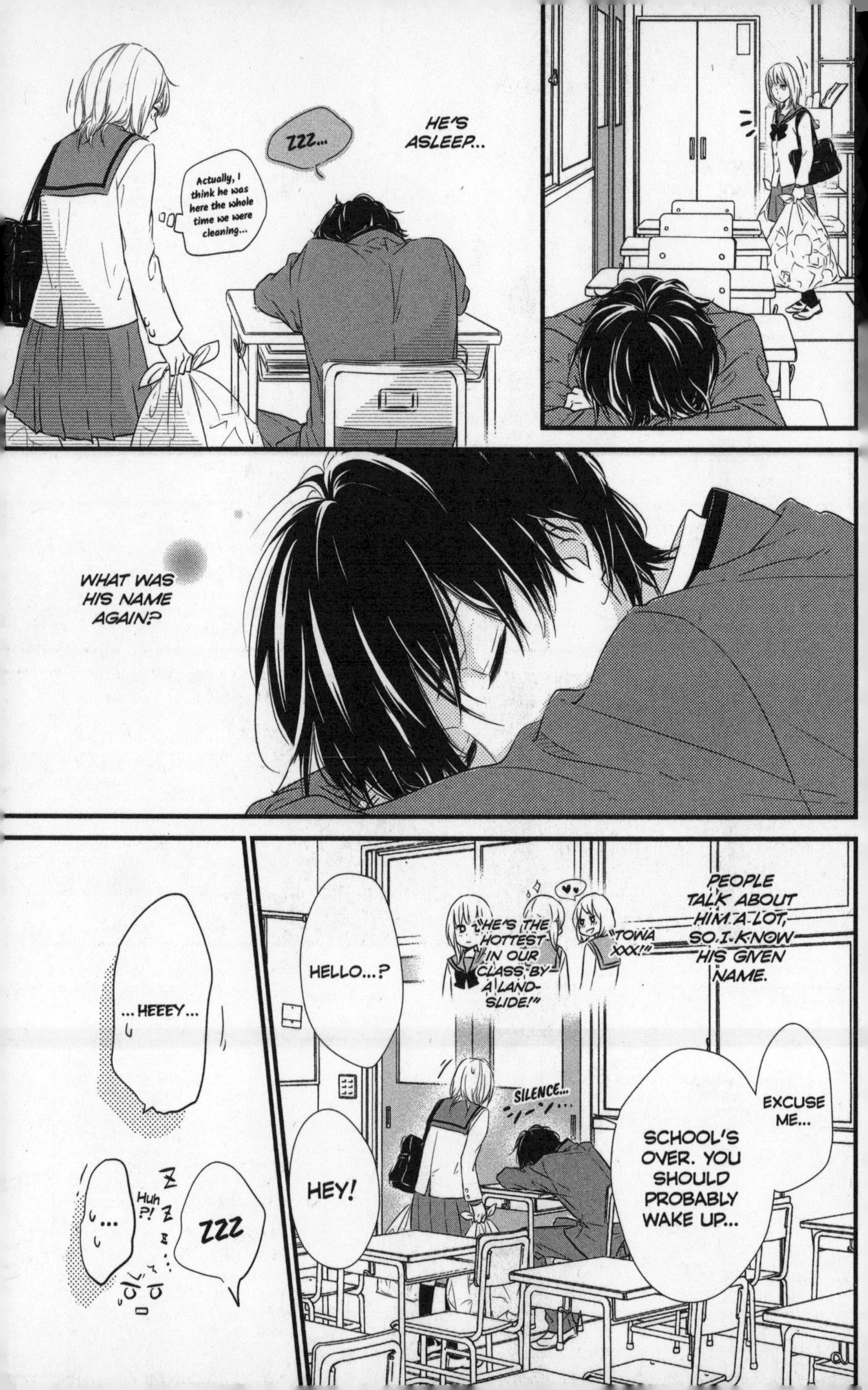
HE'S ASLEEP...
ZZZ...
Actually, I think he was here the whole time we were cleaning...
WHAT WAS HIS NAME AGAIN?
PEOPLE TALK ABOUT HIM A LOT, SO I KNOW HIS GIVEN NAME.
"TOWA XXX!"
"HE'S THE HOTTEST IN OUR CLASS BY A LANDSLIDE!"
HELLO...?
EXCUSE ME...
SCHOOL'S OVER. YOU SHOULD PROBABLY WAKE UP...
SILENCE...
HEY!
...HEEEY...
ZZZ
Huh?!
...

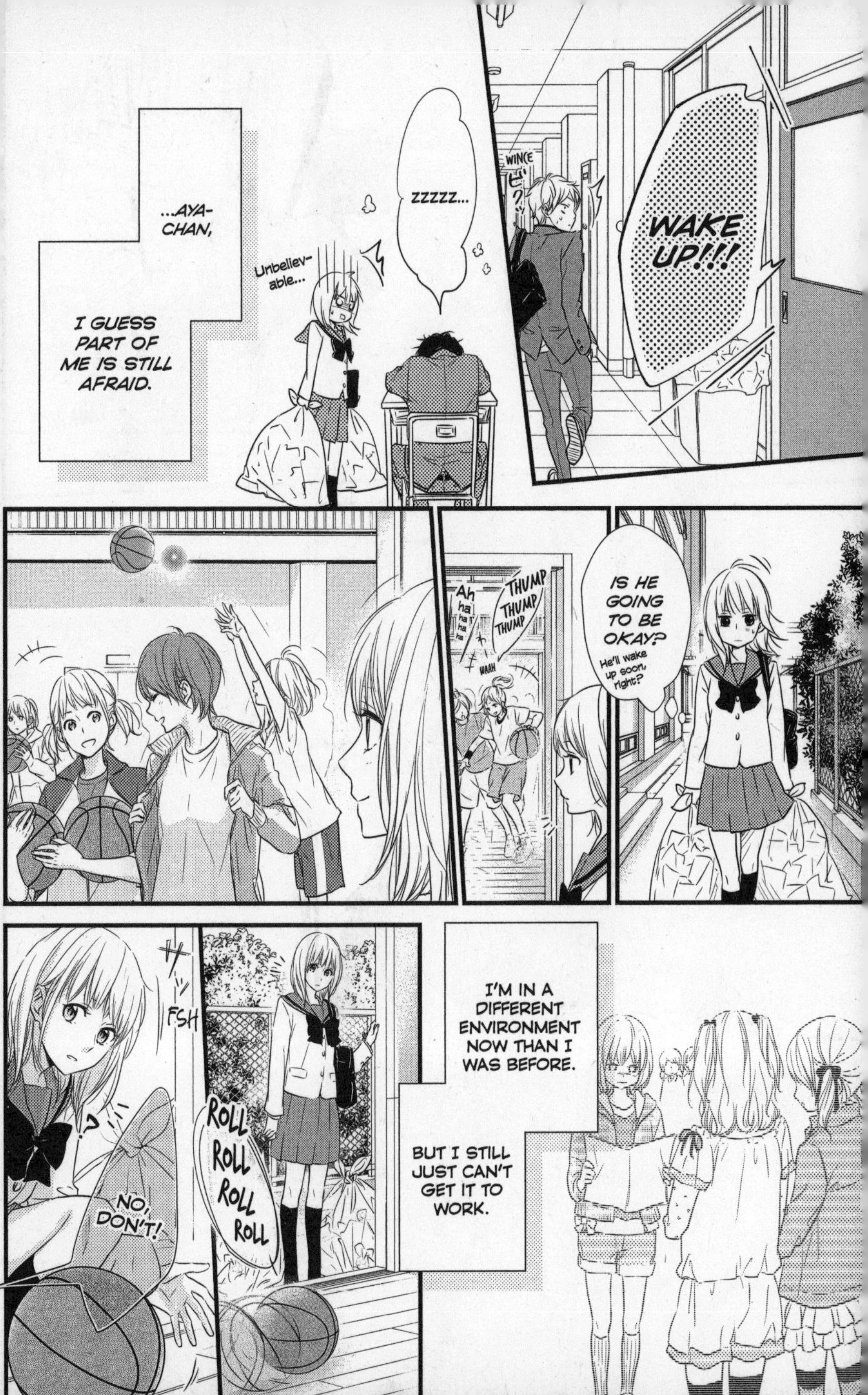
WAKE UP!!!
WINCE
ZZZZZ...
Unbeliev-able...
...AYA-CHAN,
I GUESS PART OF ME IS STILL AFRAID.
IS HE GOING TO BE OKAY?
He'll wake up soon, right?
THUMP THUMP THUMP
Ah ha ha ha ha
WAAH
I'M IN A DIFFERENT ENVIRONMENT NOW THAN I WAS BEFORE.
BUT I STILL JUST CAN'T GET IT TO WORK.
ROLL ROLL ROLL ROLL
FSH
NO, DON'T!

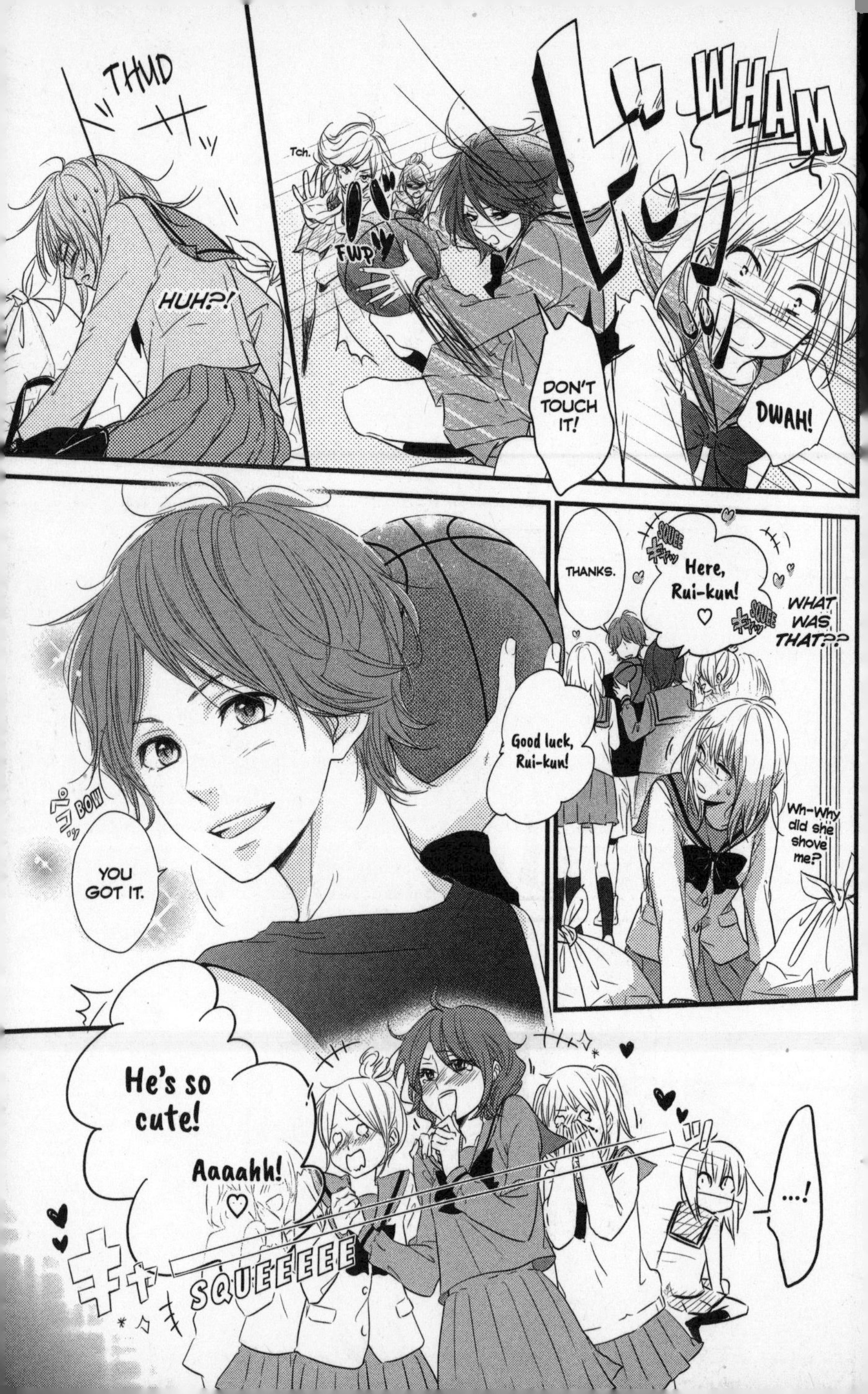
WHAM
DWAH!
DON'T TOUCH IT!
Tch.
FWP
THUD
HUH?!
SQUEE
Here, Rui-kun! ♡
SQUEE
WHAT WAS THAT??
THANKS.
Wh-Why did she shove me?
Good luck, Rui-kun!
BOW
YOU GOT IT.
...!
He's so cute!
Aaaahh! ♡
SQUEEEEEE

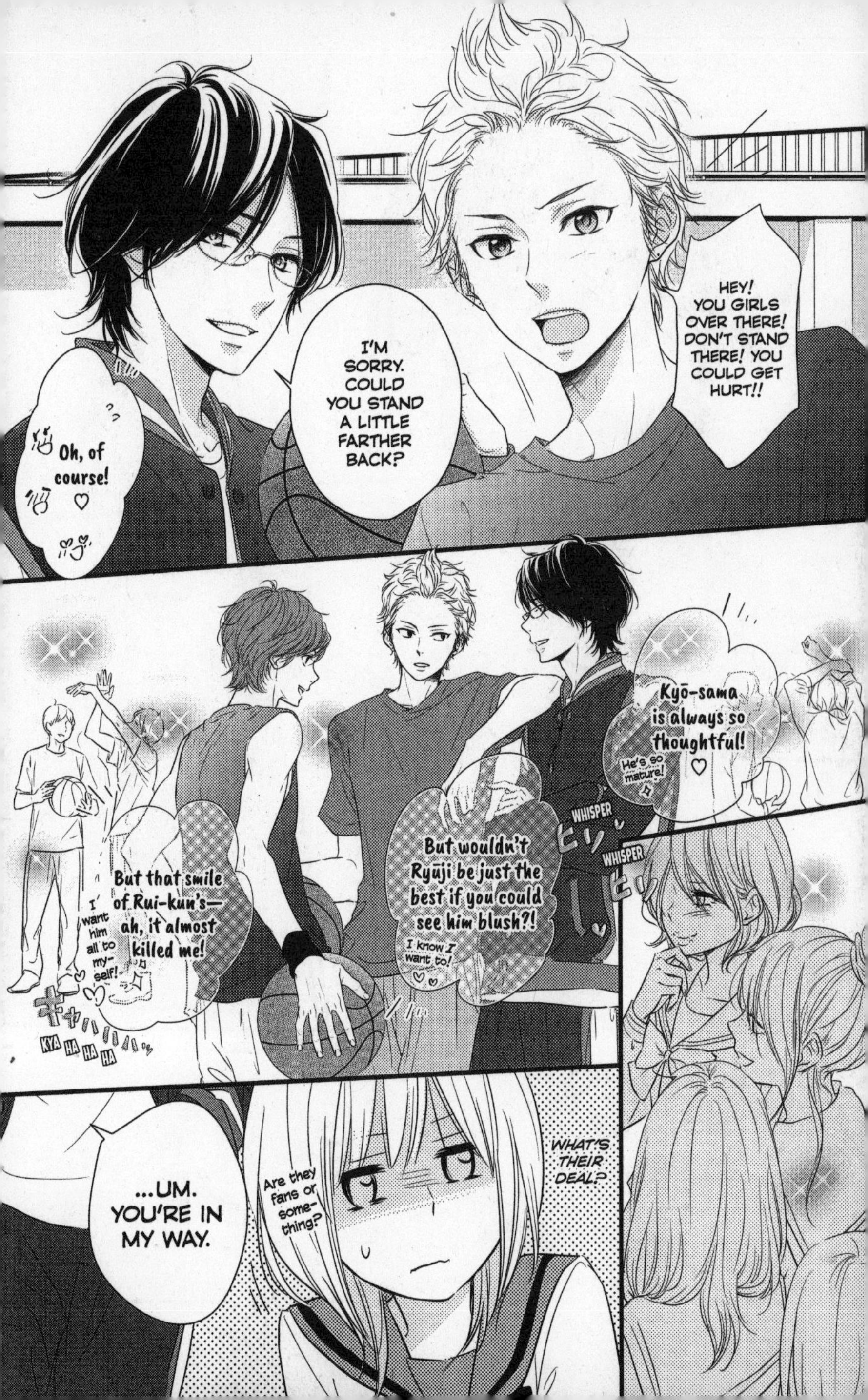
HEY! YOU GIRLS OVER THERE! DON'T STAND THERE! YOU COULD GET HURT!!
I'M SORRY. COULD YOU STAND A LITTLE FARTHER BACK?
Oh, of course! ♡
Kyō-sama is always so thoughtful! ♡
He's so mature!
WHISPER
WHISPER
But wouldn't Ryūji be just the best if you could see him blush?!
I know I want to!
But that smile of Rui-kun's—ah, it almost killed me!
I want him all to my-self!
KYA HA HA HA
WHAT'S THEIR DEAL?
Are they fans or some-thing?
...UM. YOU'RE IN MY WAY.

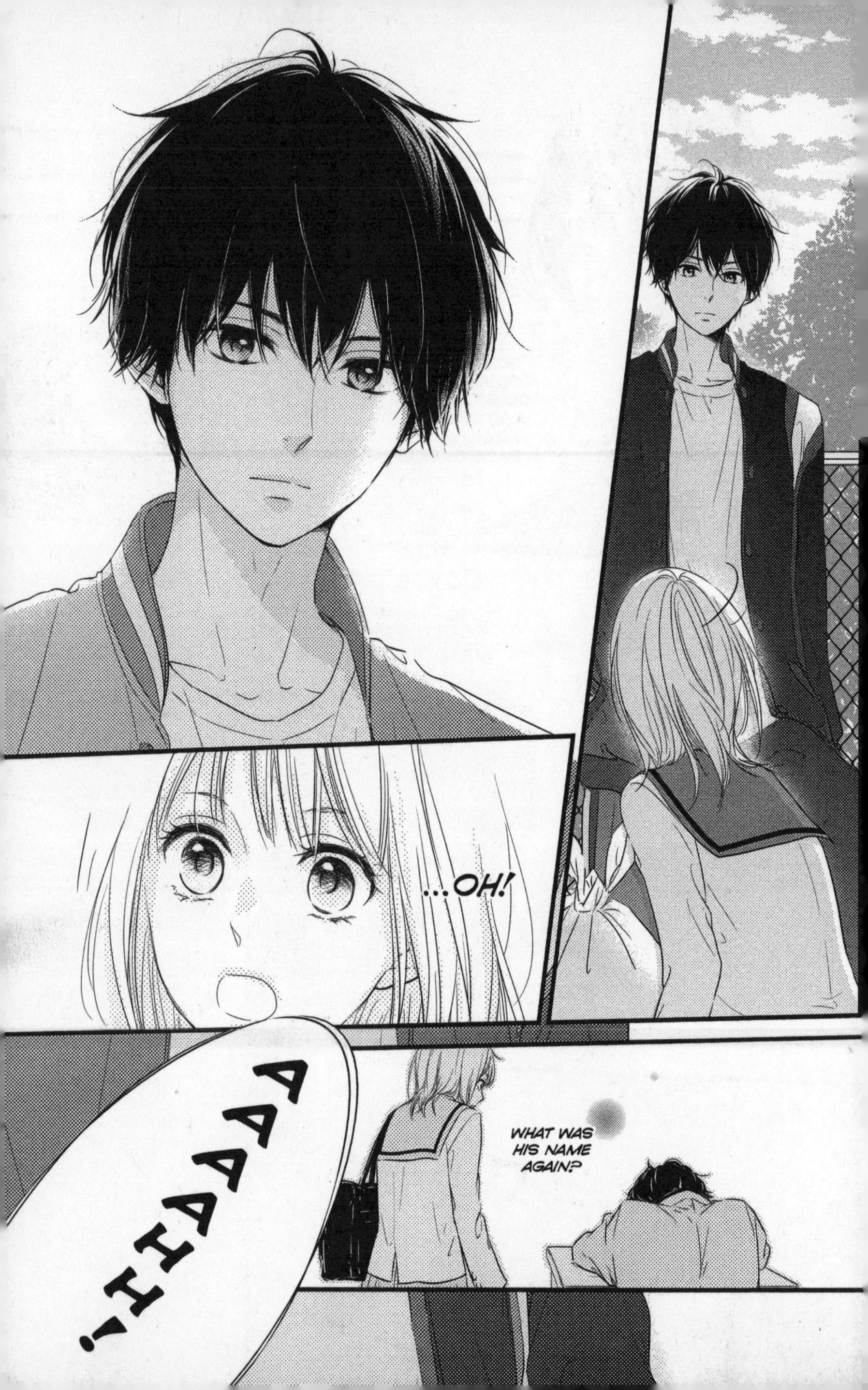
...OH!
AAAAAAHH!
WHAT WAS HIS NAME AGAIN?

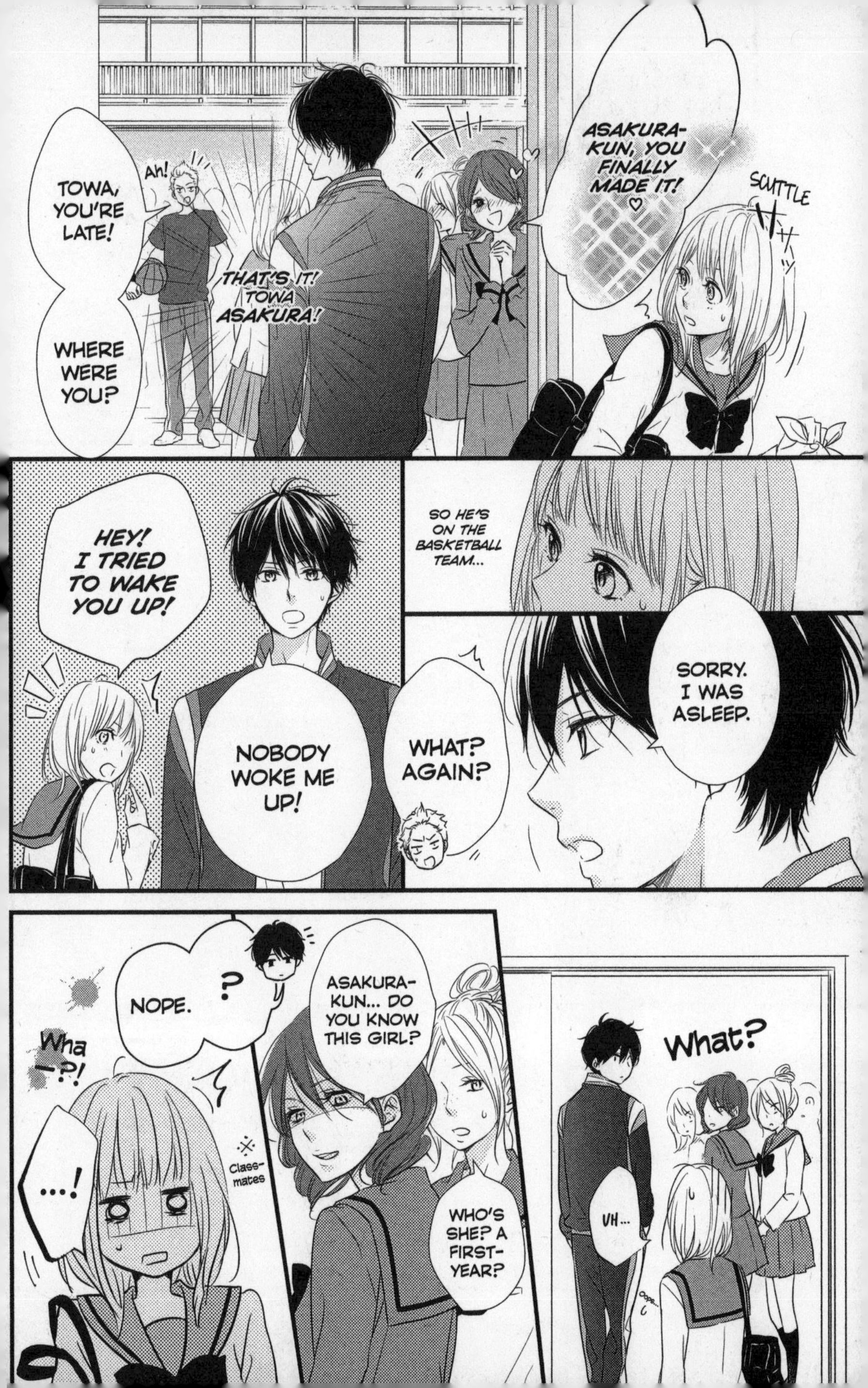
SCUTTLE
ASAKURA-KUN, YOU FINALLY MADE IT! ♡
THAT'S IT! TOWA ASAKURA!
Ah!
TOWA, YOU'RE LATE!
WHERE WERE YOU?
SO HE'S ON THE BASKETBALL TEAM...
SORRY. I WAS ASLEEP.
WHAT? AGAIN?
NOBODY WOKE ME UP!
HEY! I TRIED TO WAKE YOU UP!
What?
UH...
Oops...
ASAKURA-KUN... DO YOU KNOW THIS GIRL?
WHO'S SHE? A FIRST-YEAR?
※ Classmates
?
NOPE.
Wha-?!
...!

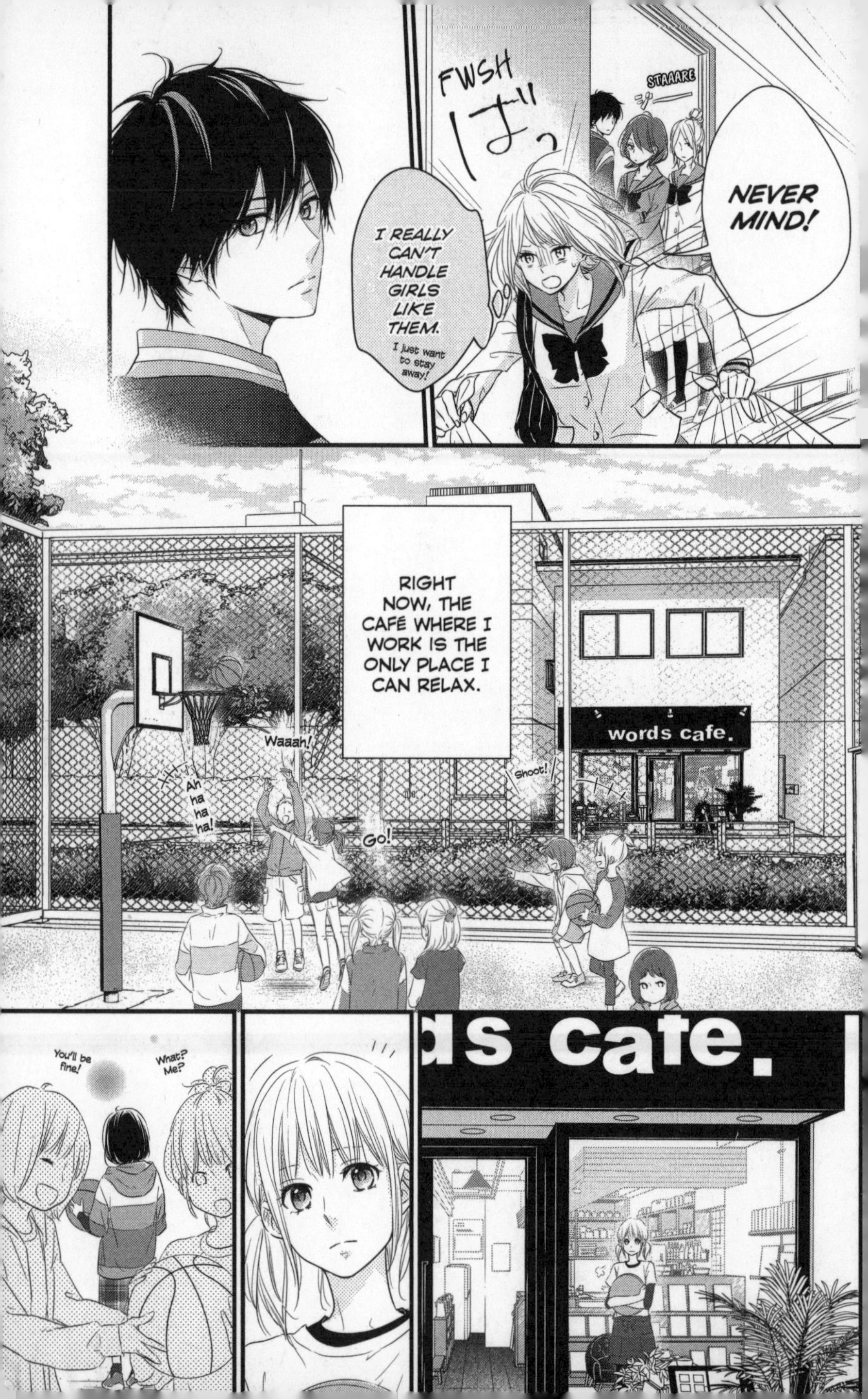
NEVER MIND!
STAAARE
FWSH
ばっ
I REALLY CAN'T HANDLE GIRLS LIKE THEM.
I just want to stay away!
RIGHT NOW, THE CAFÉ WHERE I WORK IS THE ONLY PLACE I CAN RELAX.
words cafe.
Shoot!
Go!
Waaah!
Ah ha ha ha!
ds cafe.
What? Me?
You'll be fine!

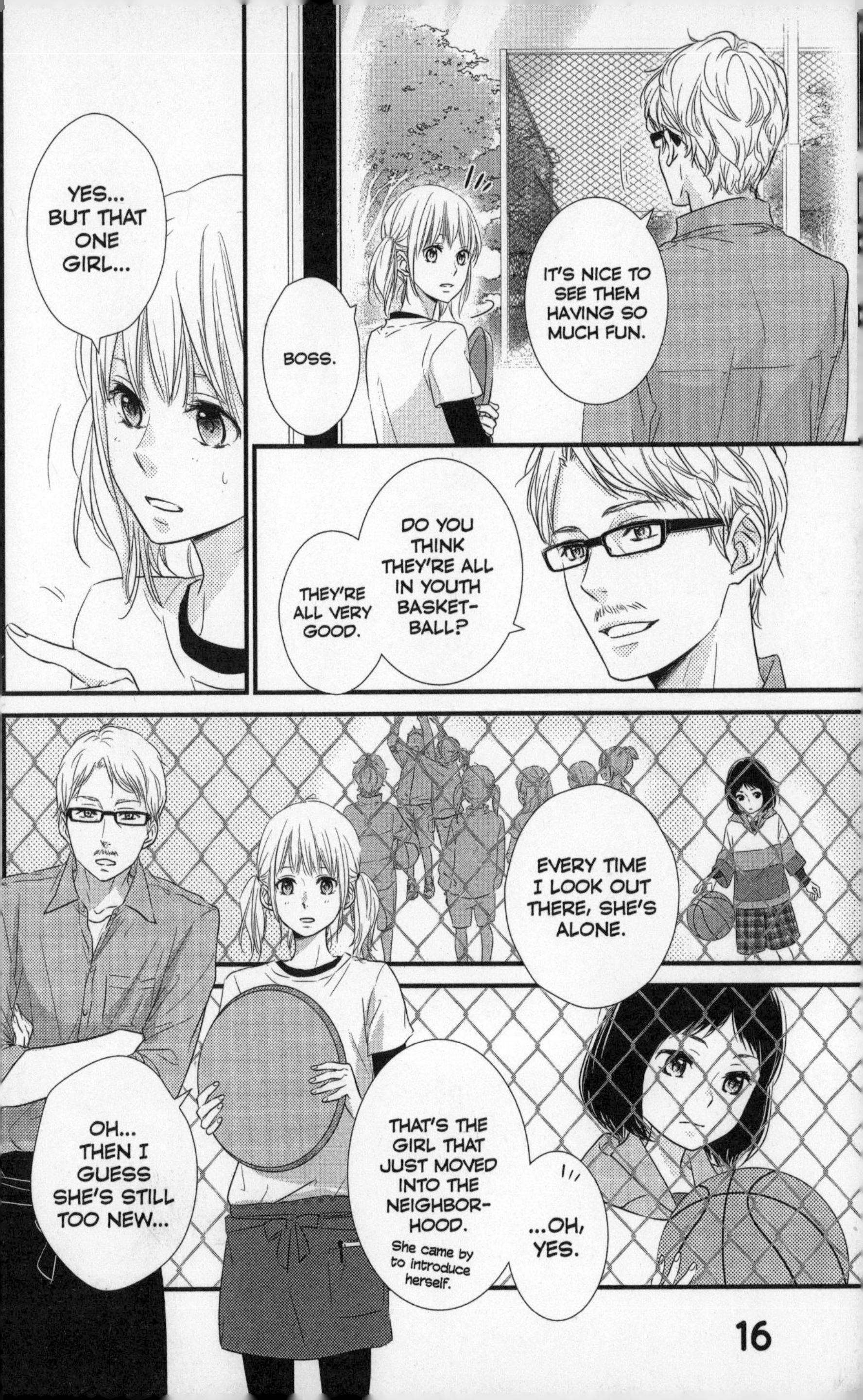
IT'S NICE TO SEE THEM HAVING SO MUCH FUN.
BOSS.
DO YOU THINK THEY'RE ALL IN YOUTH BASKET-BALL?
THEY'RE ALL VERY GOOD.
YES... BUT THAT ONE GIRL...
EVERY TIME I LOOK OUT THERE, SHE'S ALONE.
...OH, YES.
THAT'S THE GIRL THAT JUST MOVED INTO THE NEIGHBOR-HOOD.
She came by to introduce herself.
OH... THEN I GUESS SHE'S STILL TOO NEW...

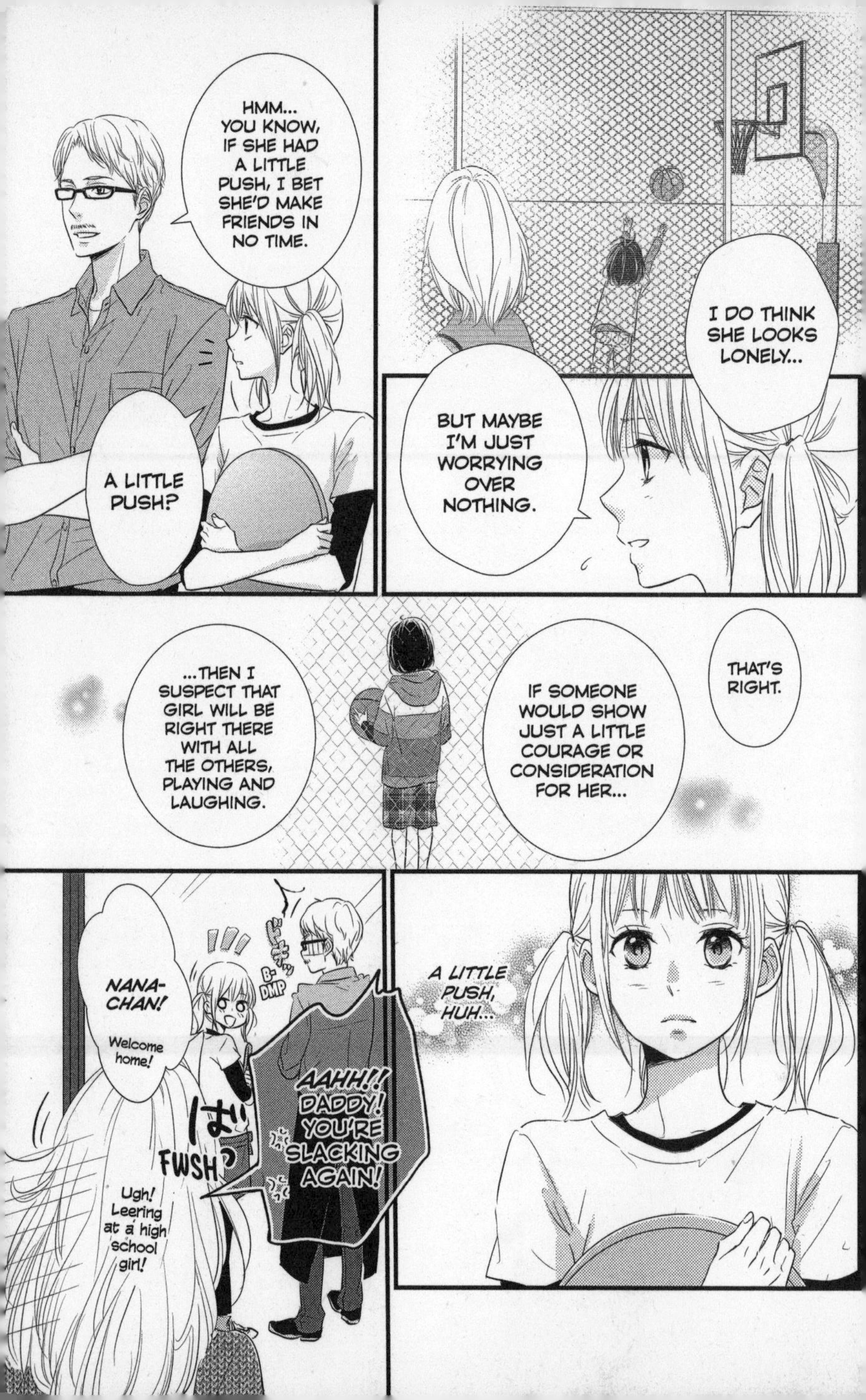
I DO THINK SHE LOOKS LONELY...
BUT MAYBE I'M JUST WORRYING OVER NOTHING.
HMM... YOU KNOW, IF SHE HAD A LITTLE PUSH, I BET SHE'D MAKE FRIENDS IN NO TIME.
A LITTLE PUSH?
THAT'S RIGHT.
IF SOMEONE WOULD SHOW JUST A LITTLE COURAGE OR CONSIDERATION FOR HER...
...THEN I SUSPECT THAT GIRL WILL BE RIGHT THERE WITH ALL THE OTHERS, PLAYING AND LAUGHING.
A LITTLE PUSH, HUH...
NANA-CHAN!
Welcome home!
B-DMP
AAHH!! DADDY! YOU'RE SLACKING AGAIN!
FWSH
Ugh! Leering at a high school girl!

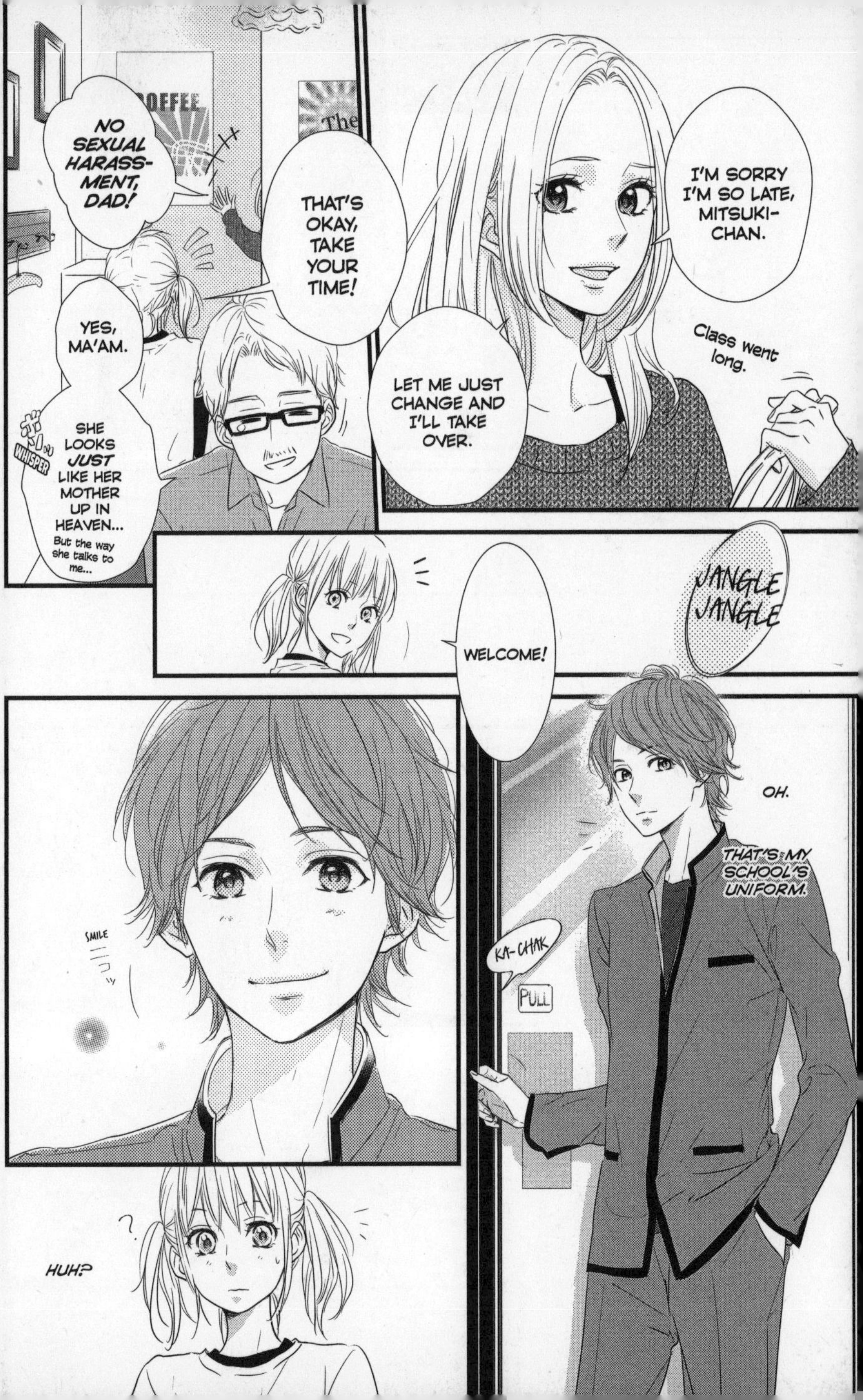
I'M SORRY I'M SO LATE, MITSUKI-CHAN.
Class went long.
LET ME JUST CHANGE AND I'LL TAKE OVER.
THAT'S OKAY, TAKE YOUR TIME!
NO SEXUAL HARASS-MENT, DAD!
YES, MA'AM.
WHISPER
SHE LOOKS JUST LIKE HER MOTHER UP IN HEAVEN...
But the way she talks to me...
JANGLE JANGLE
WELCOME!
OH.
THAT'S MY SCHOOL'S UNIFORM.
KA-CHAK
PULL
SMILE
HUH?

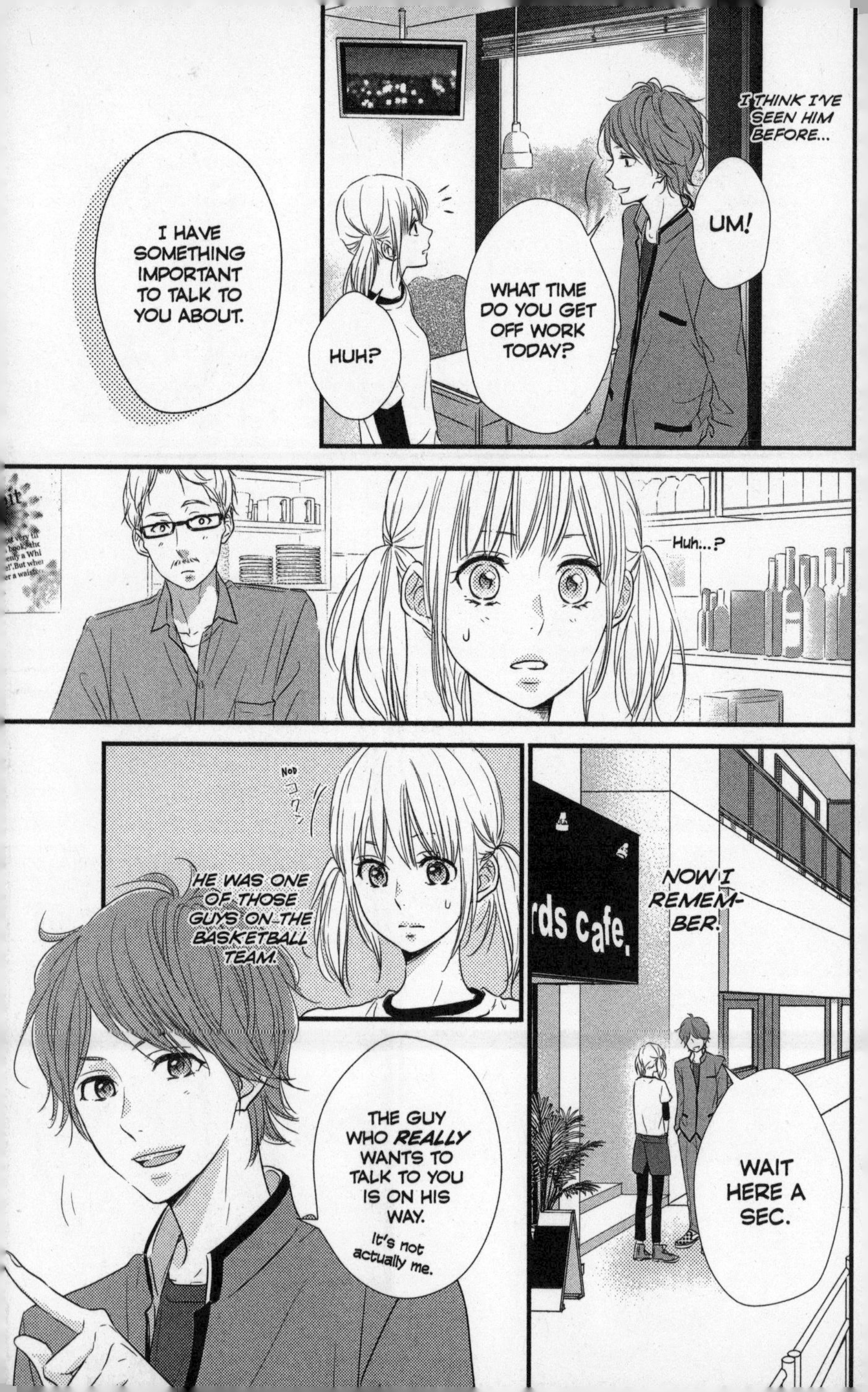
I THINK I'VE SEEN HIM BEFORE...
UM!
WHAT TIME DO YOU GET OFF WORK TODAY?
HUH?
I HAVE SOMETHING IMPORTANT TO TALK TO YOU ABOUT.
Huh...?
NOW I REMEMBER.
rds cafe.
WAIT HERE A SEC.
NOD
HE WAS ONE OF THOSE GUYS ON THE BASKETBALL TEAM.
THE GUY WHO *REALLY* WANTS TO TALK TO YOU IS ON HIS WAY.
It's not actually me.

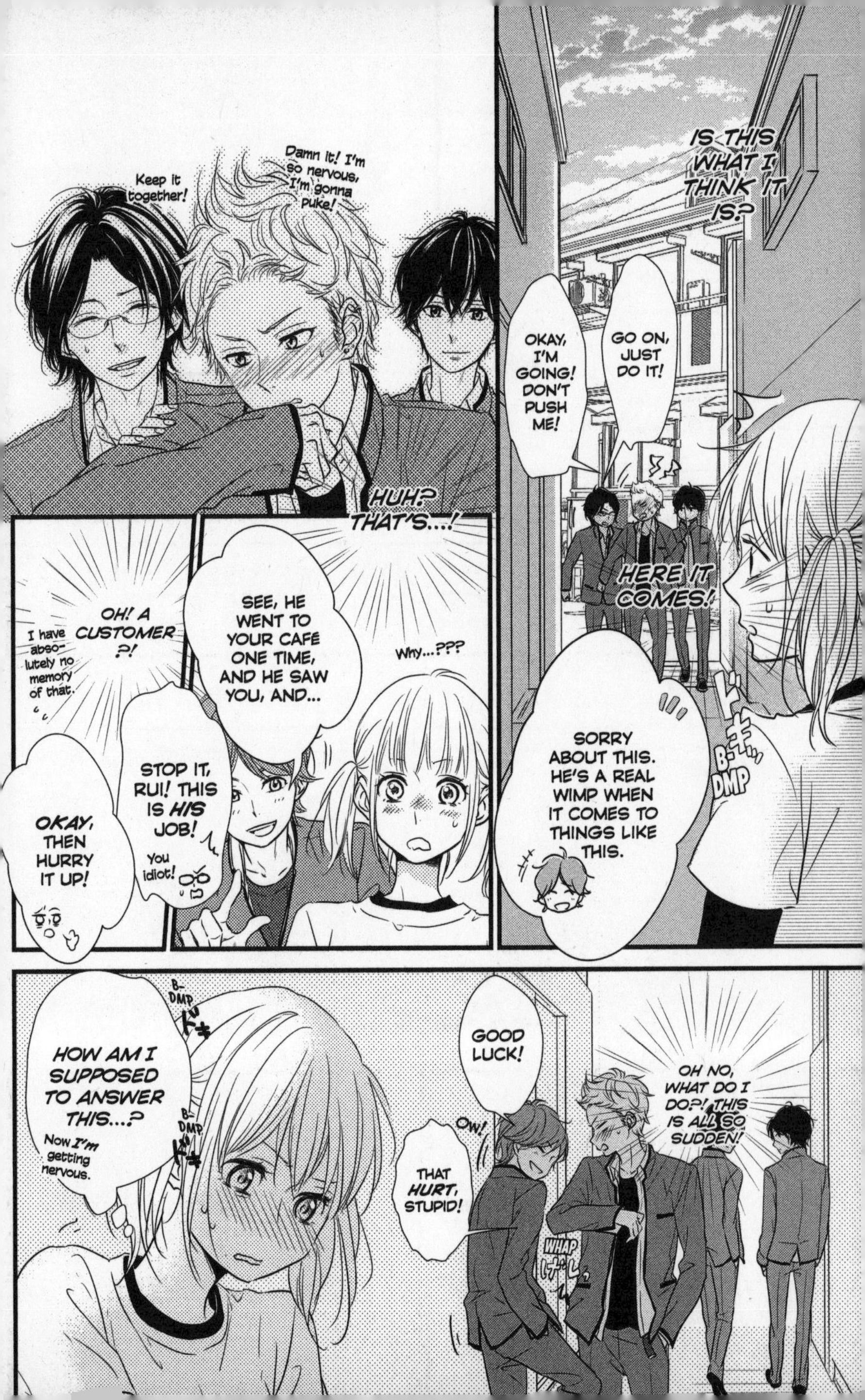
IS THIS WHAT I THINK IT IS?
GO ON, JUST DO IT!
OKAY, I'M GOING! DON'T PUSH ME!
HERE IT COMES!
B-DMP
SORRY ABOUT THIS. HE'S A REAL WIMP WHEN IT COMES TO THINGS LIKE THIS.
Damn it! I'm so nervous, I'm gonna puke!
Keep it together!
HUH? THAT'S...!
SEE, HE WENT TO YOUR CAFÉ ONE TIME, AND HE SAW YOU, AND...
Why...???
STOP IT, RUI! THIS IS HIS JOB!
You idiot!
OH! A CUSTOMER ?!
I have absolutely no memory of that.
OKAY, THEN HURRY IT UP!
OH NO, WHAT DO I DO?! THIS IS ALL SO SUDDEN!
GOOD LUCK!
OW!
THAT HURT, STUPID!
WHAP
B-DMP
HOW AM I SUPPOSED TO ANSWER THIS...?
B-DMP
Now I'm getting nervous.

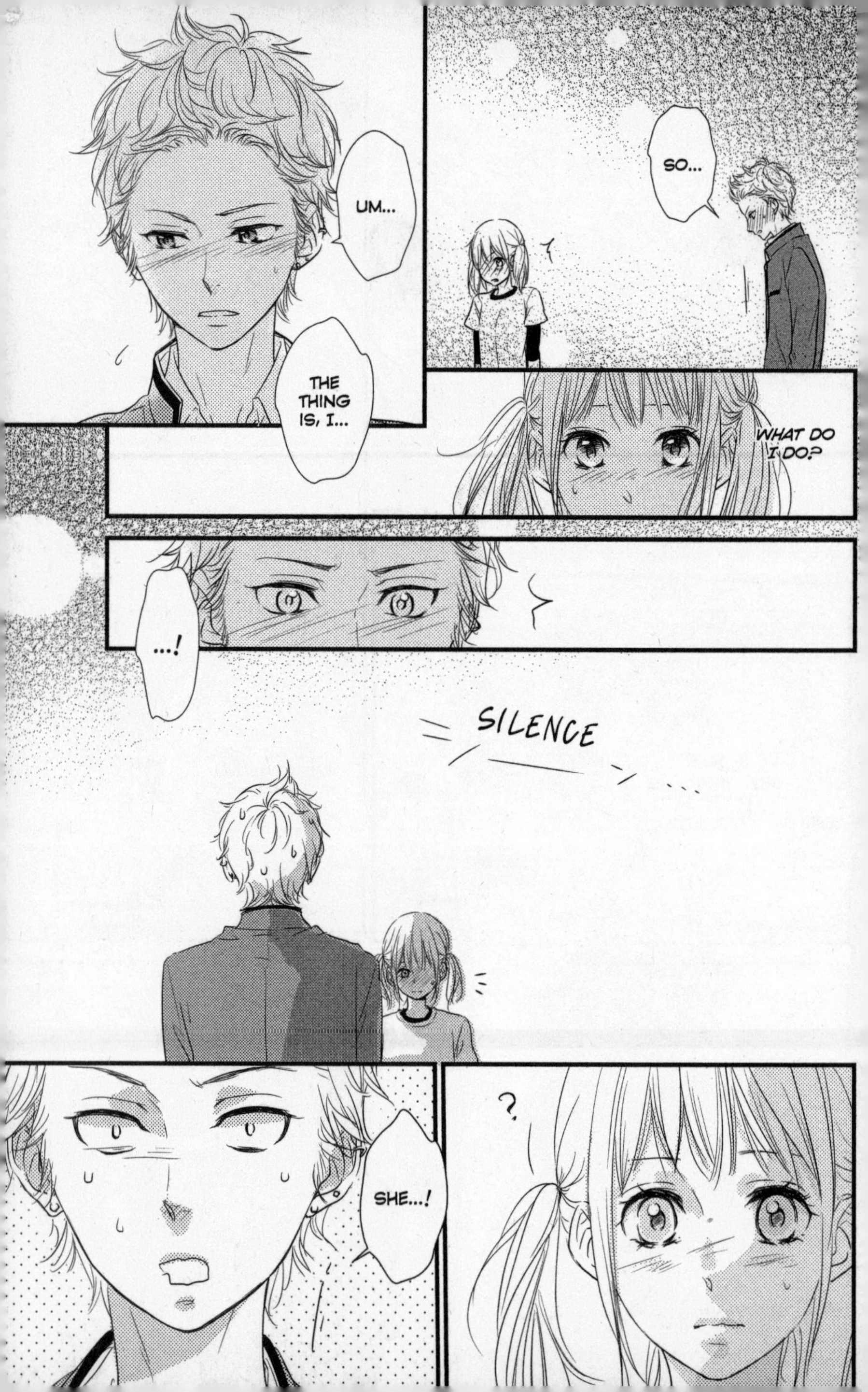
SO...
UM...
THE THING IS, I...
WHAT DO I DO?
...!
SILENCE
?
SHE...!

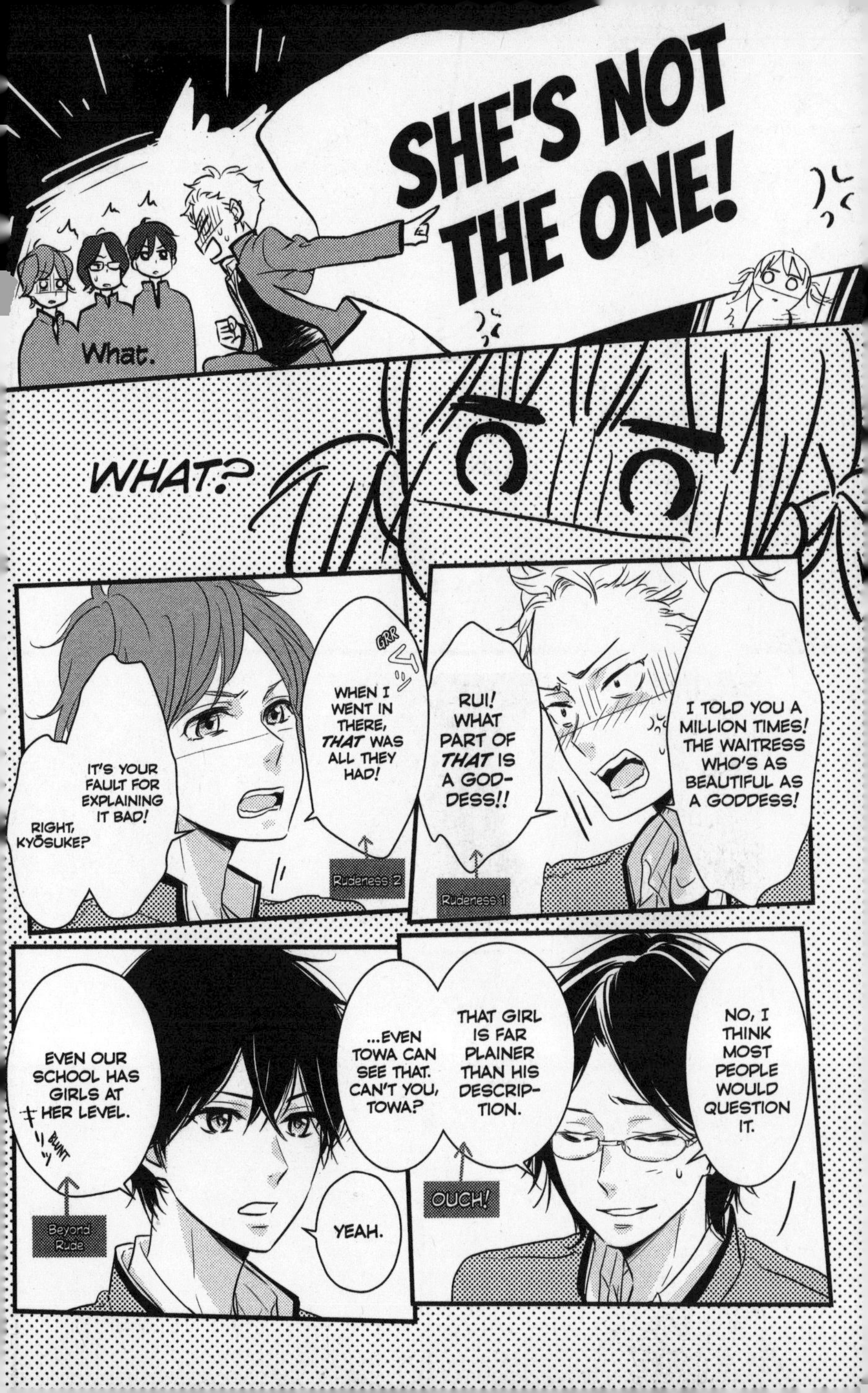
SHE'S NOT THE ONE!
What.
WHAT?
I TOLD YOU A MILLION TIMES! THE WAITRESS WHO'S AS BEAUTIFUL AS A GODDESS!
RUI! WHAT PART OF *THAT* IS A GOD-DESS!!
Rudeness 1
GRR
WHEN I WENT IN THERE, *THAT* WAS ALL THEY HAD!
Rudeness 2
IT'S YOUR FAULT FOR EXPLAINING IT BAD!
RIGHT, KYŌSUKE?
NO, I THINK MOST PEOPLE WOULD QUESTION IT.
THAT GIRL IS FAR PLAINER THAN HIS DESCRIP-TION.
OUCH!
...EVEN TOWA CAN SEE THAT. CAN'T YOU, TOWA?
YEAH.
EVEN OUR SCHOOL HAS GIRLS AT HER LEVEL.
BLUNT
Beyond Rude

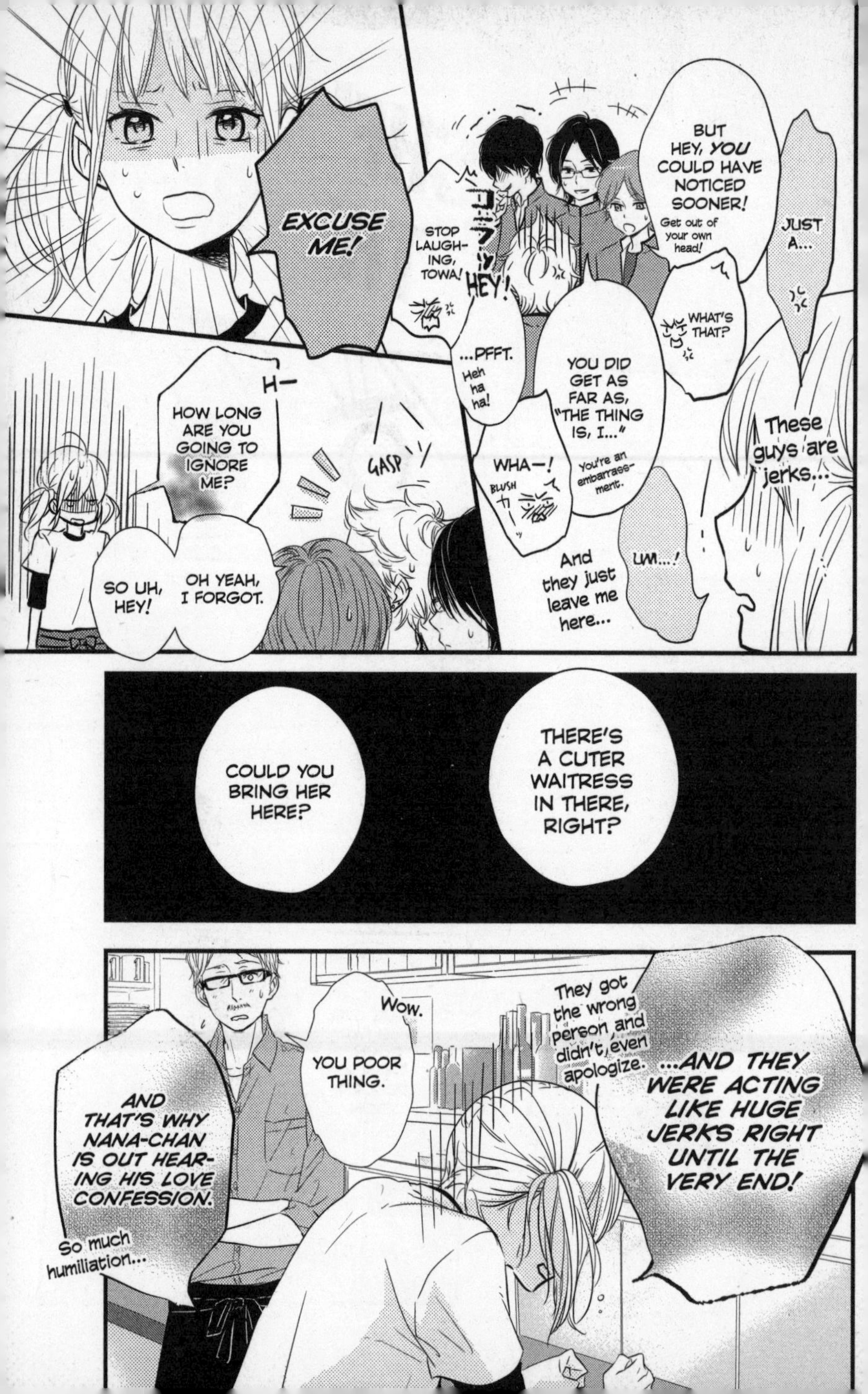
JUST A...
BUT HEY, YOU COULD HAVE NOTICED SOONER!
Get out of your own head!
WHAT'S THAT?
HEY!
STOP LAUGHING, TOWA!
...PFFT.
Heh ha ha!
YOU DID GET AS FAR AS, "THE THING IS, I..."
You're an embarrassment.
WHA—!
BLUSH
These guys are jerks...
UM...!
And they just leave me here...
EXCUSE ME!
H—
HOW LONG ARE YOU GOING TO IGNORE ME?
GASP
OH YEAH, I FORGOT.
SO UH, HEY!
THERE'S A CUTER WAITRESS IN THERE, RIGHT?
COULD YOU BRING HER HERE?
...AND THEY WERE ACTING LIKE HUGE JERKS RIGHT UNTIL THE VERY END!
They got the wrong person and didn't even apologize.
Wow.
YOU POOR THING.
AND THAT'S WHY NANA-CHAN IS OUT HEARING HIS LOVE CONFESSION.
So much humiliation...

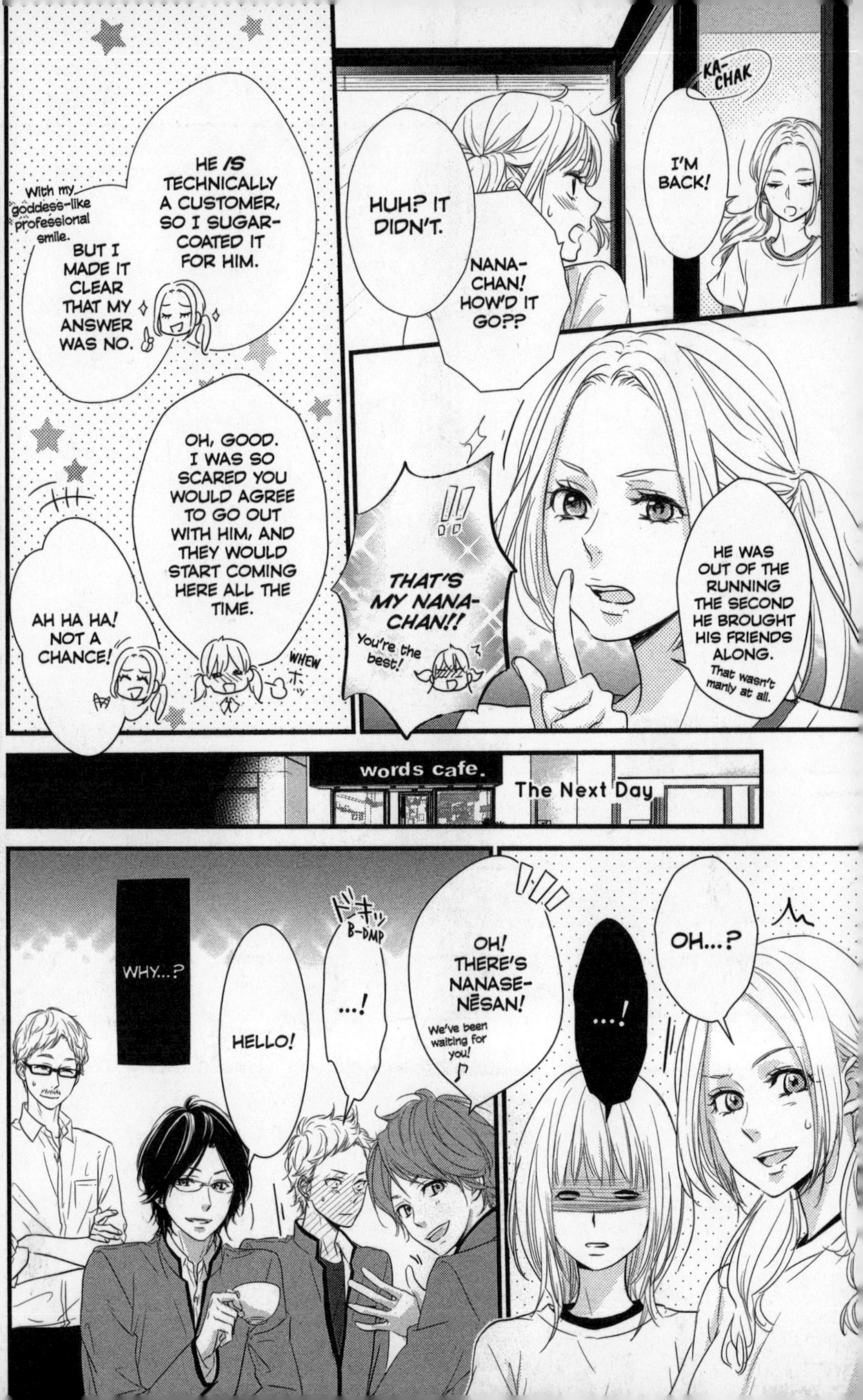
KA-CHAK
I'M BACK!
NANA-CHAN! HOW'D IT GO??
HUH? IT DIDN'T.
HE WAS OUT OF THE RUNNING THE SECOND HE BROUGHT HIS FRIENDS ALONG.
That wasn't manly at all.
THAT'S MY NANA-CHAN!!
You're the best!
HE IS TECHNICALLY A CUSTOMER, SO I SUGAR-COATED IT FOR HIM.
BUT I MADE IT CLEAR THAT MY ANSWER WAS NO.
With my goddess-like professional smile.
OH, GOOD. I WAS SO SCARED YOU WOULD AGREE TO GO OUT WITH HIM, AND THEY WOULD START COMING HERE ALL THE TIME.
WHEW
AH HA HA! NOT A CHANCE!
words cafe.
The Next Day
OH...?
...!
OH! THERE'S NANASE-NĒSAN!
We've been waiting for you!
B-DMP
...!
HELLO!
WHY...?

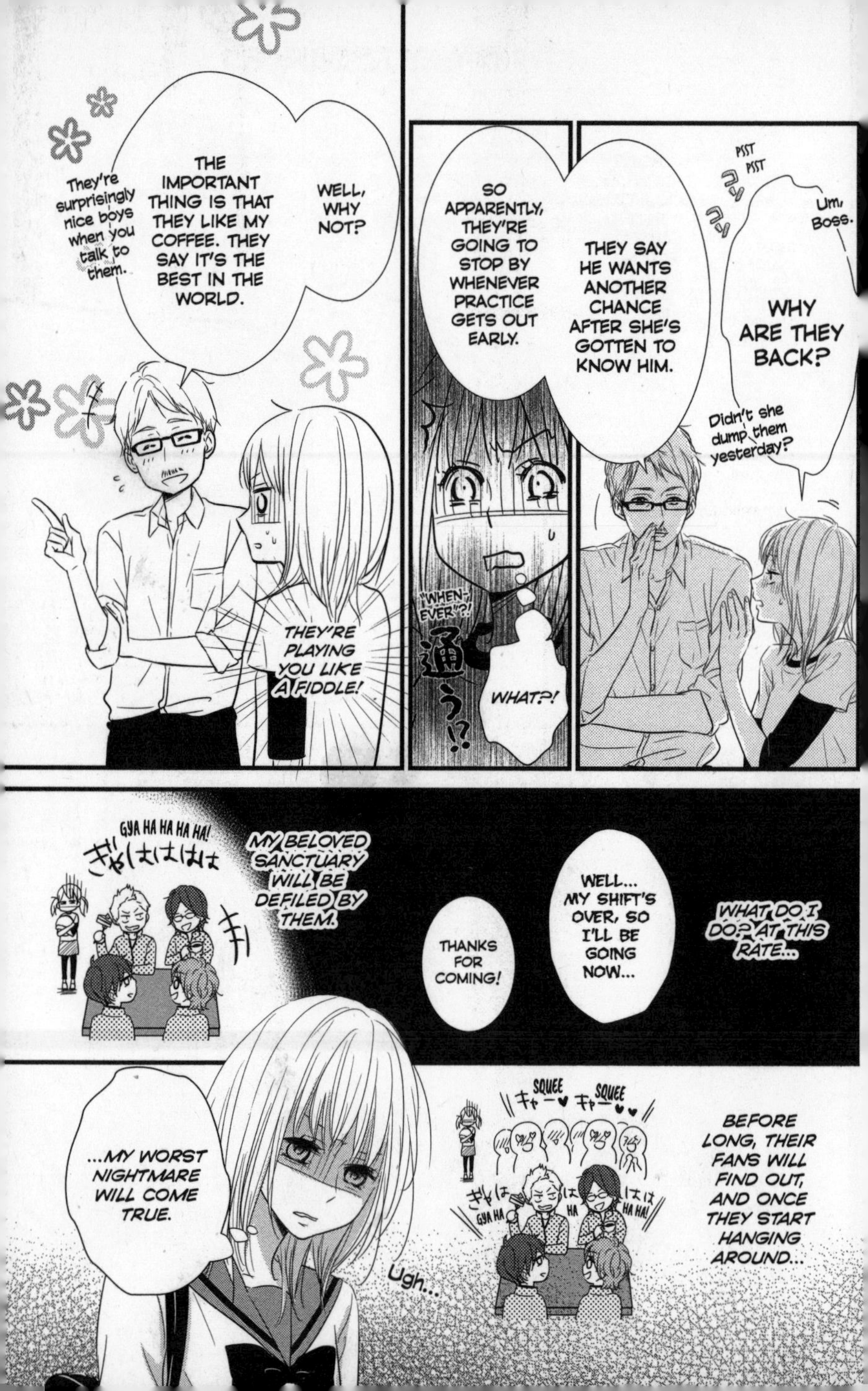
PSST PSST
Um, Boss.
WHY ARE THEY BACK?
Didn't she dump them yesterday?
SO APPARENTLY, THEY'RE GOING TO STOP BY WHENEVER PRACTICE GETS OUT EARLY.
THEY SAY HE WANTS ANOTHER CHANCE AFTER SHE'S GOTTEN TO KNOW HIM.
"WHEN-EVER"?!
通う!?
WHAT?!
WELL, WHY NOT?
THE IMPORTANT THING IS THAT THEY LIKE MY COFFEE. THEY SAY IT'S THE BEST IN THE WORLD.
They're surprisingly nice boys when you talk to them.
THEY'RE PLAYING YOU LIKE A FIDDLE!
WHAT DO I DO? AT THIS RATE...
WELL... MY SHIFT'S OVER, SO I'LL BE GOING NOW...
THANKS FOR COMING!
MY BELOVED SANCTUARY WILL BE DEFILED BY THEM.
GYA HA HA HA HA!
ぎゃはははは
BEFORE LONG, THEIR FANS WILL FIND OUT, AND ONCE THEY START HANGING AROUND...
SQUEE キャー
SQUEE キャー
ぎゃは GYA HA
は HA
はは HA HA!
Ugh...
...MY WORST NIGHTMARE WILL COME TRUE.

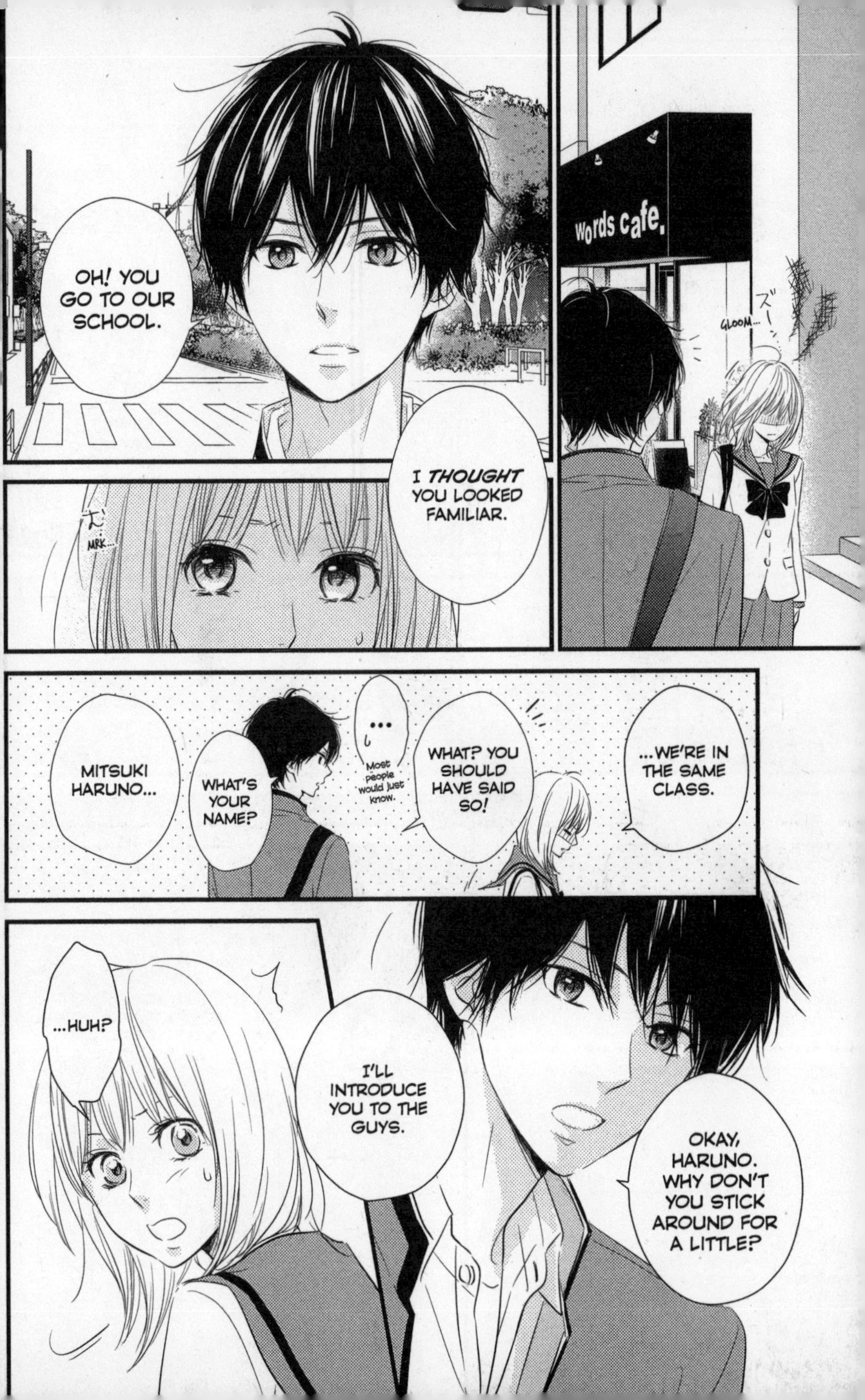
words cafe.
GLOOM...
OH! YOU GO TO OUR SCHOOL.
I *THOUGHT* YOU LOOKED FAMILIAR.
MRK...
...WE'RE IN THE SAME CLASS.
WHAT? YOU SHOULD HAVE SAID SO!
...
Most people would just know.
WHAT'S YOUR NAME?
MITSUKI HARUNO...
OKAY, HARUNO. WHY DON'T YOU STICK AROUND FOR A LITTLE?
I'LL INTRODUCE YOU TO THE GUYS.
...HUH?

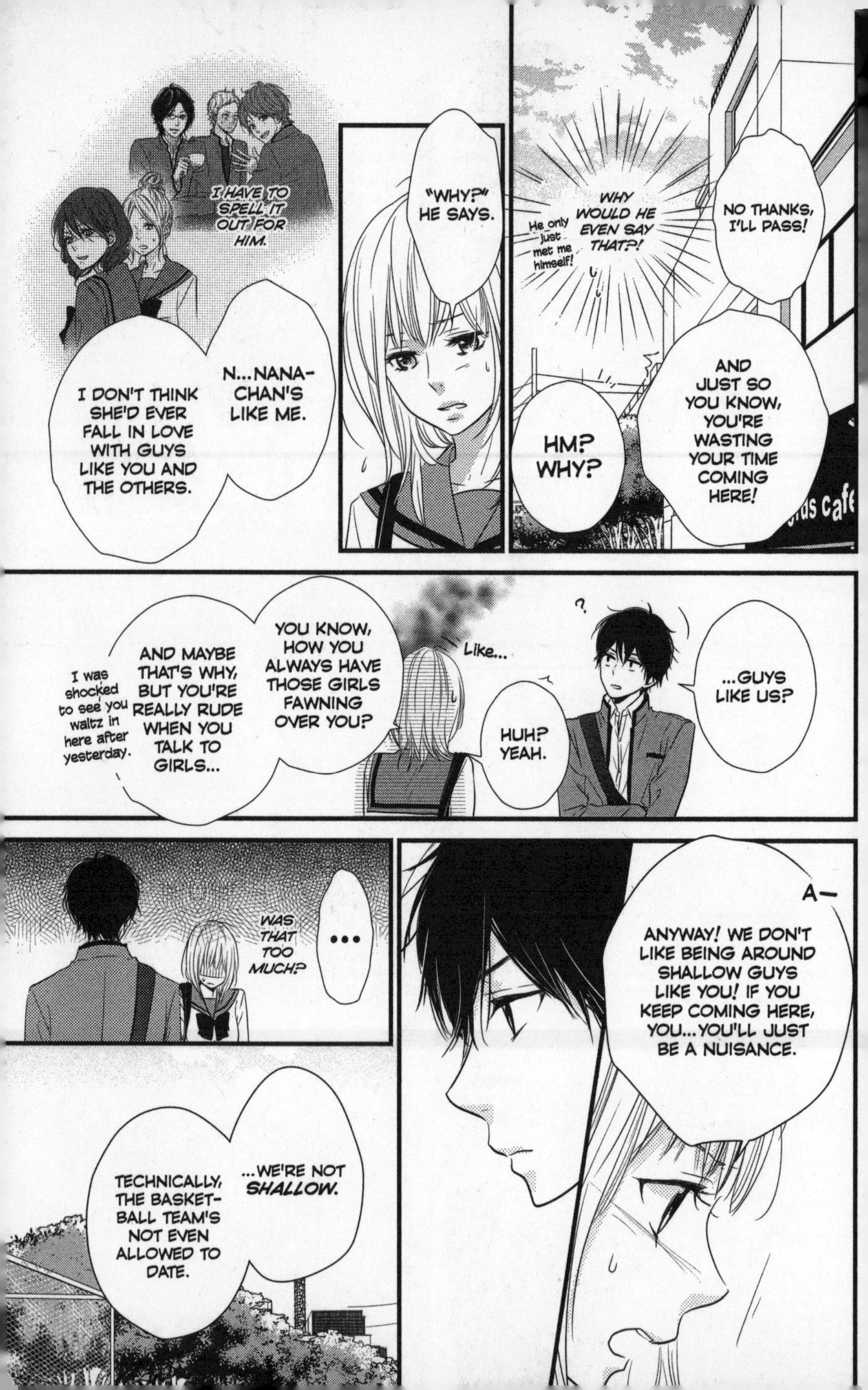
NO THANKS, I'LL PASS!
AND JUST SO YOU KNOW, YOU'RE WASTING YOUR TIME COMING HERE!
HM? WHY?
WHY WOULD HE EVEN SAY THAT?!
He only just met me himself!
"WHY?" HE SAYS.
I HAVE TO SPELL IT OUT FOR HIM.
N...NANA-CHAN'S LIKE ME.
I DON'T THINK SHE'D EVER FALL IN LOVE WITH GUYS LIKE YOU AND THE OTHERS.
...GUYS LIKE US?
HUH? YEAH.
Like...
YOU KNOW, HOW YOU ALWAYS HAVE THOSE GIRLS FAWNING OVER YOU?
AND MAYBE THAT'S WHY, BUT YOU'RE REALLY RUDE WHEN YOU TALK TO GIRLS...
I was shocked to see you waltz in here after yesterday.
A—
ANYWAY! WE DON'T LIKE BEING AROUND SHALLOW GUYS LIKE YOU! IF YOU KEEP COMING HERE, YOU...YOU'LL JUST BE A NUISANCE.
...
WAS THAT TOO MUCH?
...WE'RE NOT SHALLOW.
TECHNICALLY, THE BASKET-BALL TEAM'S NOT EVEN ALLOWED TO DATE.

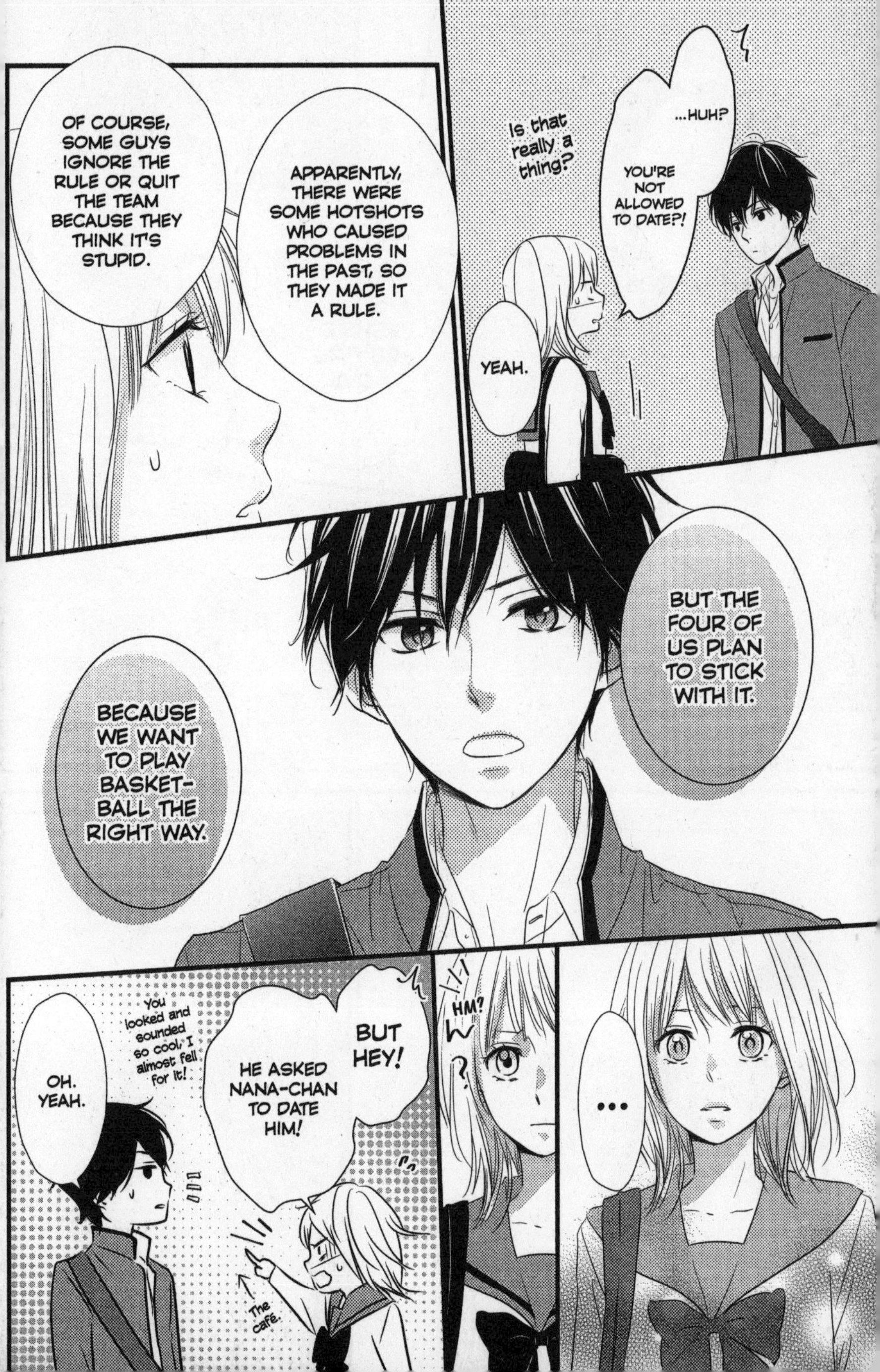
...HUH?
YOU'RE NOT ALLOWED TO DATE?!
Is that really a thing?
YEAH.
APPARENTLY, THERE WERE SOME HOTSHOTS WHO CAUSED PROBLEMS IN THE PAST, SO THEY MADE IT A RULE.
OF COURSE, SOME GUYS IGNORE THE RULE OR QUIT THE TEAM BECAUSE THEY THINK IT'S STUPID.
BUT THE FOUR OF US PLAN TO STICK WITH IT.
BECAUSE WE WANT TO PLAY BASKET-BALL THE RIGHT WAY.
...
HM?
BUT HEY!
HE ASKED NANA-CHAN TO DATE HIM!
You looked and sounded so cool, I almost fell for it!
OH. YEAH.
The café.

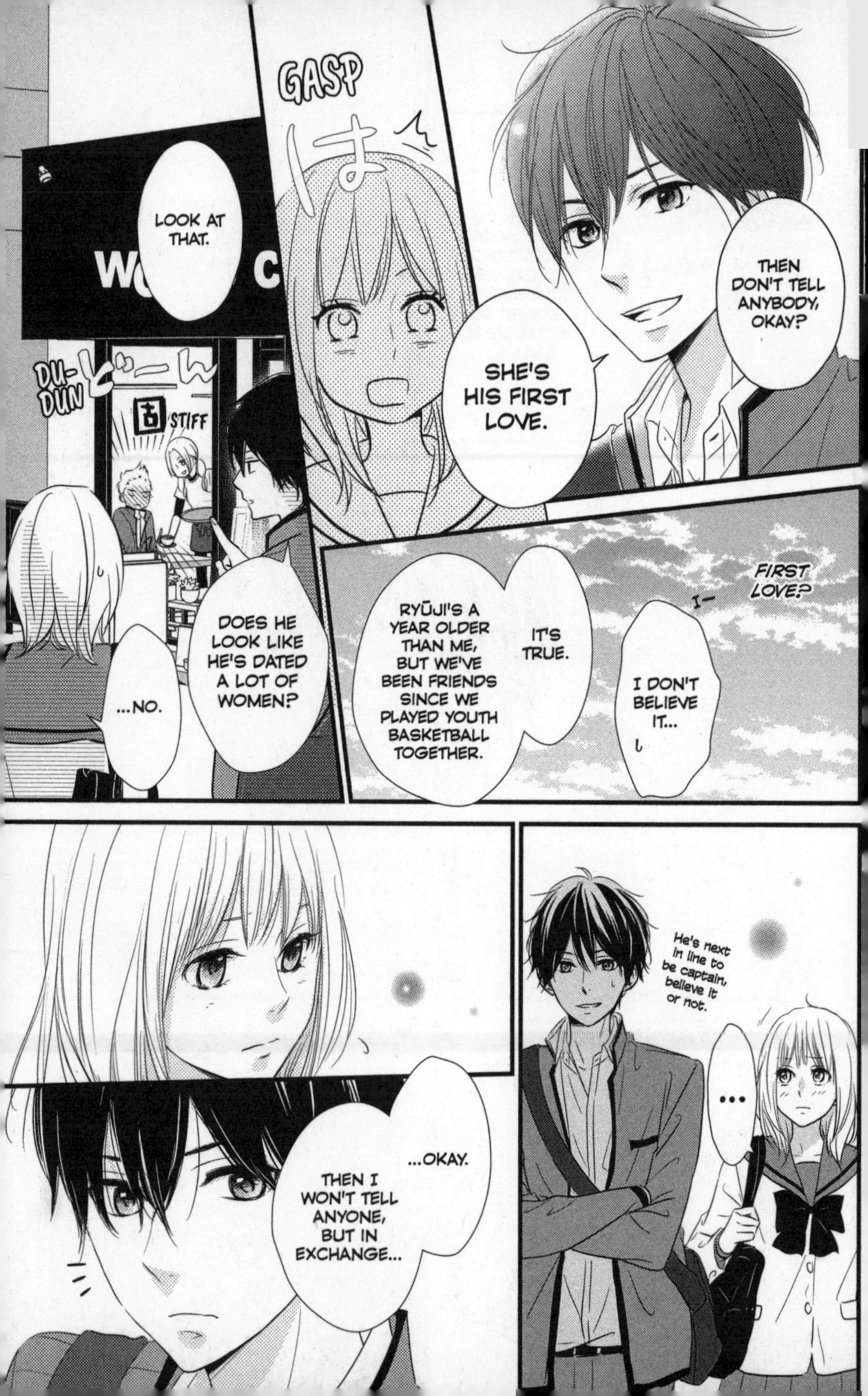
THEN DON'T TELL ANYBODY, OKAY?
GASP
は
SHE'S HIS FIRST LOVE.
FIRST LOVE?
I—
I DON'T BELIEVE IT...
IT'S TRUE.
RYŪJI'S A YEAR OLDER THAN ME, BUT WE'VE BEEN FRIENDS SINCE WE PLAYED YOUTH BASKETBALL TOGETHER.
LOOK AT THAT.
DU-DUN
STIFF
DOES HE LOOK LIKE HE'S DATED A LOT OF WOMEN?
...NO.
He's next in line to be captain, believe it or not.
...
...OKAY.
THEN I WON'T TELL ANYONE, BUT IN EXCHANGE...

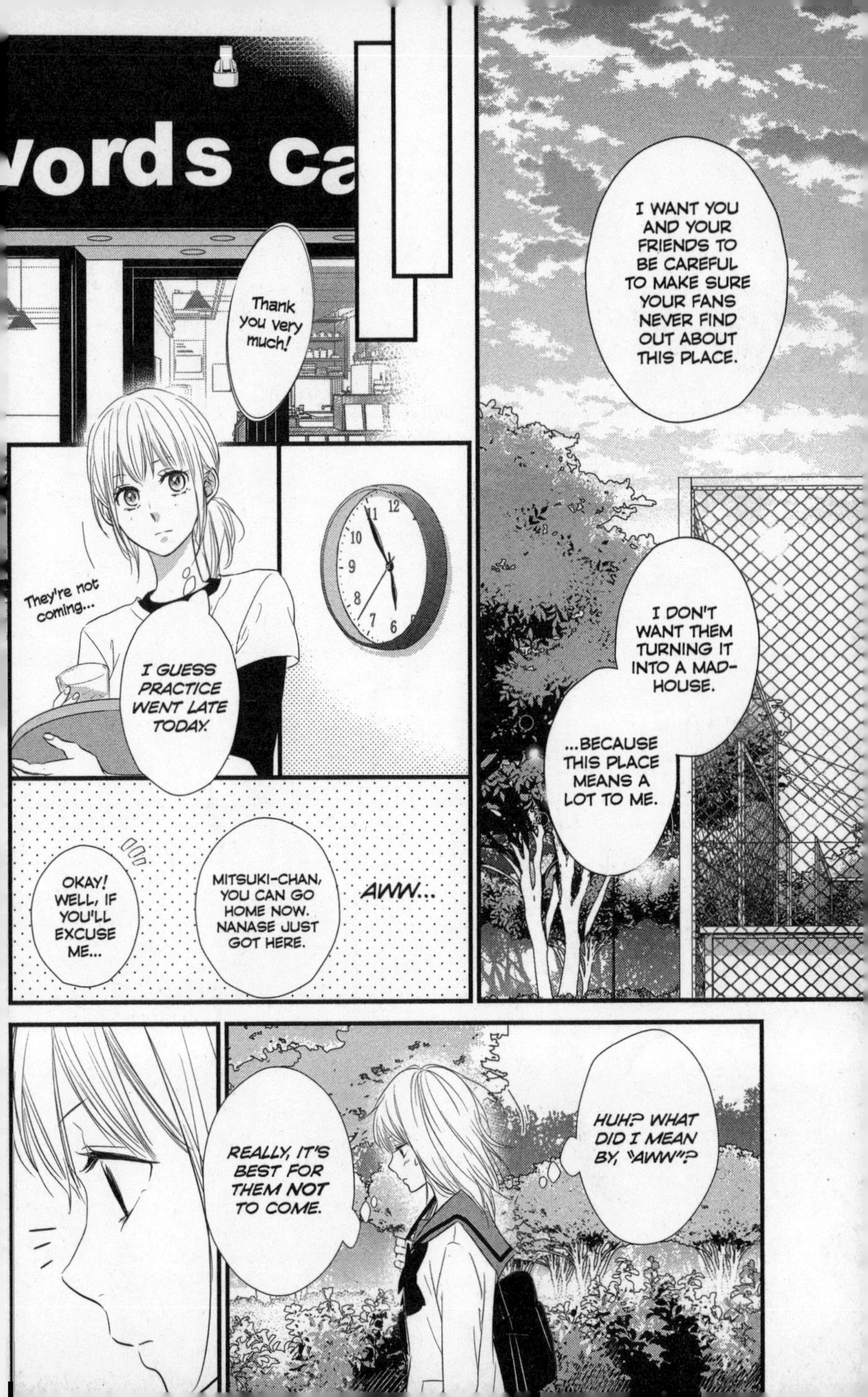
I WANT YOU AND YOUR FRIENDS TO BE CAREFUL TO MAKE SURE YOUR FANS NEVER FIND OUT ABOUT THIS PLACE.
I DON'T WANT THEM TURNING IT INTO A MAD-HOUSE.
...BECAUSE THIS PLACE MEANS A LOT TO ME.
words ca
Thank you very much!
They're not coming...
I GUESS PRACTICE WENT LATE TODAY.
AWW...
MITSUKI-CHAN, YOU CAN GO HOME NOW. NANASE JUST GOT HERE.
OKAY! WELL, IF YOU'LL EXCUSE ME...
HUH? WHAT DID I MEAN BY, "AWW"?
REALLY, IT'S BEST FOR THEM NOT TO COME.

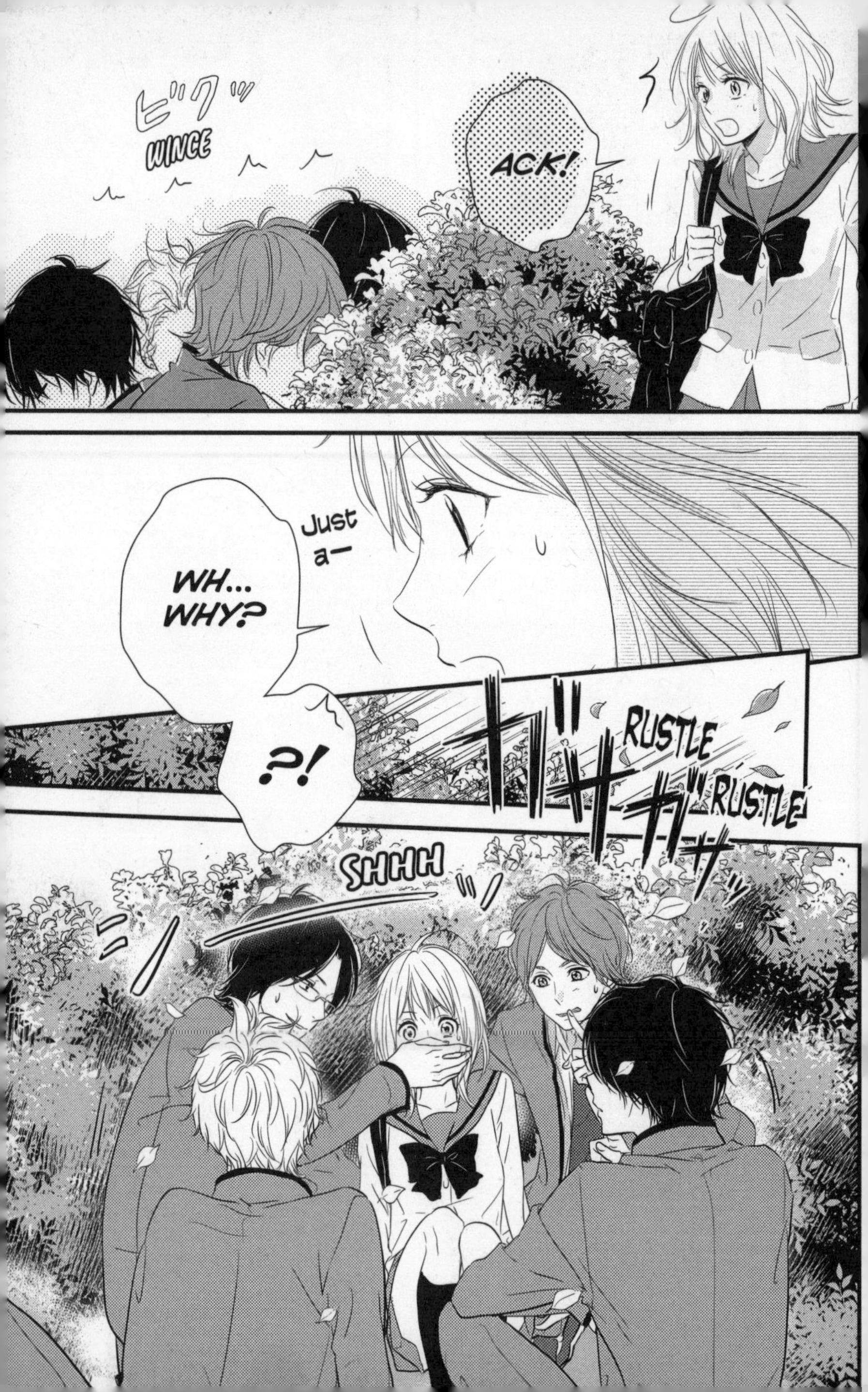
ACK!
ビクッ
WINCE
Just a—
WH... WHY?
RUSTLE
RUSTLE
?!
SHHH

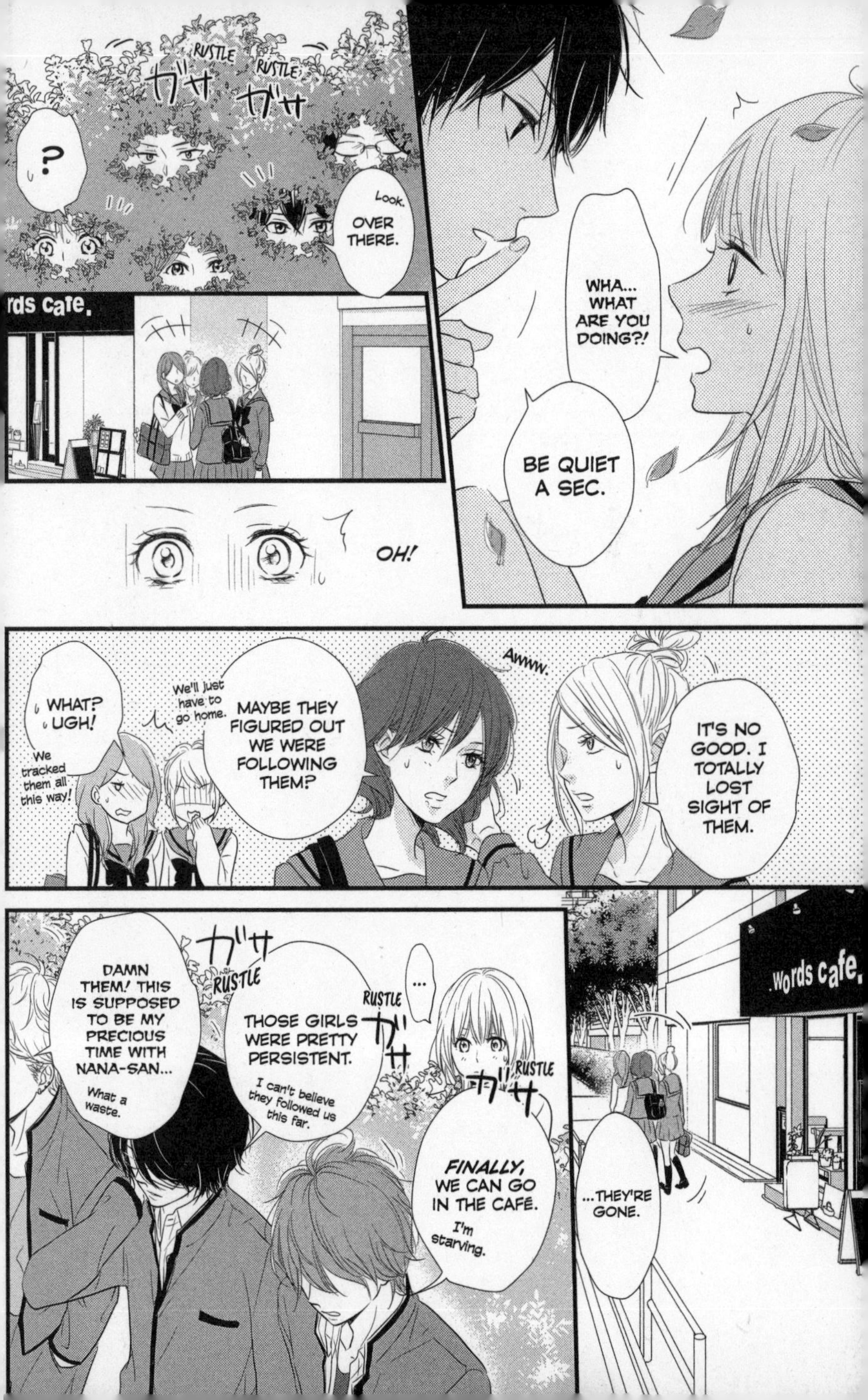
WHA... WHAT ARE YOU DOING?!
BE QUIET A SEC.
ガサ RUSTLE ガサ RUSTLE
Look. OVER THERE.
?
rds cafe.
OH!
IT'S NO GOOD. I TOTALLY LOST SIGHT OF THEM.
Awww.
MAYBE THEY FIGURED OUT WE WERE FOLLOWING THEM?
We'll just have to go home.
WHAT? UGH!
We tracked them all this way!
.Words cafe.
...THEY'RE GONE.
ガサ RUSTLE
FINALLY, WE CAN GO IN THE CAFÉ.
I'm starving.
...
ガサ RUSTLE
THOSE GIRLS WERE PRETTY PERSISTENT.
I can't believe they followed us this far.
ガサ RUSTLE
DAMN THEM! THIS IS SUPPOSED TO BE MY PRECIOUS TIME WITH NANA-SAN...
What a waste.

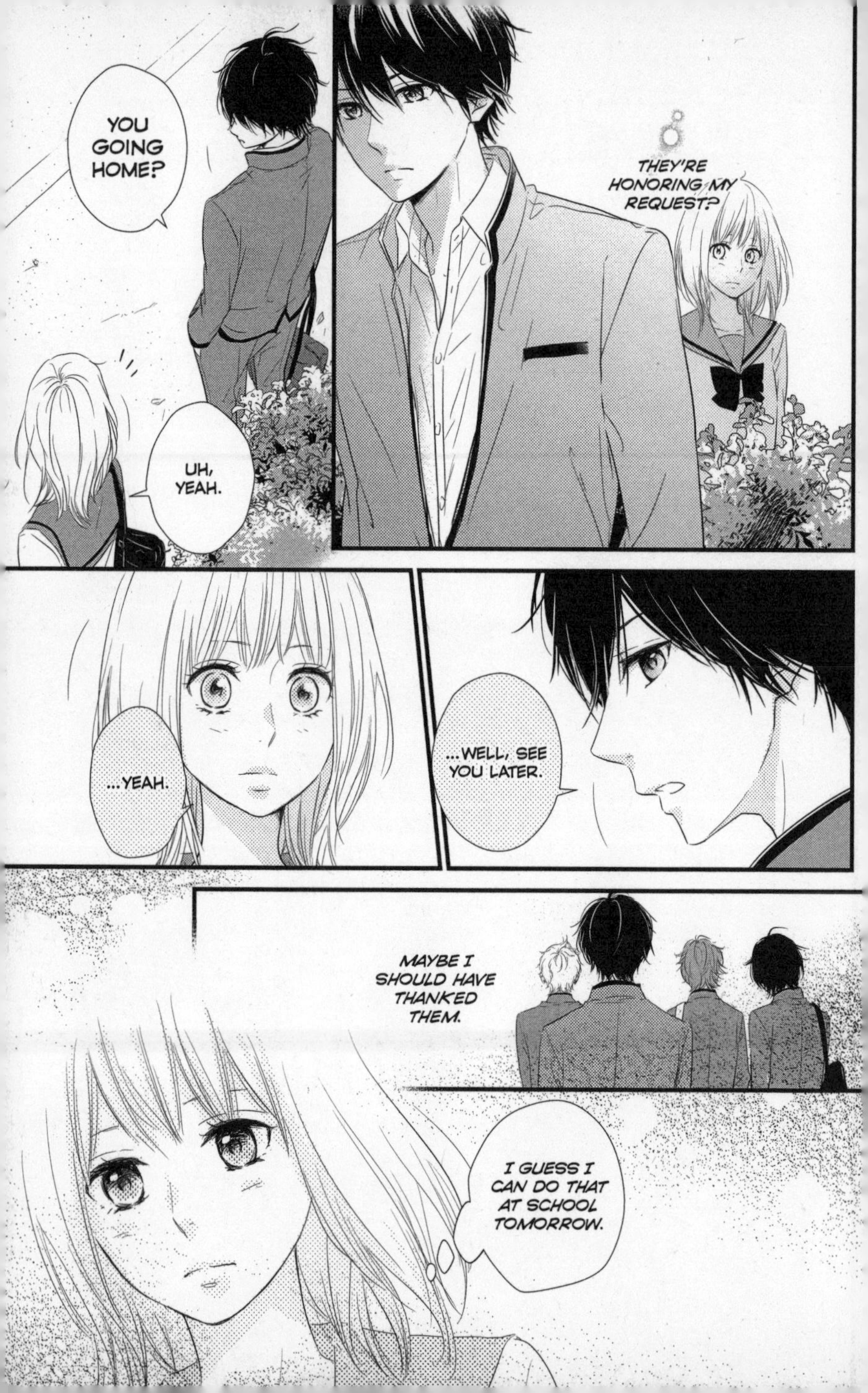
THEY'RE HONORING MY REQUEST?
YOU GOING HOME?
UH, YEAH.
...WELL, SEE YOU LATER.
...YEAH.
MAYBE I SHOULD HAVE THANKED THEM.
I GUESS I CAN DO THAT AT SCHOOL TOMORROW.

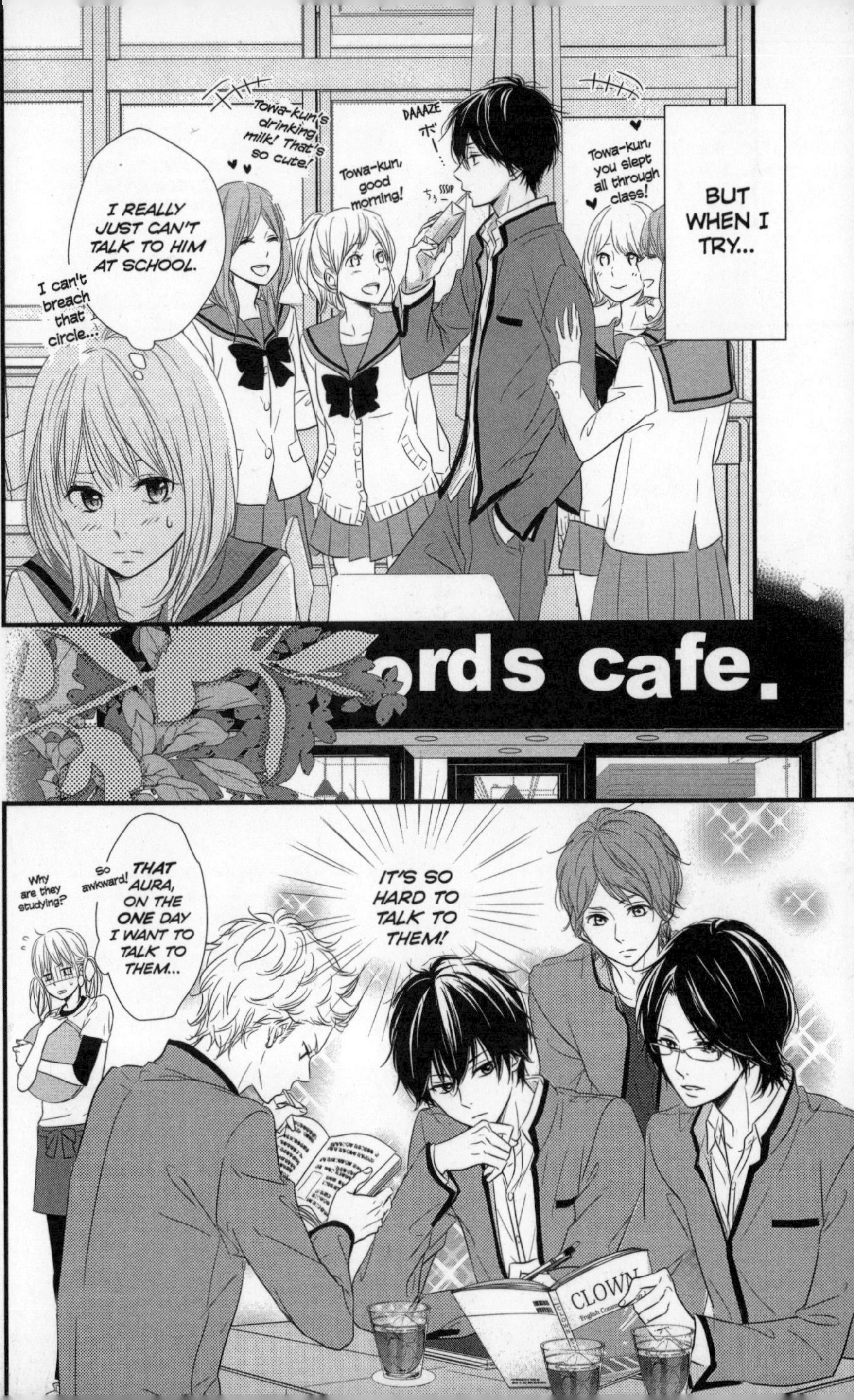
BUT WHEN I TRY...
Towa-kun, you slept all through class!
DAAAZE
ボー
SSSIP
Towa-kun, good morning!
Towa-kun's drinking milk! That's so cute!
I REALLY JUST CAN'T TALK TO HIM AT SCHOOL.
I can't breach that circle...
ords cafe.
IT'S SO HARD TO TALK TO THEM!
THAT AURA, ON THE ONE DAY I WANT TO TALK TO THEM...
So awkward!
Why are they studying?
CLOWN

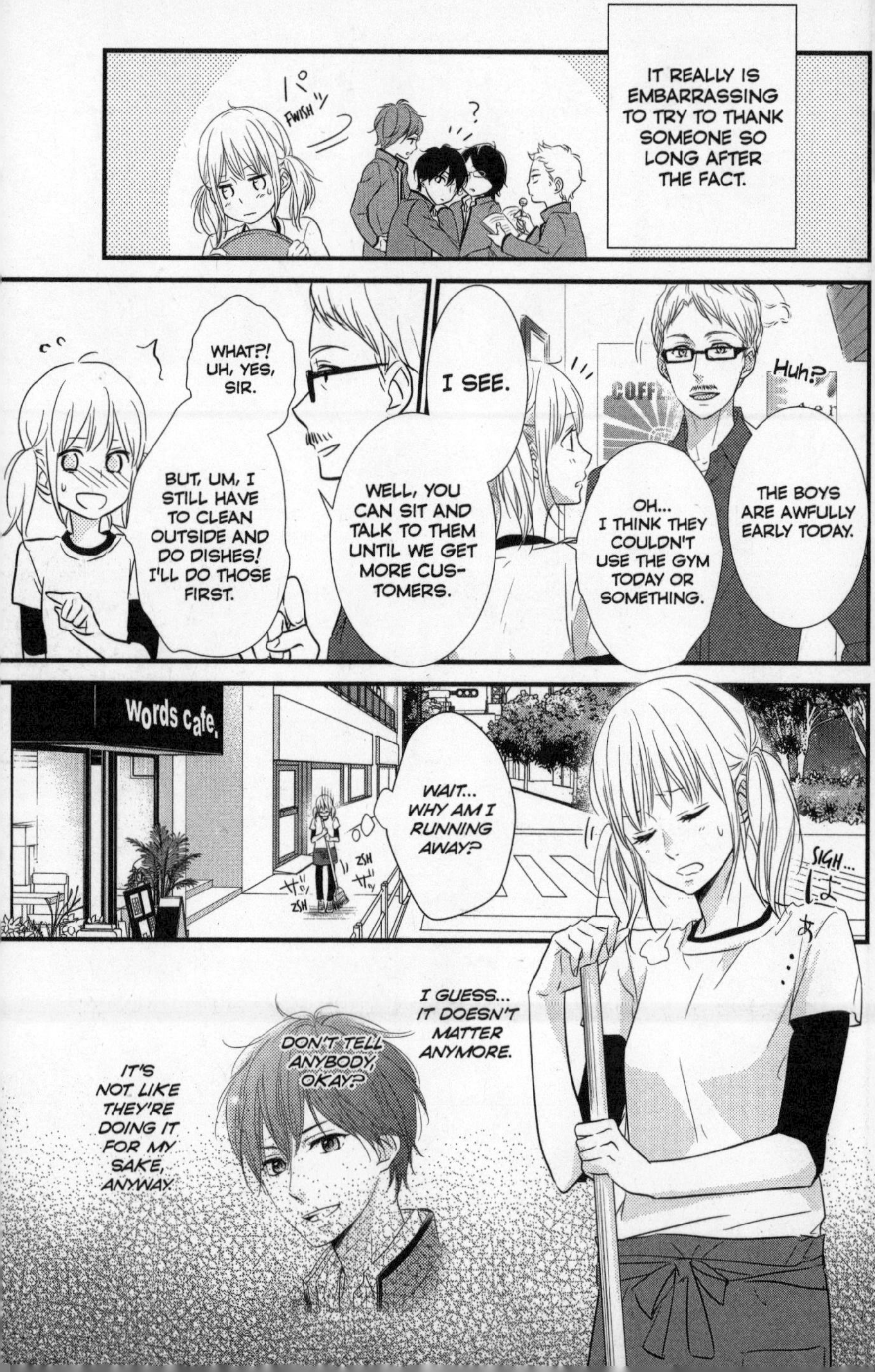
IT REALLY IS EMBARRASSING TO TRY TO THANK SOMEONE SO LONG AFTER THE FACT.
パッ
FWISH
?
Huh?
THE BOYS ARE AWFULLY EARLY TODAY.
OH... I THINK THEY COULDN'T USE THE GYM TODAY OR SOMETHING.
I SEE.
WELL, YOU CAN SIT AND TALK TO THEM UNTIL WE GET MORE CUS-TOMERS.
WHAT?! UH, YES, SIR.
BUT, UM, I STILL HAVE TO CLEAN OUTSIDE AND DO DISHES! I'LL DO THOSE FIRST.
SIGH...
はあ
WAIT... WHY AM I RUNNING AWAY?
Words cafe.
ZSH
ザッ
ZSH
ザッ
I GUESS... IT DOESN'T MATTER ANYMORE.
DON'T TELL ANYBODY, OKAY?
IT'S NOT LIKE THEY'RE DOING IT FOR MY SAKE, ANYWAY.

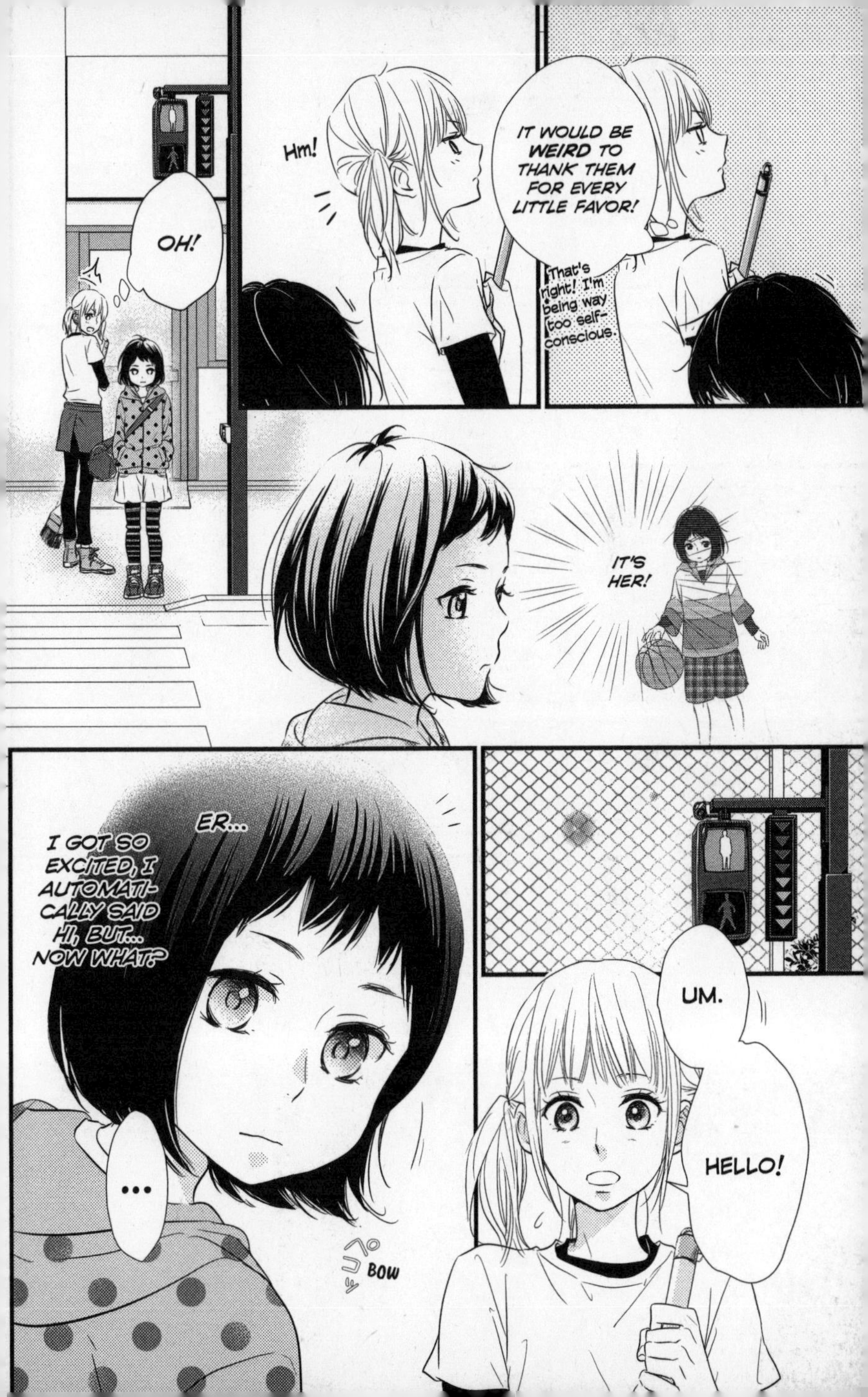
IT WOULD BE *WEIRD* TO THANK THEM FOR EVERY LITTLE FAVOR!
That's right! I'm being way too self-conscious.
Hm!
IT'S HER!
OH!
UM.
HELLO!
ER...
I GOT SO EXCITED, I AUTOMATICALLY SAID HI, BUT... NOW WHAT?
...
BOW

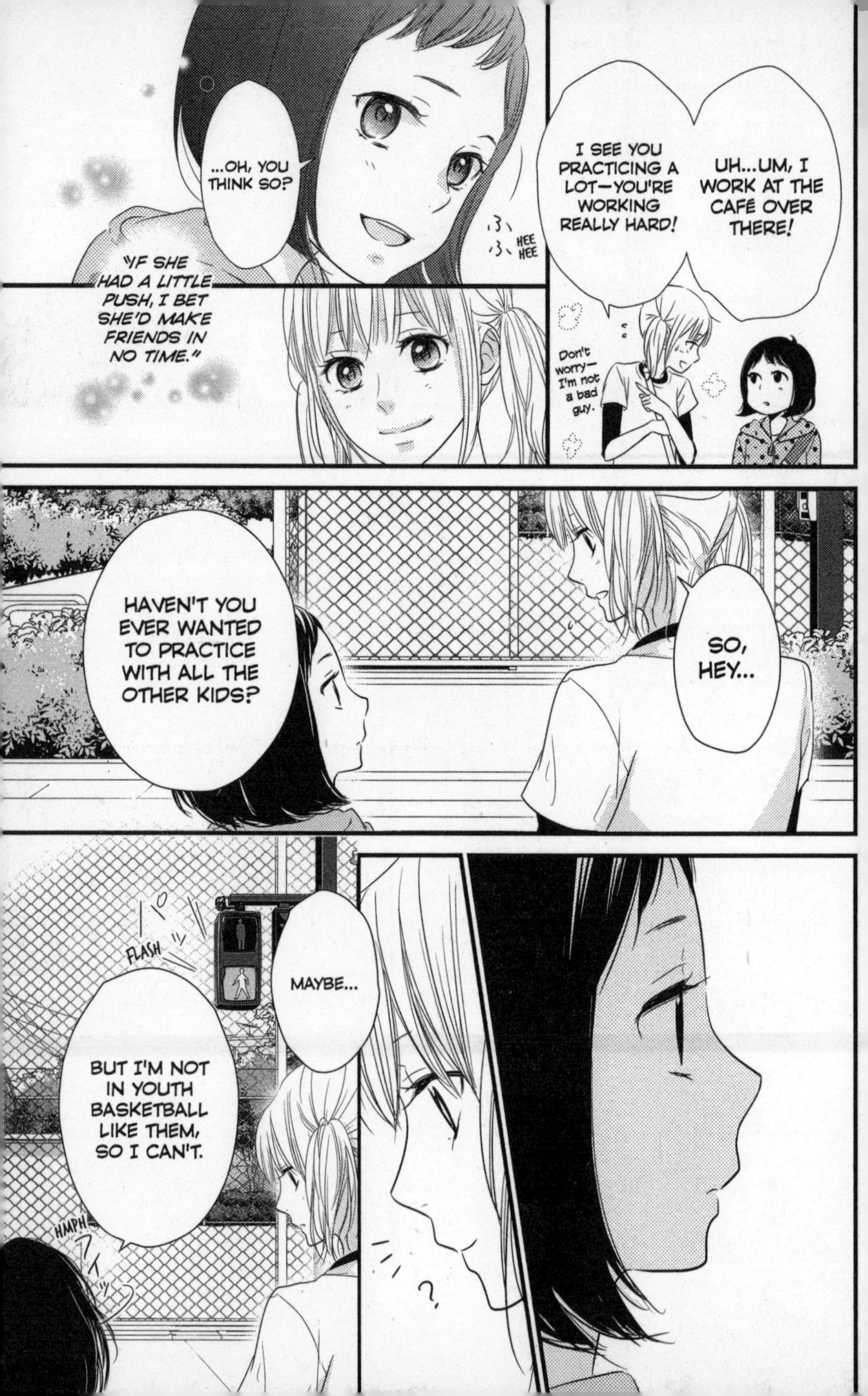
UH...UM, I WORK AT THE CAFÉ OVER THERE!
I SEE YOU PRACTICING A LOT—YOU'RE WORKING REALLY HARD!
Don't worry—I'm not a bad guy.
...OH, YOU THINK SO?
HEE HEE
"IF SHE HAD A LITTLE PUSH, I BET SHE'D MAKE FRIENDS IN NO TIME."
SO, HEY...
HAVEN'T YOU EVER WANTED TO PRACTICE WITH ALL THE OTHER KIDS?
FLASH
MAYBE...
BUT I'M NOT IN YOUTH BASKETBALL LIKE THEM, SO I CAN'T.
HMPH

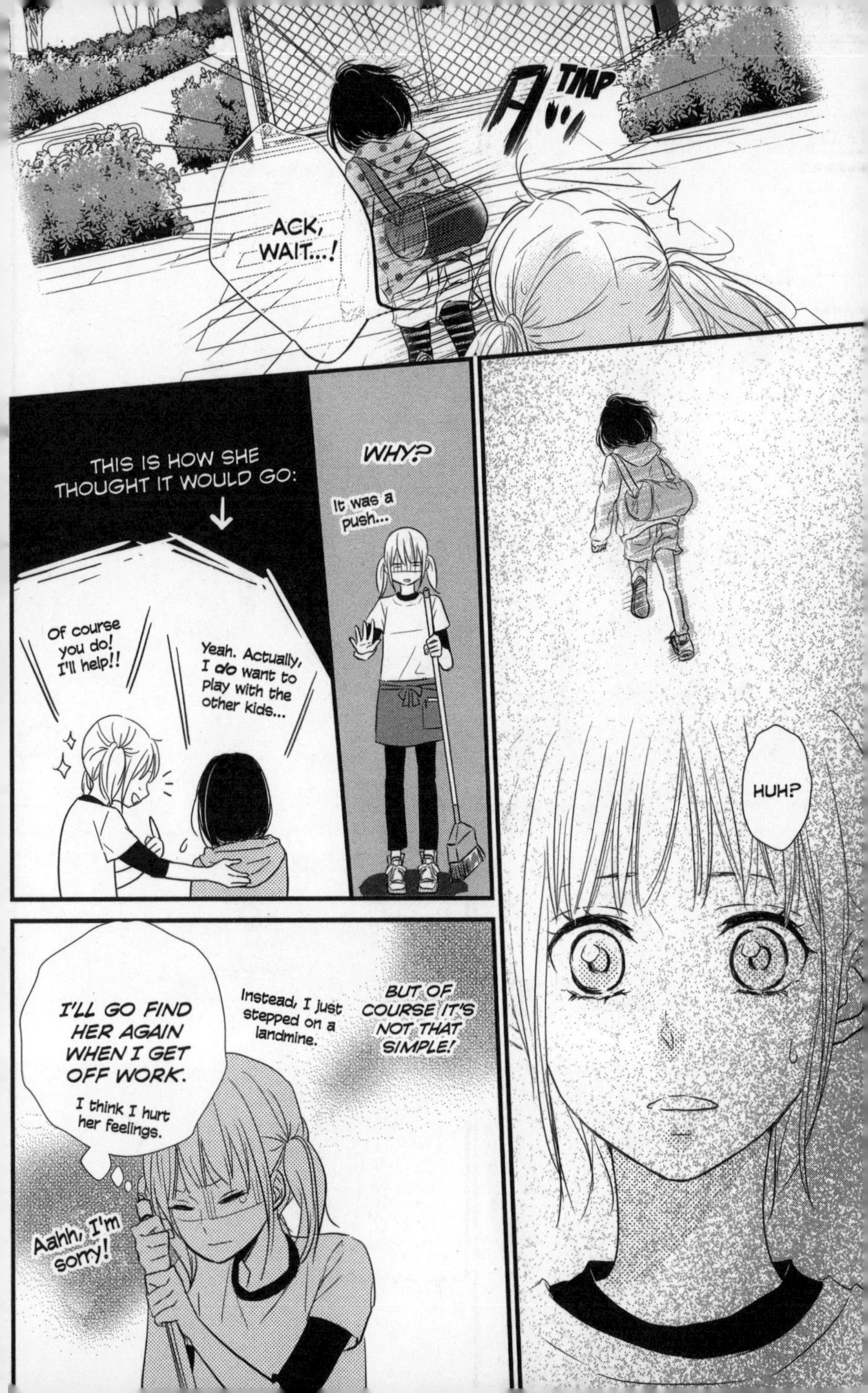
TMP
ACK, WAIT...!
HUH?
WHY?
It was a push...
THIS IS HOW SHE THOUGHT IT WOULD GO:
Yeah. Actually, I *do* want to play with the other kids...
Of course you do! I'll help!!
BUT OF COURSE IT'S NOT THAT SIMPLE!
Instead, I just stepped on a landmine.
I'LL GO FIND HER AGAIN WHEN I GET OFF WORK.
I think I hurt her feelings.
Aahh, I'm sorry!

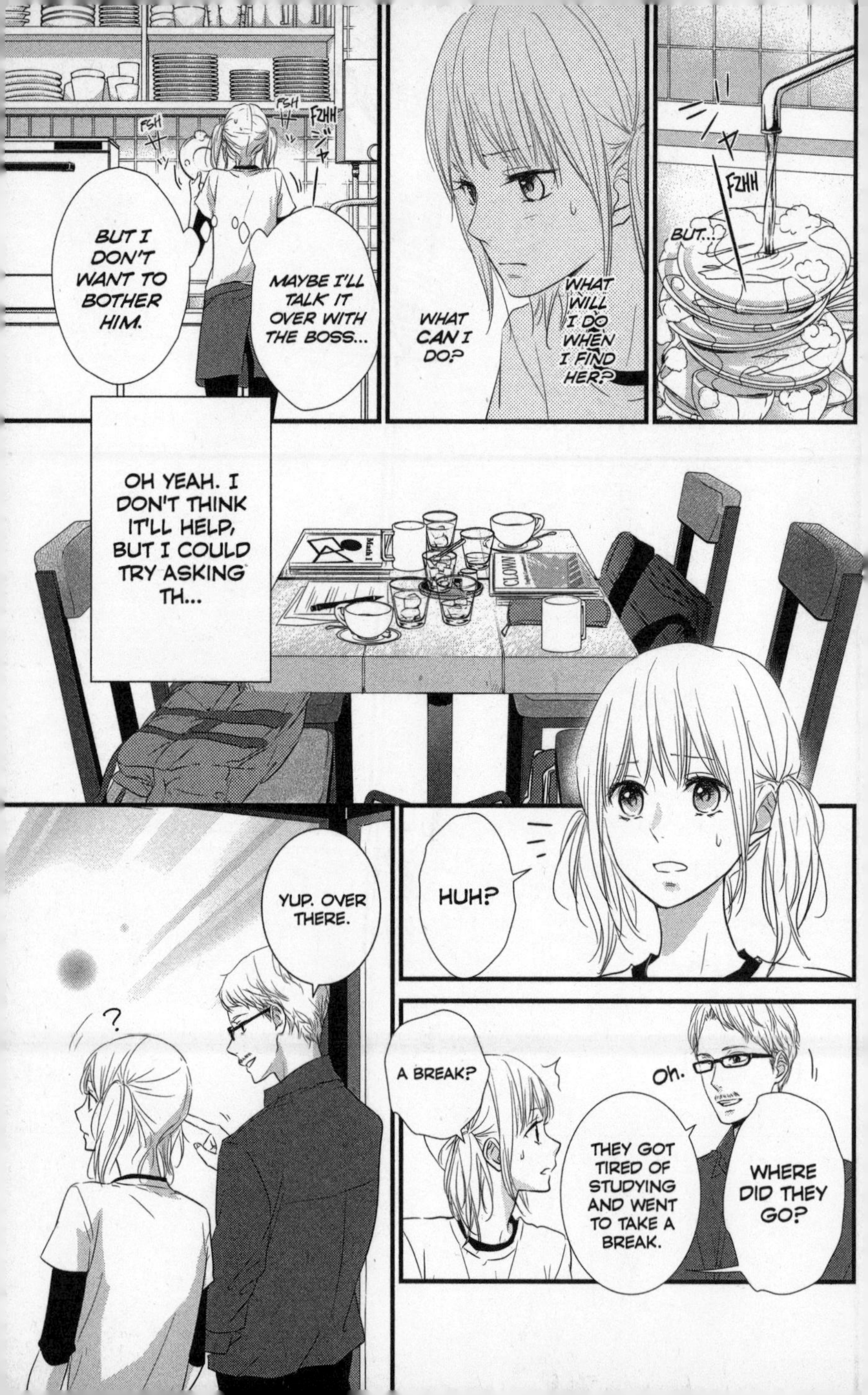
FZHH
BUT...
WHAT WILL I DO WHEN I FIND HER?
WHAT CAN I DO?
FZHH
FSH
FSH
MAYBE I'LL TALK IT OVER WITH THE BOSS...
BUT I DON'T WANT TO BOTHER HIM.
OH YEAH. I DON'T THINK IT'LL HELP, BUT I COULD TRY ASKING TH...
HUH?
WHERE DID THEY GO?
Oh.
THEY GOT TIRED OF STUDYING AND WENT TO TAKE A BREAK.
A BREAK?
YUP. OVER THERE.
?

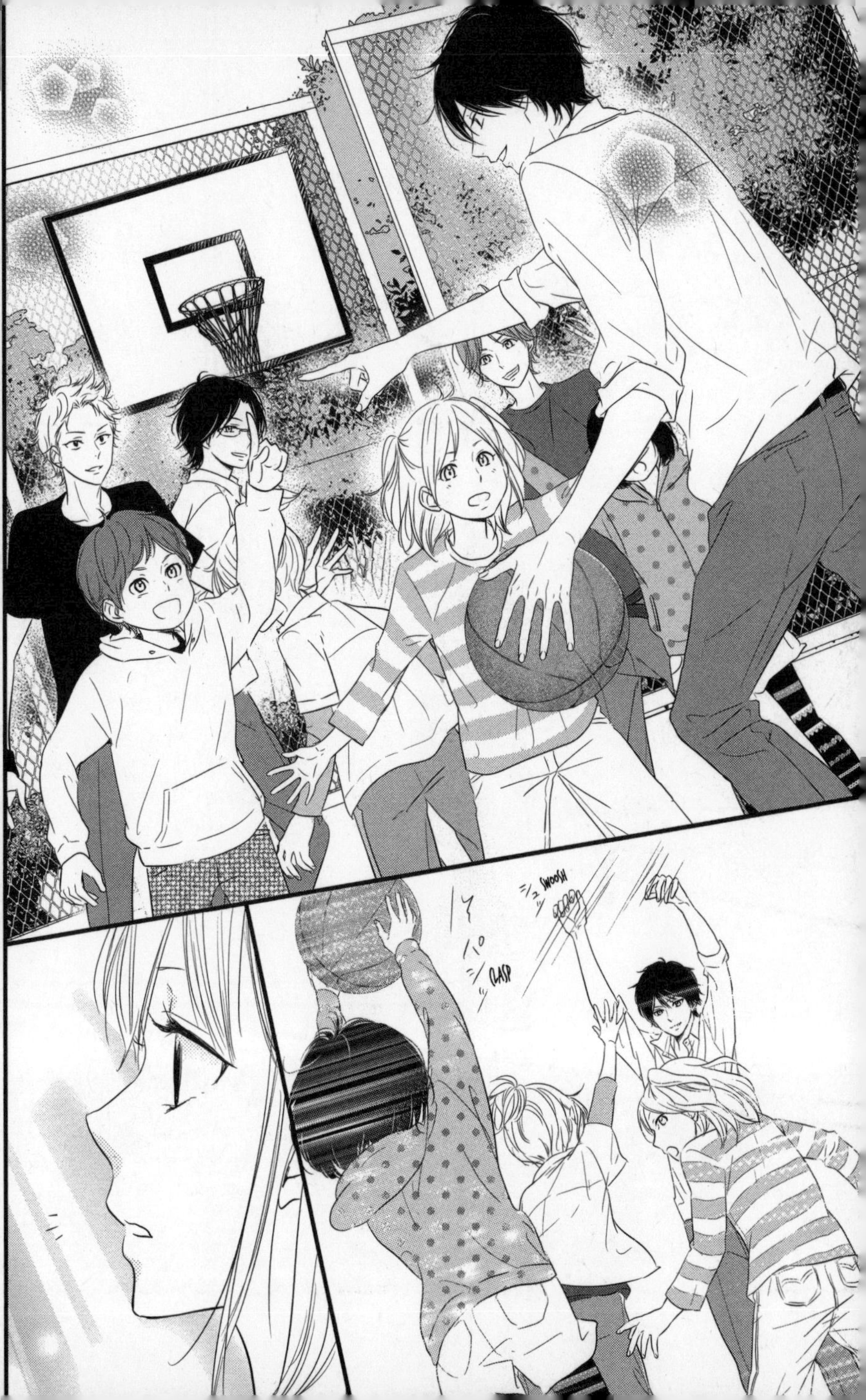
SWOOSH
CLASP

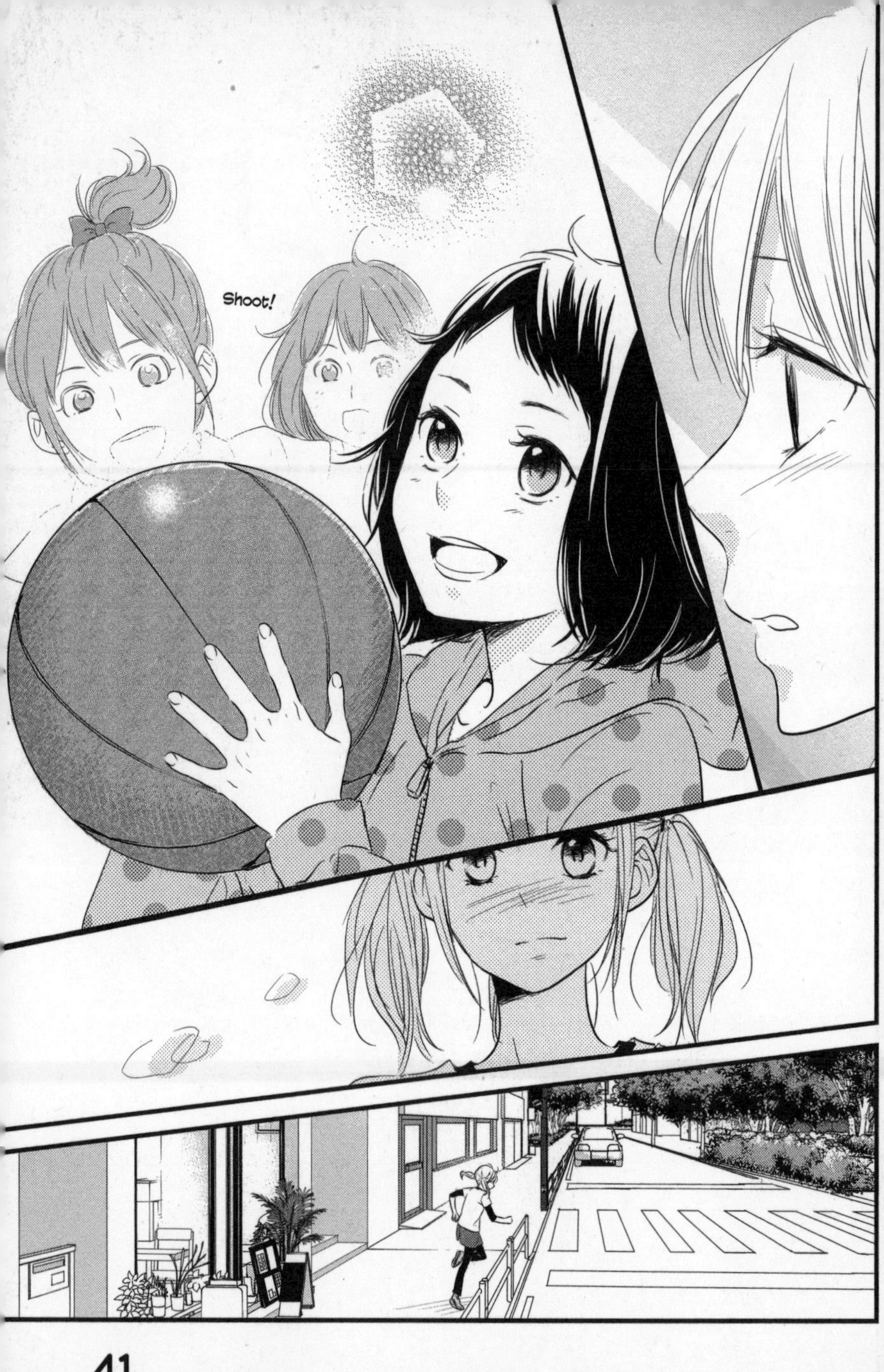
Shoot!

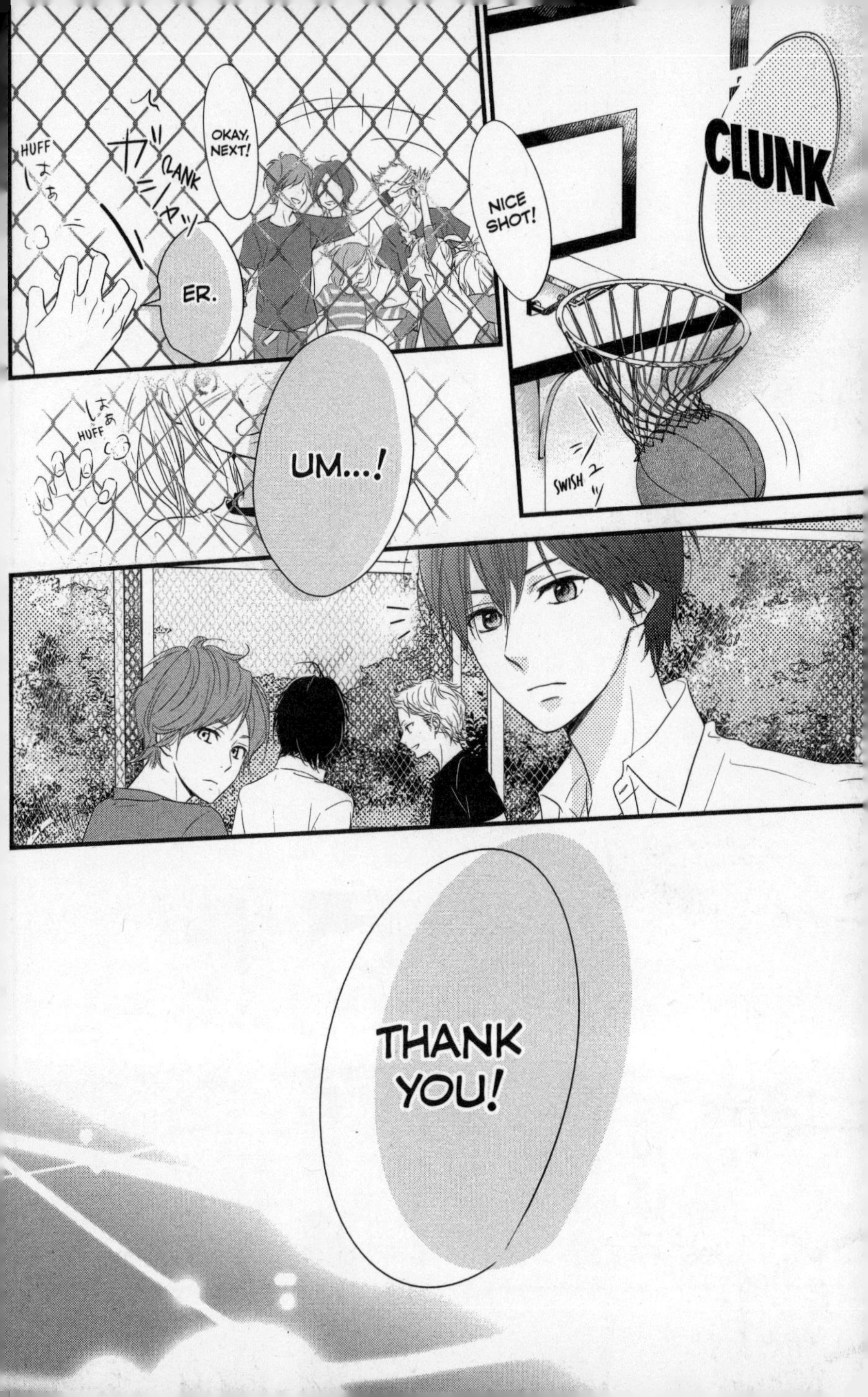
CLUNK
NICE SHOT!
SWISH
OKAY, NEXT!
CLANK
HUFF はぁ
ER.
HUFF はぁ
UM...!
THANK YOU!

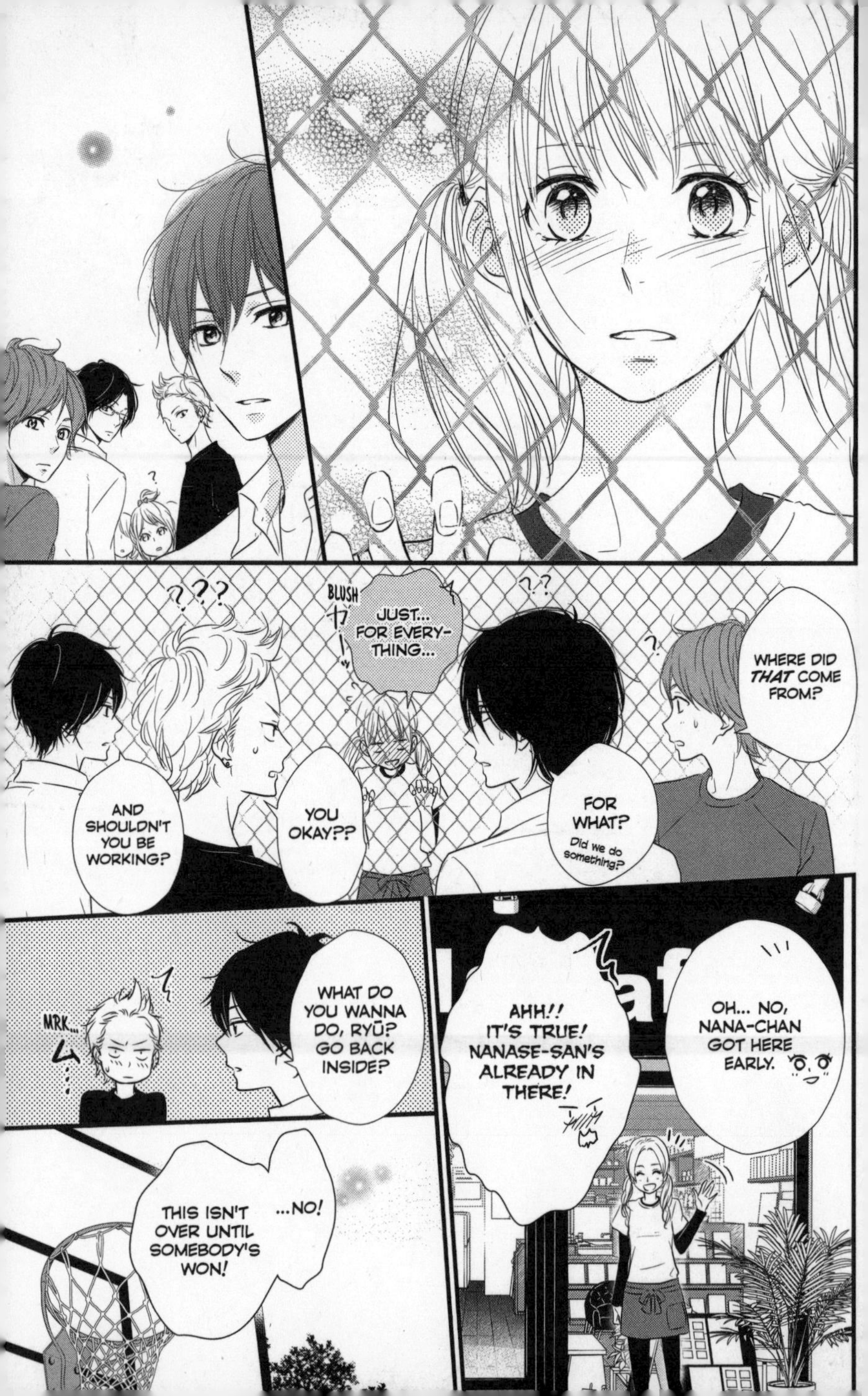
WHERE DID *THAT* COME FROM?
FOR WHAT?
Did we do something?
JUST... FOR EVERY-THING...
BLUSH
YOU OKAY??
AND SHOULDN'T YOU BE WORKING?
OH... NO, NANA-CHAN GOT HERE EARLY.
AHH!! IT'S TRUE! NANASE-SAN'S ALREADY IN THERE!
WHAT DO YOU WANNA DO, RYŪ? GO BACK INSIDE?
MRK...
...NO!
THIS ISN'T OVER UNTIL SOMEBODY'S WON!

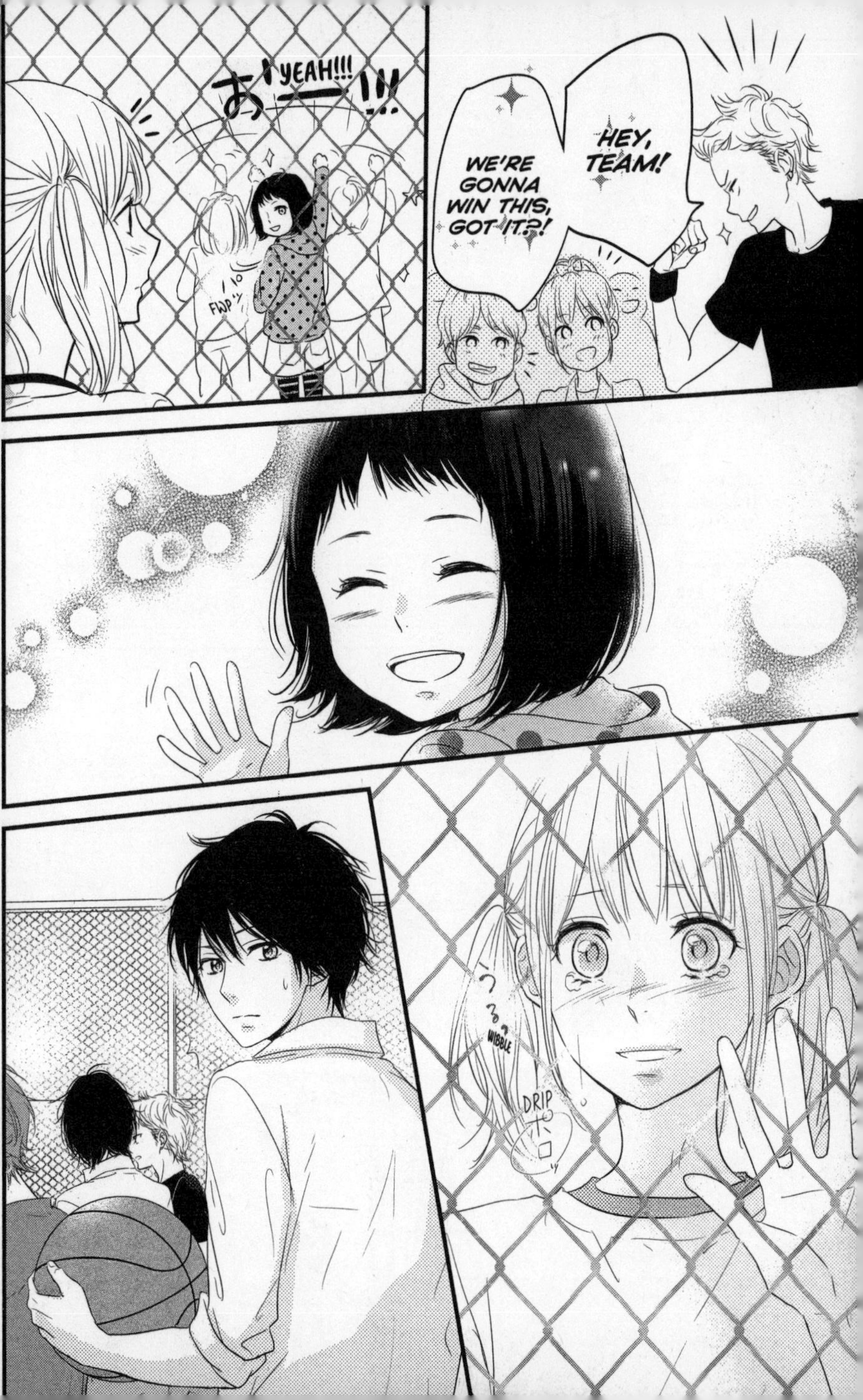
HEY, TEAM!
WE'RE GONNA WIN THIS, GOT IT?!
あー!!!
YEAH!!!
FWP
WIBBLE
DRIP

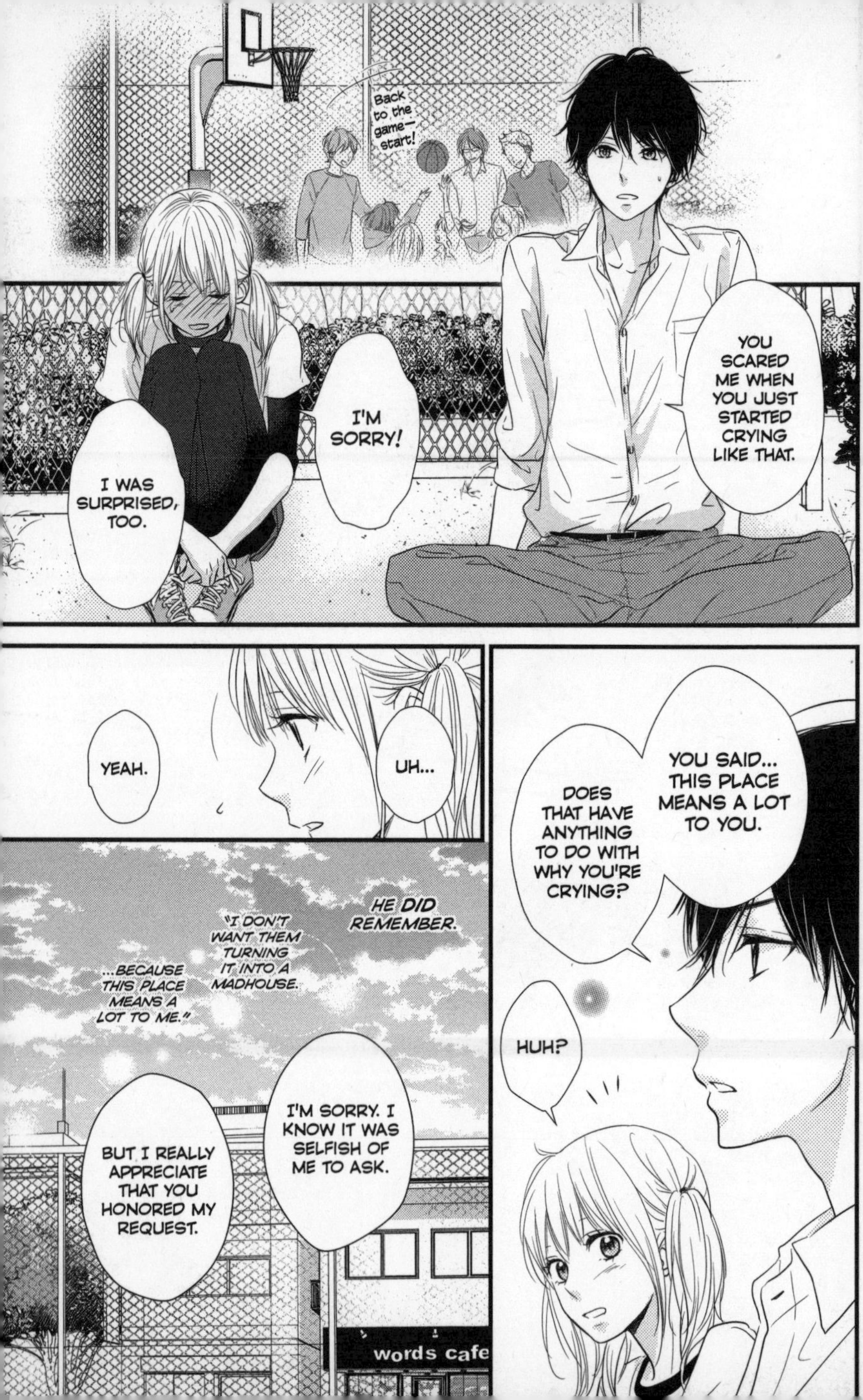
YOU SCARED ME WHEN YOU JUST STARTED CRYING LIKE THAT.
Back to the game—start!
I'M SORRY!
I WAS SURPRISED, TOO.
YOU SAID... THIS PLACE MEANS A LOT TO YOU.
DOES THAT HAVE ANYTHING TO DO WITH WHY YOU'RE CRYING?
HUH?
UH...
YEAH.
HE DID REMEMBER.
"I DON'T WANT THEM TURNING IT INTO A MADHOUSE.
...BECAUSE THIS PLACE MEANS A LOT TO ME."
I'M SORRY. I KNOW IT WAS SELFISH OF ME TO ASK.
BUT I REALLY APPRECIATE THAT YOU HONORED MY REQUEST.
words cafe

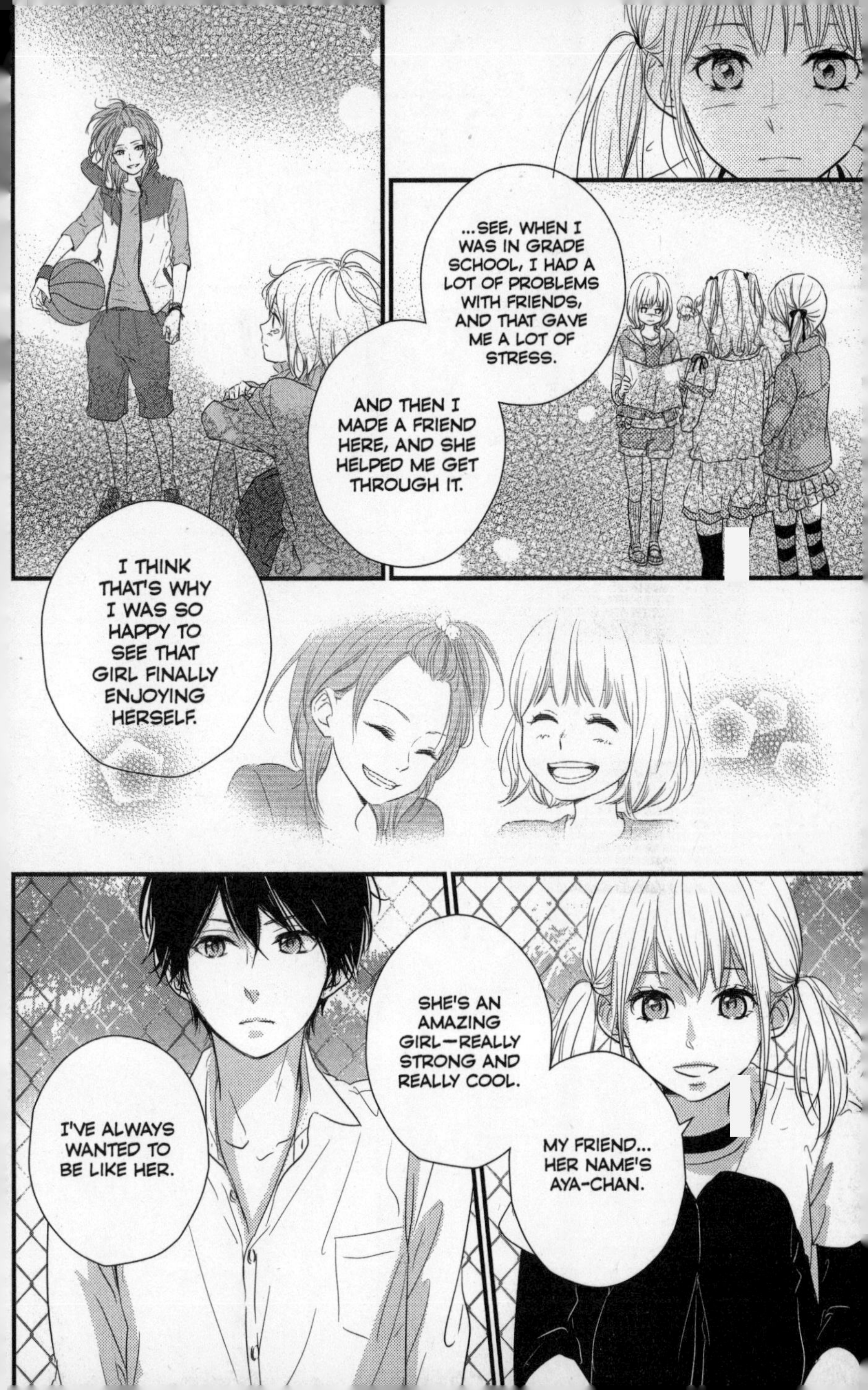
...SEE, WHEN I WAS IN GRADE SCHOOL, I HAD A LOT OF PROBLEMS WITH FRIENDS, AND THAT GAVE ME A LOT OF STRESS.
AND THEN I MADE A FRIEND HERE, AND SHE HELPED ME GET THROUGH IT.
I THINK THAT'S WHY I WAS SO HAPPY TO SEE THAT GIRL FINALLY ENJOYING HERSELF.
MY FRIEND... HER NAME'S AYA-CHAN.
SHE'S AN AMAZING GIRL—REALLY STRONG AND REALLY COOL.
I'VE ALWAYS WANTED TO BE LIKE HER.

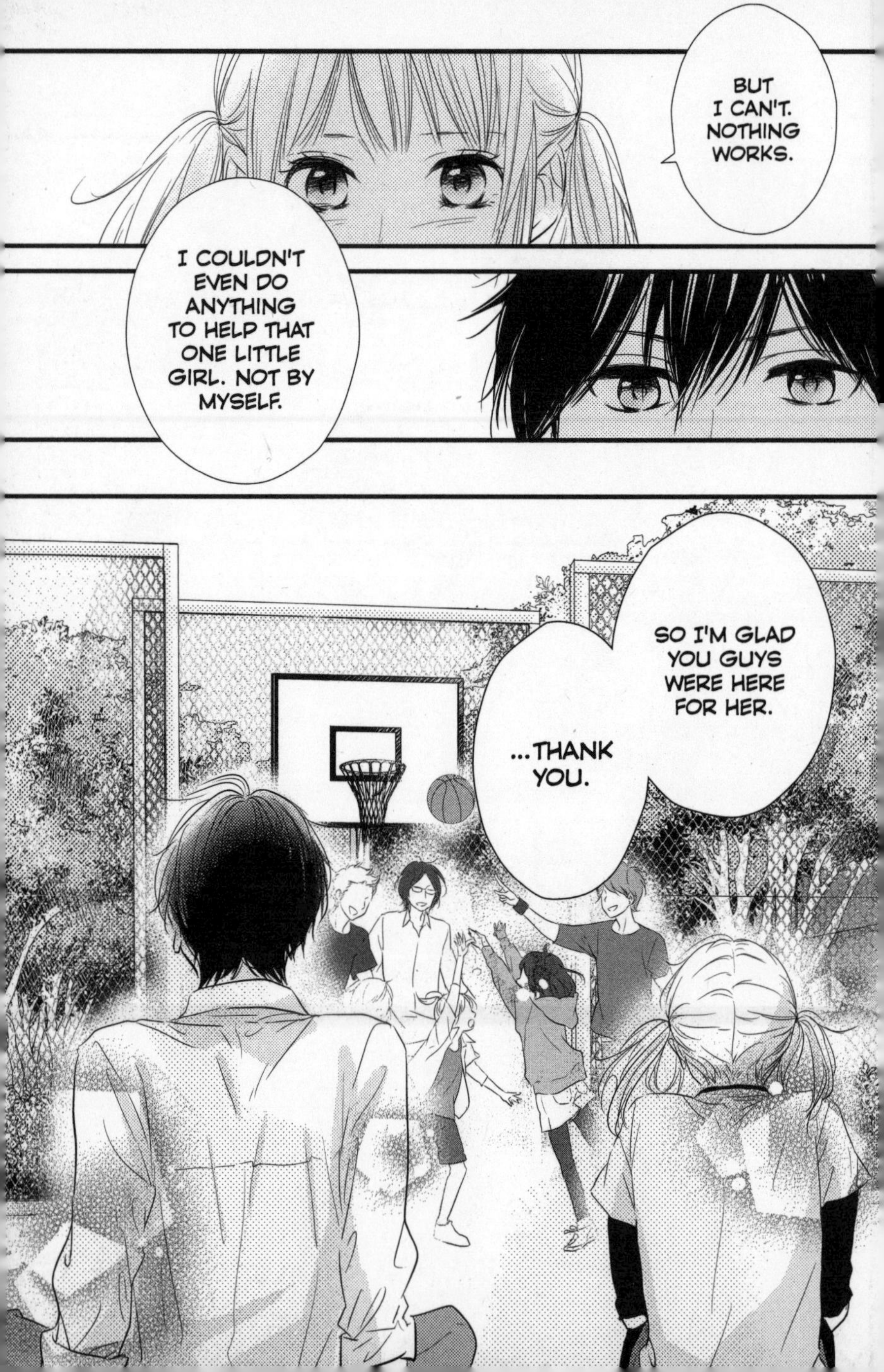
BUT I CAN'T. NOTHING WORKS.
I COULDN'T EVEN DO ANYTHING TO HELP THAT ONE LITTLE GIRL. NOT BY MYSELF.
SO I'M GLAD YOU GUYS WERE HERE FOR HER.
...THANK YOU.

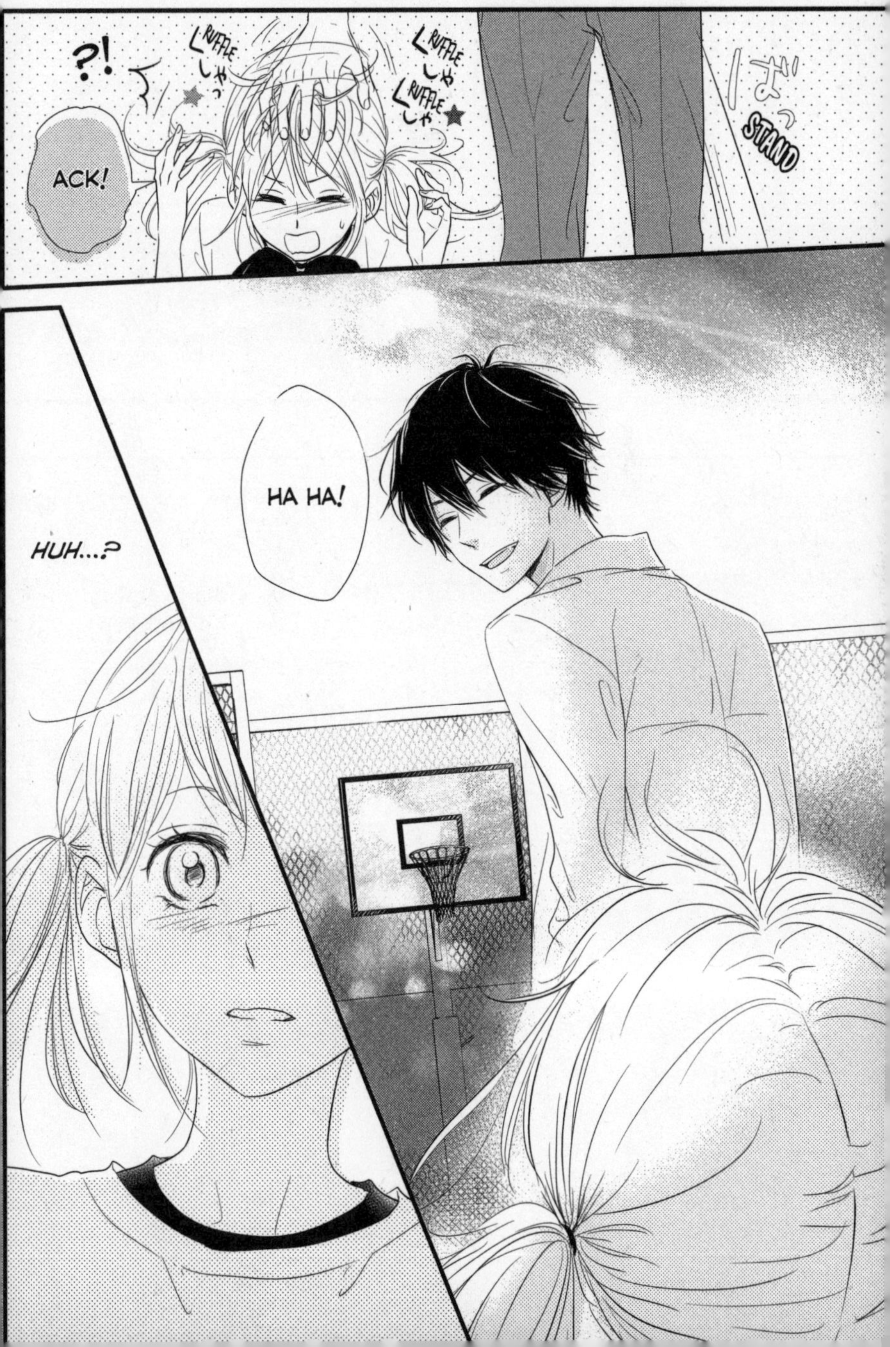

ぱっ
STAND
くしゃ
RUFFLE
くしゃ
RUFFLE
?!
くしゃっ
RUFFLE
ACK!
HA HA!
HUH...?

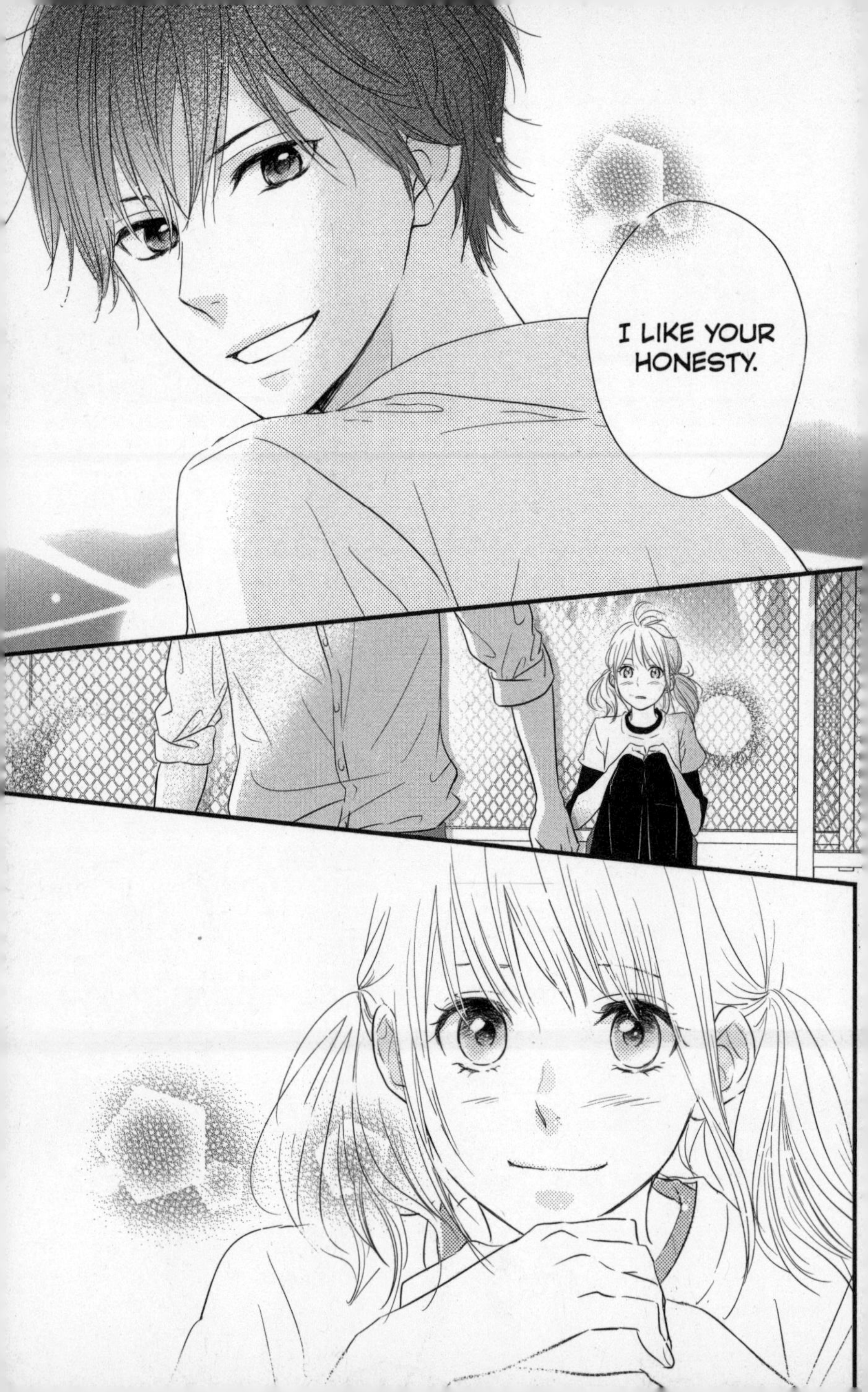
I LIKE YOUR HONESTY.

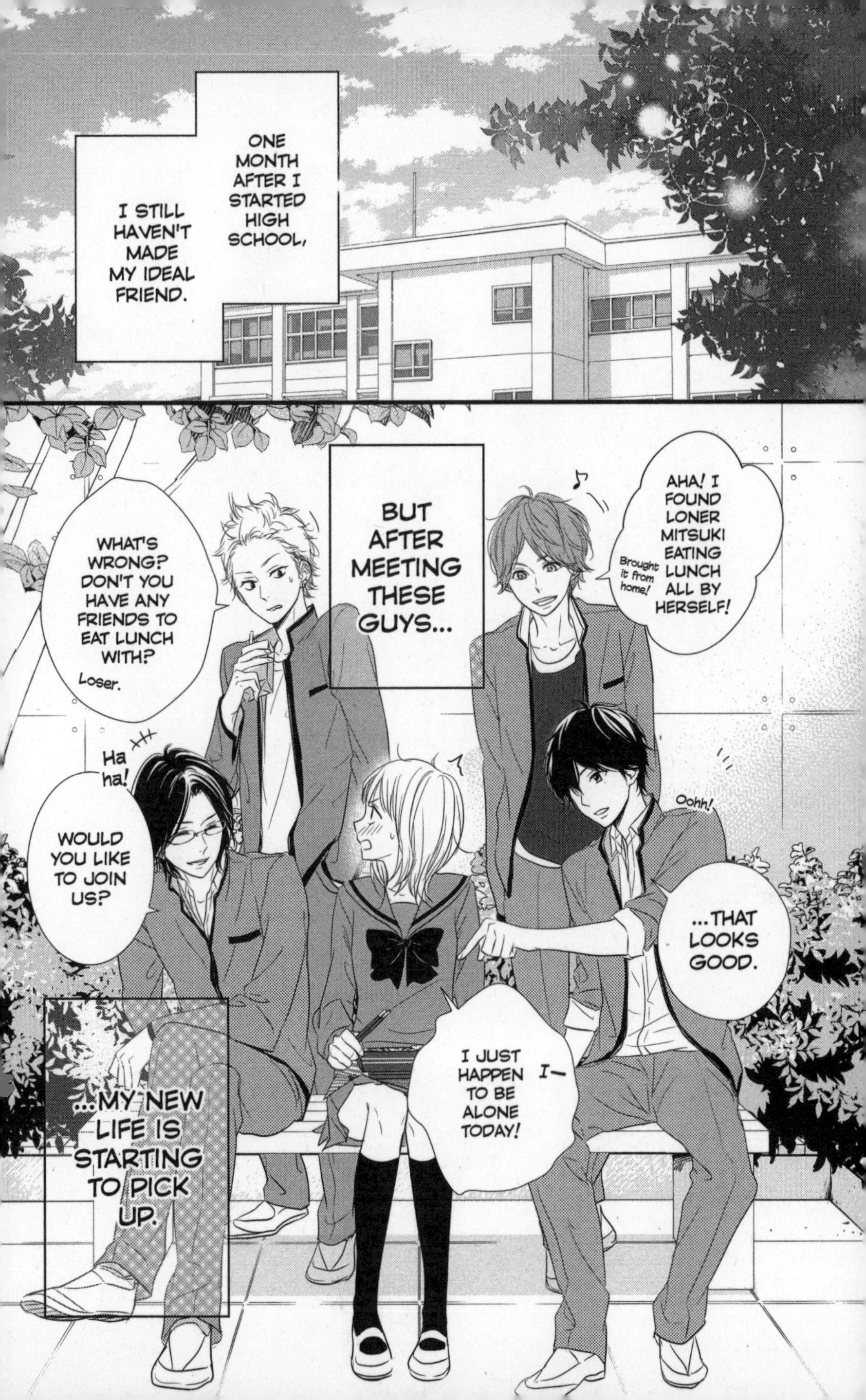
ONE MONTH AFTER I STARTED HIGH SCHOOL,
I STILL HAVEN'T MADE MY IDEAL FRIEND.
AHA! I FOUND LONER MITSUKI EATING LUNCH ALL BY HERSELF!
Brought it from home!
BUT AFTER MEETING THESE GUYS...
WHAT'S WRONG? DON'T YOU HAVE ANY FRIENDS TO EAT LUNCH WITH?
Loser.
Oohh!
...THAT LOOKS GOOD.
Ha ha!
WOULD YOU LIKE TO JOIN US?
I— I JUST HAPPEN TO BE ALONE TODAY!
...MY NEW LIFE IS STARTING TO PICK UP.

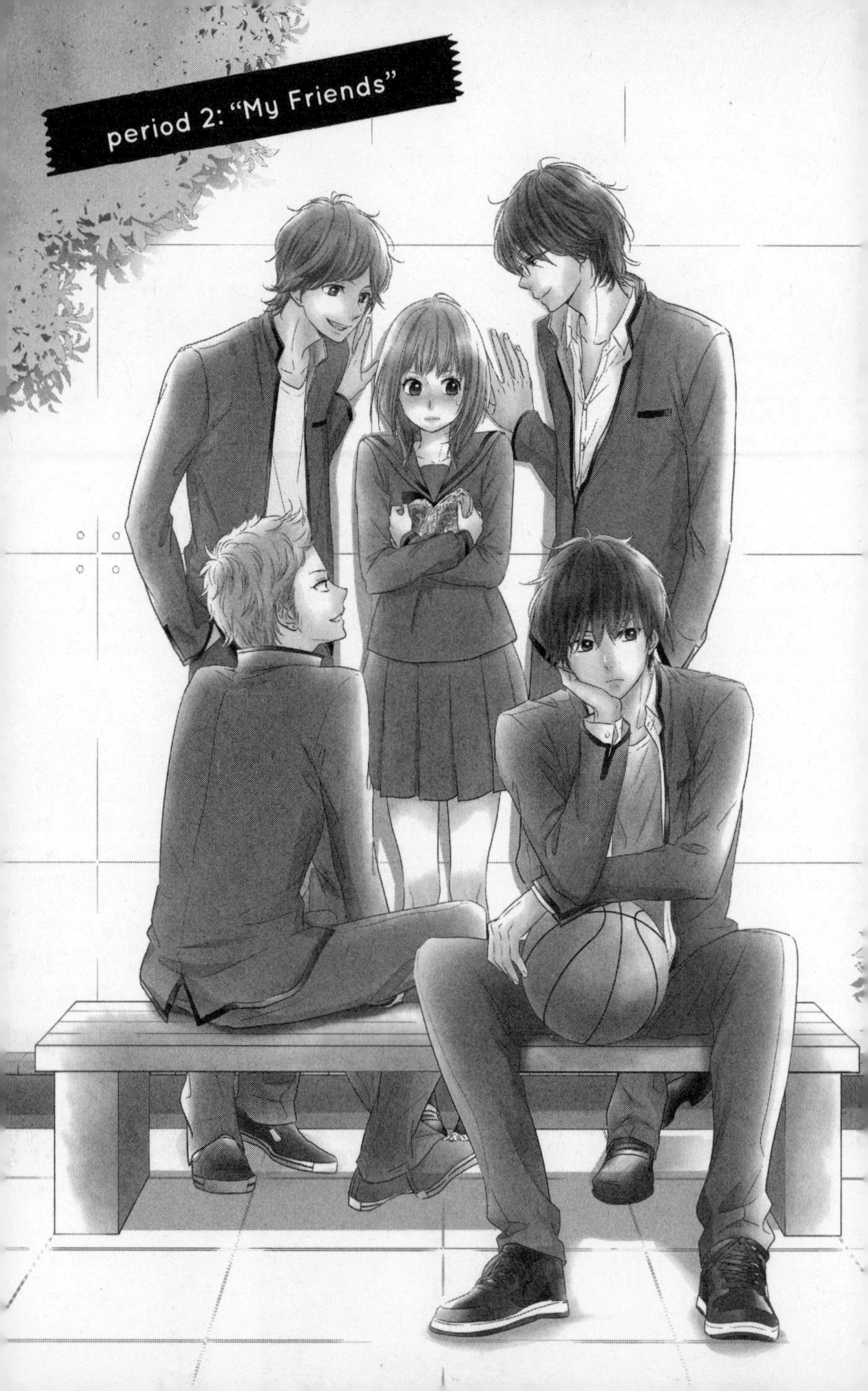
period 2: "My Friends"

The answer to the silhouette quiz on
page 6 is...

Rui & Towa

The first-
year duo.

It is the first volume...

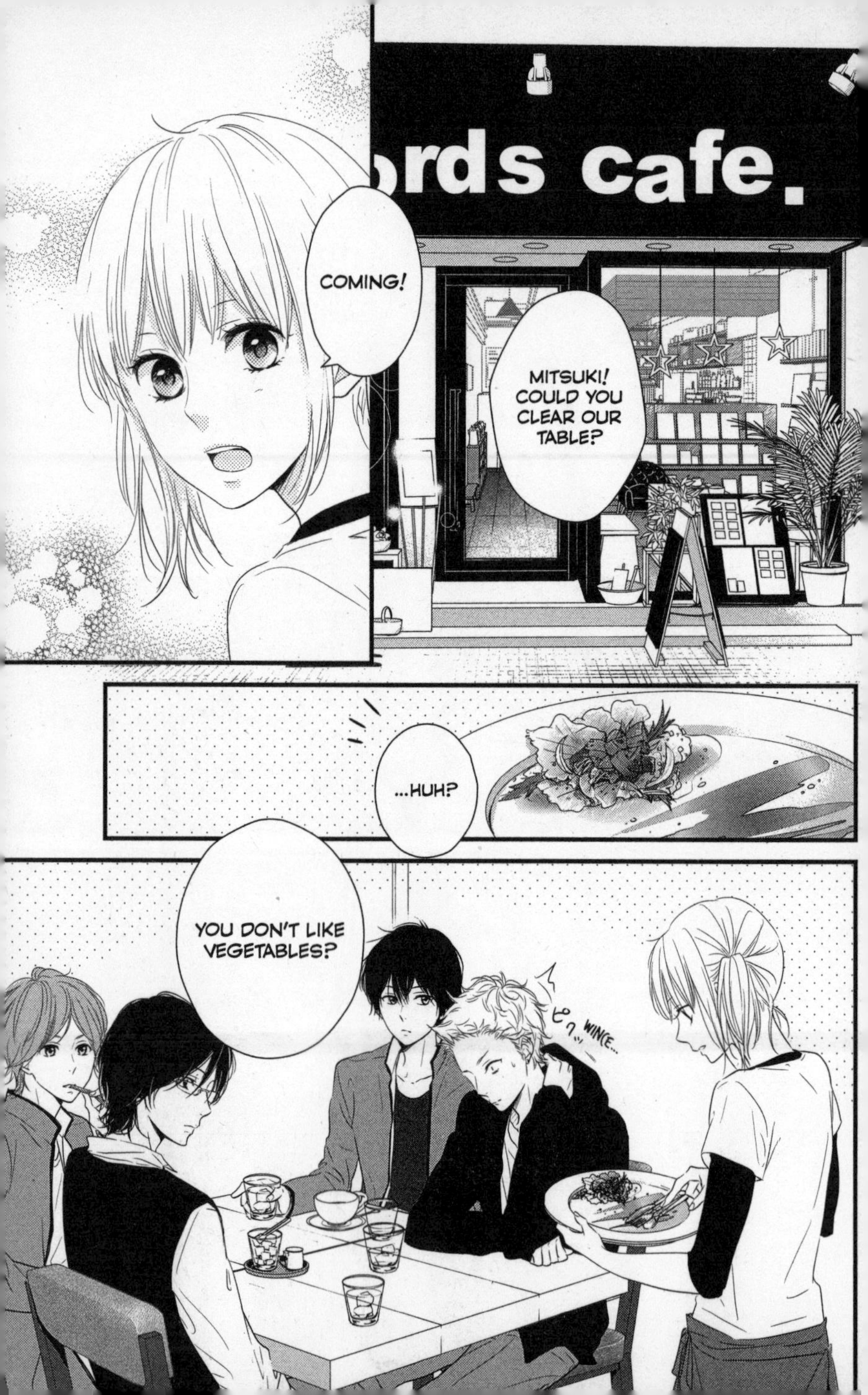
ords cafe.
MITSUKI! COULD YOU CLEAR OUR TABLE?
COMING!
...HUH?
YOU DON'T LIKE VEGETABLES?
ピクッ
WINCE...

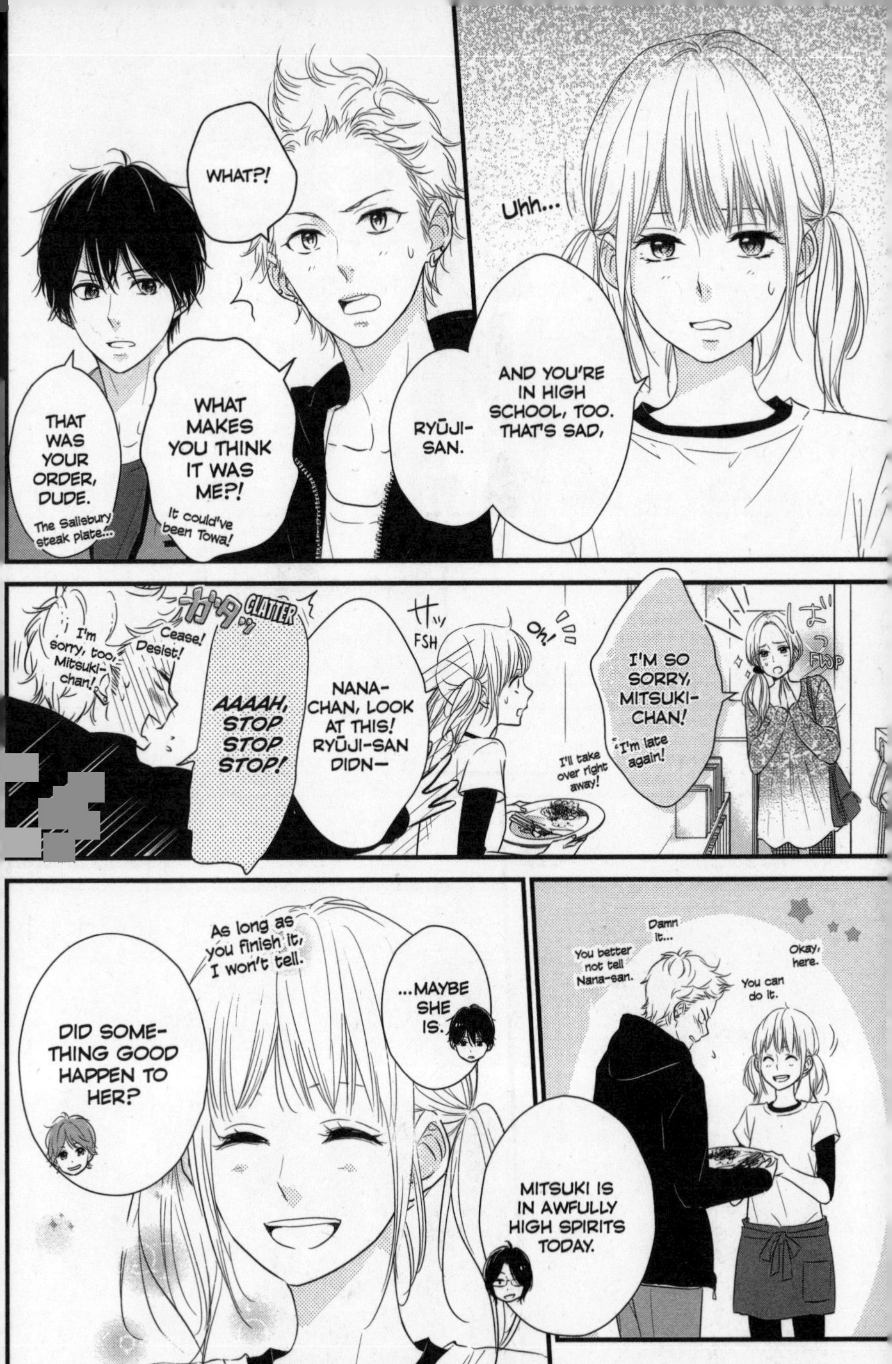
Uhh...
AND YOU'RE IN HIGH SCHOOL, TOO. THAT'S SAD,
RYŪJI-SAN.
WHAT?!
WHAT MAKES YOU THINK IT WAS ME?!
It could've been Towa!
THAT WAS YOUR ORDER, DUDE.
The Salisbury steak plate...
FWP
I'M SO SORRY, MITSUKI-CHAN!
I'm late again!
I'll take over right away!
Oh!
FSH
NANA-CHAN, LOOK AT THIS! RYŪJI-SAN DIDN—
AAAAH, STOP STOP STOP!
CLATTER
Cease! Desist!
I'm sorry, too, Mitsuki-chan!
Damn it...
You better not tell Nana-san.
Okay, here.
You can do it.
MITSUKI IS IN AWFULLY HIGH SPIRITS TODAY.
...MAYBE SHE IS.
As long as you finish it, I won't tell.
DID SOMETHING GOOD HAPPEN TO HER?

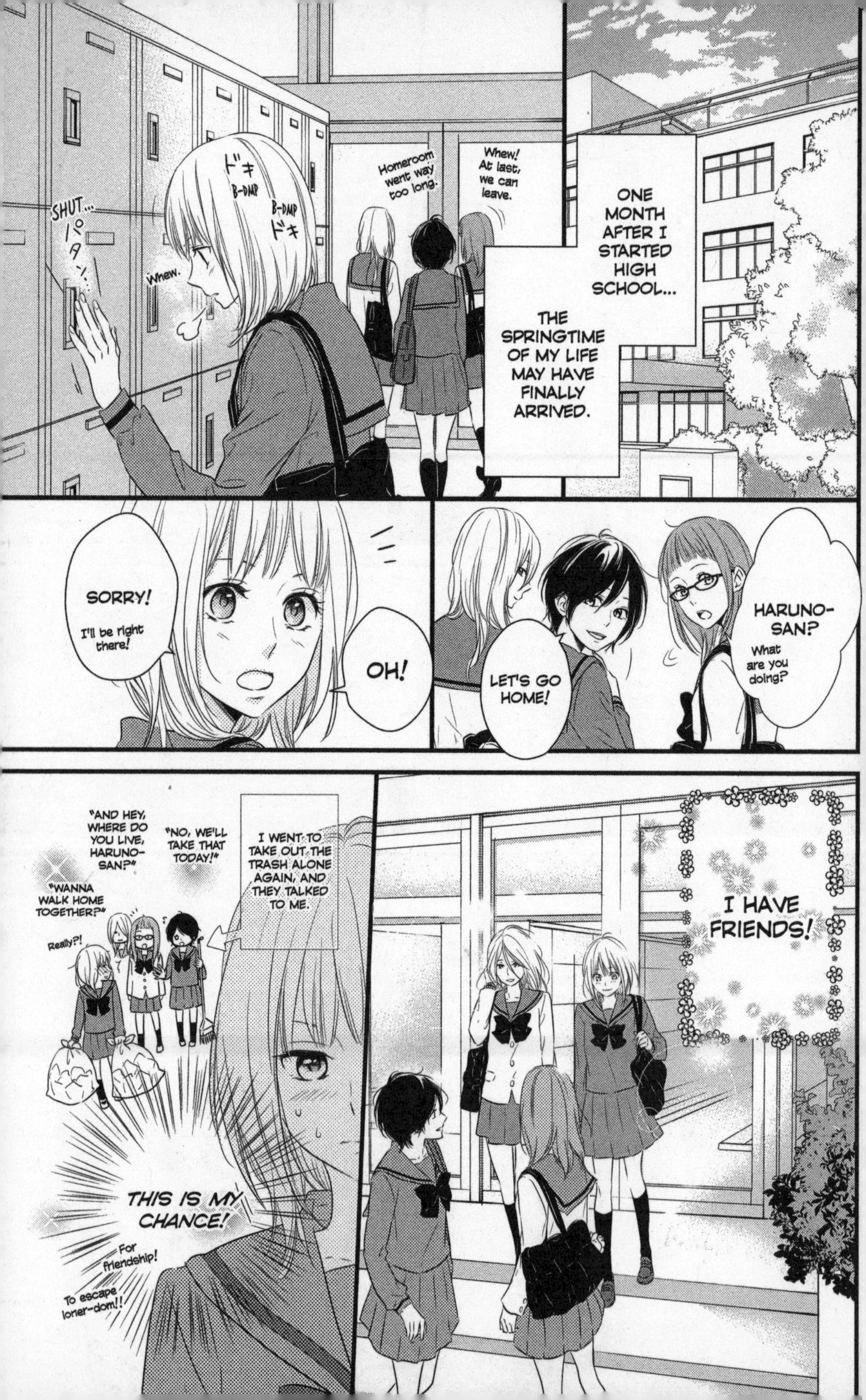
ONE MONTH AFTER I STARTED HIGH SCHOOL...
THE SPRINGTIME OF MY LIFE MAY HAVE FINALLY ARRIVED.
Whew! At last, we can leave.
Homeroom went way too long.
ドキ B-DMP
B-DMP ドキ
SHUT... パタン…
Whew.
HARUNO-SAN? What are you doing?
LET'S GO HOME!
OH!
SORRY! I'll be right there!
I HAVE FRIENDS!
I WENT TO TAKE OUT THE TRASH ALONE AGAIN, AND THEY TALKED TO ME.
"NO, WE'LL TAKE THAT TODAY!"
"AND HEY, WHERE DO YOU LIVE, HARUNO-SAN?"
"WANNA WALK HOME TOGETHER?"
Really?!
THIS IS MY CHANCE!
For friendship!
To escape loner-dom!!

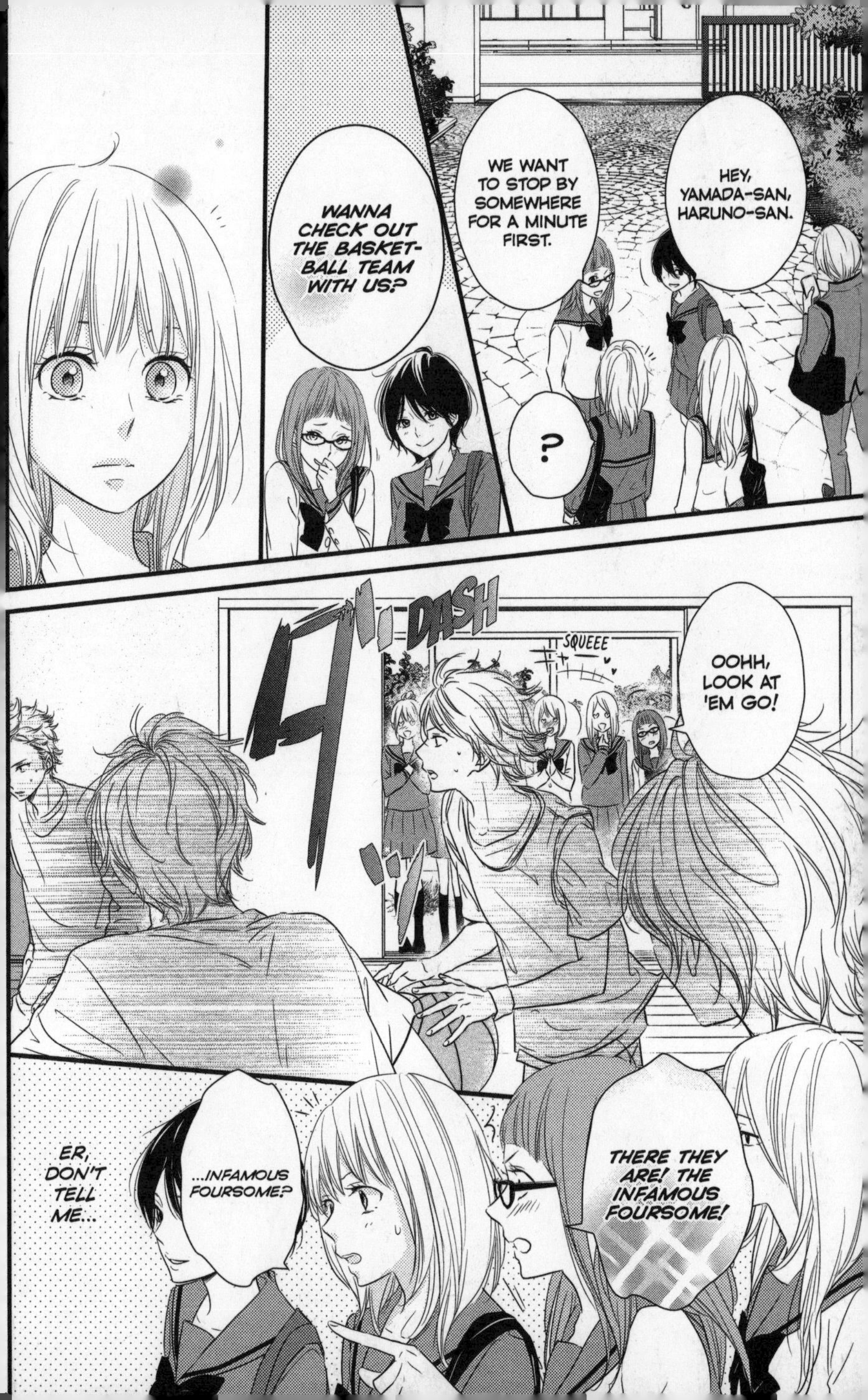
HEY, YAMADA-SAN, HARUNO-SAN.
WE WANT TO STOP BY SOMEWHERE FOR A MINUTE FIRST.
?
WANNA CHECK OUT THE BASKET-BALL TEAM WITH US?
OOHH, LOOK AT 'EM GO!
SQUEEE
DASH
THERE THEY ARE! THE INFAMOUS FOURSOME!
...INFAMOUS FOURSOME?
ER, DON'T TELL ME...

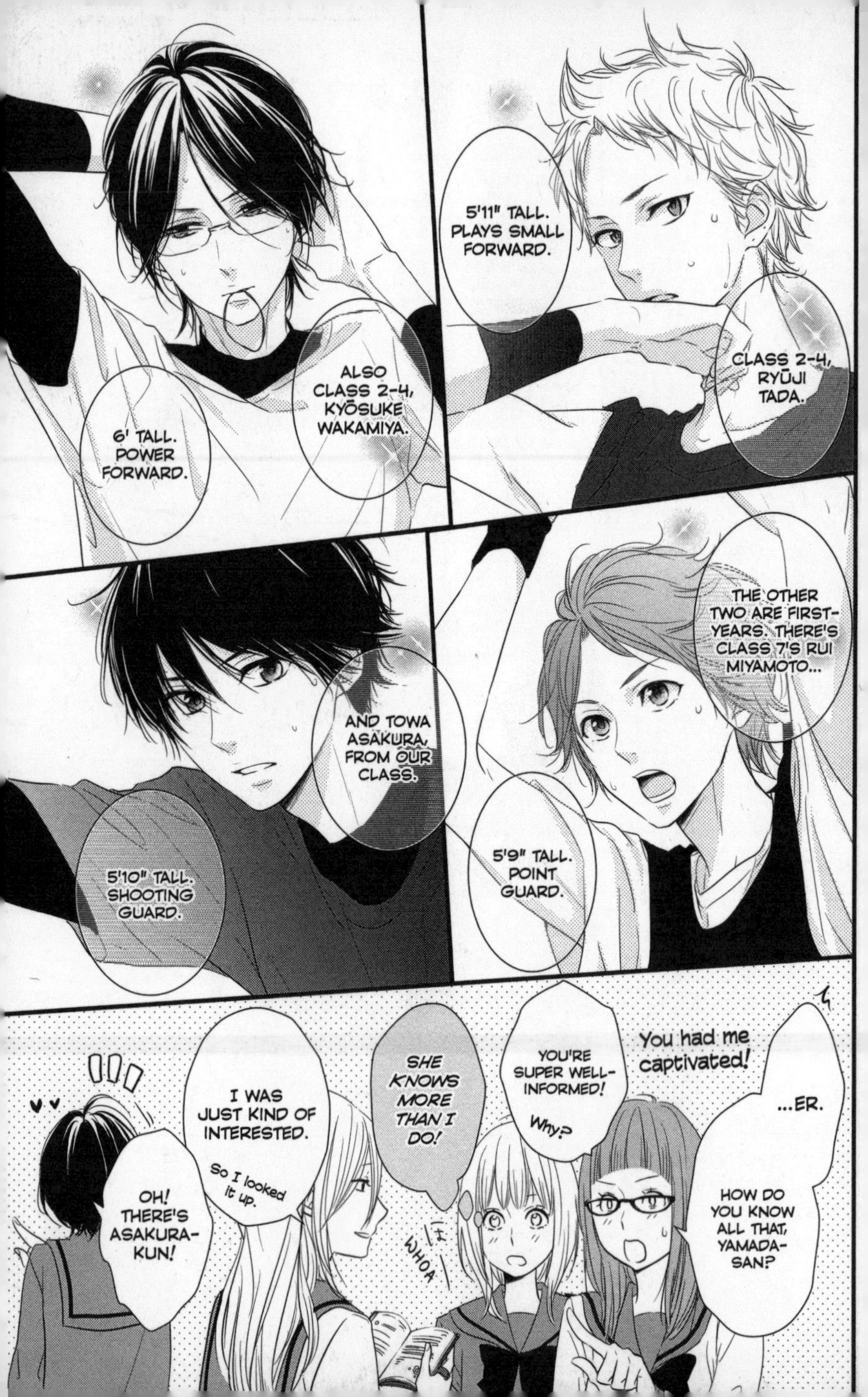
CLASS 2-4, RYŪJI TADA.
5'11" TALL. PLAYS SMALL FORWARD.
ALSO CLASS 2-4, KYŌSUKE WAKAMIYA.
6' TALL. POWER FORWARD.
THE OTHER TWO ARE FIRST-YEARS. THERE'S CLASS 7'S RUI MIYAMOTO...
5'9" TALL. POINT GUARD.
AND TOWA ASAKURA, FROM OUR CLASS.
5'10" TALL. SHOOTING GUARD.
...ER.
HOW DO YOU KNOW ALL THAT, YAMADA-SAN?
You had me captivated!
YOU'RE SUPER WELL-INFORMED!
Why?
SHE KNOWS MORE THAN I DO!
WHOA
I WAS JUST KIND OF INTERESTED.
So I looked it up.
OH! THERE'S ASAKURA-KUN!

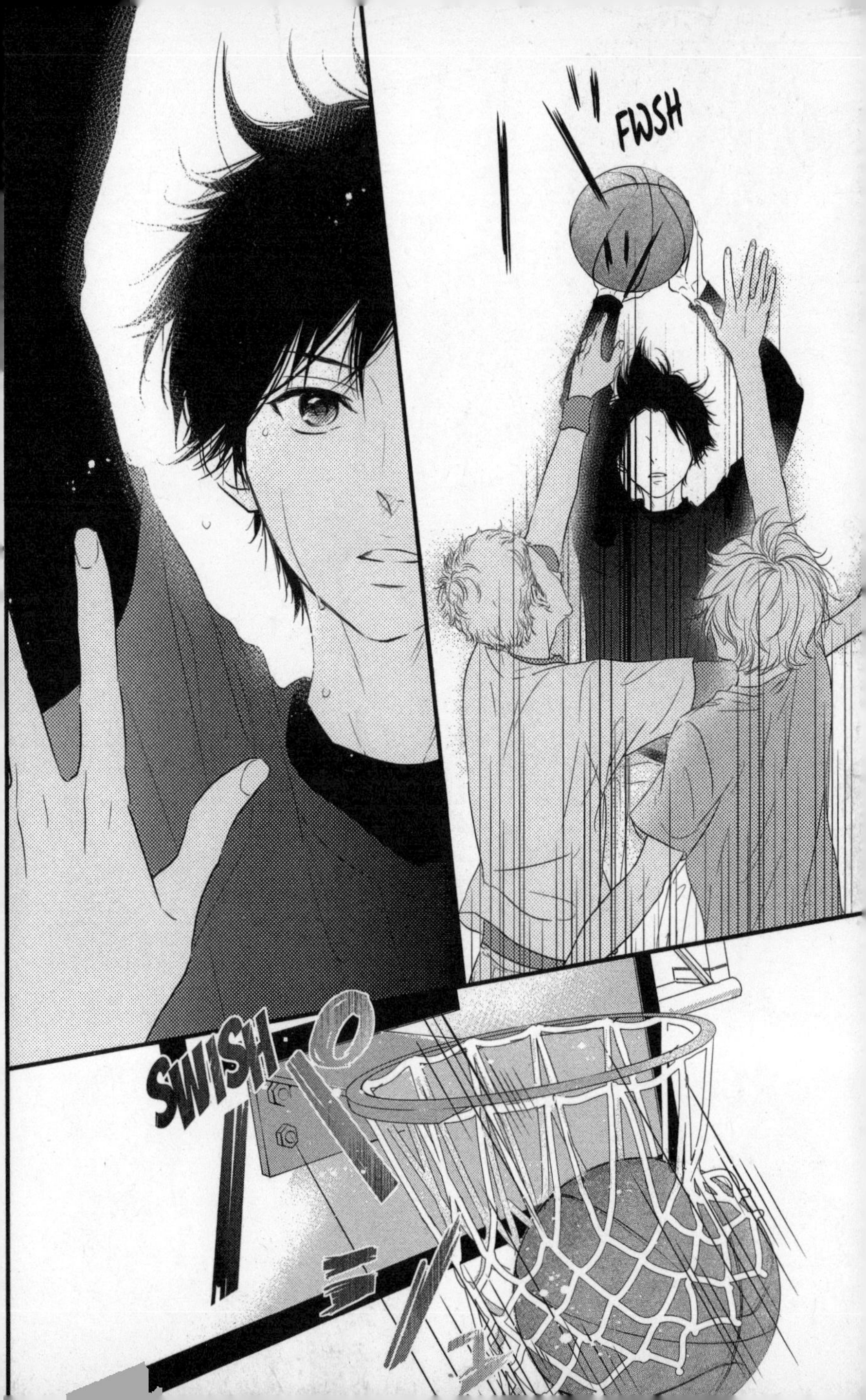
FWSH
SWISH

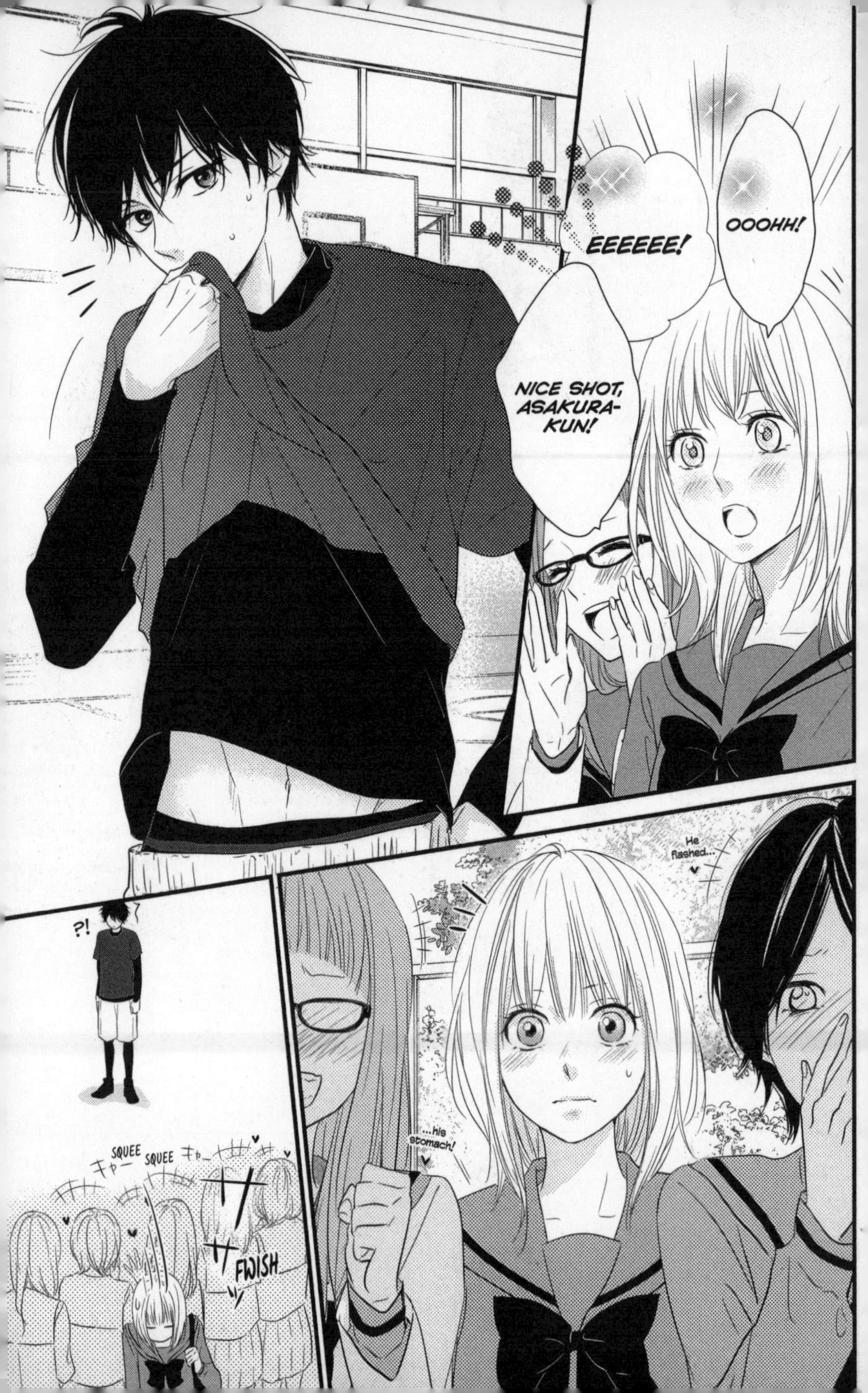
OOOHH!
EEEEEE!
NICE SHOT, ASAKURA-KUN!
He flashed...
...his stomach!
?!
SQUEE
キャー
SQUEE
キャー
FWISH

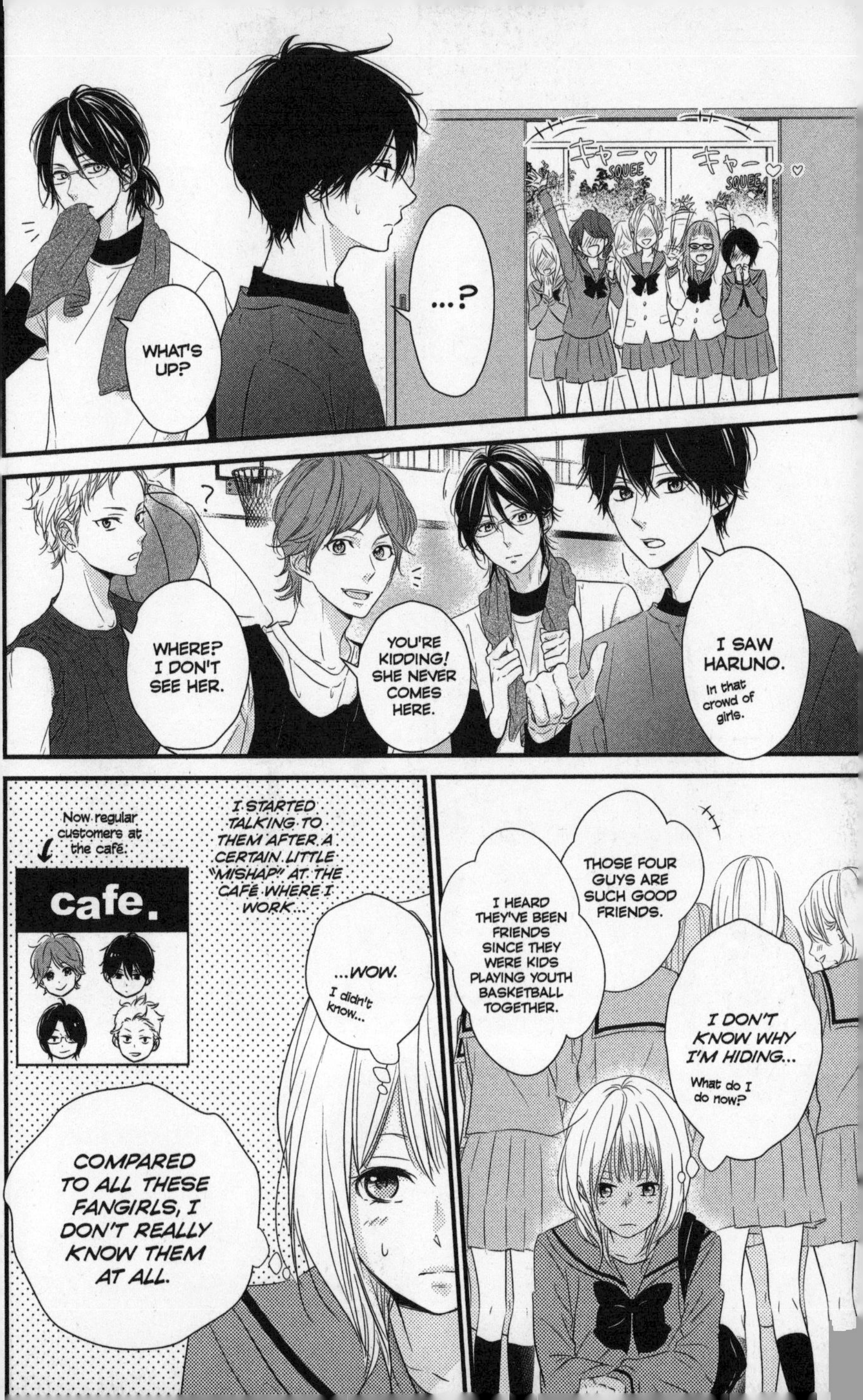
キャー SQUEE
キャー SQUEE
...?
WHAT'S UP?
I SAW HARUNO. In that crowd of girls.
YOU'RE KIDDING! SHE NEVER COMES HERE.
WHERE? I DON'T SEE HER.
THOSE FOUR GUYS ARE SUCH GOOD FRIENDS.
I HEARD THEY'VE BEEN FRIENDS SINCE THEY WERE KIDS PLAYING YOUTH BASKETBALL TOGETHER.
I DON'T KNOW WHY I'M HIDING... What do I do now?
I STARTED TALKING TO THEM AFTER A CERTAIN LITTLE "MISHAP" AT THE CAFÉ WHERE I WORK...
Now regular customers at the café.
cafe.
...WOW. I didn't know...
COMPARED TO ALL THESE FANGIRLS, I DON'T REALLY KNOW THEM AT ALL.

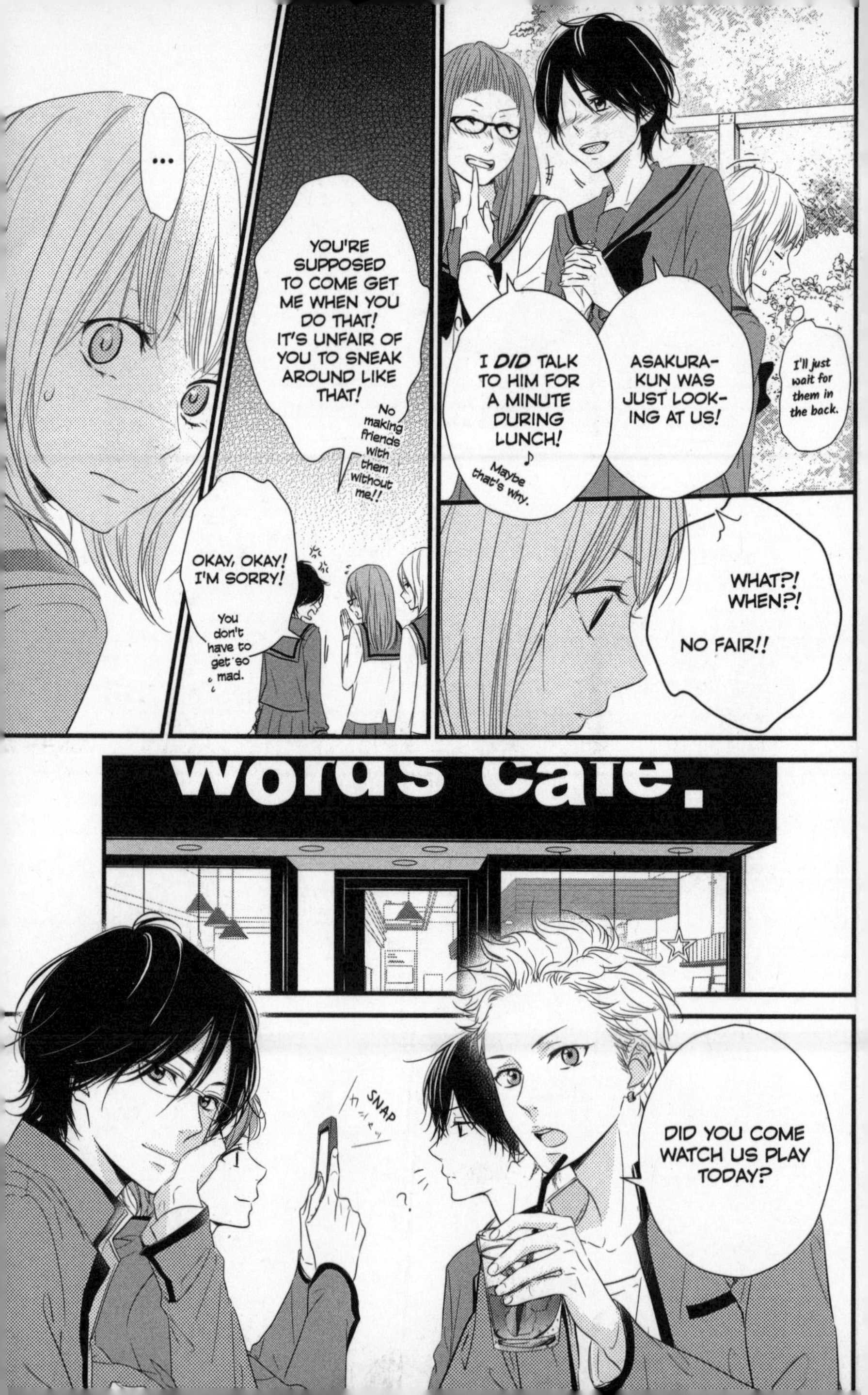

I'll just wait for them in the back.
ASAKURA-KUN WAS JUST LOOKING AT US!
I *DID* TALK TO HIM FOR A MINUTE DURING LUNCH! ♪
Maybe that's why.
WHAT?! WHEN?!
NO FAIR!!
YOU'RE SUPPOSED TO COME GET ME WHEN YOU DO THAT! IT'S UNFAIR OF YOU TO SNEAK AROUND LIKE THAT!
No making friends with them without me!!
OKAY, OKAY! I'M SORRY!
You don't have to get so mad.
...
words cafe.
DID YOU COME WATCH US PLAY TODAY?
SNAP

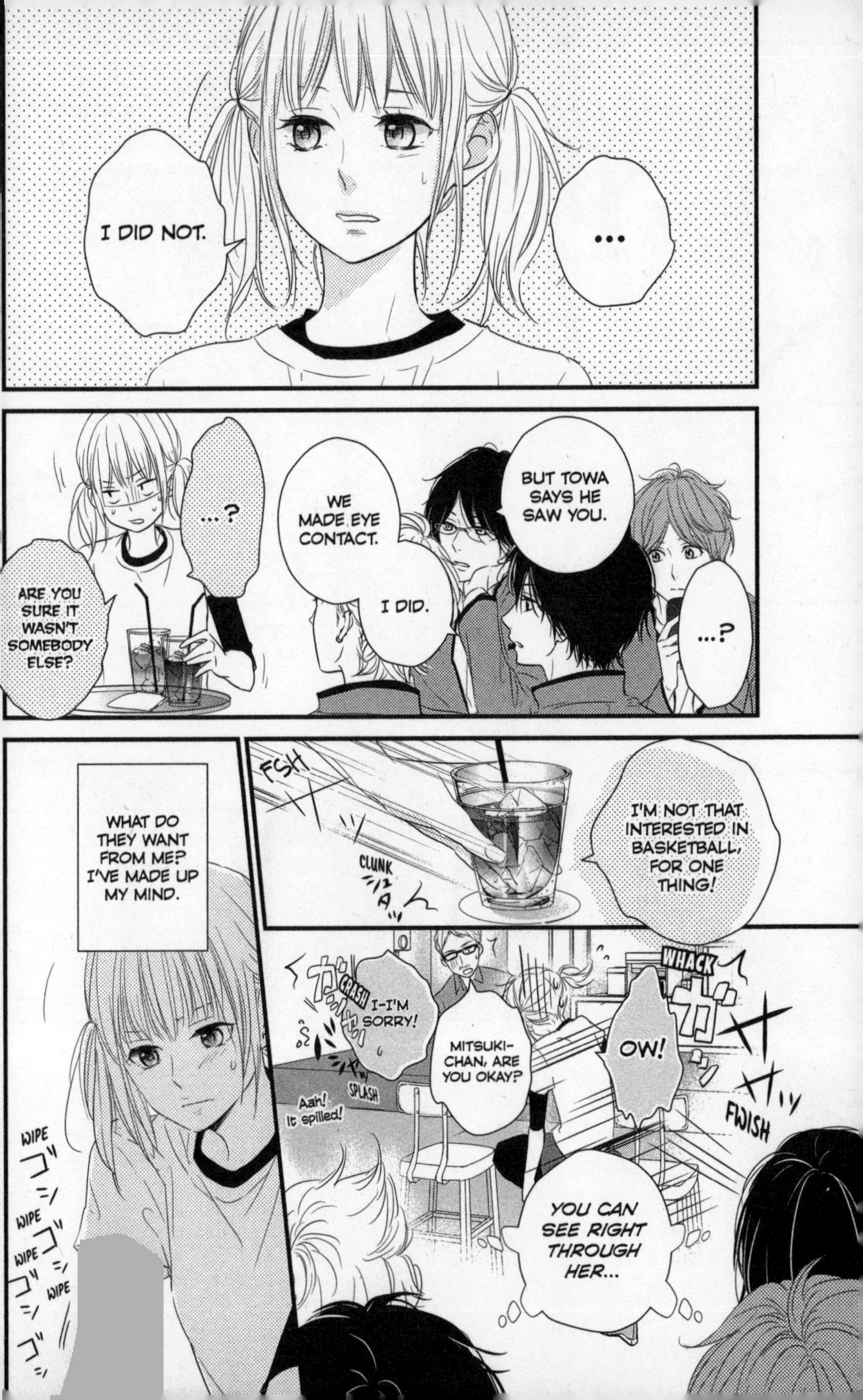
...
I DID NOT.
...?
BUT TOWA SAYS HE SAW YOU.
WE MADE EYE CONTACT.
I DID.
...?
ARE YOU SURE IT WASN'T SOMEBODY ELSE?
I'M NOT THAT INTERESTED IN BASKETBALL, FOR ONE THING!
FSH
CLUNK
WHAT DO THEY WANT FROM ME? I'VE MADE UP MY MIND.
WHACK
FWISH
OW!
MITSUKI-CHAN, ARE YOU OKAY?
CRASH
I-I'M SORRY!
SPLASH
Aah! It spilled!
YOU CAN SEE RIGHT THROUGH HER...
WIPE
WIPE
WIPE
WIPE

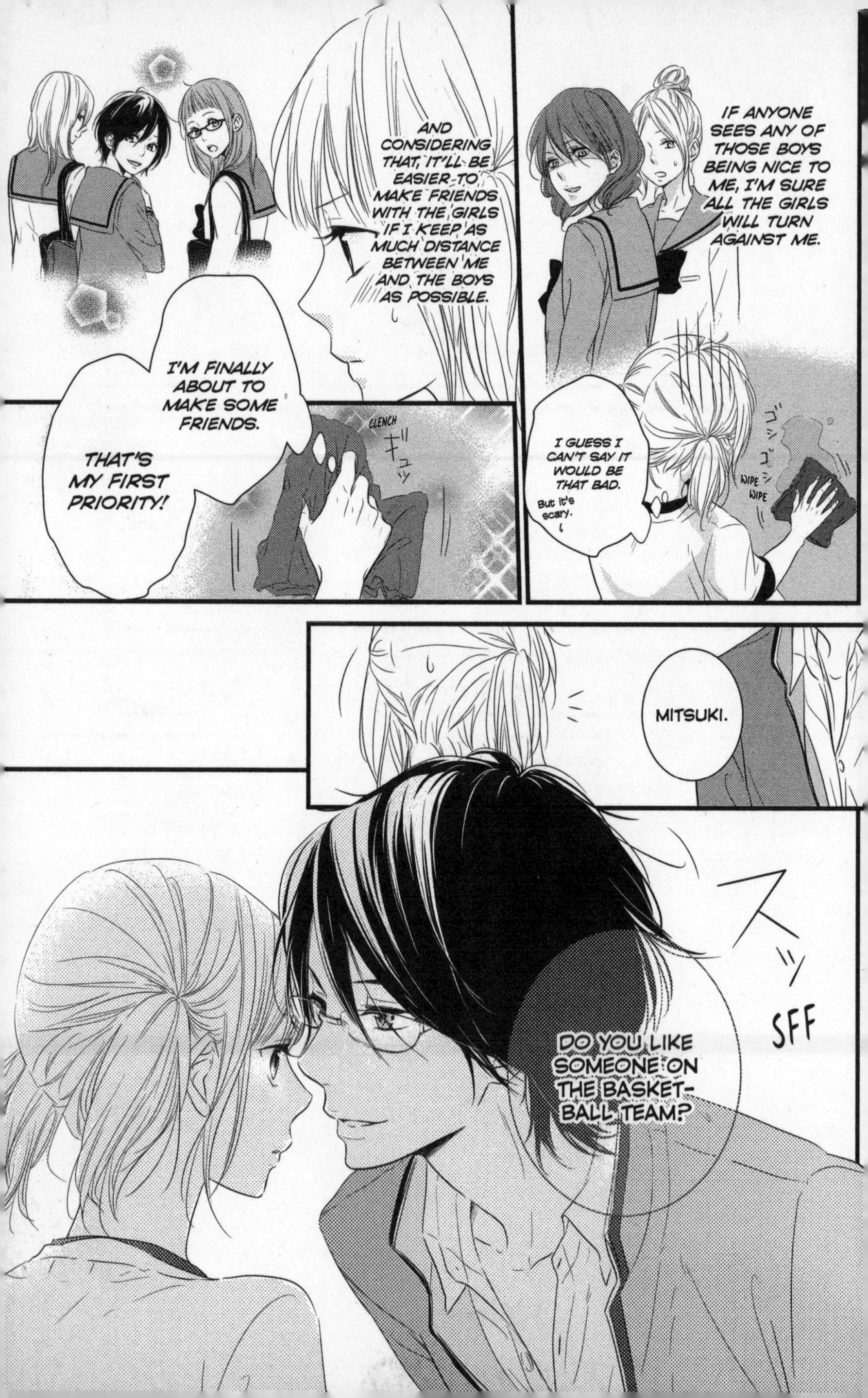
IF ANYONE SEES ANY OF THOSE BOYS BEING NICE TO ME, I'M SURE ALL THE GIRLS WILL TURN AGAINST ME.
AND CONSIDERING THAT, IT'LL BE EASIER TO MAKE FRIENDS WITH THE GIRLS IF I KEEP AS MUCH DISTANCE BETWEEN ME AND THE BOYS AS POSSIBLE.
I'M FINALLY ABOUT TO MAKE SOME FRIENDS.
THAT'S MY FIRST PRIORITY!
CLENCH
ギュッ
ゴシゴシ
WIPE WIPE
I GUESS I CAN'T SAY IT WOULD BE THAT BAD.
But it's scary.
MITSUKI.
スッ
SFF
DO YOU LIKE SOMEONE ON THE BASKET-BALL TEAM?

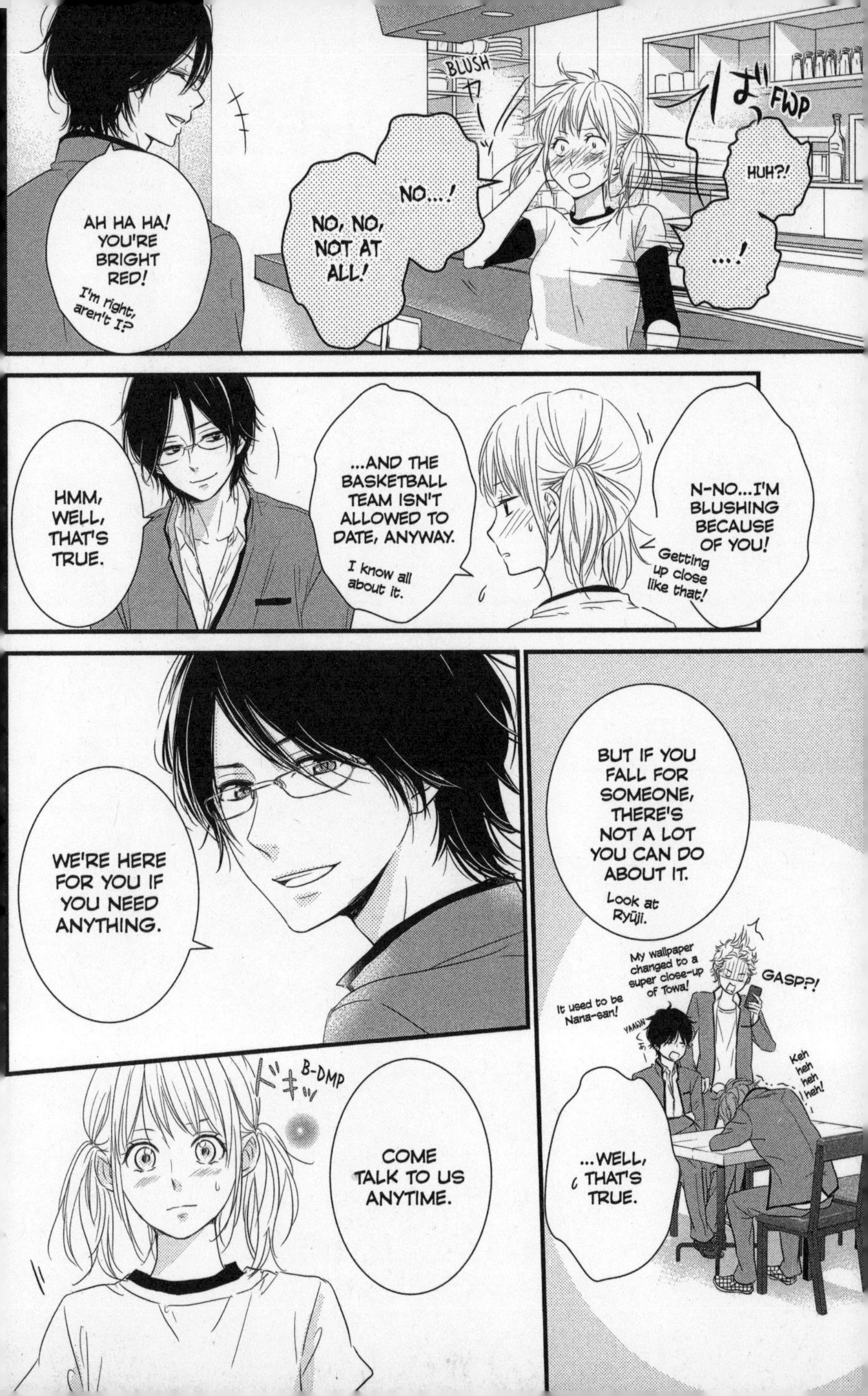
HUH?!
FWP
...!
BLUSH
NO...!
NO, NO, NOT AT ALL!
AH HA HA! YOU'RE BRIGHT RED!
I'm right, aren't I?
N-NO...I'M BLUSHING BECAUSE OF YOU!
Getting up close like that!
...AND THE BASKETBALL TEAM ISN'T ALLOWED TO DATE, ANYWAY.
I know all about it.
HMM, WELL, THAT'S TRUE.
BUT IF YOU FALL FOR SOMEONE, THERE'S NOT A LOT YOU CAN DO ABOUT IT.
Look at Ryūji.
GASP?!
My wallpaper changed to a super close-up of Towa!
It used to be Nana-san!
YAAWN
Keh heh heh heh!
...WELL, THAT'S TRUE.
WE'RE HERE FOR YOU IF YOU NEED ANYTHING.
B-DMP
COME TALK TO US ANYTIME.

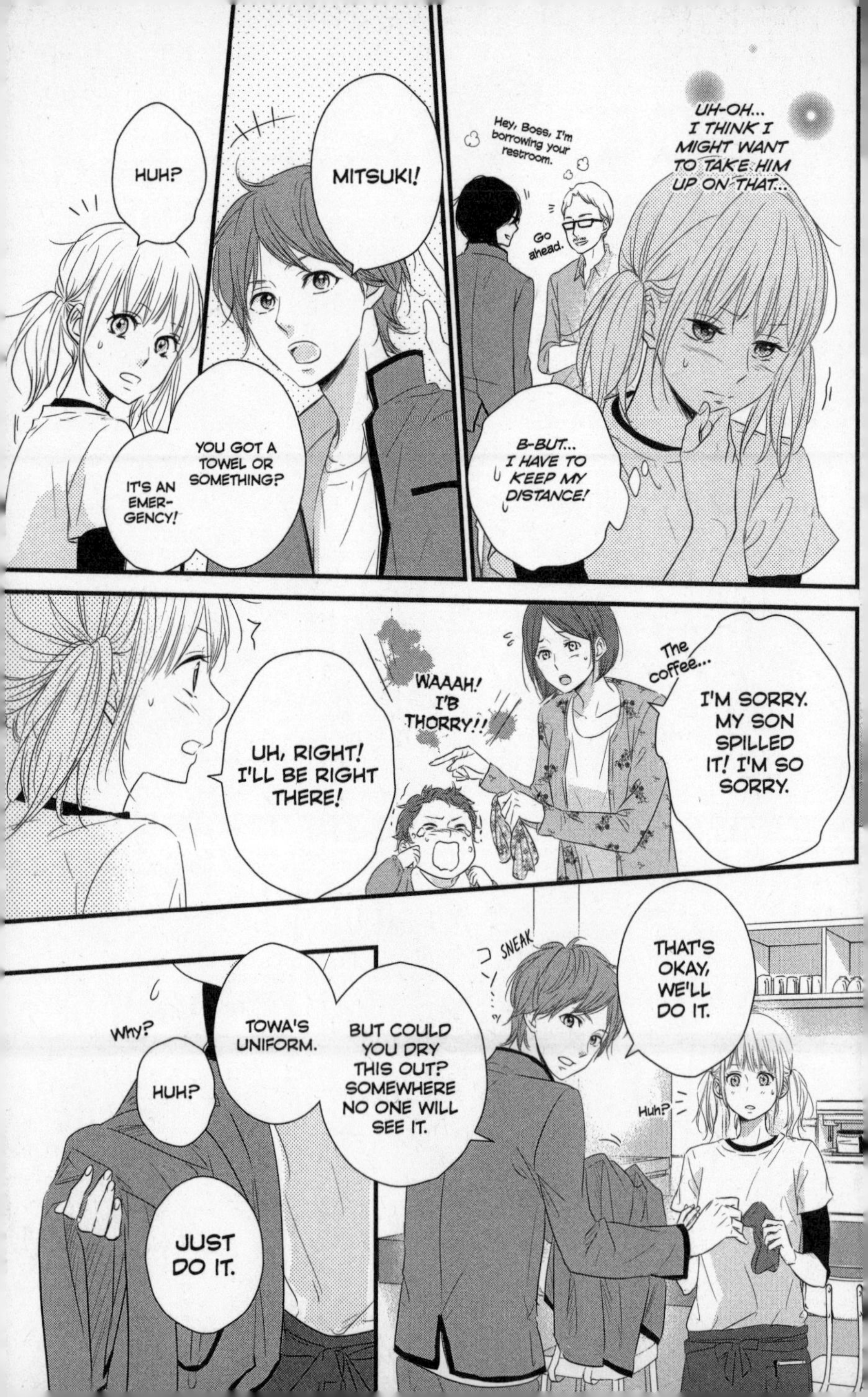
UH-OH... I THINK I MIGHT WANT TO TAKE HIM UP ON THAT...
Hey, Boss, I'm borrowing your restroom.
Go ahead.
B-BUT... I HAVE TO KEEP MY DISTANCE!
MITSUKI!
YOU GOT A TOWEL OR SOMETHING?
IT'S AN EMERGENCY!
HUH?
The coffee...
I'M SORRY. MY SON SPILLED IT! I'M SO SORRY.
WAAAH! I'B THORRY!!
UH, RIGHT! I'LL BE RIGHT THERE!
SNEAK
THAT'S OKAY, WE'LL DO IT.
Huh?
BUT COULD YOU DRY THIS OUT? SOMEWHERE NO ONE WILL SEE IT.
TOWA'S UNIFORM.
Why?
HUH?
JUST DO IT.

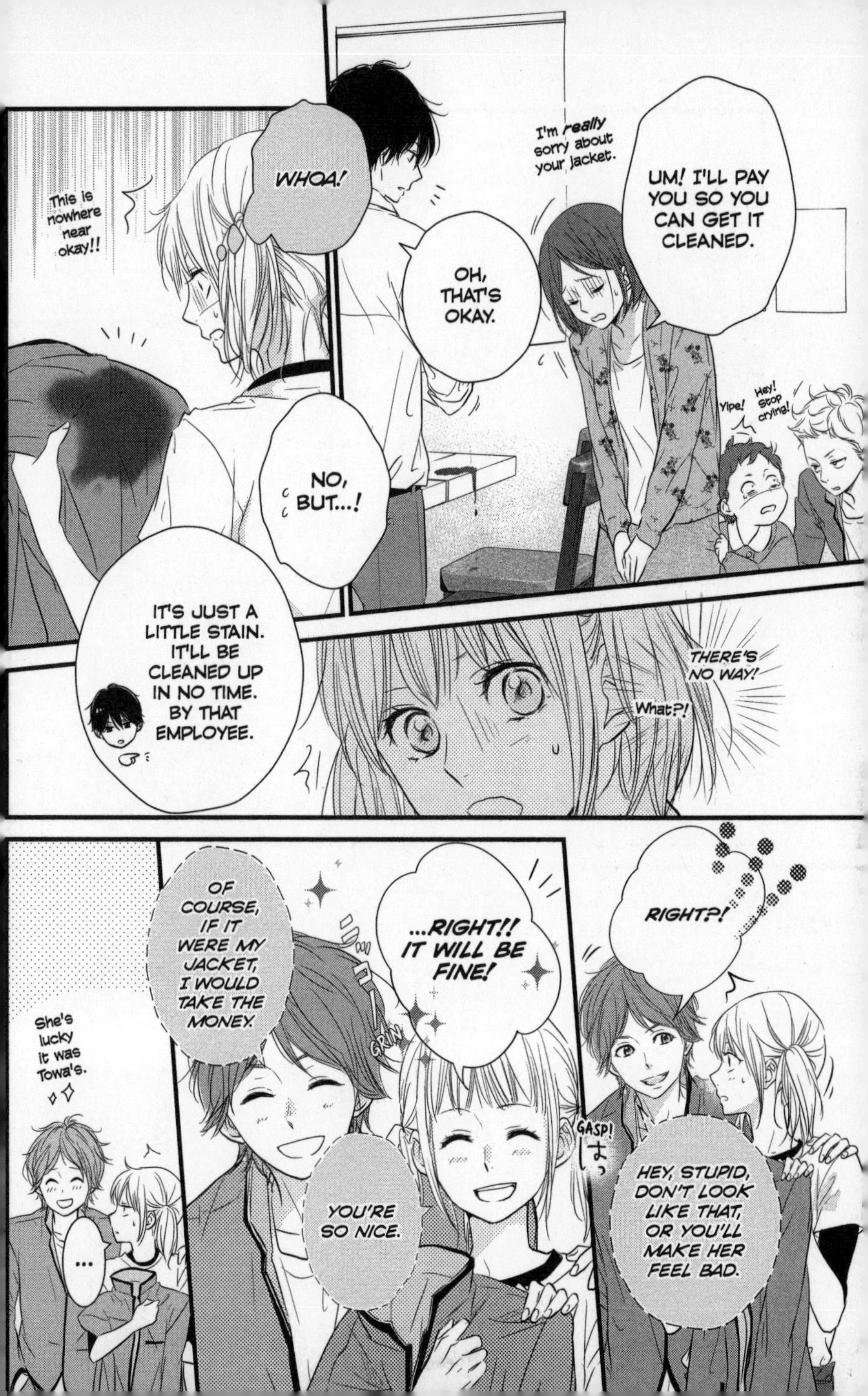
I'm really sorry about your jacket.
UM! I'LL PAY YOU SO YOU CAN GET IT CLEANED.
OH, THAT'S OKAY.
Hey! Stop crying!
Yipe!
WHOA!
This is nowhere near okay!!
NO, BUT...!
THERE'S NO WAY!
What?!
IT'S JUST A LITTLE STAIN. IT'LL BE CLEANED UP IN NO TIME. BY THAT EMPLOYEE.
RIGHT?!
HEY, STUPID, DON'T LOOK LIKE THAT, OR YOU'LL MAKE HER FEEL BAD.
GASP!
...RIGHT!! IT WILL BE FINE!
YOU'RE SO NICE.
GRIN
OF COURSE, IF IT WERE MY JACKET, I WOULD TAKE THE MONEY.
She's lucky it was Towa's.
...

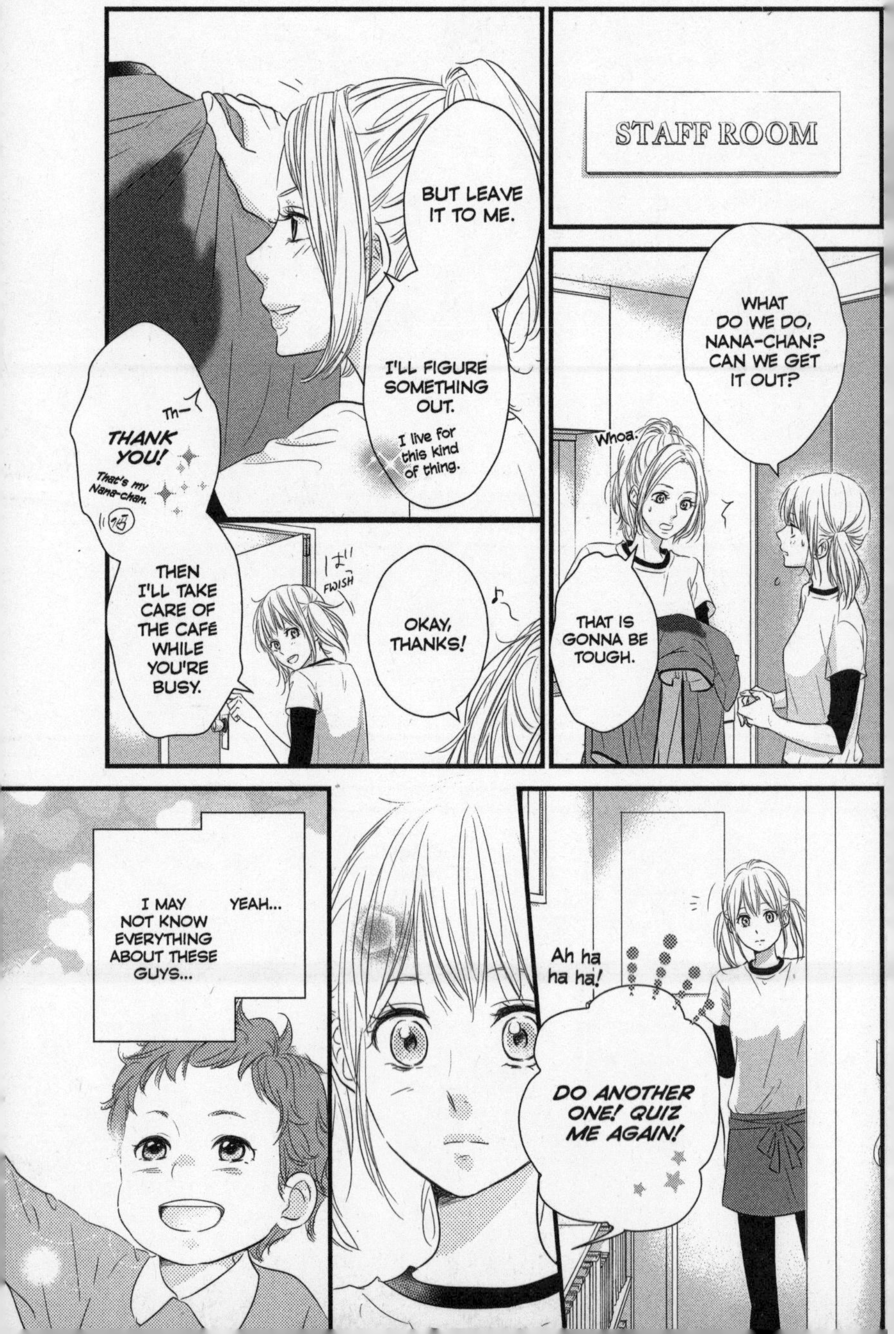
STAFF ROOM
WHAT DO WE DO, NANA-CHAN? CAN WE GET IT OUT?
Whoa.
THAT IS GONNA BE TOUGH.
BUT LEAVE IT TO ME.
I'LL FIGURE SOMETHING OUT.
I live for this kind of thing.
Th- THANK YOU!
That's my Nana-chan.
OKAY, THANKS!
FWISH
THEN I'LL TAKE CARE OF THE CAFÉ WHILE YOU'RE BUSY.
Ah ha ha ha!
DO ANOTHER ONE! QUIZ ME AGAIN!
YEAH...
I MAY NOT KNOW EVERYTHING ABOUT THESE GUYS...

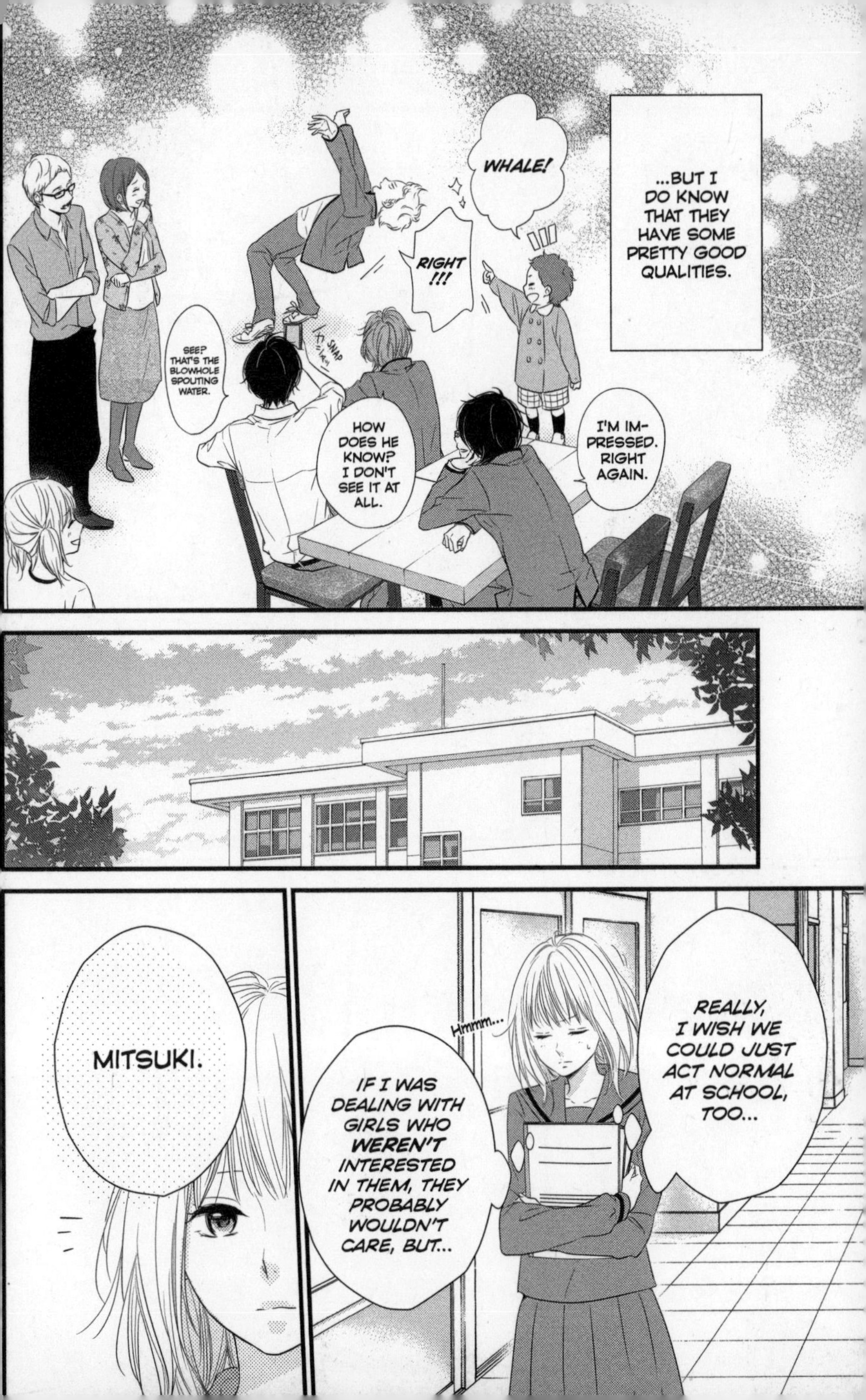
...BUT I DO KNOW THAT THEY HAVE SOME PRETTY GOOD QUALITIES.
WHALE!
RIGHT !!!
I'M IM-PRESSED. RIGHT AGAIN.
HOW DOES HE KNOW? I DON'T SEE IT AT ALL.
SNAP
SEE? THAT'S THE BLOWHOLE SPOUTING WATER.
REALLY, I WISH WE COULD JUST ACT NORMAL AT SCHOOL, TOO...
Hmmm...
IF I WAS DEALING WITH GIRLS WHO WEREN'T INTERESTED IN THEM, THEY PROBABLY WOULDN'T CARE, BUT...
MITSUKI.

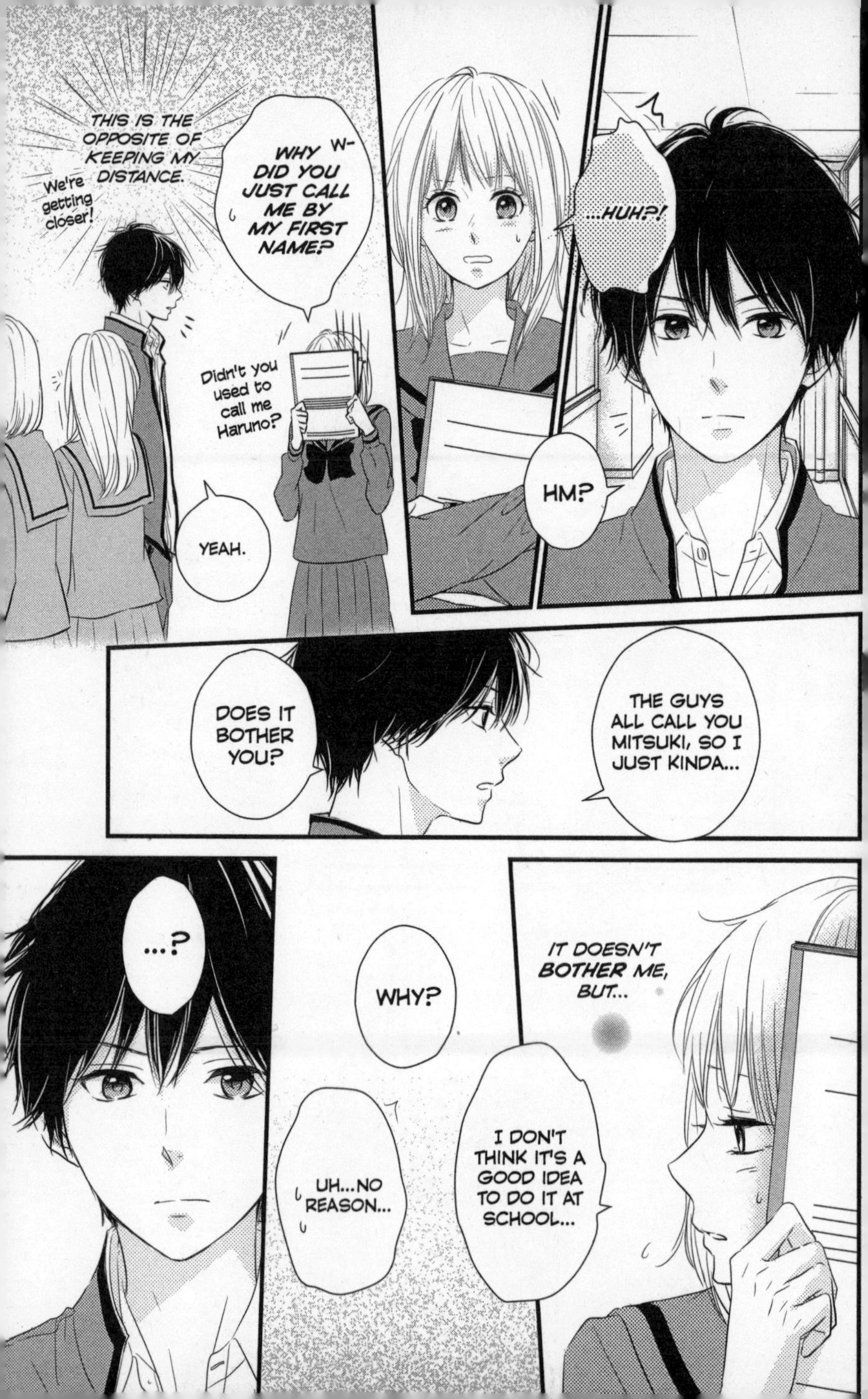
...HUH?!
HM?
WHY W-DID YOU JUST CALL ME BY MY FIRST NAME?
THIS IS THE OPPOSITE OF KEEPING MY DISTANCE.
We're getting closer!
Didn't you used to call me Haruno?
YEAH.
THE GUYS ALL CALL YOU MITSUKI, SO I JUST KINDA...
DOES IT BOTHER YOU?
IT DOESN'T BOTHER ME, BUT...
I DON'T THINK IT'S A GOOD IDEA TO DO IT AT SCHOOL...
WHY?
...?
UH...NO REASON...

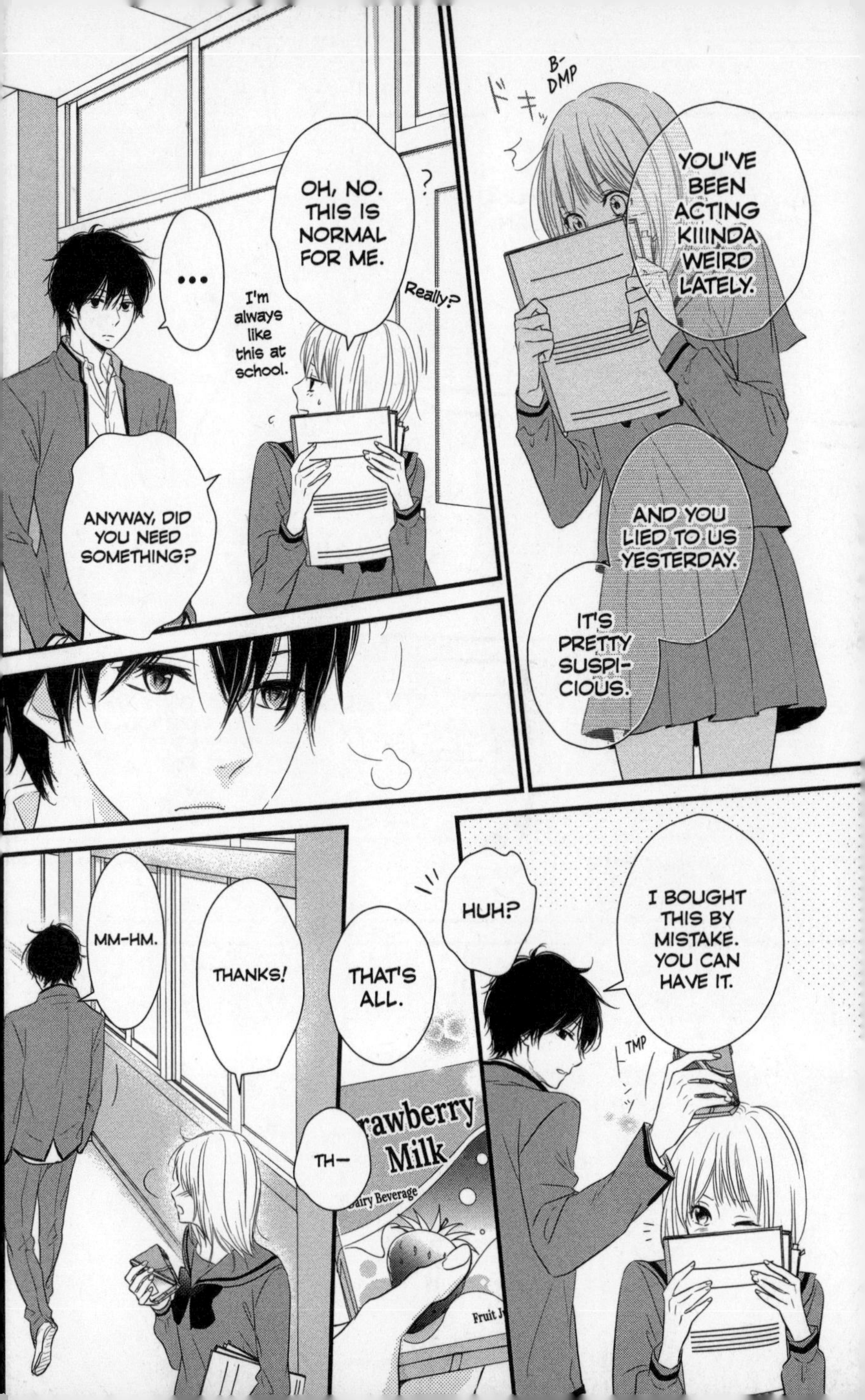
B-DMP
YOU'VE BEEN ACTING KIIINDA WEIRD LATELY.
AND YOU LIED TO US YESTERDAY.
IT'S PRETTY SUSPICIOUS.
?
OH, NO. THIS IS NORMAL FOR ME.
Really?
I'm always like this at school.
...
ANYWAY, DID YOU NEED SOMETHING?
I BOUGHT THIS BY MISTAKE. YOU CAN HAVE IT.
TMP
HUH?
THAT'S ALL.
TH—
Strawberry Milk
Dairy Beverage
THANKS!
MM-HM.

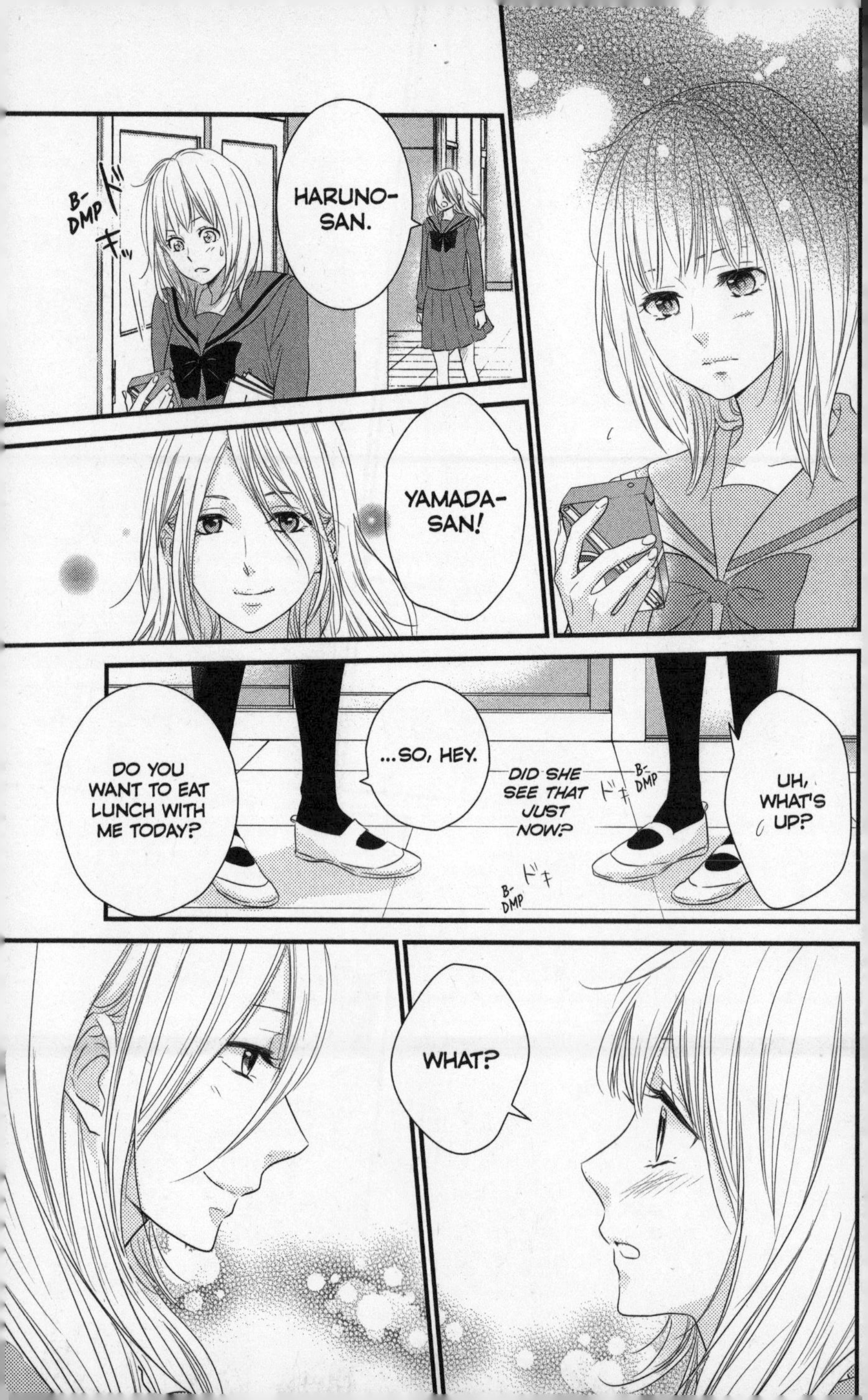
B-DMP
HARUNO-SAN.
YAMADA-SAN!
UH, WHAT'S UP?
DID SHE SEE THAT JUST NOW?
B-DMP
B-DMP
...SO, HEY.
DO YOU WANT TO EAT LUNCH WITH ME TODAY?
WHAT?

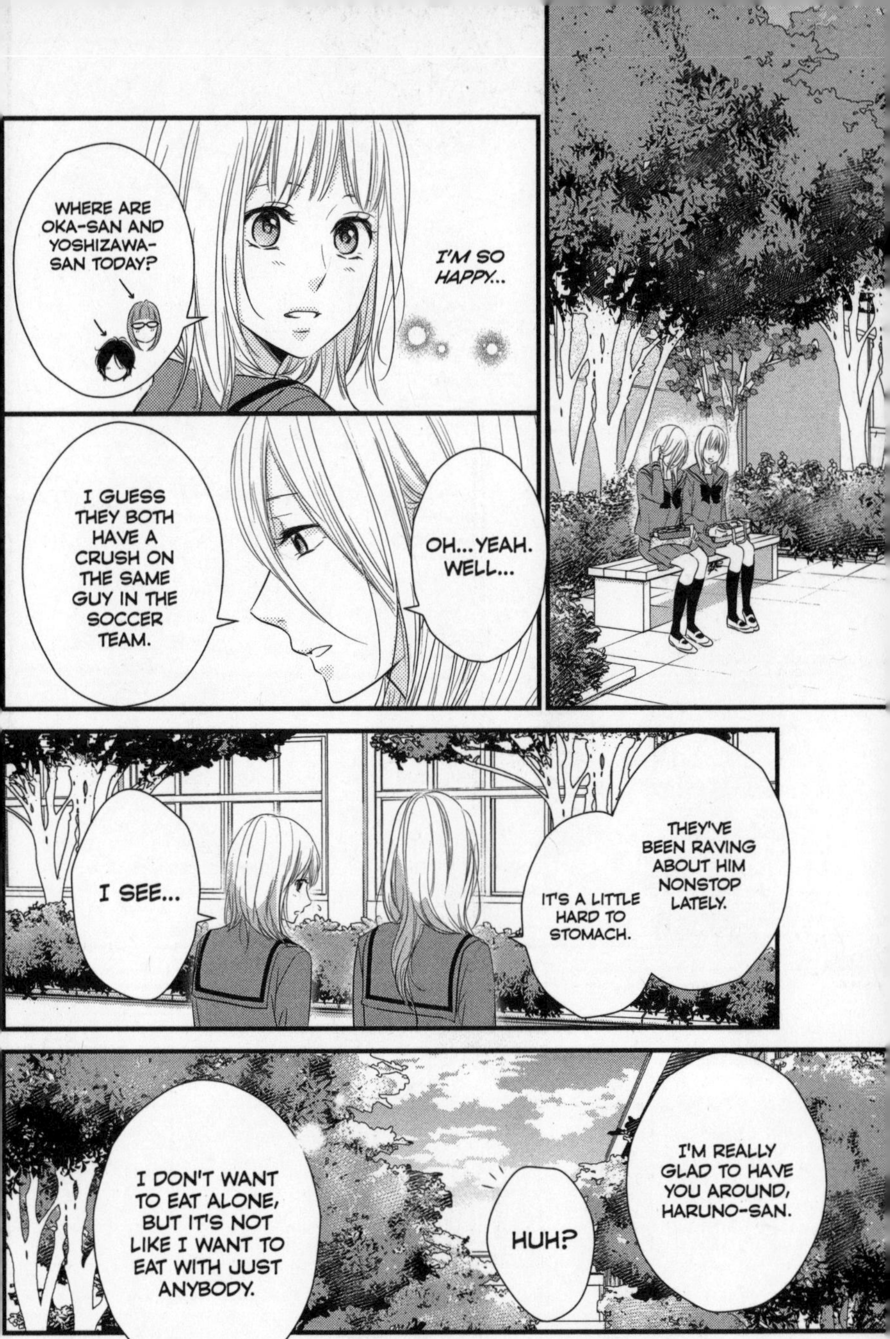
I'M SO HAPPY...
WHERE ARE OKA-SAN AND YOSHIZAWA-SAN TODAY?
OH...YEAH. WELL...
I GUESS THEY BOTH HAVE A CRUSH ON THE SAME GUY IN THE SOCCER TEAM.
THEY'VE BEEN RAVING ABOUT HIM NONSTOP LATELY.
IT'S A LITTLE HARD TO STOMACH.
I SEE...
I'M REALLY GLAD TO HAVE YOU AROUND, HARUNO-SAN.
HUH?
I DON'T WANT TO EAT ALONE, BUT IT'S NOT LIKE I WANT TO EAT WITH JUST ANYBODY.

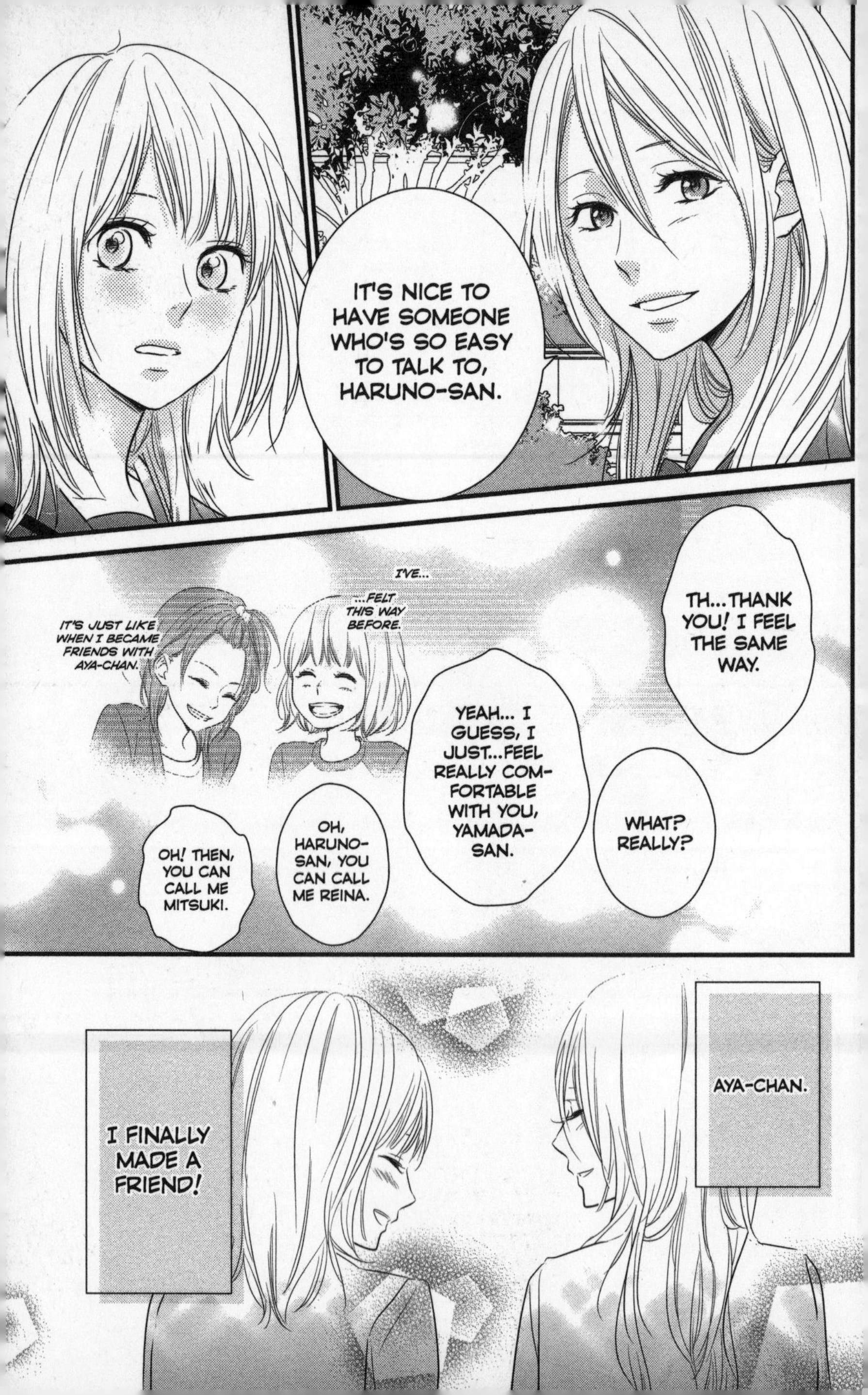
IT'S NICE TO HAVE SOMEONE WHO'S SO EASY TO TALK TO, HARUNO-SAN.
TH...THANK YOU! I FEEL THE SAME WAY.
WHAT? REALLY?
YEAH... I GUESS, I JUST...FEEL REALLY COM-FORTABLE WITH YOU, YAMADA-SAN.
I'VE...
...FELT THIS WAY BEFORE.
IT'S JUST LIKE WHEN I BECAME FRIENDS WITH AYA-CHAN.
OH, HARUNO-SAN, YOU CAN CALL ME REINA.
OH! THEN, YOU CAN CALL ME MITSUKI.
AYA-CHAN.
I FINALLY MADE A FRIEND!

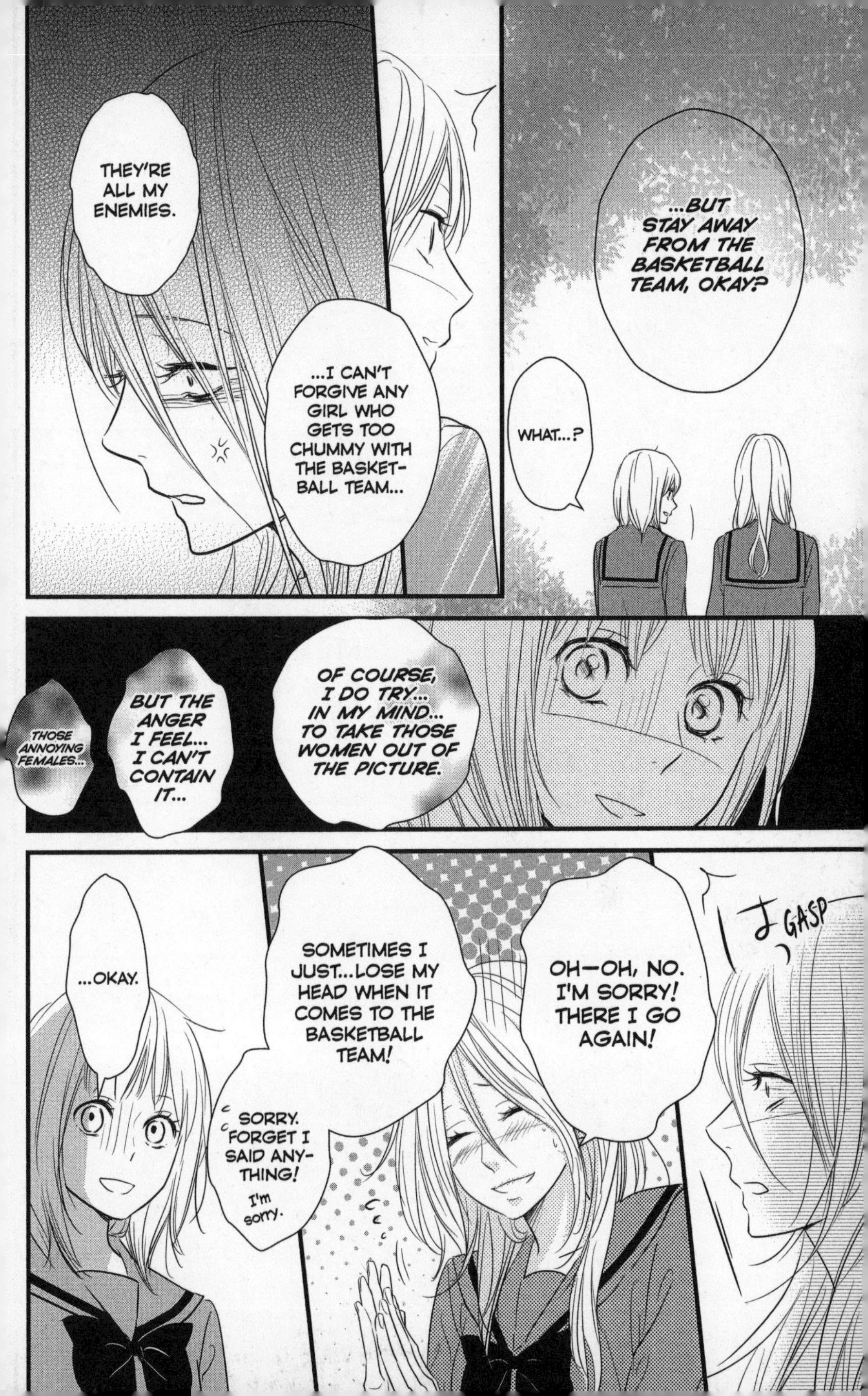
...BUT STAY AWAY FROM THE BASKETBALL TEAM, OKAY?
WHAT...?
...I CAN'T FORGIVE ANY GIRL WHO GETS TOO CHUMMY WITH THE BASKET-BALL TEAM...
THEY'RE ALL MY ENEMIES.
OF COURSE, I DO TRY... IN MY MIND... TO TAKE THOSE WOMEN OUT OF THE PICTURE.
BUT THE ANGER I FEEL... I CAN'T CONTAIN IT...
THOSE ANNOYING FEMALES...
GASP
OH—OH, NO. I'M SORRY! THERE I GO AGAIN!
SOMETIMES I JUST...LOSE MY HEAD WHEN IT COMES TO THE BASKETBALL TEAM!
SORRY. FORGET I SAID ANY-THING!
I'm sorry.
...OKAY.

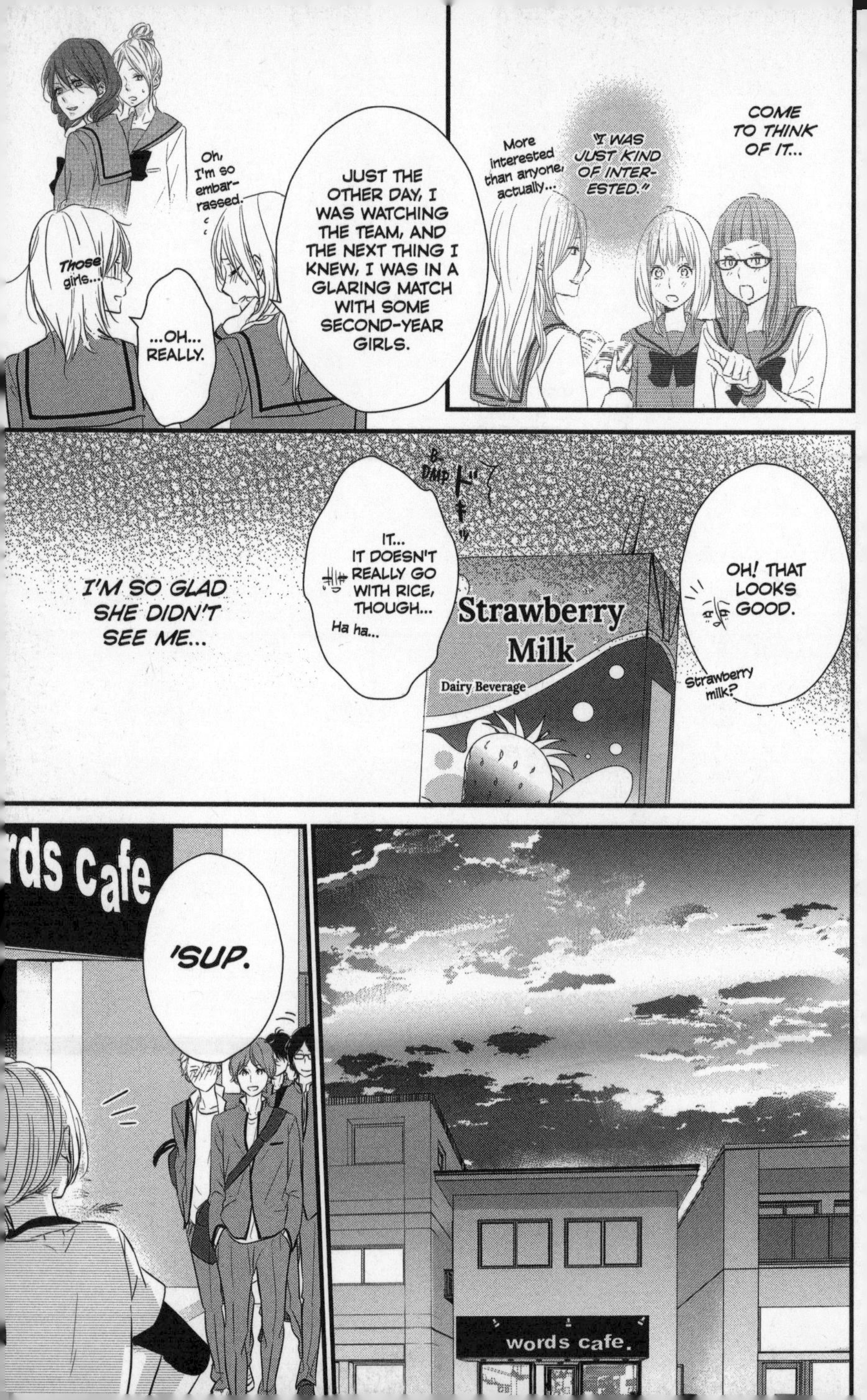
COME TO THINK OF IT...
"I WAS JUST KIND OF INTERESTED."
More interested than anyone, actually...
JUST THE OTHER DAY, I WAS WATCHING THE TEAM, AND THE NEXT THING I KNEW, I WAS IN A GLARING MATCH WITH SOME SECOND-YEAR GIRLS.
Oh, I'm so embarrassed.
Those girls...
...OH... REALLY.
OH! THAT LOOKS GOOD.
Strawberry milk?
B-DMP
Strawberry Milk
Dairy Beverage
IT... IT DOESN'T REALLY GO WITH RICE, THOUGH...
Ha ha...
I'M SO GLAD SHE DIDN'T SEE ME...
words cafe.
rds cafe
'SUP.

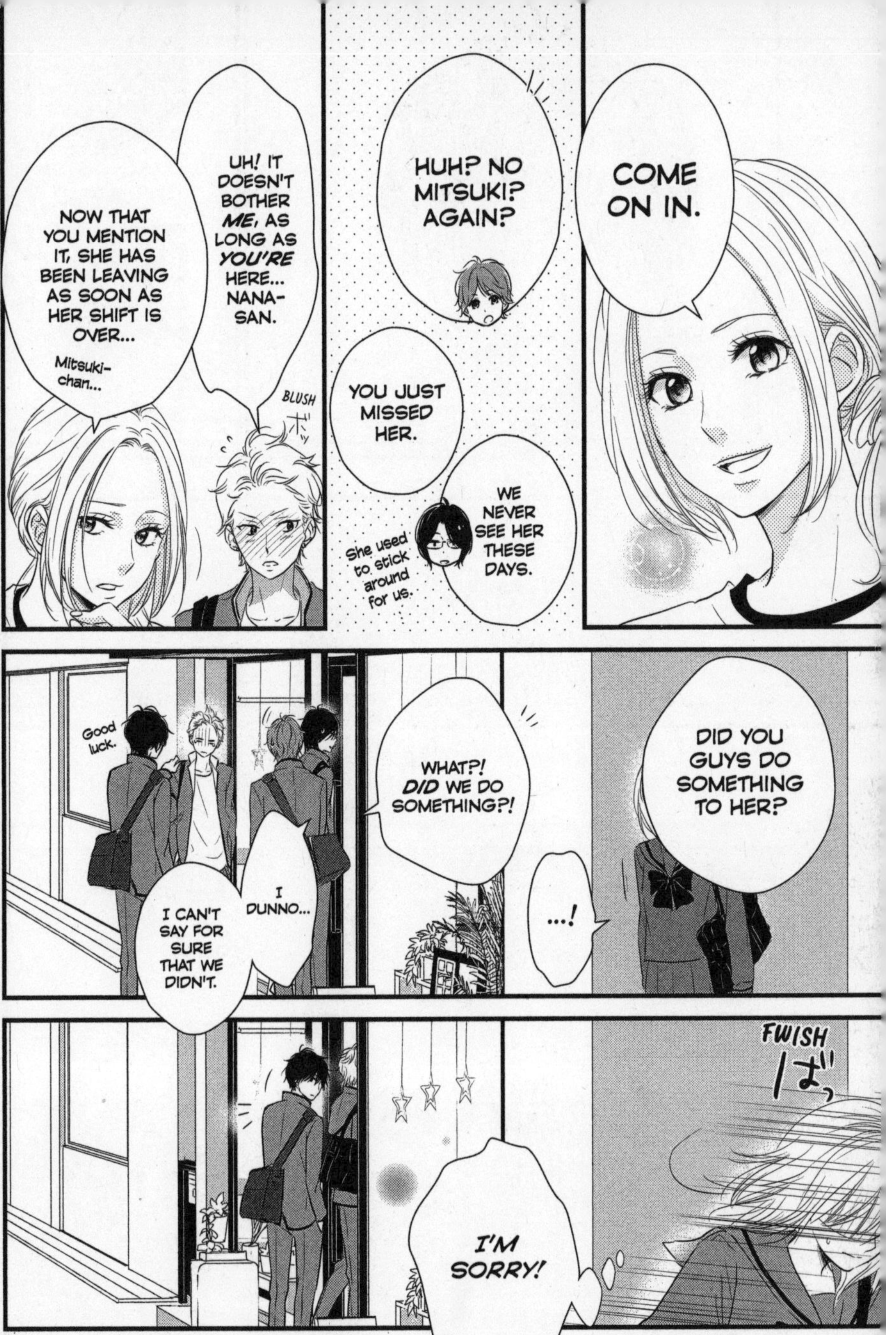
COME ON IN.
HUH? NO MITSUKI? AGAIN?
YOU JUST MISSED HER.
WE NEVER SEE HER THESE DAYS.
She used to stick around for us.
UH! IT DOESN'T BOTHER *ME*, AS LONG AS *YOU'RE* HERE... NANA-SAN.
BLUSH
NOW THAT YOU MENTION IT, SHE HAS BEEN LEAVING AS SOON AS HER SHIFT IS OVER...
Mitsuki-chan...
DID YOU GUYS DO SOMETHING TO HER?
...!
WHAT?! *DID* WE DO SOMETHING?!
I DUNNO...
I CAN'T SAY FOR SURE THAT WE DIDN'T.
Good luck.
FWISH
I'M SORRY!

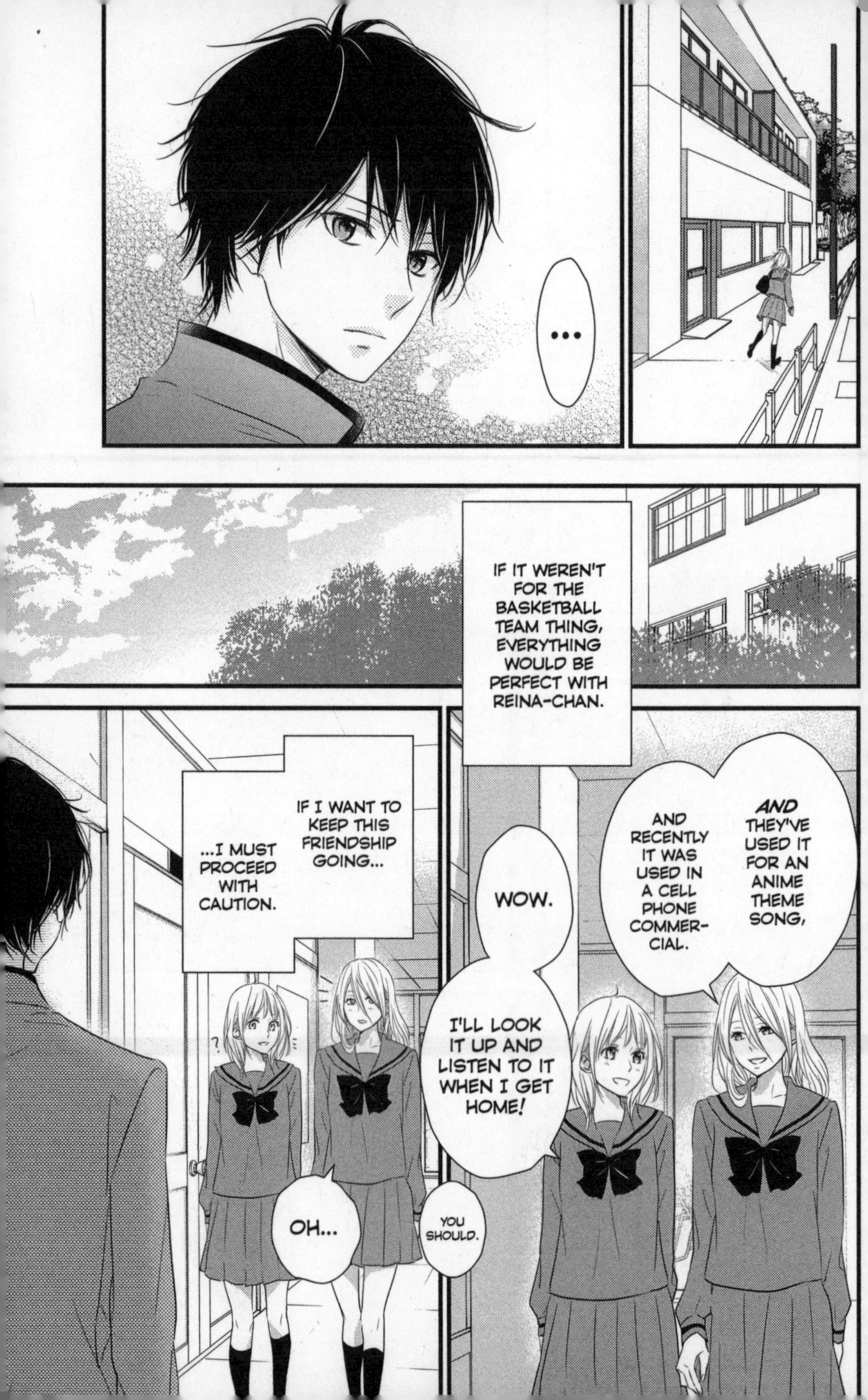
...
IF IT WEREN'T FOR THE BASKETBALL TEAM THING, EVERYTHING WOULD BE PERFECT WITH REINA-CHAN.
AND THEY'VE USED IT FOR AN ANIME THEME SONG,
AND RECENTLY IT WAS USED IN A CELL PHONE COMMER-CIAL.
WOW.
I'LL LOOK IT UP AND LISTEN TO IT WHEN I GET HOME!
IF I WANT TO KEEP THIS FRIENDSHIP GOING...
...I MUST PROCEED WITH CAUTION.
YOU SHOULD.
OH...

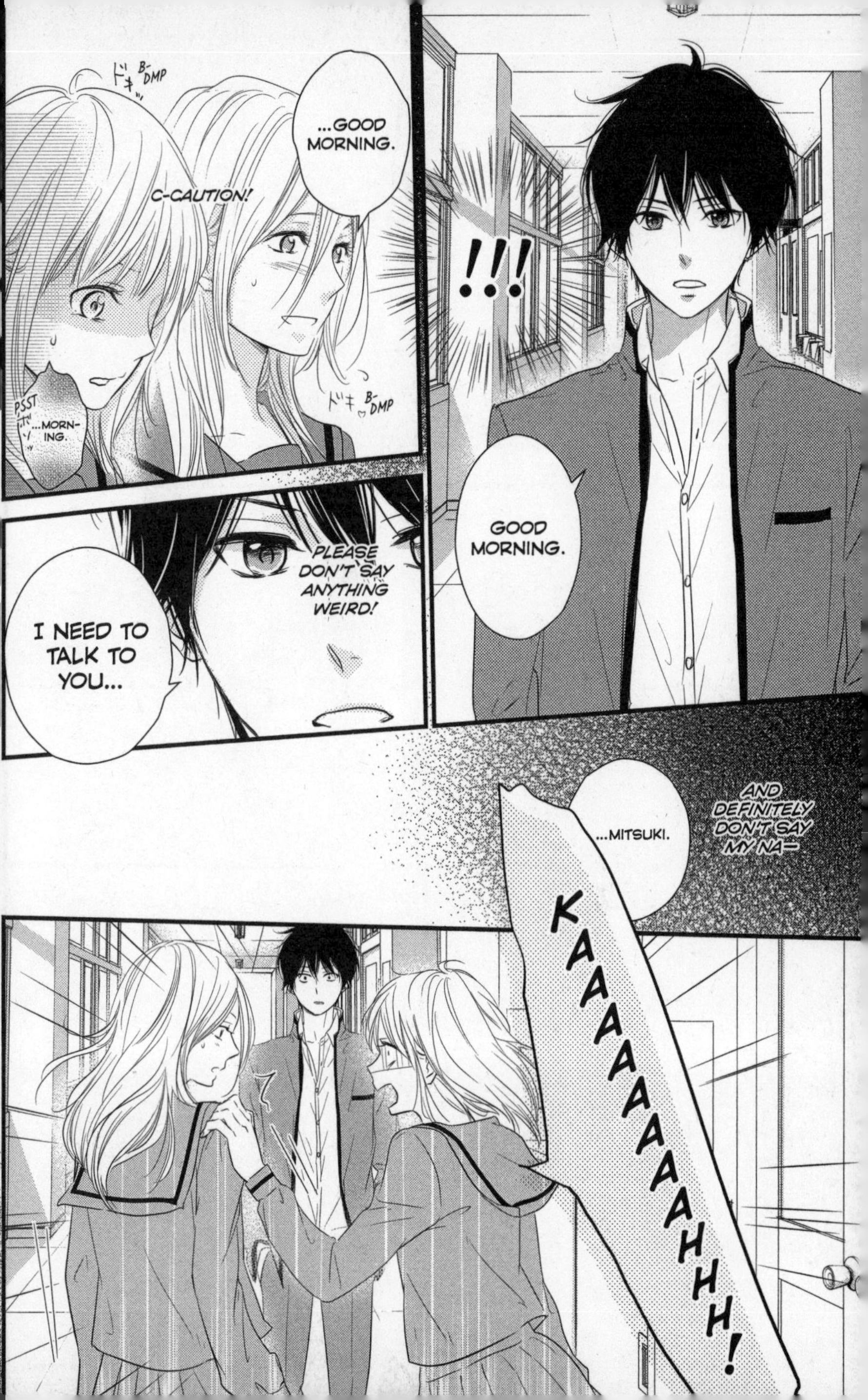
!!!
GOOD MORNING.
...GOOD MORNING.
B-DMP
C-CAUTION!
B-DMP
PSST
...MORN-ING.
PLEASE DON'T SAY ANYTHING WEIRD!
I NEED TO TALK TO YOU...
AND DEFINITELY DON'T SAY MY NA—
...MITSUKI.
KAAAAAAAAHHH!

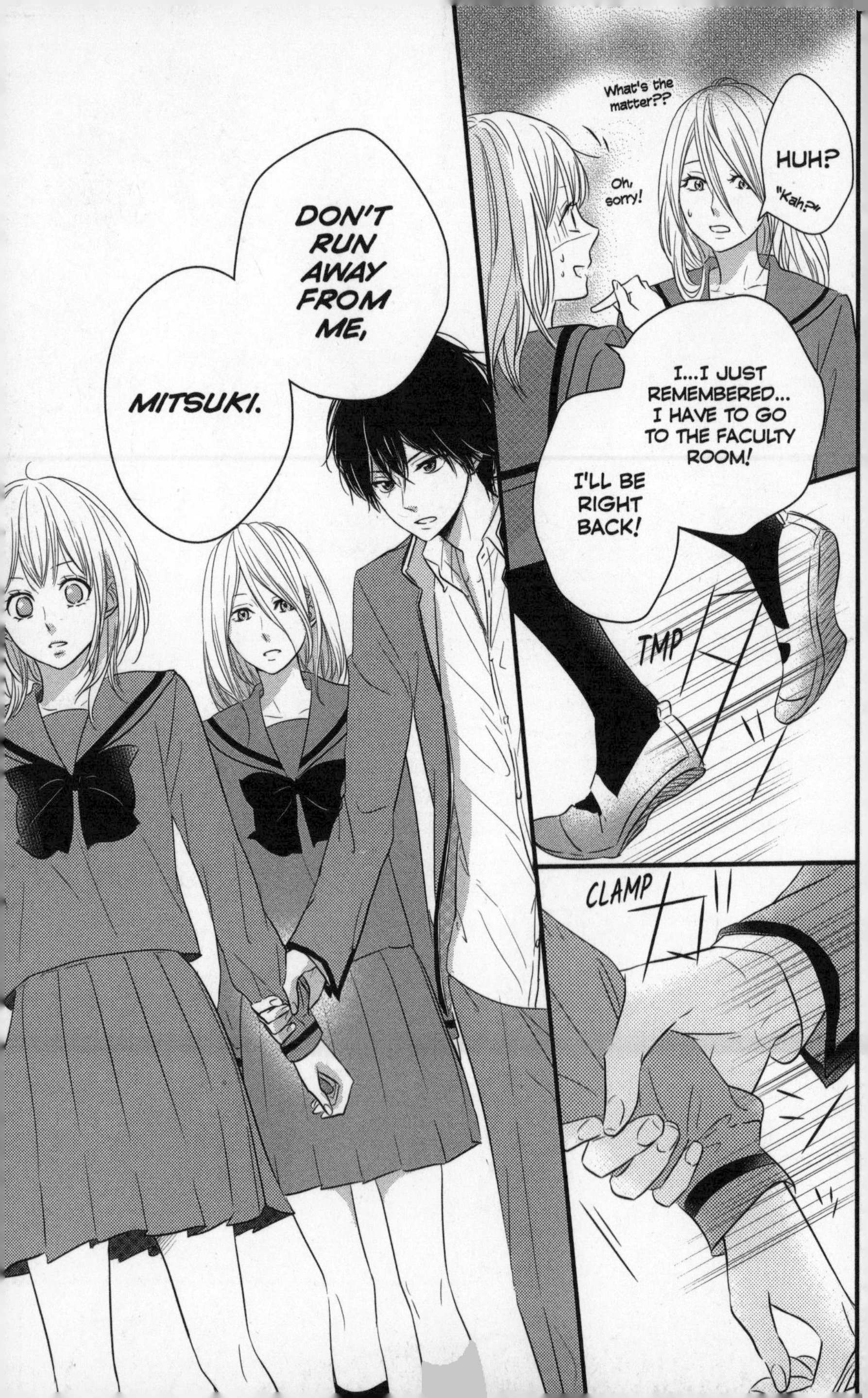
HUH?
"Kah?"
What's the matter??
Oh, sorry!
I...I JUST REMEMBERED... I HAVE TO GO TO THE FACULTY ROOM!
I'LL BE RIGHT BACK!
TMP
CLAMP
DON'T RUN AWAY FROM ME,
MITSUKI.

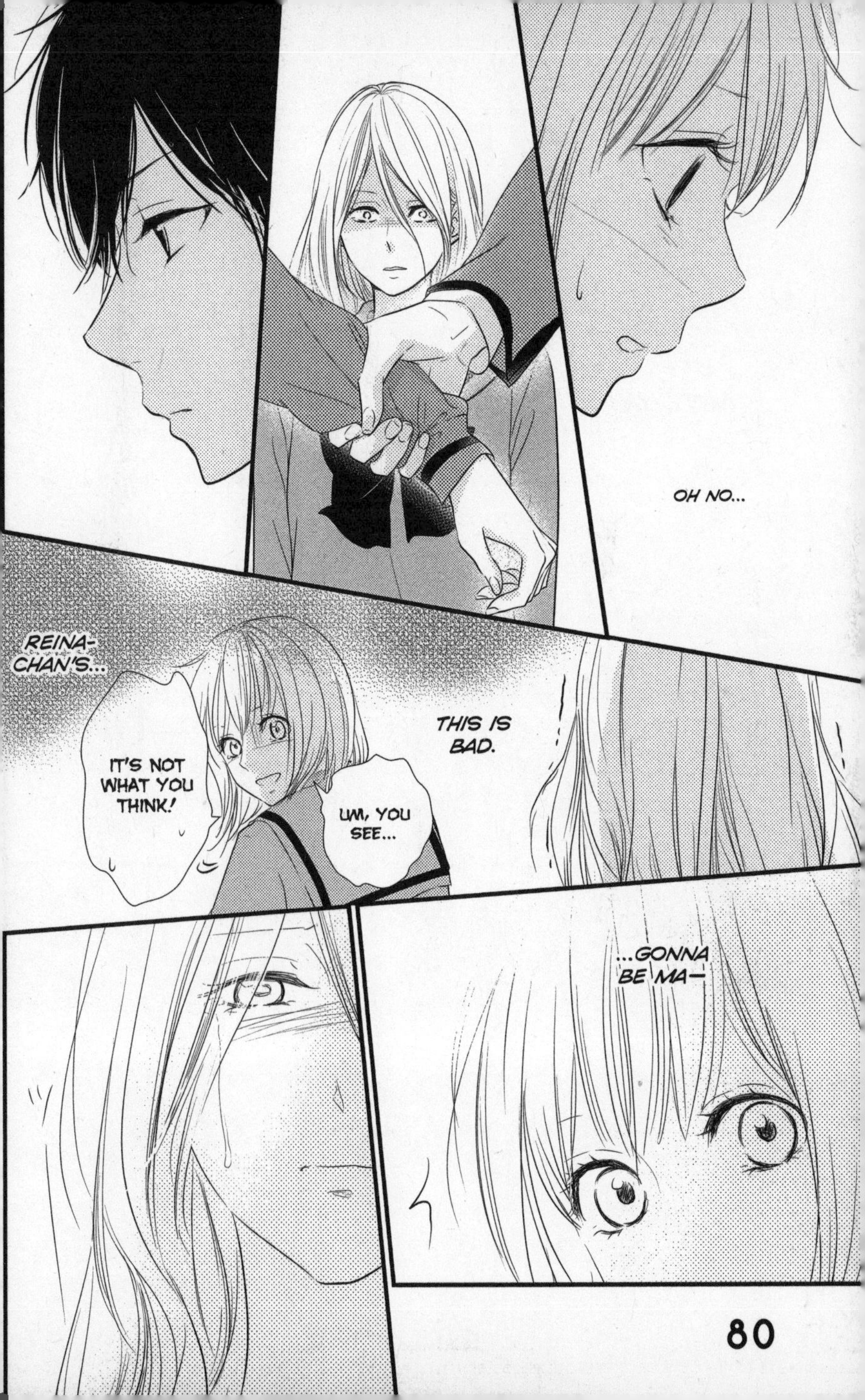
OH NO...
THIS IS BAD.
UM, YOU SEE...
IT'S NOT WHAT YOU THINK!
REINA-CHAN'S...
...GONNA BE MA—

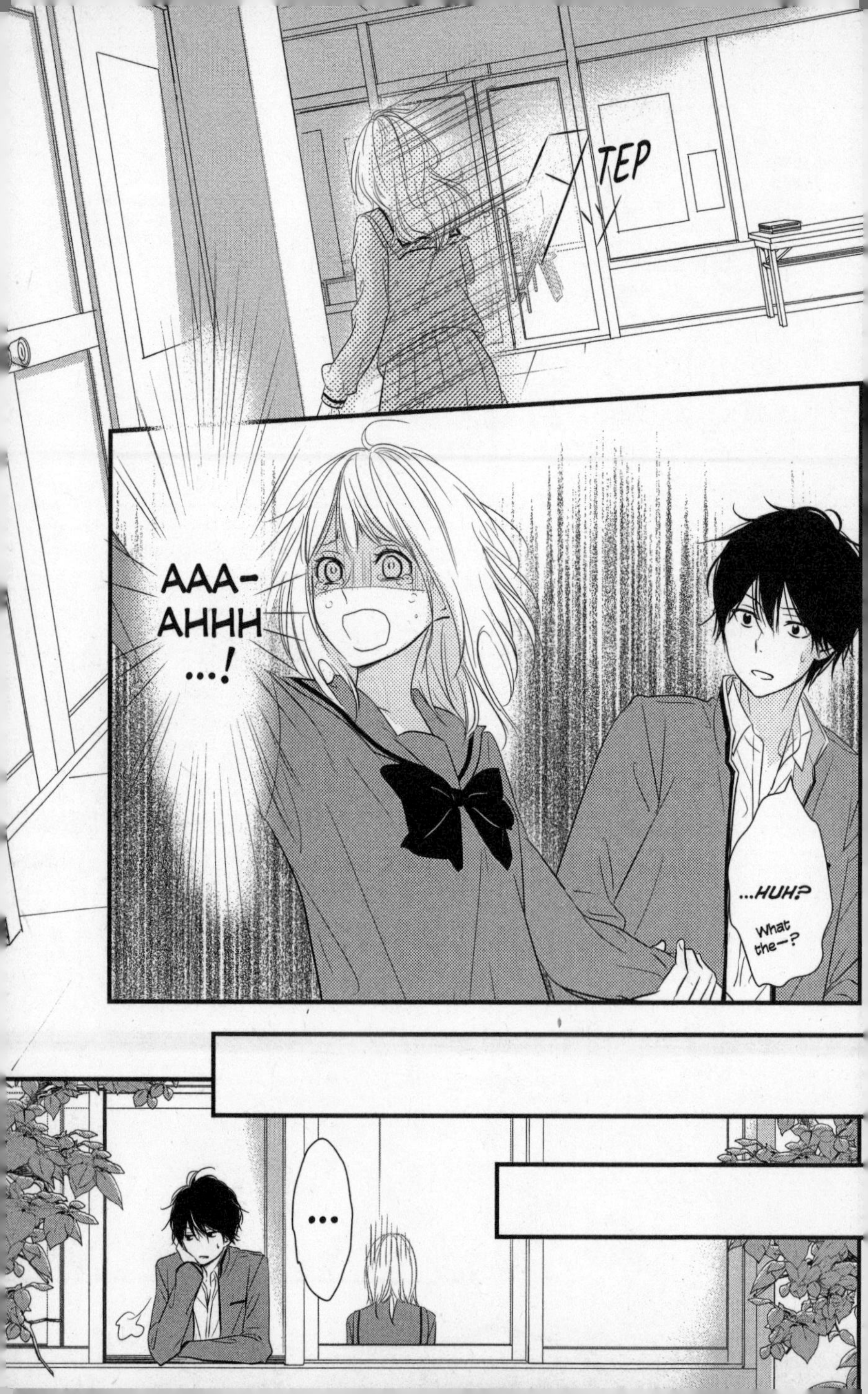
TEP
AAA-AHHH...!
...HUH?
What the—?
...

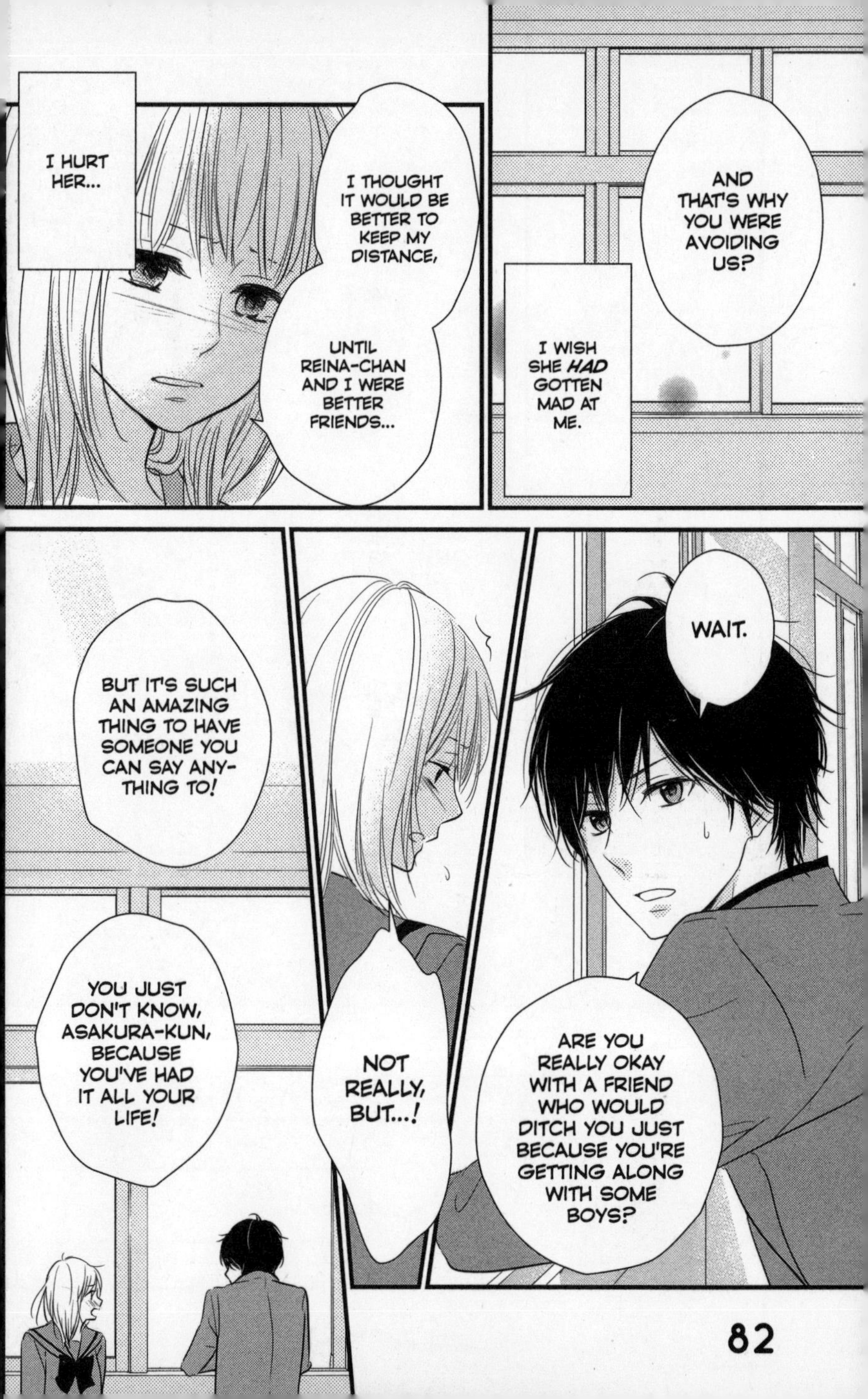
AND THAT'S WHY YOU WERE AVOIDING US?
I WISH SHE *HAD* GOTTEN MAD AT ME.
I THOUGHT IT WOULD BE BETTER TO KEEP MY DISTANCE,
UNTIL REINA-CHAN AND I WERE BETTER FRIENDS...
I HURT HER...
WAIT.
ARE YOU REALLY OKAY WITH A FRIEND WHO WOULD DITCH YOU JUST BECAUSE YOU'RE GETTING ALONG WITH SOME BOYS?
NOT REALLY, BUT...!
BUT IT'S SUCH AN AMAZING THING TO HAVE SOMEONE YOU CAN SAY ANY-THING TO!
YOU JUST DON'T KNOW, ASAKURA-KUN, BECAUSE YOU'VE HAD IT ALL YOUR LIFE!

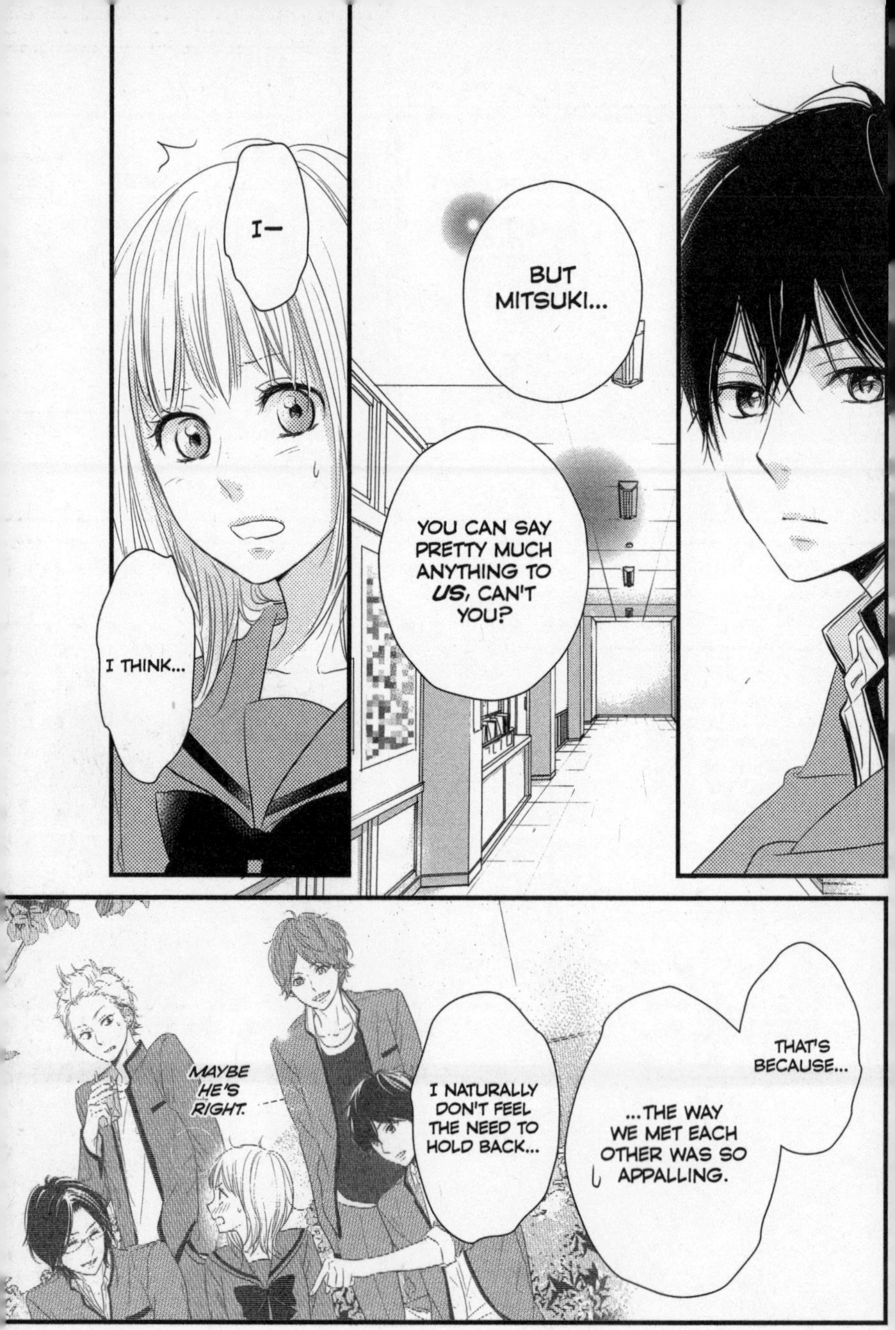
BUT MITSUKI...
YOU CAN SAY PRETTY MUCH ANYTHING TO *US*, CAN'T YOU?
I—
I THINK...
THAT'S BECAUSE...
...THE WAY WE MET EACH OTHER WAS SO APPALLING.
I NATURALLY DON'T FEEL THE NEED TO HOLD BACK...
MAYBE HE'S RIGHT.

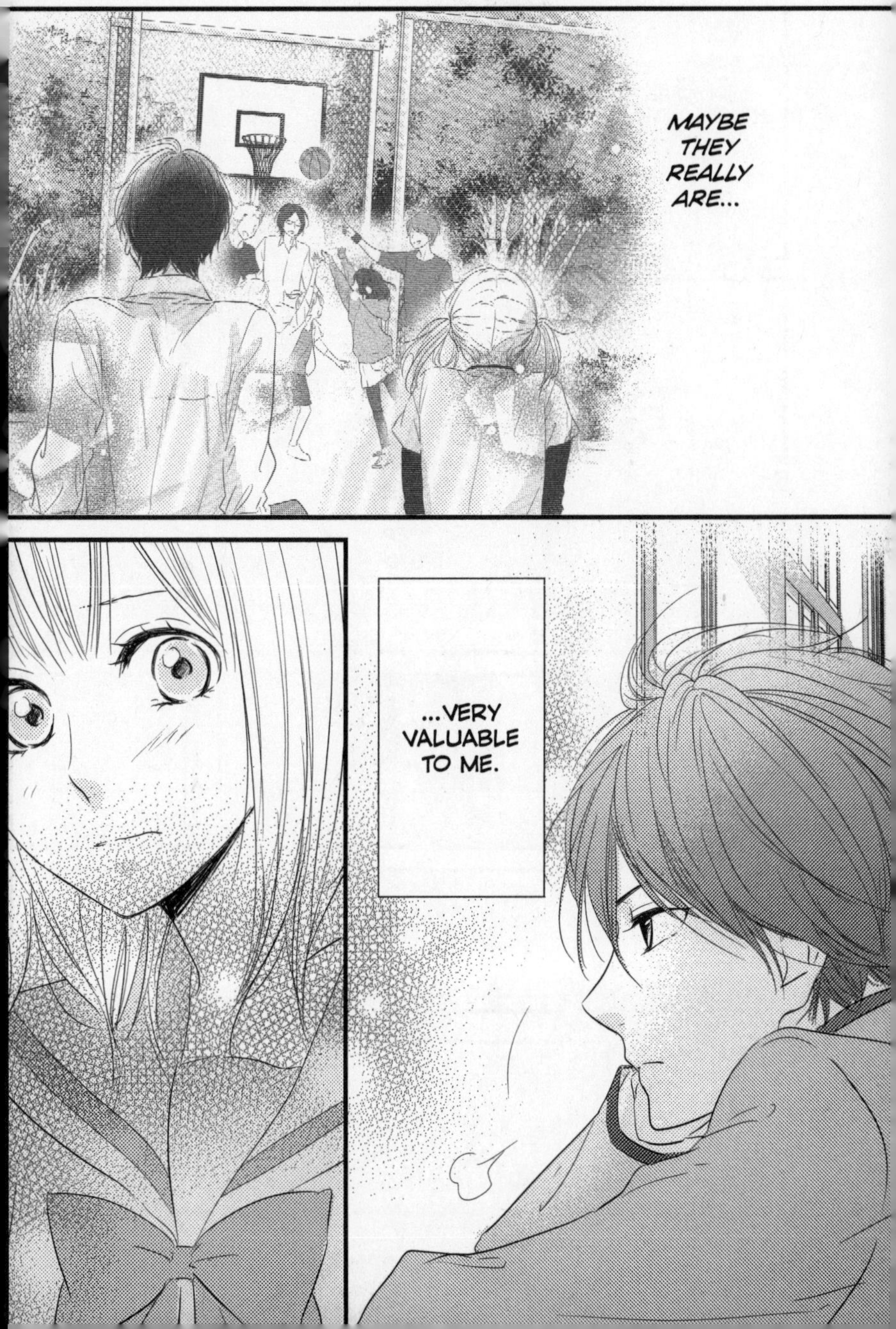
MAYBE THEY REALLY ARE...
...VERY VALUABLE TO ME.

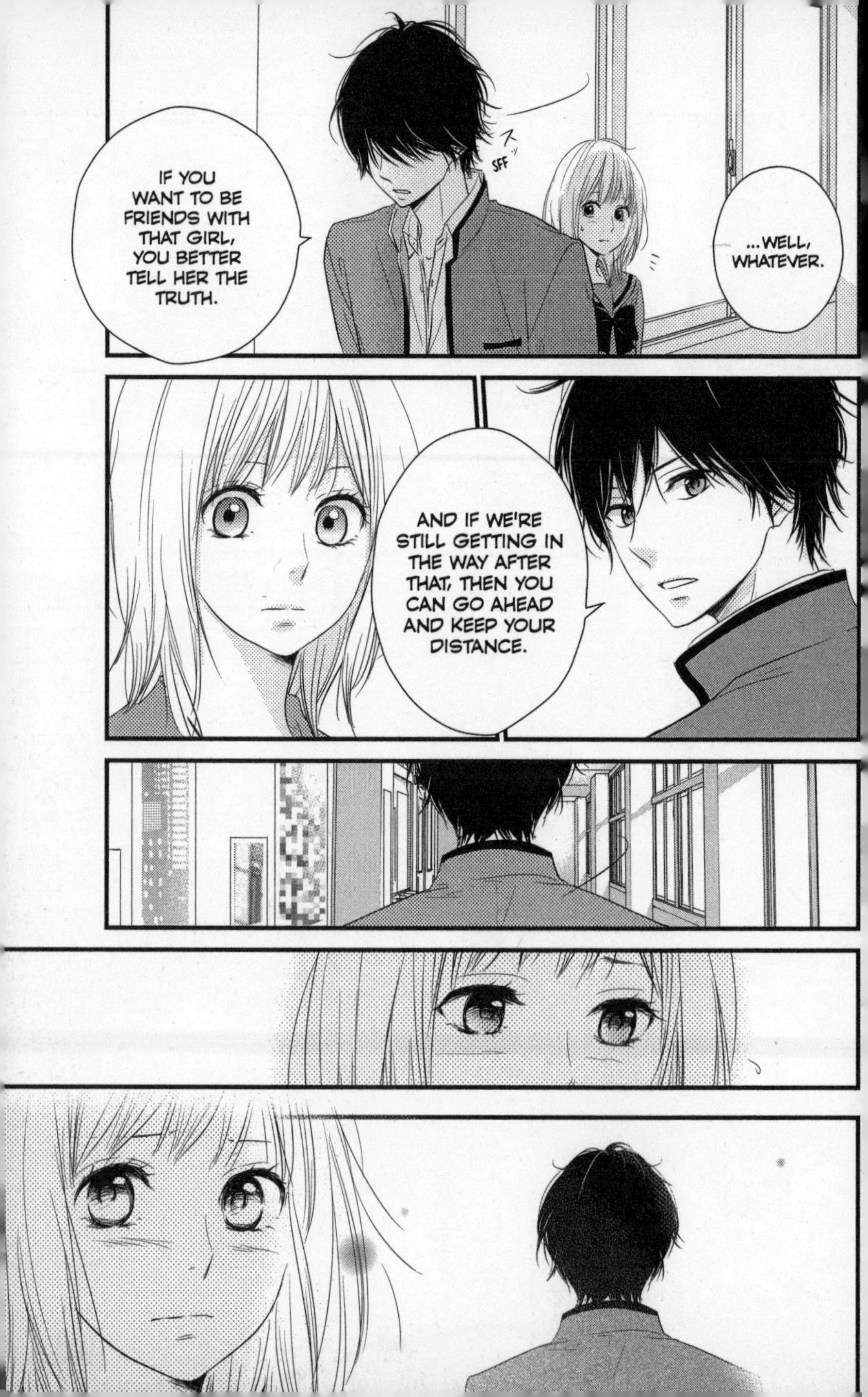
...WELL, WHATEVER.
SFF
IF YOU WANT TO BE FRIENDS WITH THAT GIRL, YOU BETTER TELL HER THE TRUTH.
AND IF WE'RE STILL GETTING IN THE WAY AFTER THAT, THEN YOU CAN GO AHEAD AND KEEP YOUR DISTANCE.

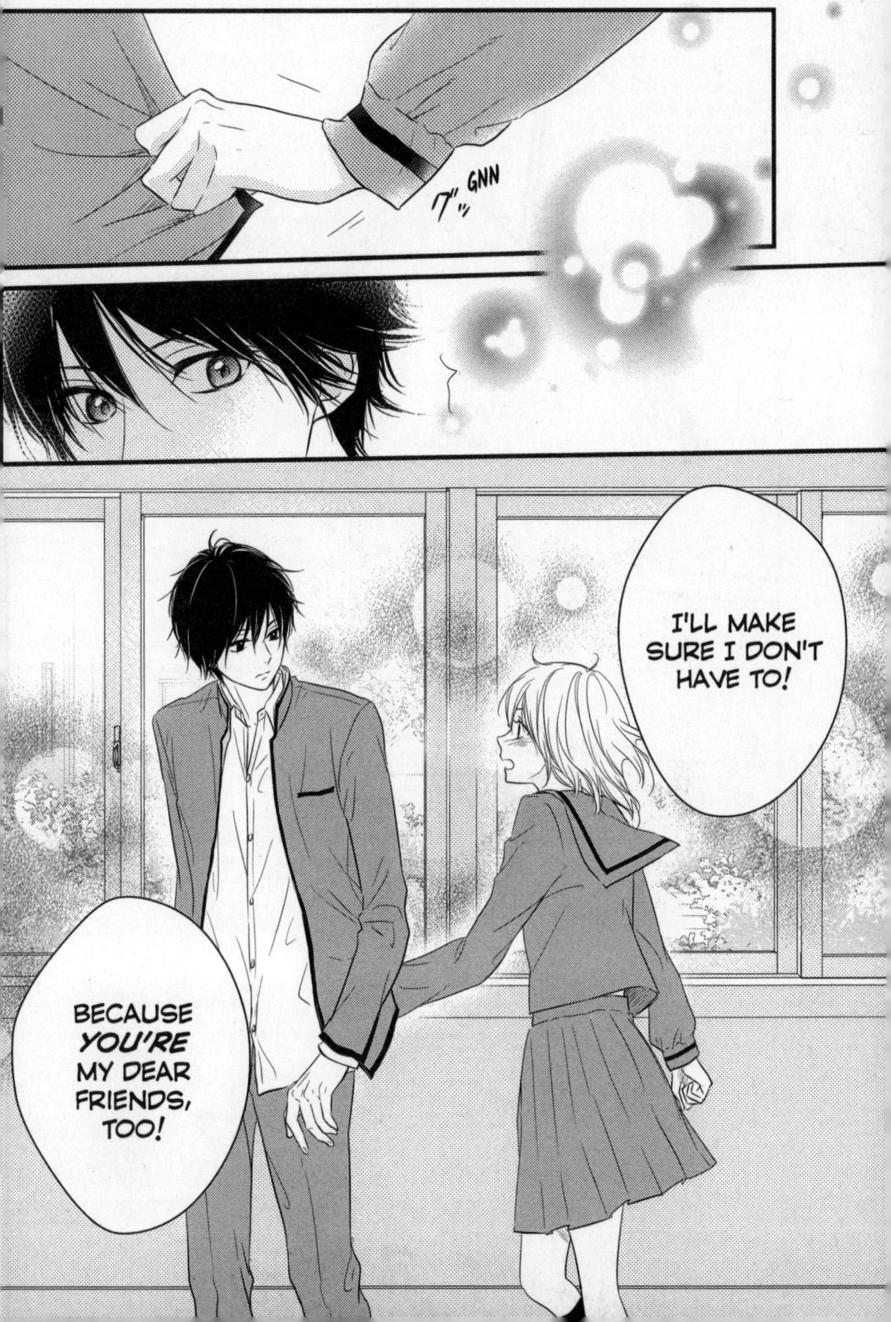
グッ GNN
I'LL MAKE SURE I DON'T HAVE TO!
BECAUSE *YOU'RE* MY DEAR FRIENDS, TOO!

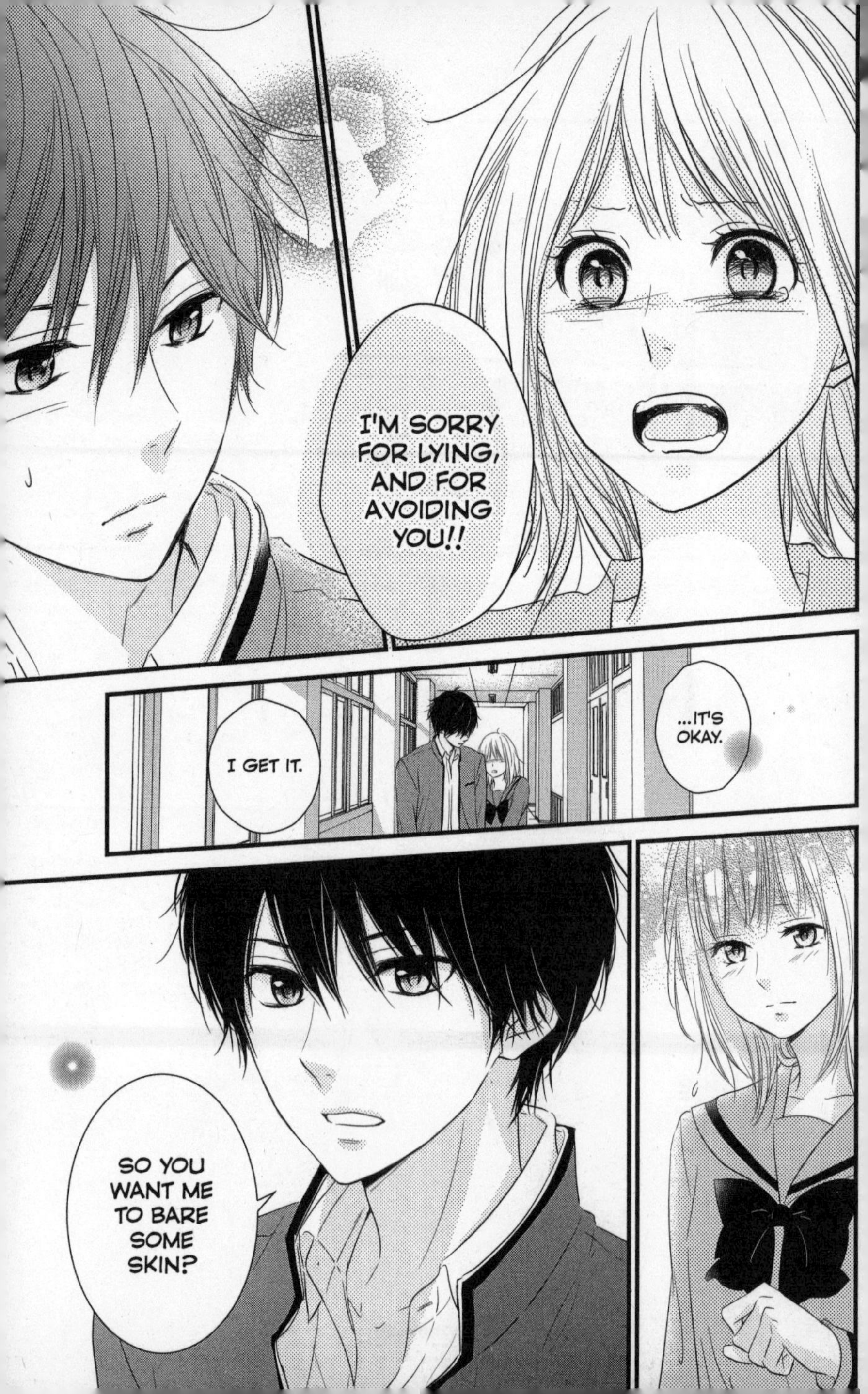
I'M SORRY FOR LYING, AND FOR AVOIDING YOU!!
...IT'S OKAY.
I GET IT.
SO YOU WANT ME TO BARE SOME SKIN?

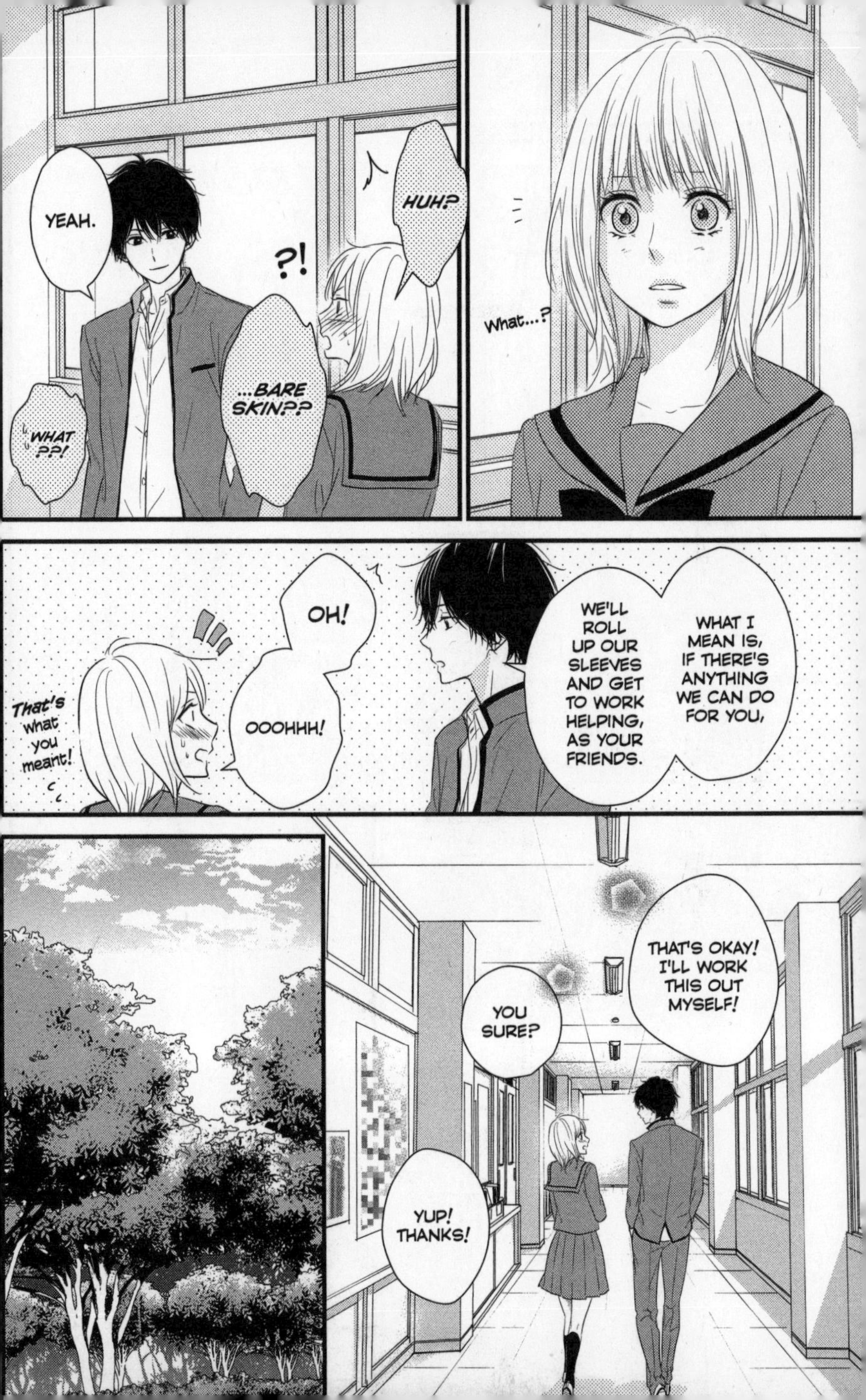
What...?
HUH?
?!
YEAH.
...BARE SKIN??
WHAT ??!
WHAT I MEAN IS, IF THERE'S ANYTHING WE CAN DO FOR YOU,
WE'LL ROLL UP OUR SLEEVES AND GET TO WORK HELPING, AS YOUR FRIENDS.
OH!
OOOHHH!
That's what you meant!
THAT'S OKAY! I'LL WORK THIS OUT MYSELF!
YOU SURE?
YUP! THANKS!

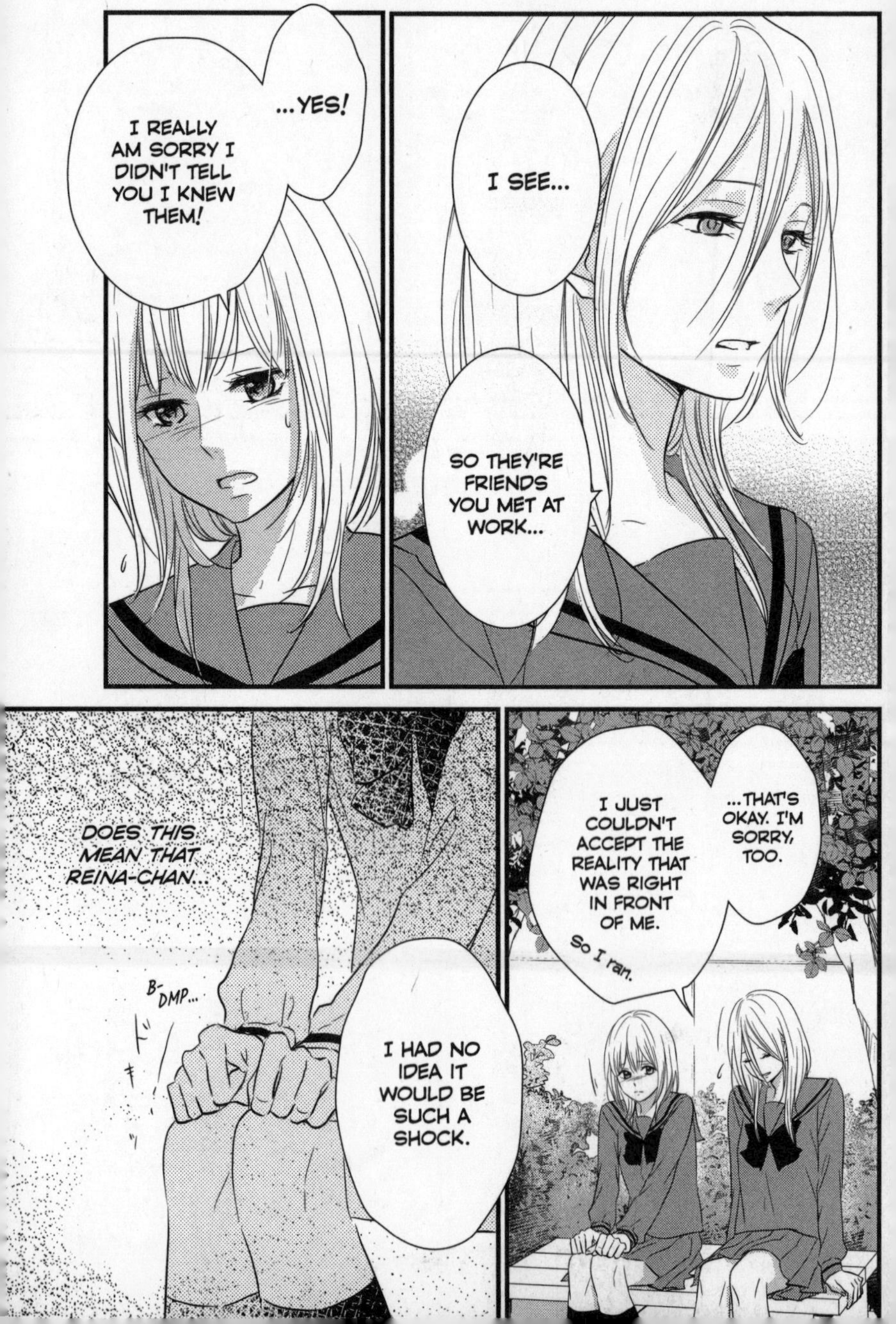
I SEE...
SO THEY'RE FRIENDS YOU MET AT WORK...
...YES!
I REALLY AM SORRY I DIDN'T TELL YOU I KNEW THEM!
...THAT'S OKAY. I'M SORRY, TOO.
I JUST COULDN'T ACCEPT THE REALITY THAT WAS RIGHT IN FRONT OF ME.
So I ran.
DOES THIS MEAN THAT REINA-CHAN...
B-DMP...
ドキッ
I HAD NO IDEA IT WOULD BE SUCH A SHOCK.

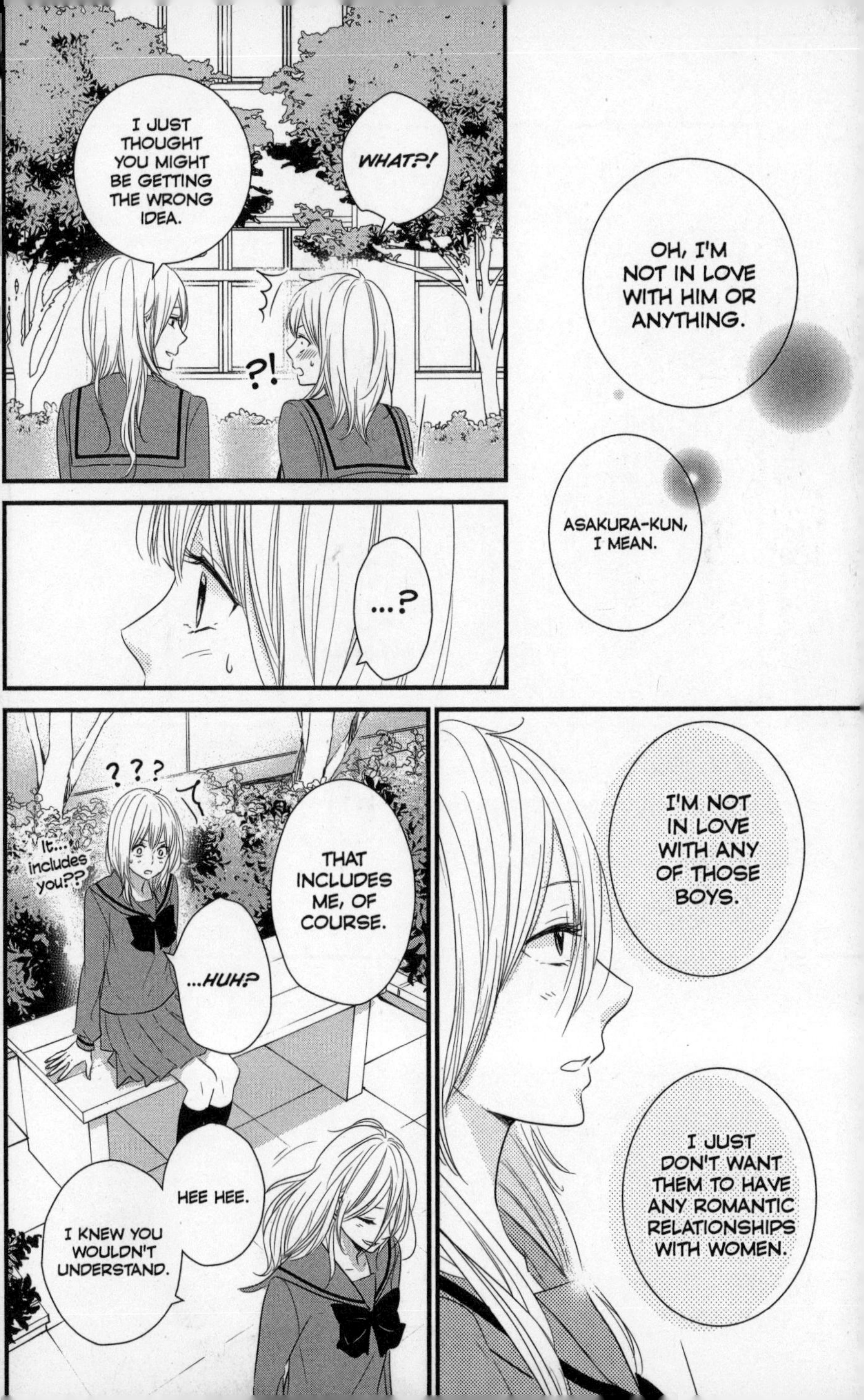

OH, I'M NOT IN LOVE WITH HIM OR ANYTHING.
ASAKURA-KUN, I MEAN.
I JUST THOUGHT YOU MIGHT BE GETTING THE WRONG IDEA.
WHAT?!
?!
...?
I'M NOT IN LOVE WITH ANY OF THOSE BOYS.
I JUST DON'T WANT THEM TO HAVE ANY ROMANTIC RELATIONSHIPS WITH WOMEN.
THAT INCLUDES ME, OF COURSE.
???
It... includes you??
...HUH?
HEE HEE.
I KNEW YOU WOULDN'T UNDERSTAND.

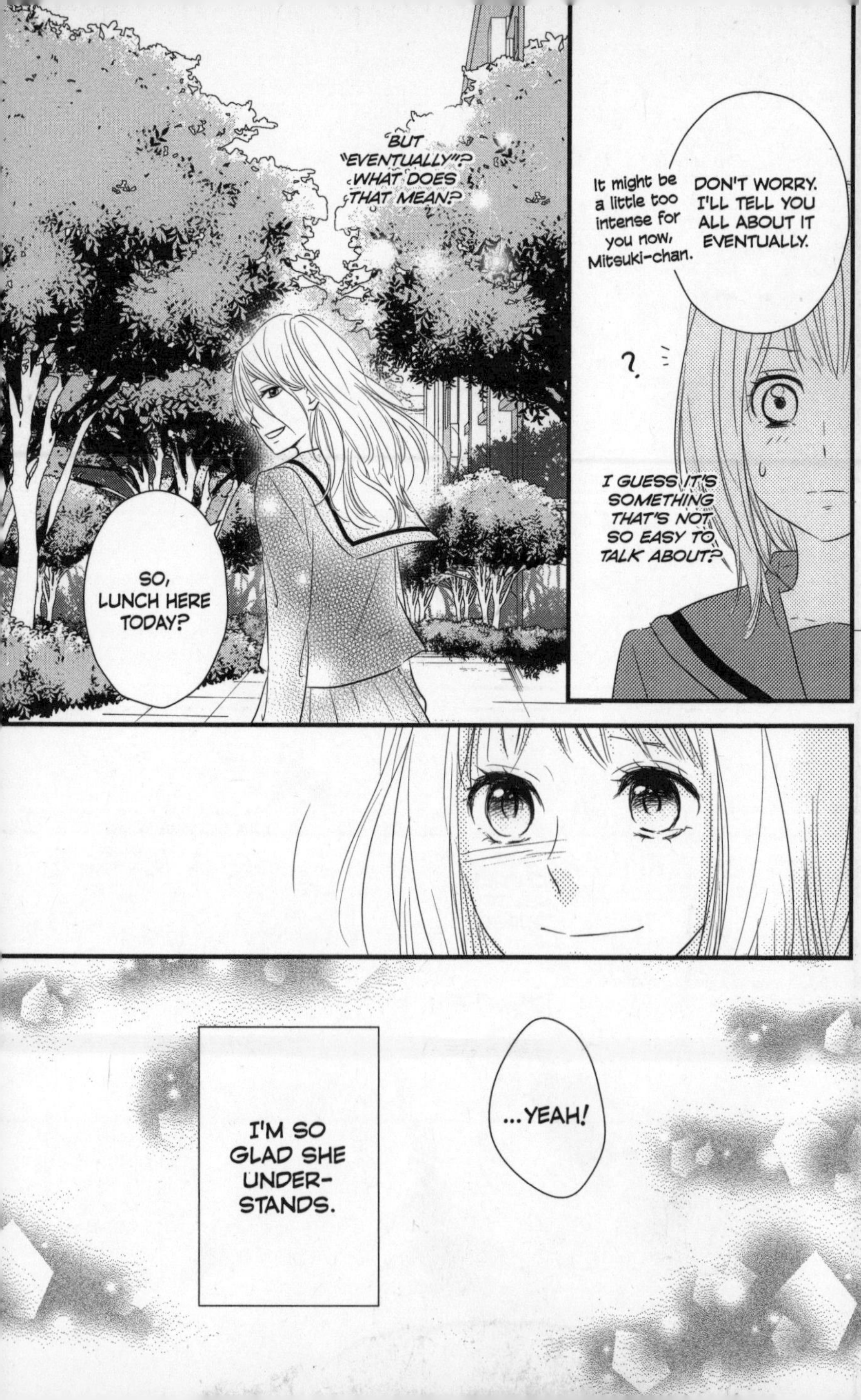
DON'T WORRY. I'LL TELL YOU ALL ABOUT IT EVENTUALLY.
It might be a little too intense for you now, Mitsuki-chan.
?
I GUESS IT'S SOMETHING THAT'S NOT SO EASY TO TALK ABOUT?
BUT "EVENTUALLY"? WHAT DOES THAT MEAN?
SO, LUNCH HERE TODAY?
...YEAH!
I'M SO GLAD SHE UNDER-STANDS.

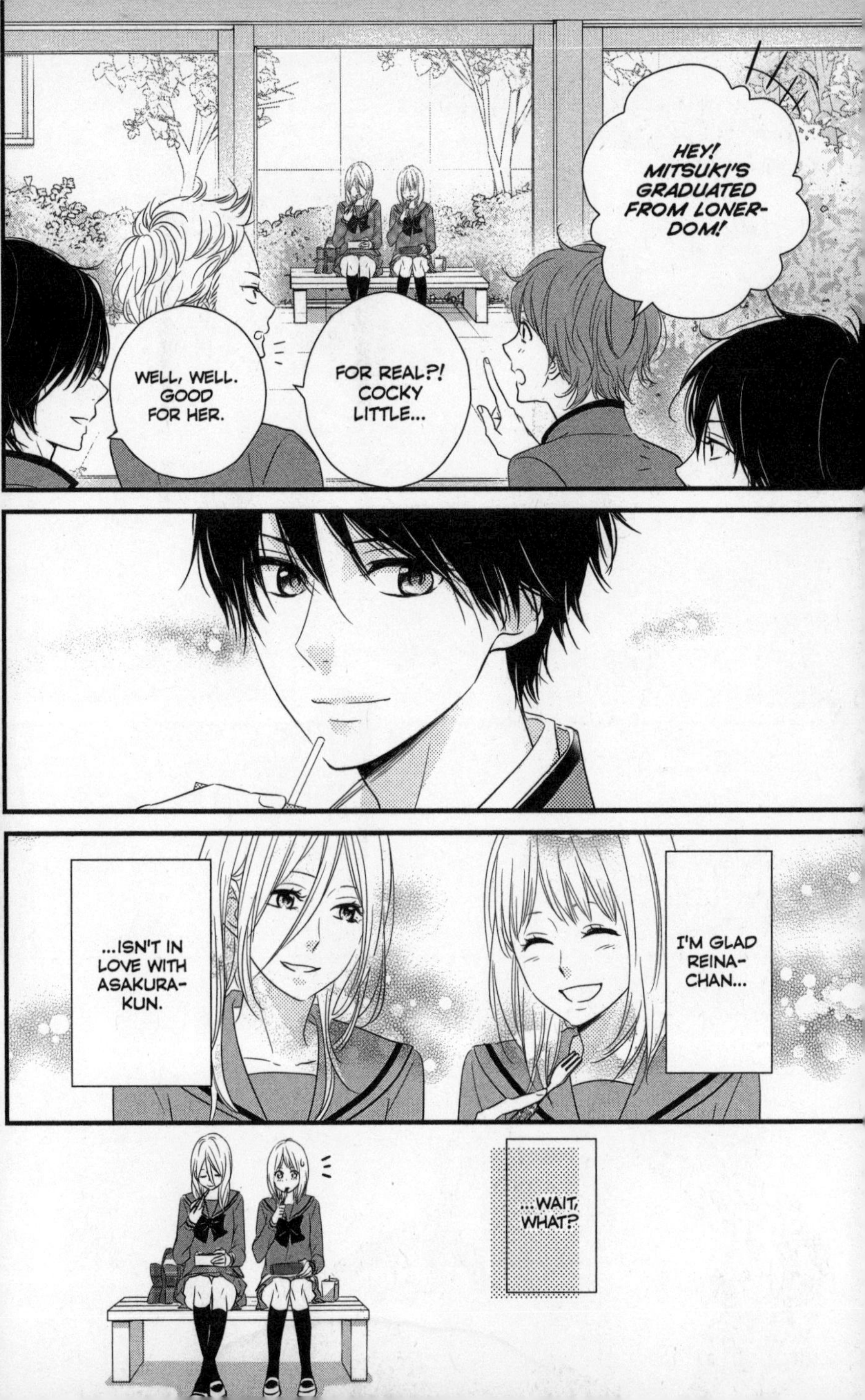
HEY! MITSUKI'S GRADUATED FROM LONER-DOM!
FOR REAL?! COCKY LITTLE...
WELL, WELL. GOOD FOR HER.
I'M GLAD REINA-CHAN...
...ISN'T IN LOVE WITH ASAKURA-KUN.
...WAIT, WHAT?

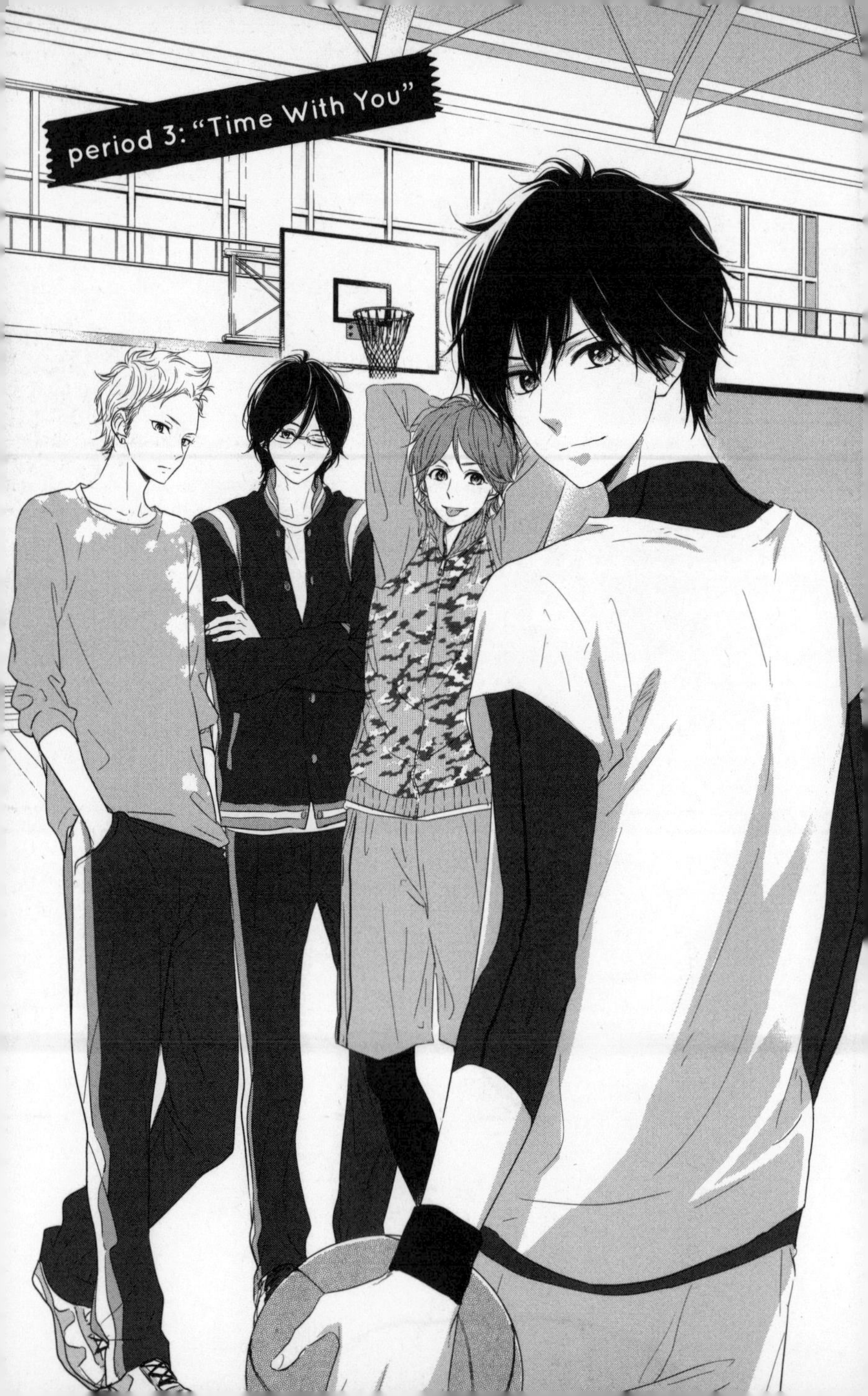
period 3: "Time With You"

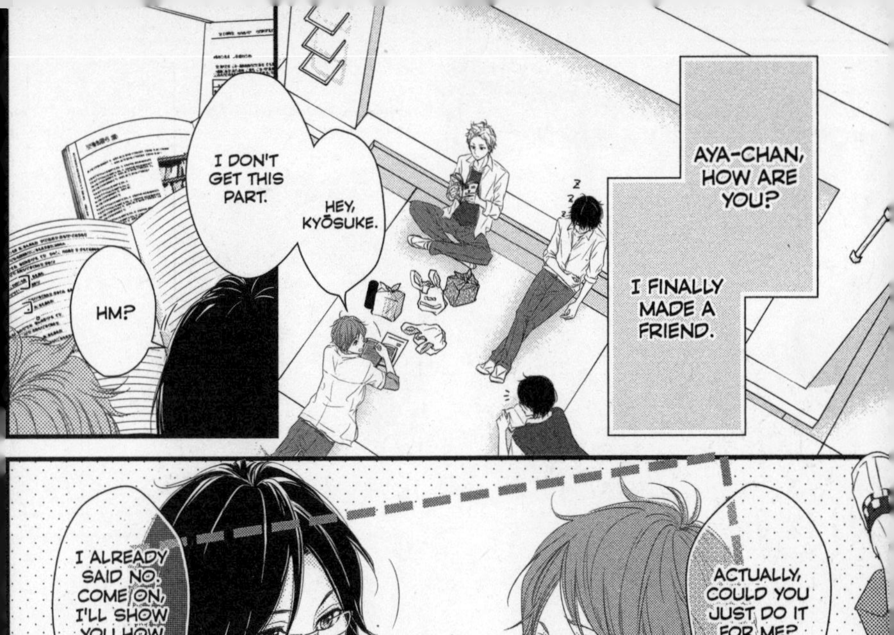
AYA-CHAN, HOW ARE YOU?
I FINALLY MADE A FRIEND.
HEY, KYŌSUKE.
I DON'T GET THIS PART.
HM?
ACTUALLY, COULD YOU JUST DO IT FOR ME?
I ALREADY SAID NO. COME ON, I'LL SHOW YOU HOW TO DO IT.
...SNAP

Mitsuki Haruno

5'4"/99.2 lbs.

Blood type O

Born April 3

Favorite food: The Boss's apple pie

What she's putting effort into lately:

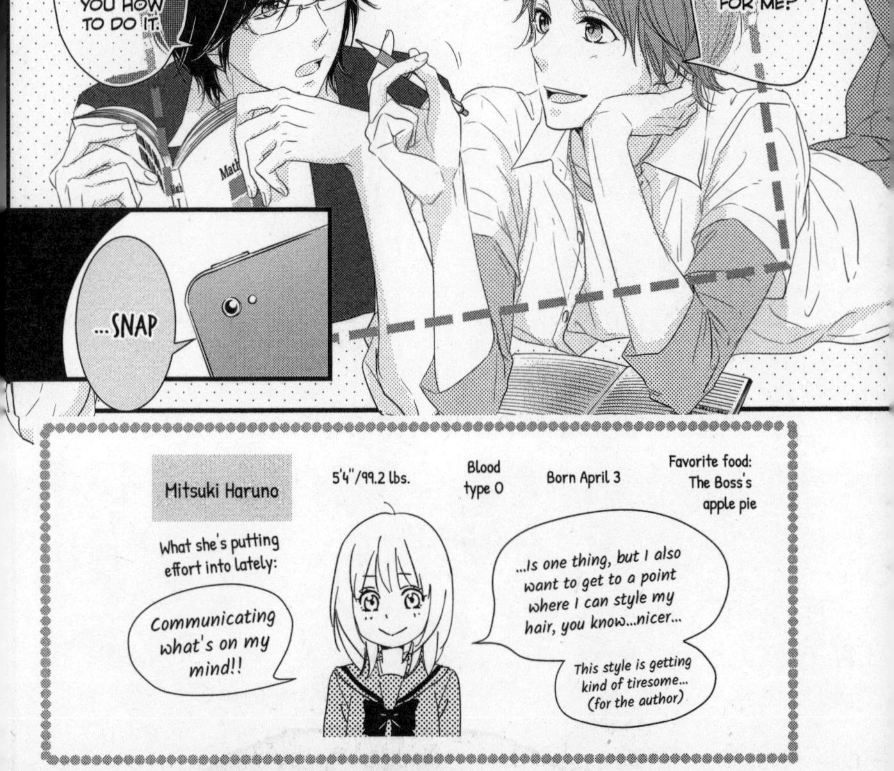
Communicating what's on my mind!!
...Is one thing, but I also want to get to a point where I can style my hair, you know...nicer...
This style is getting kind of tiresome... (for the author)

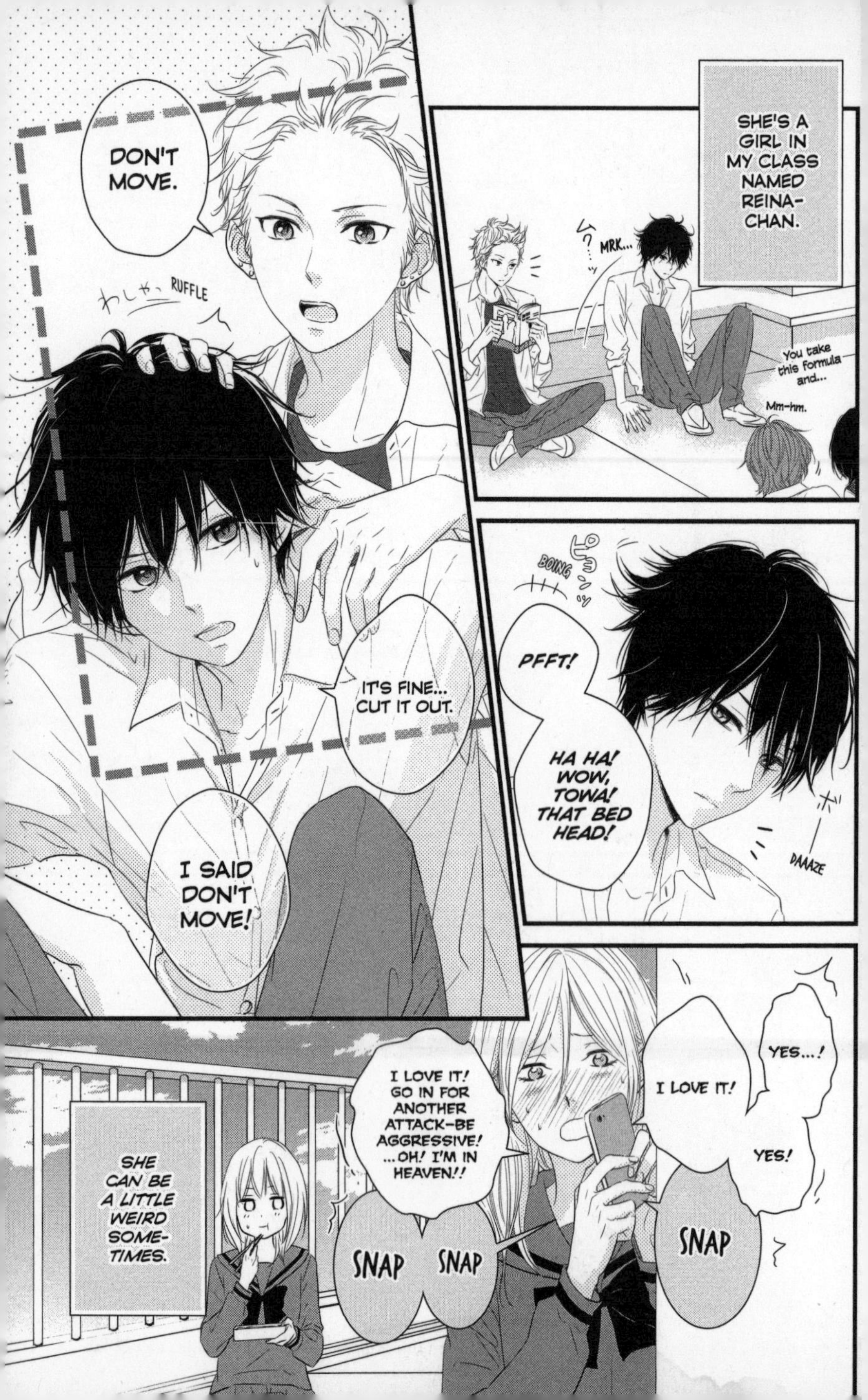
SHE'S A GIRL IN MY CLASS NAMED REINA-CHAN.
MRK...
You take this formula and...
Mm-hm.
BOING
PFFT!
HA HA! WOW, TOWA! THAT BED HEAD!
DAAAZE
DON'T MOVE.
RUFFLE
IT'S FINE... CUT IT OUT.
I SAID DON'T MOVE!
YES...!
I LOVE IT!
YES!
SNAP
I LOVE IT! GO IN FOR ANOTHER ATTACK—BE AGGRESSIVE! ...OH! I'M IN HEAVEN!!
SNAP
SNAP
SHE CAN BE A LITTLE WEIRD SOME-TIMES.

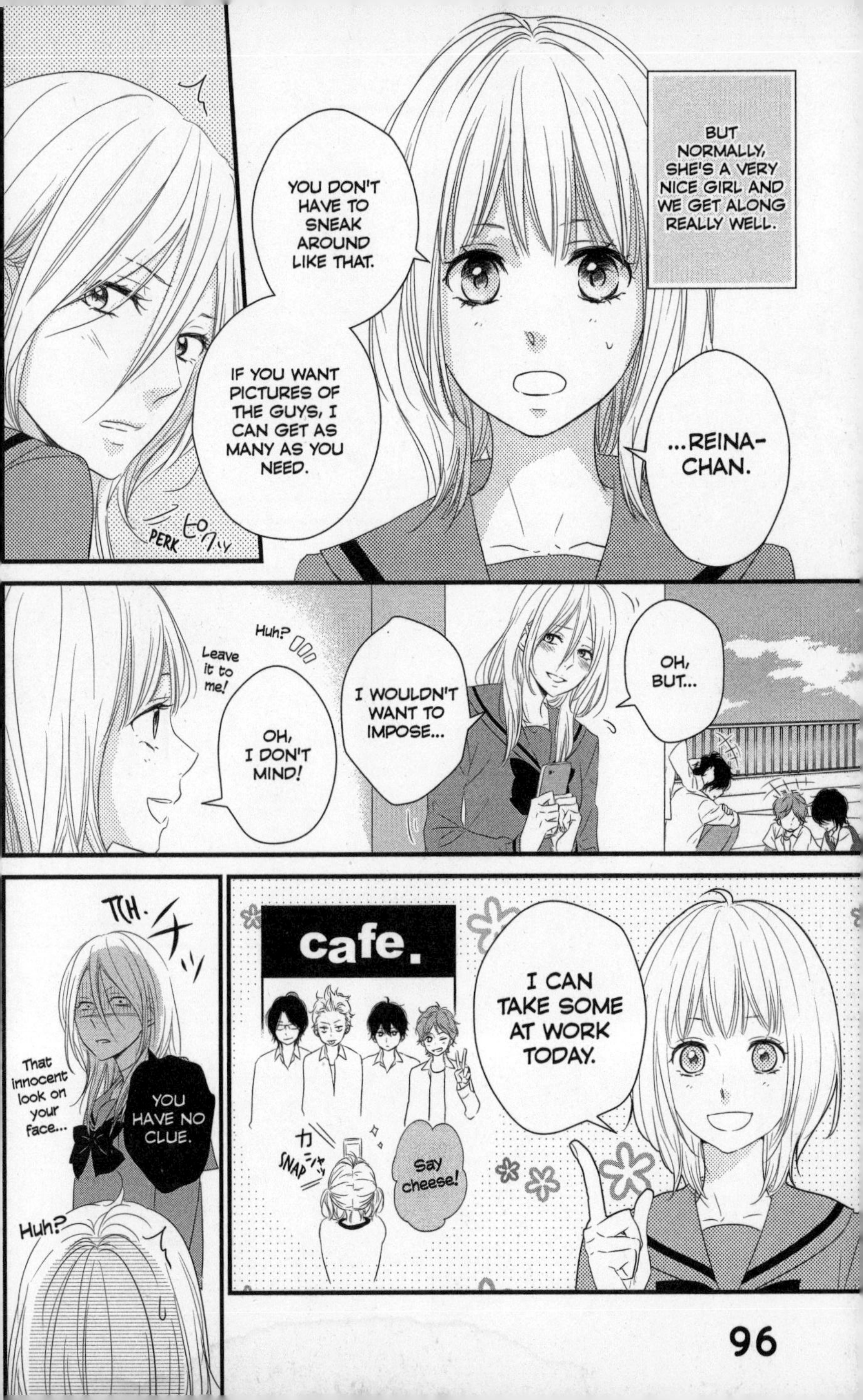

BUT NORMALLY, SHE'S A VERY NICE GIRL AND WE GET ALONG REALLY WELL.
...REINA-CHAN.
YOU DON'T HAVE TO SNEAK AROUND LIKE THAT.
IF YOU WANT PICTURES OF THE GUYS, I CAN GET AS MANY AS YOU NEED.
PERK ピクッ
OH, BUT...
I WOULDN'T WANT TO IMPOSE...
Huh?
Leave it to me!
OH, I DON'T MIND!
I CAN TAKE SOME AT WORK TODAY.
cafe.
Say cheese!
SNAP カシャッ
TCH. チッ
That innocent look on your face...
YOU HAVE NO CLUE.
Huh?

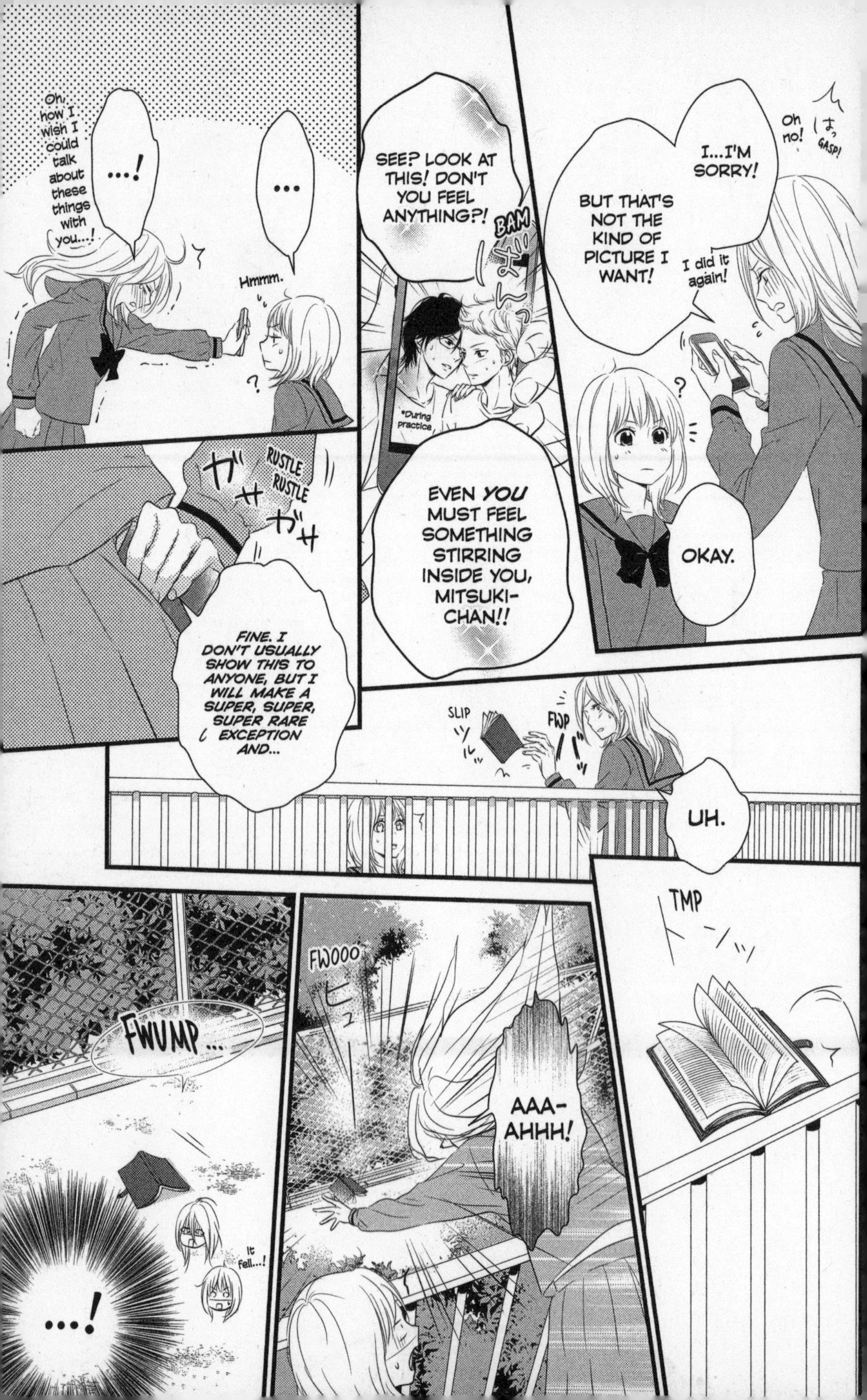

Oh no!
GASP!
I...I'M SORRY!
BUT THAT'S NOT THE KIND OF PICTURE I WANT!
I did it again!
OKAY.
SEE? LOOK AT THIS! DON'T YOU FEEL ANYTHING?!
BAM
*During practice
EVEN YOU MUST FEEL SOMETHING STIRRING INSIDE YOU, MITSUKI-CHAN!!
...!
...
Hmmm.
Oh, how I wish I could talk about these things with you...!
RUSTLE RUSTLE
FINE. I DON'T USUALLY SHOW THIS TO ANYONE, BUT I WILL MAKE A SUPER, SUPER, SUPER RARE EXCEPTION AND...
FWP
SLIP
UH.
TMP
FWOOO
AAA-AHHH!
FWUMP...
It fell...!
...!

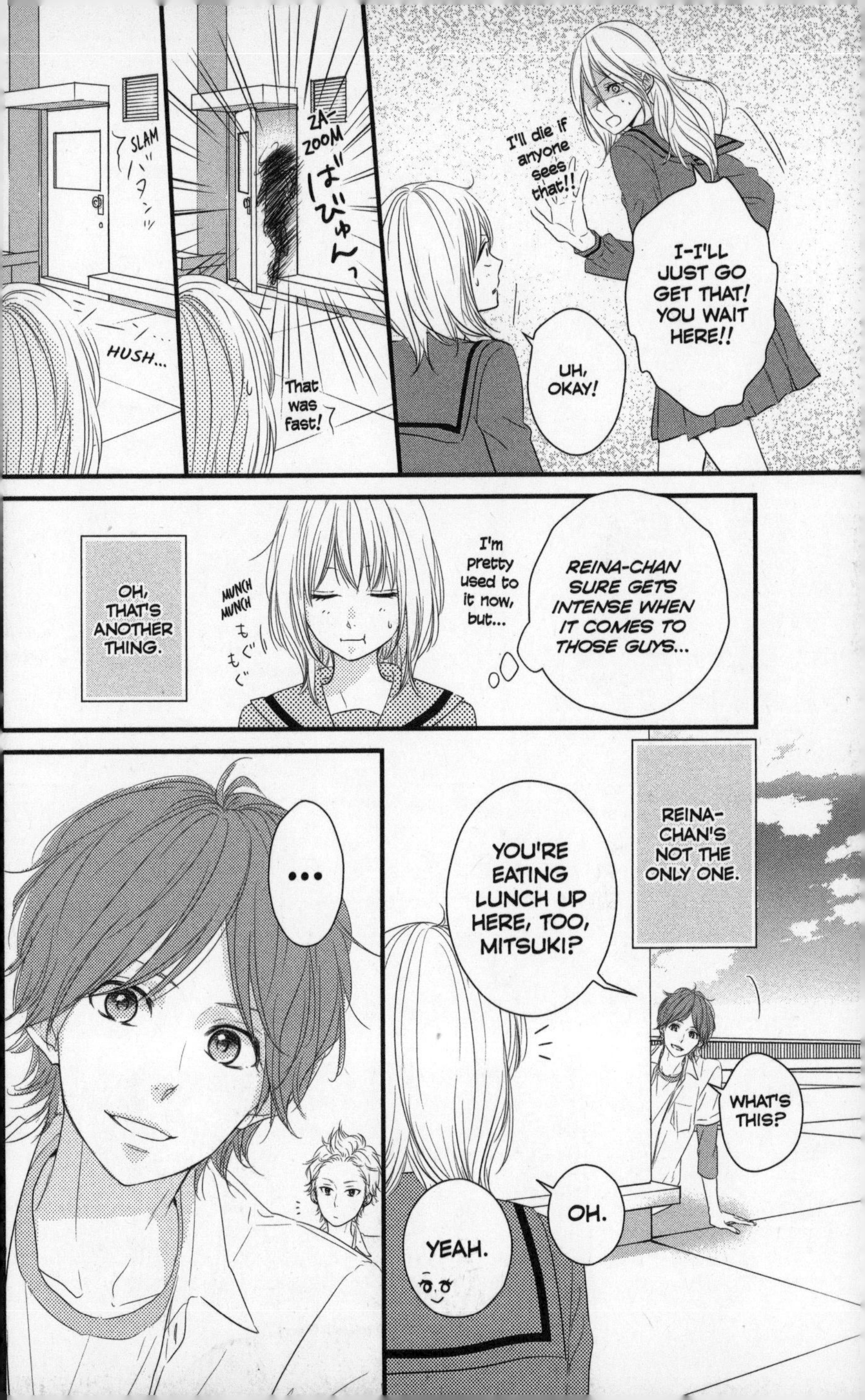

I-I'LL JUST GO GET THAT! YOU WAIT HERE!!
I'll die if anyone sees that!!
UH, OKAY!
ZA-ZOOM
ばびゅんっ
That was fast!
SLAM
バタンッ
HUSH...
REINA-CHAN SURE GETS INTENSE WHEN IT COMES TO THOSE GUYS...
I'm pretty used to it now, but...
MUNCH MUNCH
もぐもぐ
OH, THAT'S ANOTHER THING.
REINA-CHAN'S NOT THE ONLY ONE.
YOU'RE EATING LUNCH UP HERE, TOO, MITSUKI?
WHAT'S THIS?
OH.
YEAH.
...

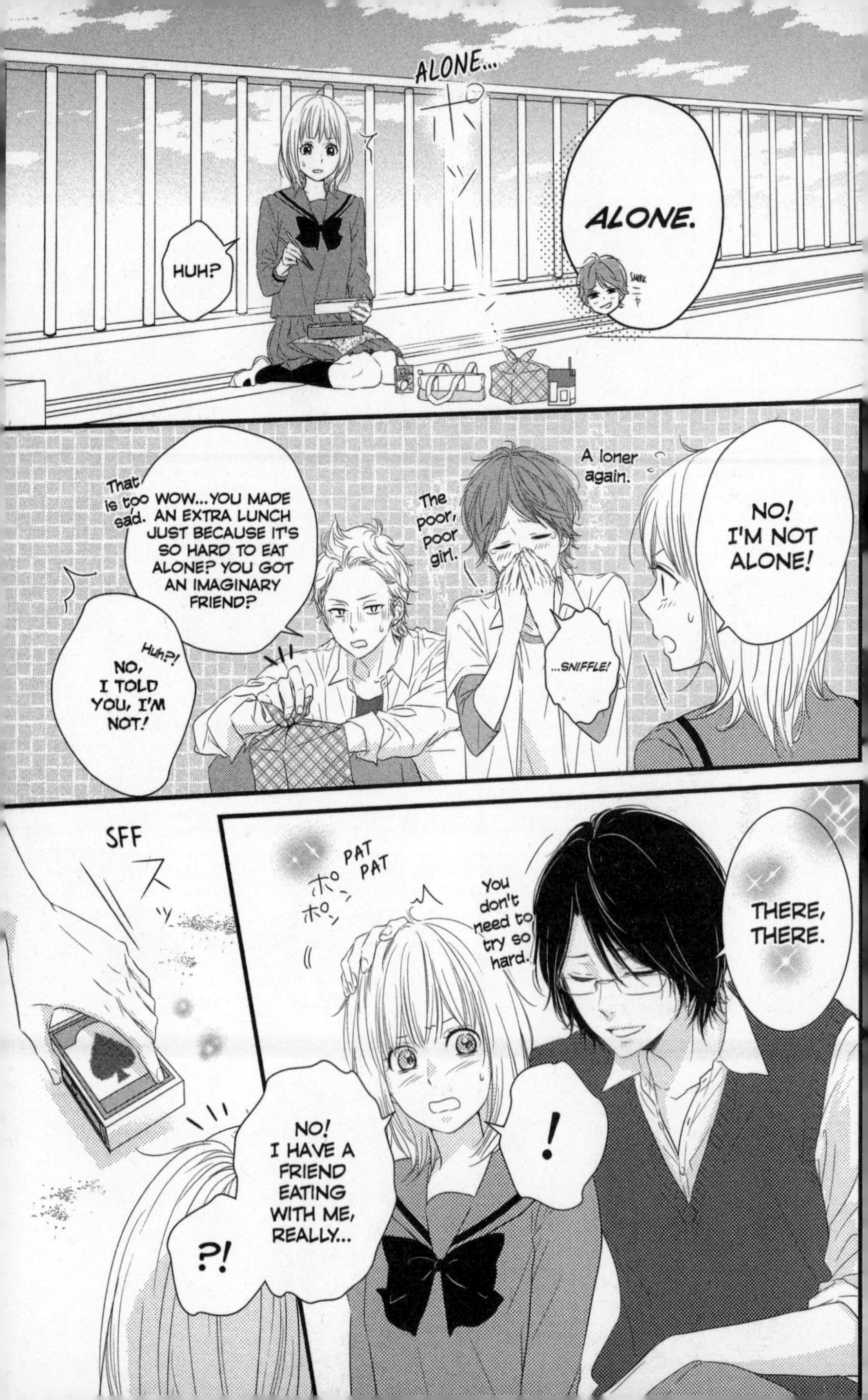
ALONE.
SMIRK
ALONE...
HUH?
NO! I'M NOT ALONE!
A loner again.
...SNIFFLE!
The poor, poor girl.
WOW...YOU MADE AN EXTRA LUNCH JUST BECAUSE IT'S SO HARD TO EAT ALONE? YOU GOT AN IMAGINARY FRIEND?
That is too sad.
Huh?!
NO, I TOLD YOU, I'M NOT!
THERE, THERE.
You don't need to try so hard.
PAT PAT
!
NO! I HAVE A FRIEND EATING WITH ME, REALLY...
SFF
?!

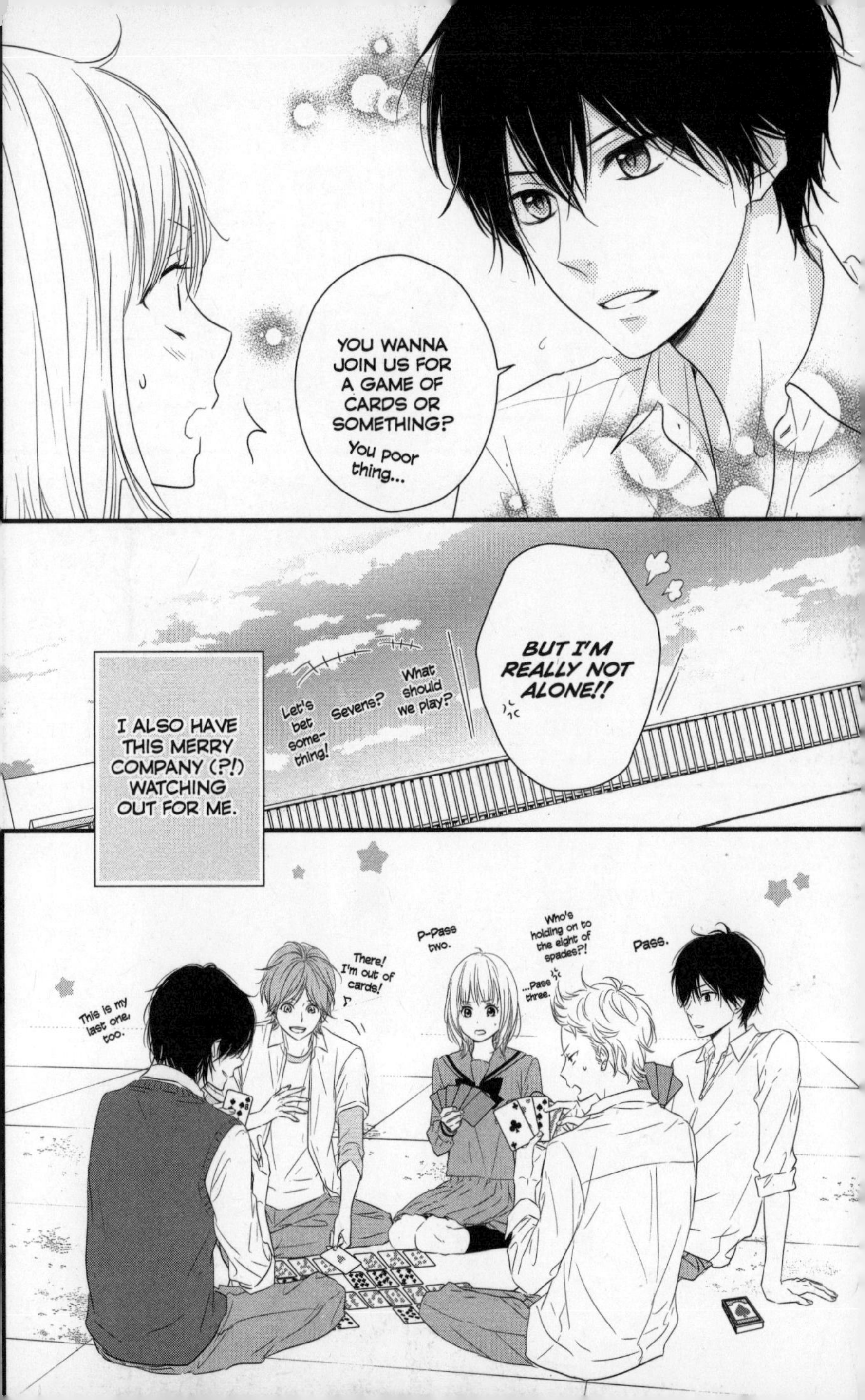
YOU WANNA JOIN US FOR A GAME OF CARDS OR SOMETHING?
You poor thing...
BUT I'M REALLY NOT ALONE!!
What should we play?
Sevens?
Let's bet some-thing!
I ALSO HAVE THIS MERRY COMPANY (?!) WATCHING OUT FOR ME.
Pass.
Who's holding on to the eight of spades?!
...Pass three.
P-Pass two.
There! I'm out of cards!
This is my last one, too.

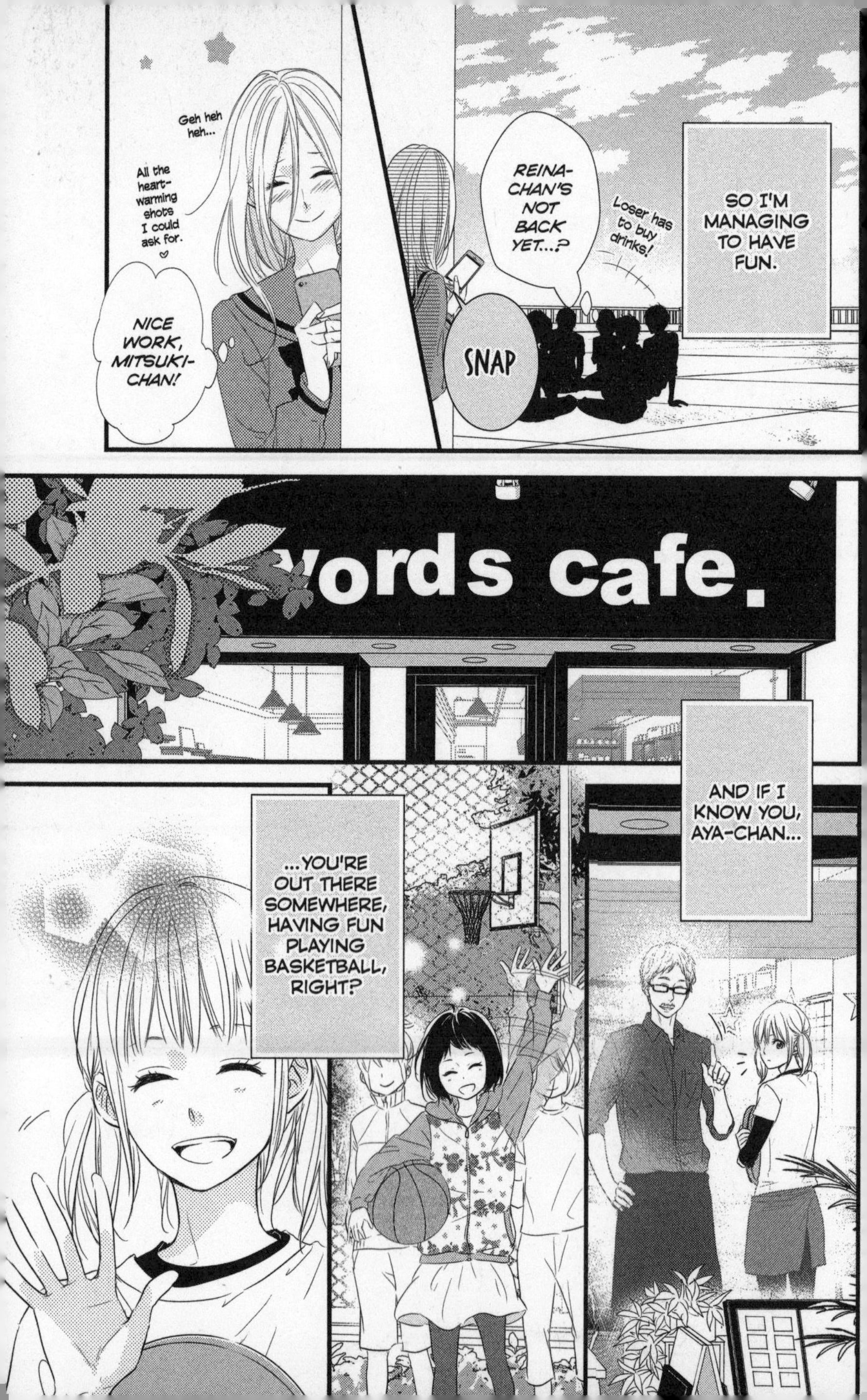
SO I'M MANAGING TO HAVE FUN.
Loser has to buy drinks!
REINA-CHAN'S NOT BACK YET...?
SNAP
Geh heh heh...
All the heart-warming shots I could ask for. ♡
NICE WORK, MITSUKI-CHAN!
ords cafe.
AND IF I KNOW YOU, AYA-CHAN...
...YOU'RE OUT THERE SOMEWHERE, HAVING FUN PLAYING BASKETBALL, RIGHT?

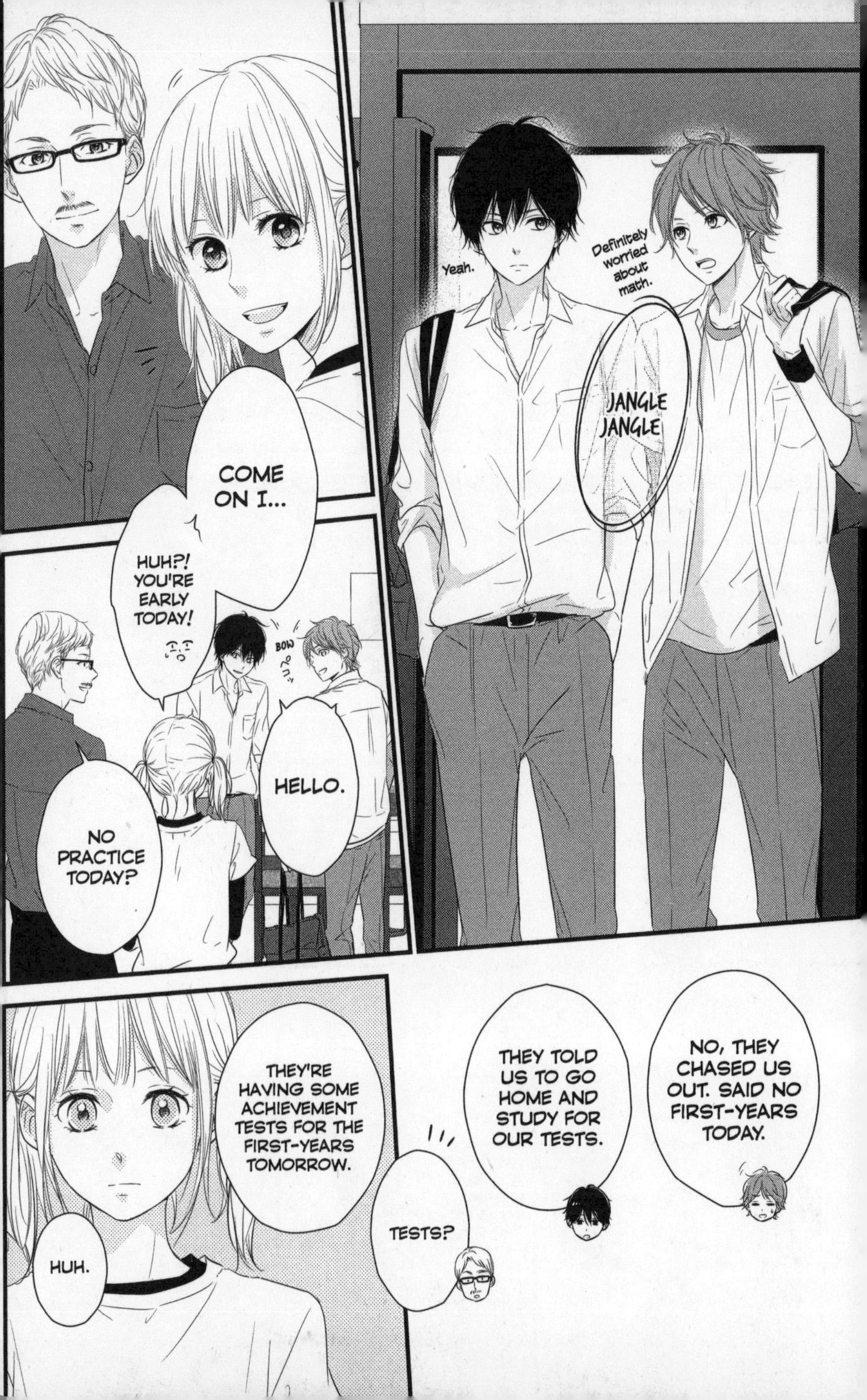
Definitely worried about math.
Yeah.
JANGLE JANGLE
COME ON I...
HUH?! YOU'RE EARLY TODAY!
BOW
HELLO.
NO PRACTICE TODAY?
NO, THEY CHASED US OUT. SAID NO FIRST-YEARS TODAY.
THEY TOLD US TO GO HOME AND STUDY FOR OUR TESTS.
TESTS?
THEY'RE HAVING SOME ACHIEVEMENT TESTS FOR THE FIRST-YEARS TOMORROW.
HUH.

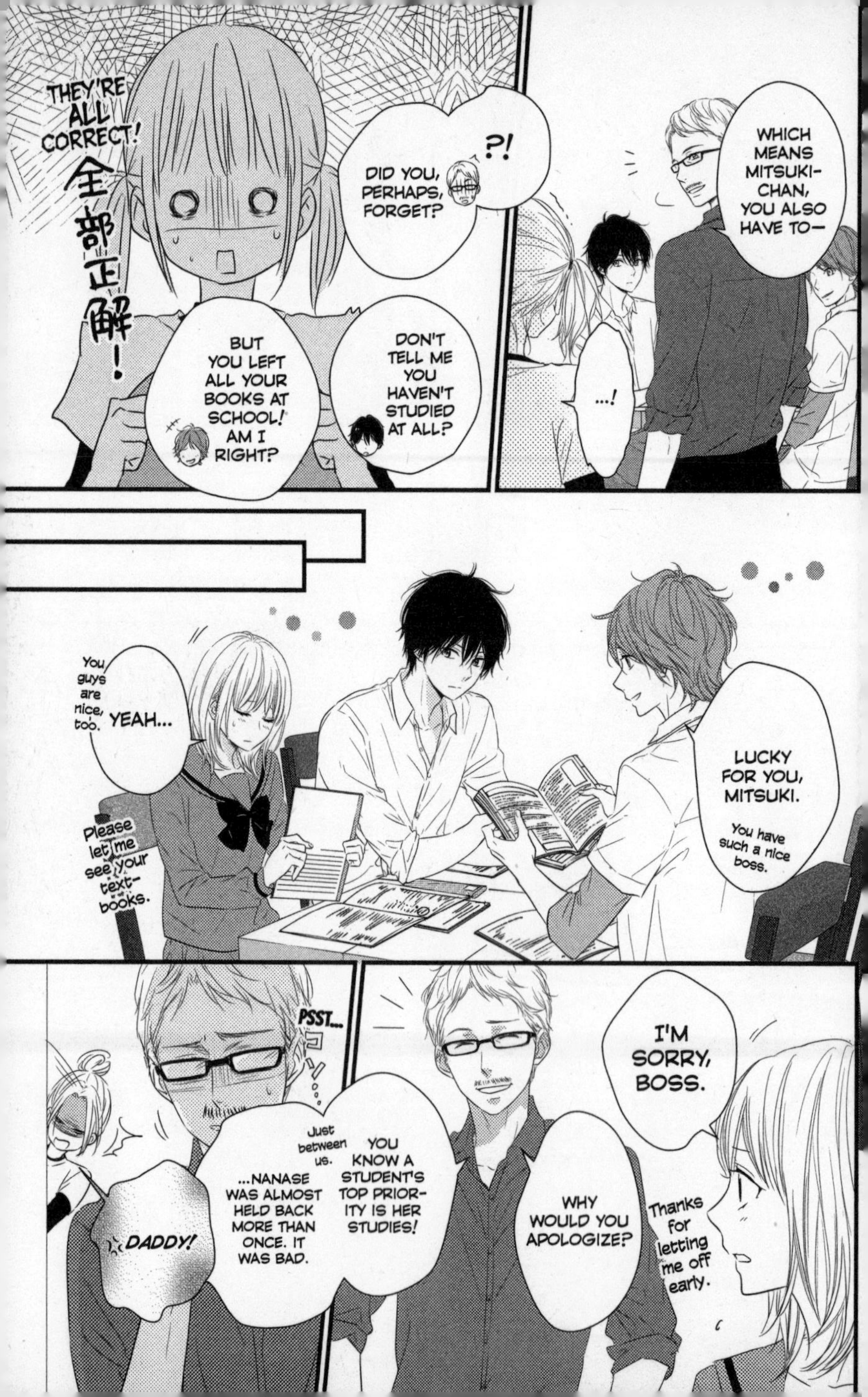

WHICH MEANS MITSUKI-CHAN, YOU ALSO HAVE TO—
...!
DID YOU, PERHAPS, FORGET?
?!
THEY'RE ALL CORRECT!
全部正解!
DON'T TELL ME YOU HAVEN'T STUDIED AT ALL?
BUT YOU LEFT ALL YOUR BOOKS AT SCHOOL! AM I RIGHT?
LUCKY FOR YOU, MITSUKI.
You have such a nice boss.
YEAH...
You guys are nice, too.
Please let me see your textbooks.
I'M SORRY, BOSS.
Thanks for letting me off early.
WHY WOULD YOU APOLOGIZE?
YOU KNOW A STUDENT'S TOP PRIORITY IS HER STUDIES!
PSST...
Just between us.
...NANASE WAS ALMOST HELD BACK MORE THAN ONCE. IT WAS BAD.
DADDY!

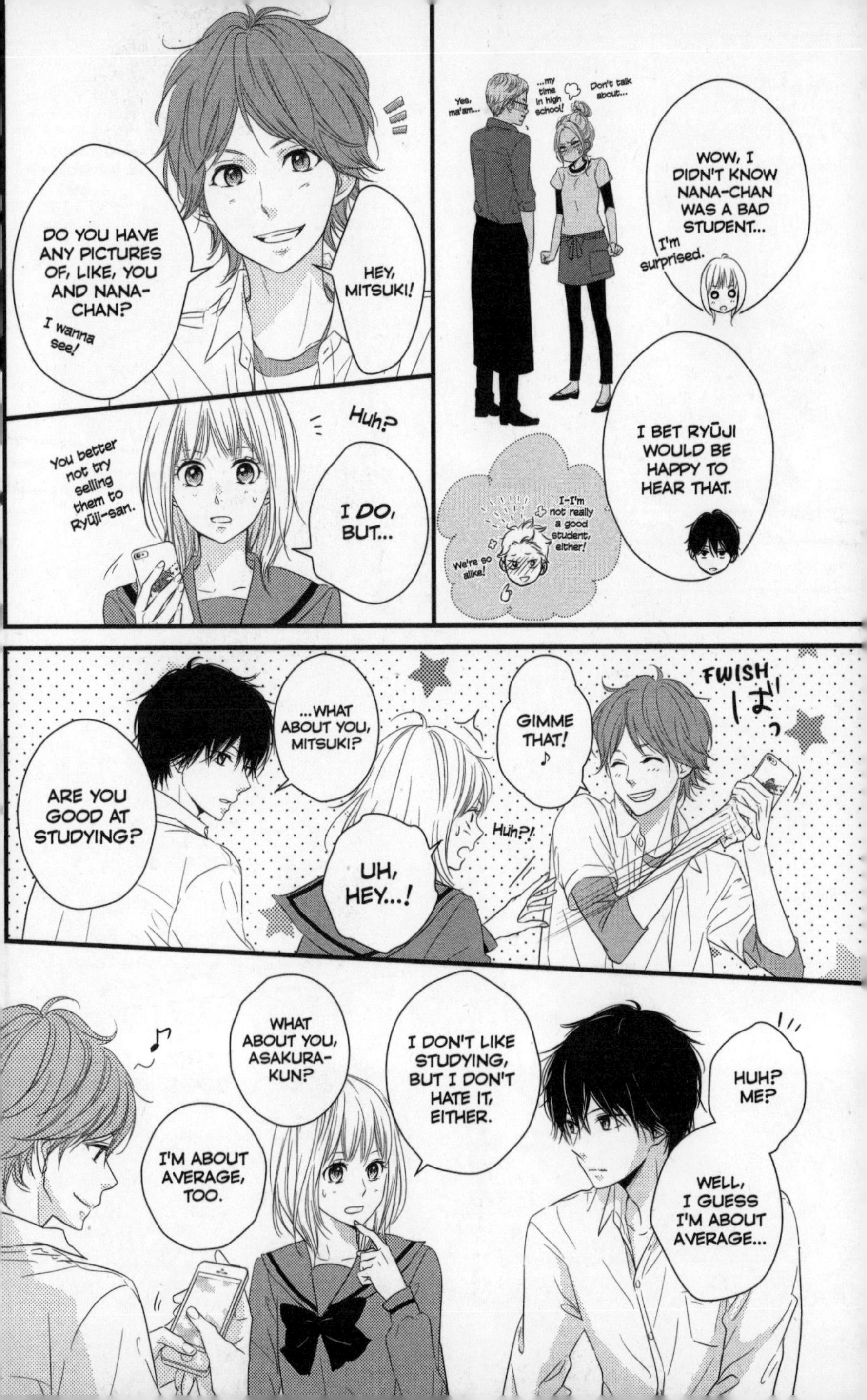
Don't talk about...
...my time in high school!
Yes, ma'am...
WOW, I DIDN'T KNOW NANA-CHAN WAS A BAD STUDENT...
I'm surprised.
I BET RYŪJI WOULD BE HAPPY TO HEAR THAT.
I-I'm not really a good student, either!
We're so alike!
HEY, MITSUKI!
DO YOU HAVE ANY PICTURES OF, LIKE, YOU AND NANA-CHAN?
I wanna see!
Huh?
I DO, BUT...
You better not try selling them to Ryūji-san.
FWISH
GIMME THAT! ♪
UH, HEY...!
Huh?!
...WHAT ABOUT YOU, MITSUKI?
ARE YOU GOOD AT STUDYING?
HUH? ME?
WELL, I GUESS I'M ABOUT AVERAGE...
I DON'T LIKE STUDYING, BUT I DON'T HATE IT, EITHER.
WHAT ABOUT YOU, ASAKURA-KUN?
I'M ABOUT AVERAGE, TOO.

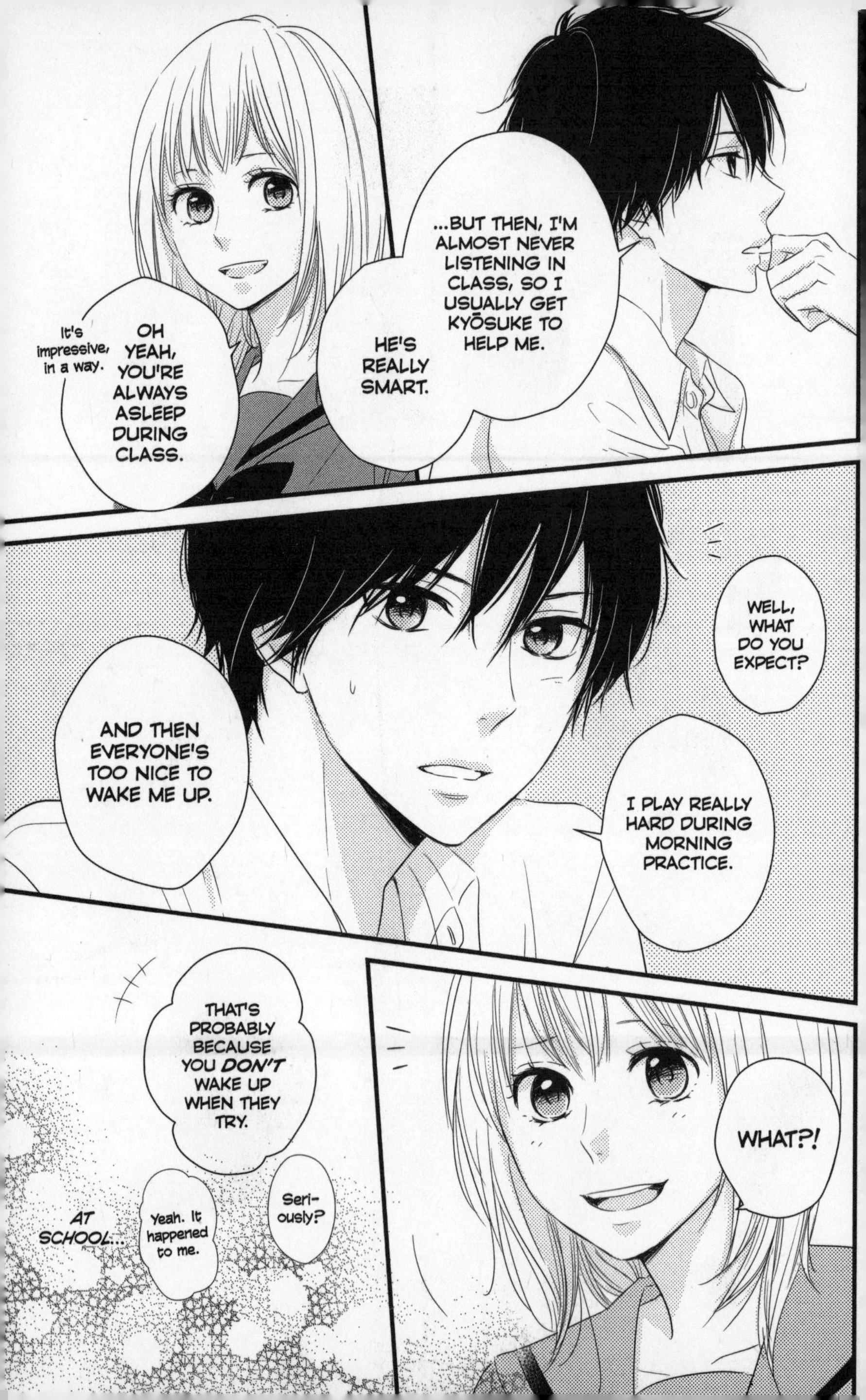
...BUT THEN, I'M ALMOST NEVER LISTENING IN CLASS, SO I USUALLY GET KYŌSUKE TO HELP ME.
HE'S REALLY SMART.
OH YEAH, YOU'RE ALWAYS ASLEEP DURING CLASS.
It's impressive, in a way.
WELL, WHAT DO YOU EXPECT?
I PLAY REALLY HARD DURING MORNING PRACTICE.
AND THEN EVERYONE'S TOO NICE TO WAKE ME UP.
THAT'S PROBABLY BECAUSE YOU *DON'T* WAKE UP WHEN THEY TRY.
WHAT?!
Seri-ously?
Yeah. It happened to me.
AT SCHOOL...

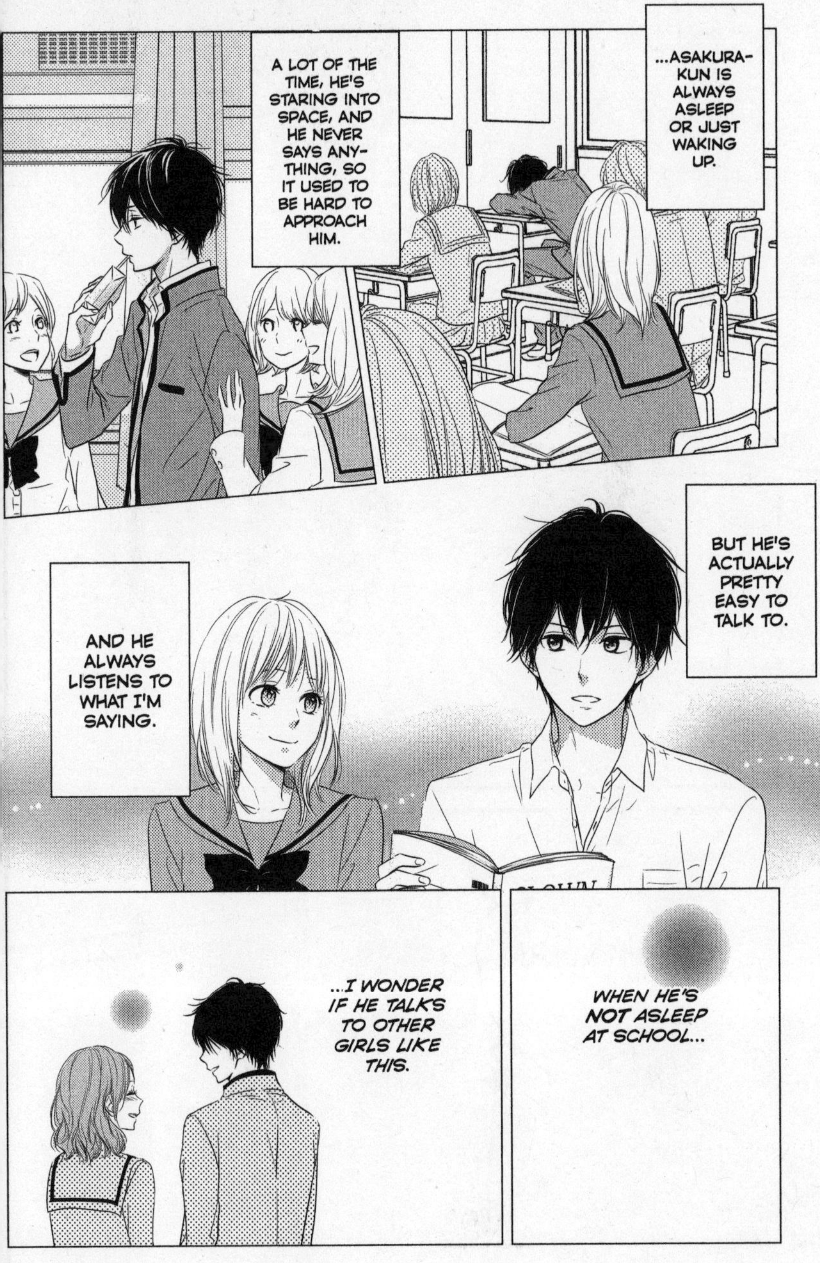
...ASAKURA-KUN IS ALWAYS ASLEEP OR JUST WAKING UP.
A LOT OF THE TIME, HE'S STARING INTO SPACE, AND HE NEVER SAYS ANY-THING, SO IT USED TO BE HARD TO APPROACH HIM.
BUT HE'S ACTUALLY PRETTY EASY TO TALK TO.
AND HE ALWAYS LISTENS TO WHAT I'M SAYING.
WHEN HE'S NOT ASLEEP AT SCHOOL...
...I WONDER IF HE TALKS TO OTHER GIRLS LIKE THIS.

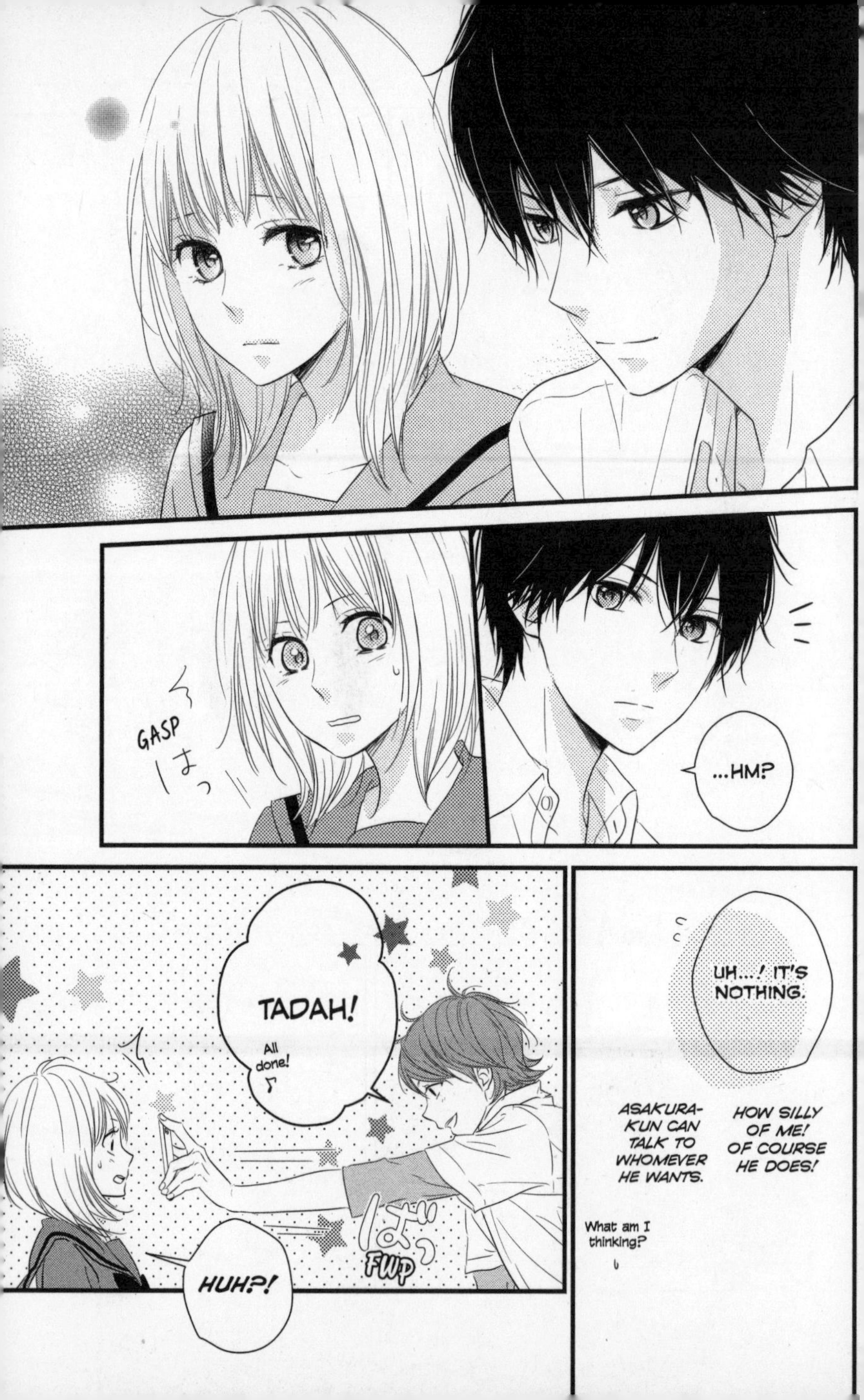
...HM?
GASP
はっ
UH...! IT'S NOTHING.
HOW SILLY OF ME! OF COURSE HE DOES!
ASAKURA-KUN CAN TALK TO WHOMEVER HE WANTS.
What am I thinking?
TADAH!
All done! ♪
FWP
ぱっ
HUH?!

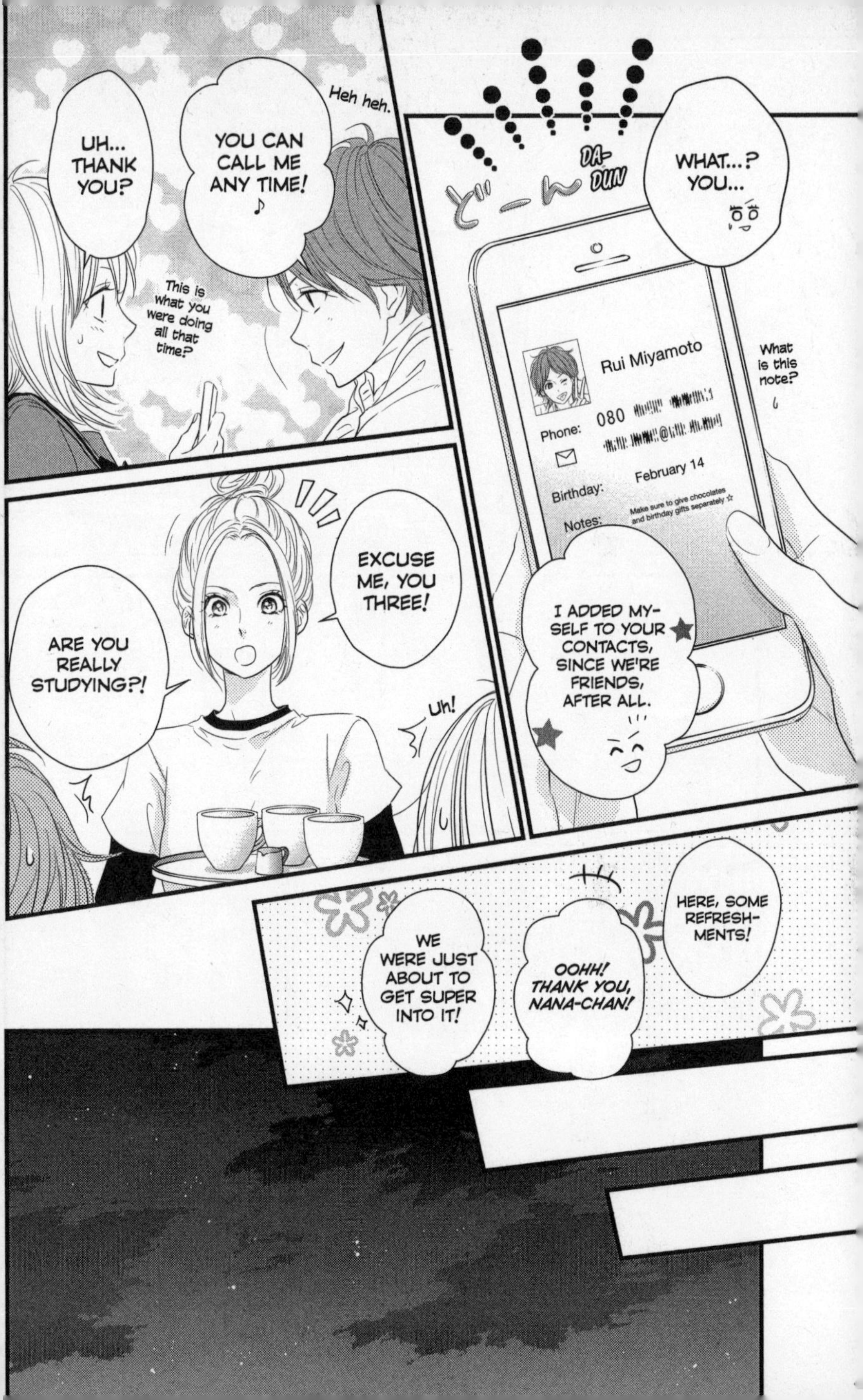
WHAT...? YOU...
どーん DA-DUN
Rui Miyamoto
Phone: 080
Birthday: February 14
Notes: Make sure to give chocolates and birthday gifts separately ☆
What is this note?
I ADDED MY-SELF TO YOUR CONTACTS, SINCE WE'RE FRIENDS, AFTER ALL.
Heh heh.
YOU CAN CALL ME ANY TIME! ♪
UH... THANK YOU?
This is what you were doing all that time?
EXCUSE ME, YOU THREE!
ARE YOU REALLY STUDYING?!
Uh!
HERE, SOME REFRESH-MENTS!
OOHH! THANK YOU, NANA-CHAN!
WE WERE JUST ABOUT TO GET SUPER INTO IT!

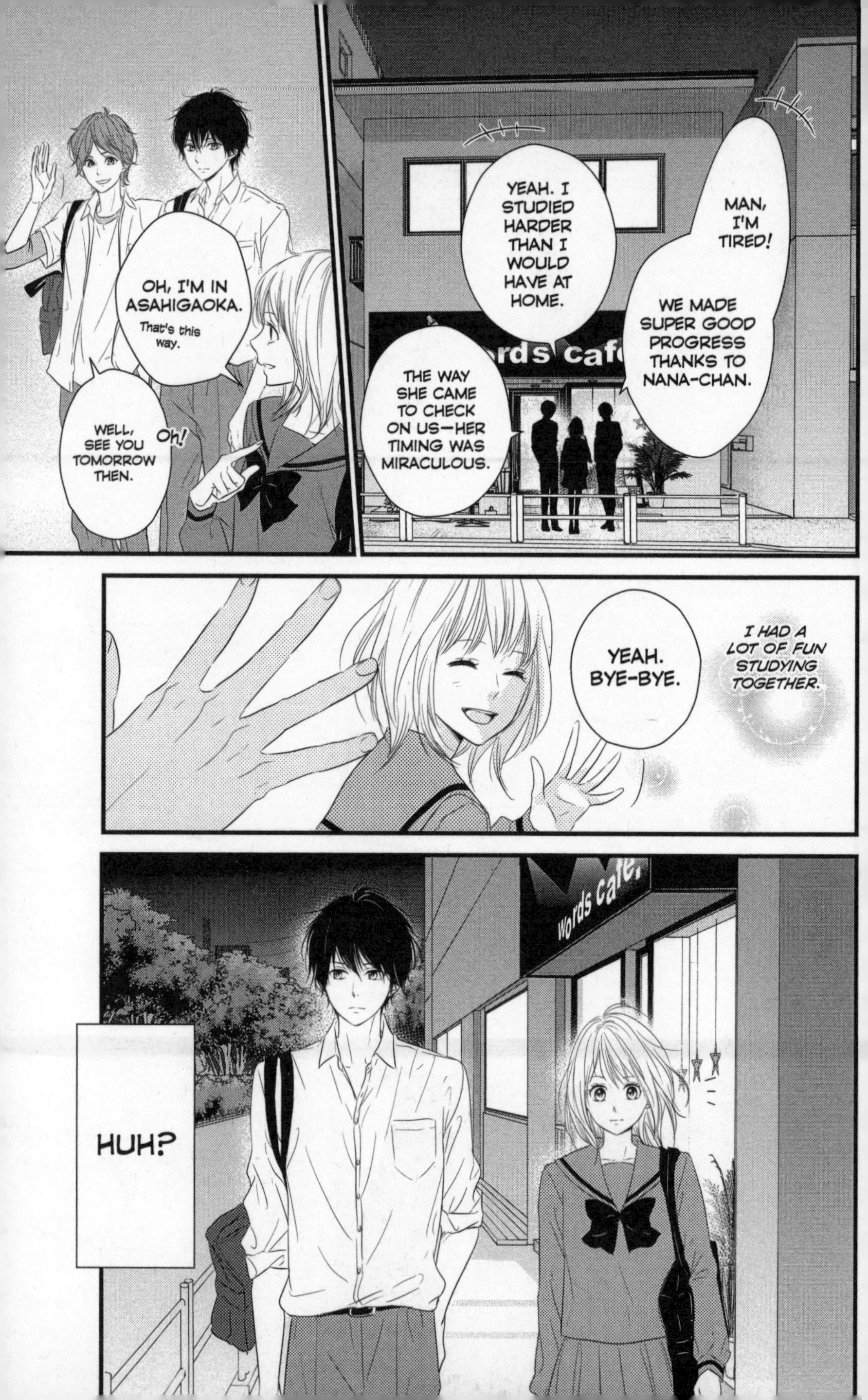
MAN, I'M TIRED!
WE MADE SUPER GOOD PROGRESS THANKS TO NANA-CHAN.
YEAH. I STUDIED HARDER THAN I WOULD HAVE AT HOME.
THE WAY SHE CAME TO CHECK ON US—HER TIMING WAS MIRACULOUS.
OH, I'M IN ASAHIGAOKA.
That's this way.
Oh!
WELL, SEE YOU TOMORROW THEN.
I HAD A LOT OF FUN STUDYING TOGETHER.
YEAH. BYE-BYE.
words cafe
HUH?

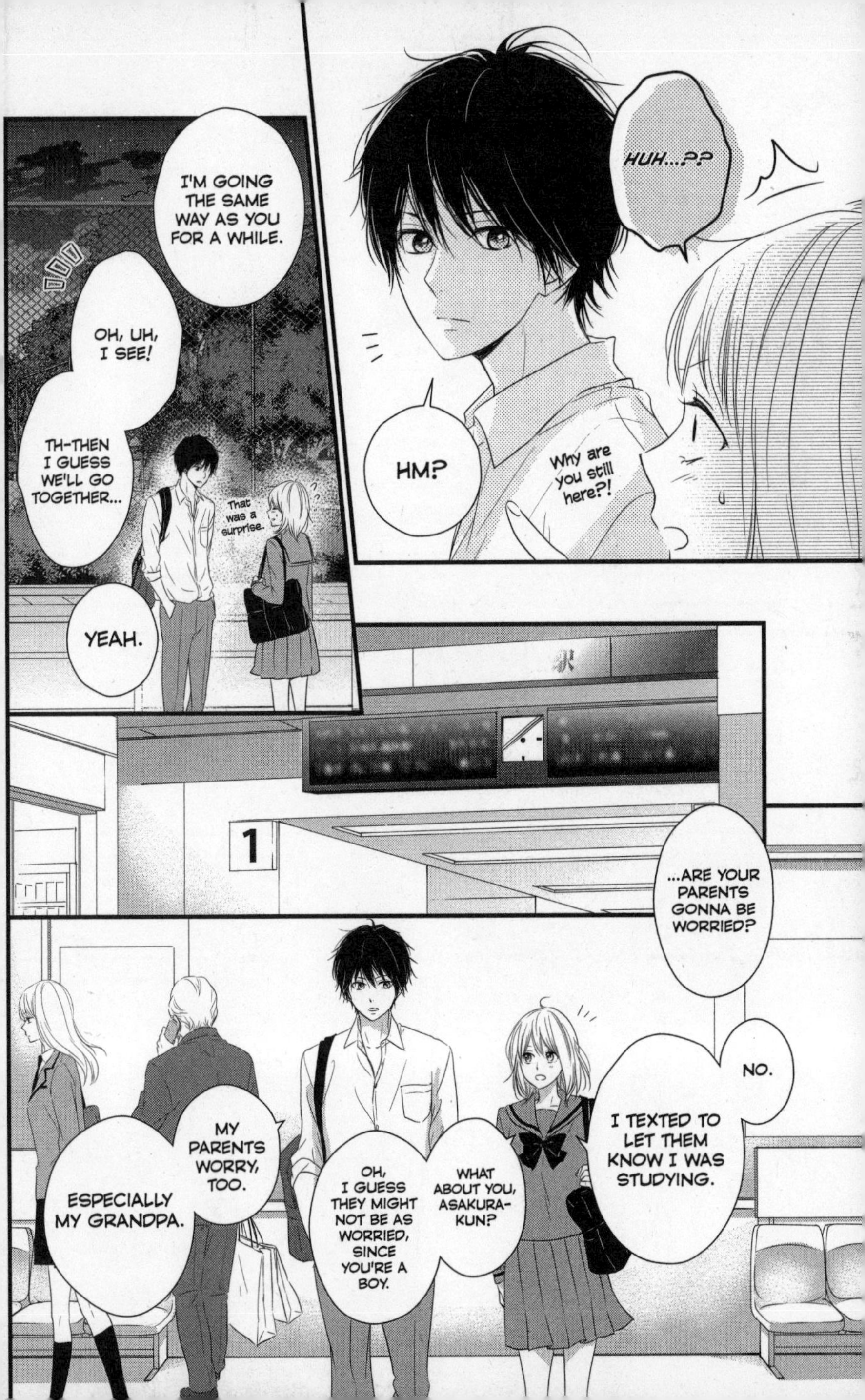
HUH...??
HM?
Why are you still here?!
I'M GOING THE SAME WAY AS YOU FOR A WHILE.
OH, UH, I SEE!
TH-THEN I GUESS WE'LL GO TOGETHER...
That was a surprise.
YEAH.
1
...ARE YOUR PARENTS GONNA BE WORRIED?
NO.
I TEXTED TO LET THEM KNOW I WAS STUDYING.
WHAT ABOUT YOU, ASAKURA-KUN?
OH, I GUESS THEY MIGHT NOT BE AS WORRIED, SINCE YOU'RE A BOY.
MY PARENTS WORRY, TOO.
ESPECIALLY MY GRANDPA.

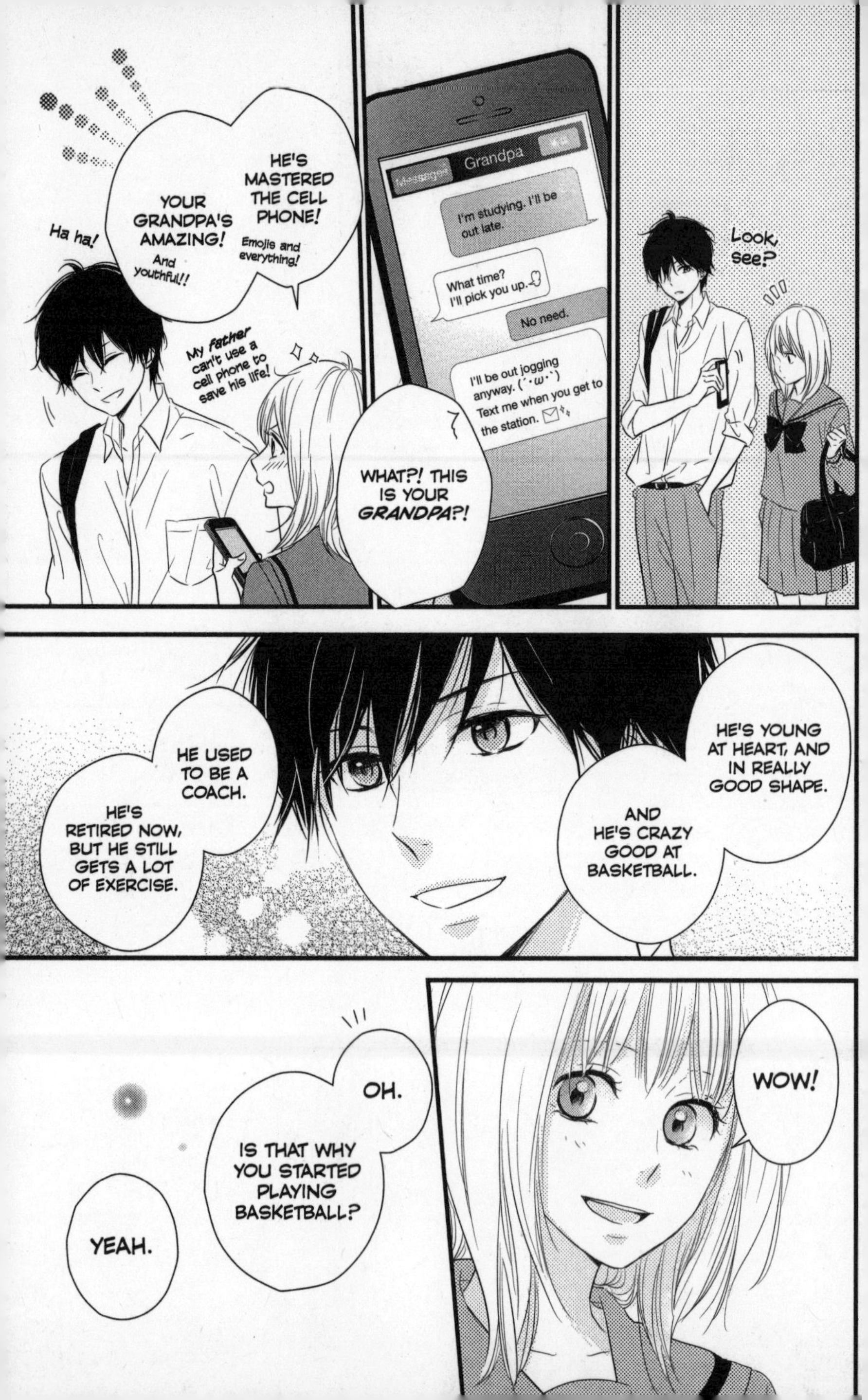
Look, see?
Messages
Grandpa
I'm studying. I'll be out late.
What time? I'll pick you up.
No need.
I'll be out jogging anyway. (´・ω・`) Text me when you get to the station.
WHAT?! THIS IS YOUR *GRANDPA*?!
HE'S MASTERED THE CELL PHONE!
Emojis and everything!
YOUR GRANDPA'S AMAZING!
And youthful!!
Ha ha!
My *father* can't use a cell phone to save his life!
HE'S YOUNG AT HEART, AND IN REALLY GOOD SHAPE.
AND HE'S CRAZY GOOD AT BASKETBALL.
HE USED TO BE A COACH.
HE'S RETIRED NOW, BUT HE STILL GETS A LOT OF EXERCISE.
WOW!
OH.
IS THAT WHY YOU STARTED PLAYING BASKETBALL?
YEAH.

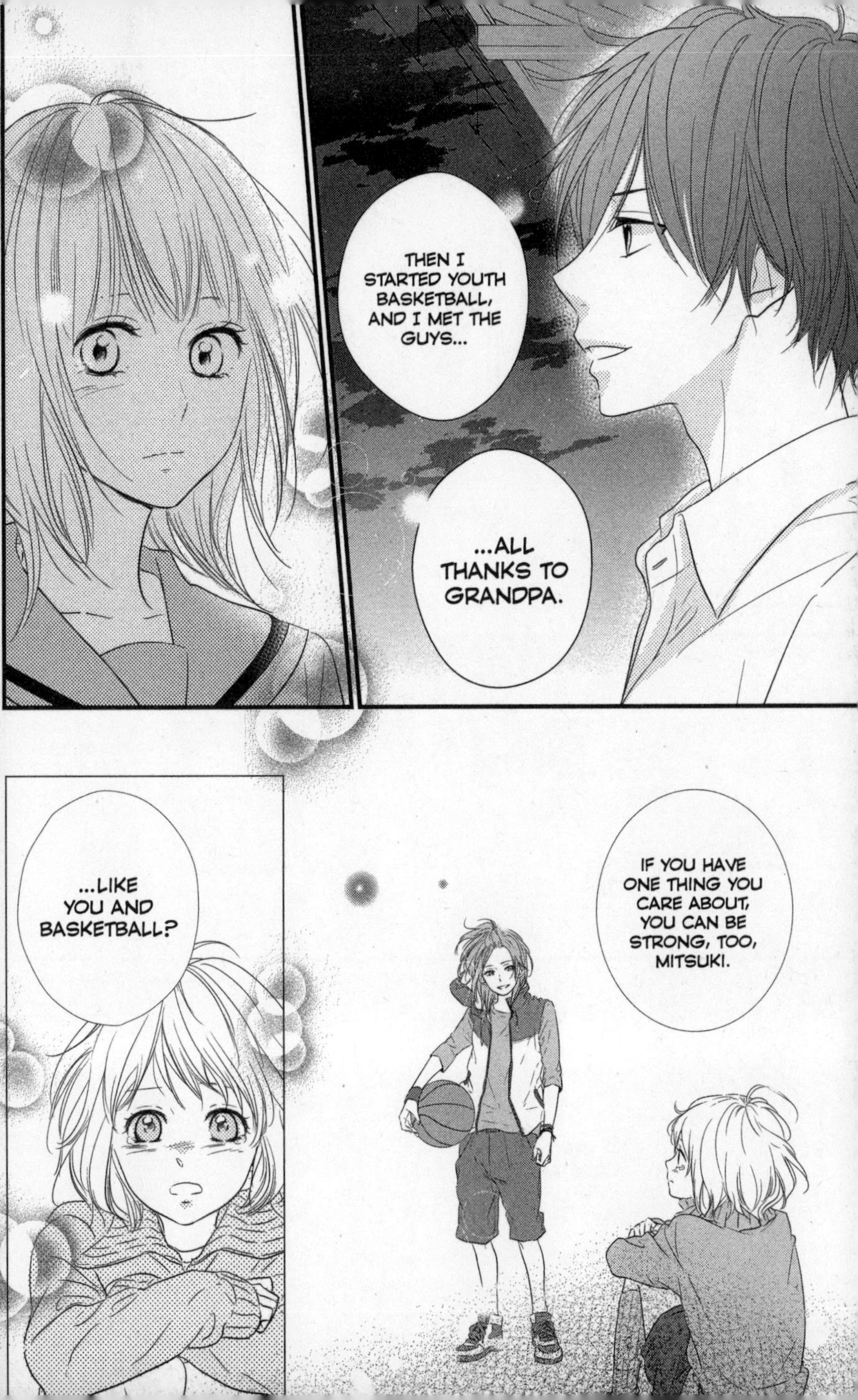
THEN I STARTED YOUTH BASKETBALL, AND I MET THE GUYS...
...ALL THANKS TO GRANDPA.
IF YOU HAVE ONE THING YOU CARE ABOUT, YOU CAN BE STRONG, TOO, MITSUKI.
...LIKE YOU AND BASKETBALL?

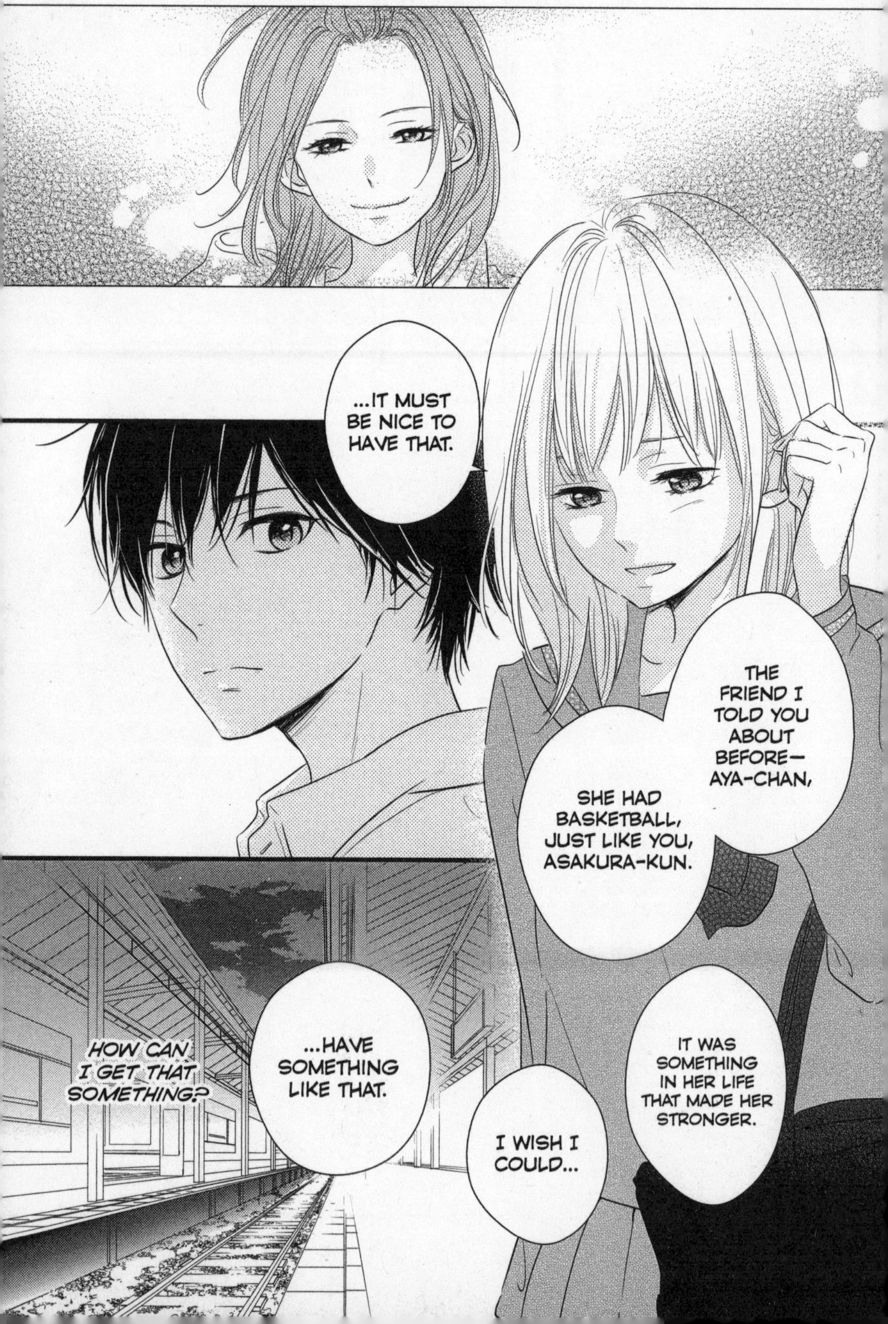
...IT MUST BE NICE TO HAVE THAT.
THE FRIEND I TOLD YOU ABOUT BEFORE—AYA-CHAN,
SHE HAD BASKETBALL, JUST LIKE YOU, ASAKURA-KUN.
IT WAS SOMETHING IN HER LIFE THAT MADE HER STRONGER.
I WISH I COULD...
...HAVE SOMETHING LIKE THAT.
HOW CAN I GET THAT SOMETHING?

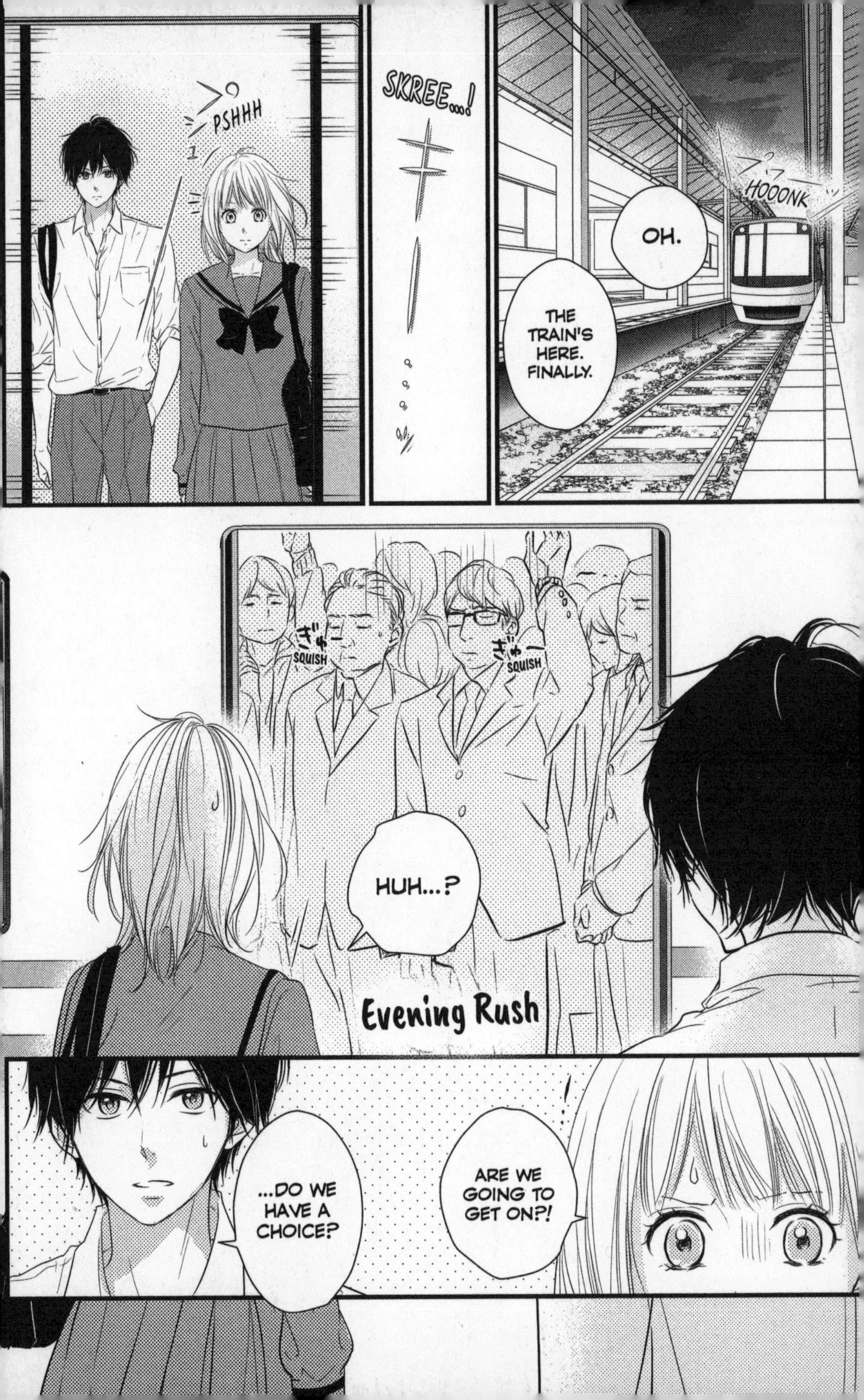
HOOONK
OH.
THE TRAIN'S HERE. FINALLY.
SKREE...!
PSHHH
SQUISH
SQUISH
HUH...?
Evening Rush
ARE WE GOING TO GET ON?!
...DO WE HAVE A CHOICE?

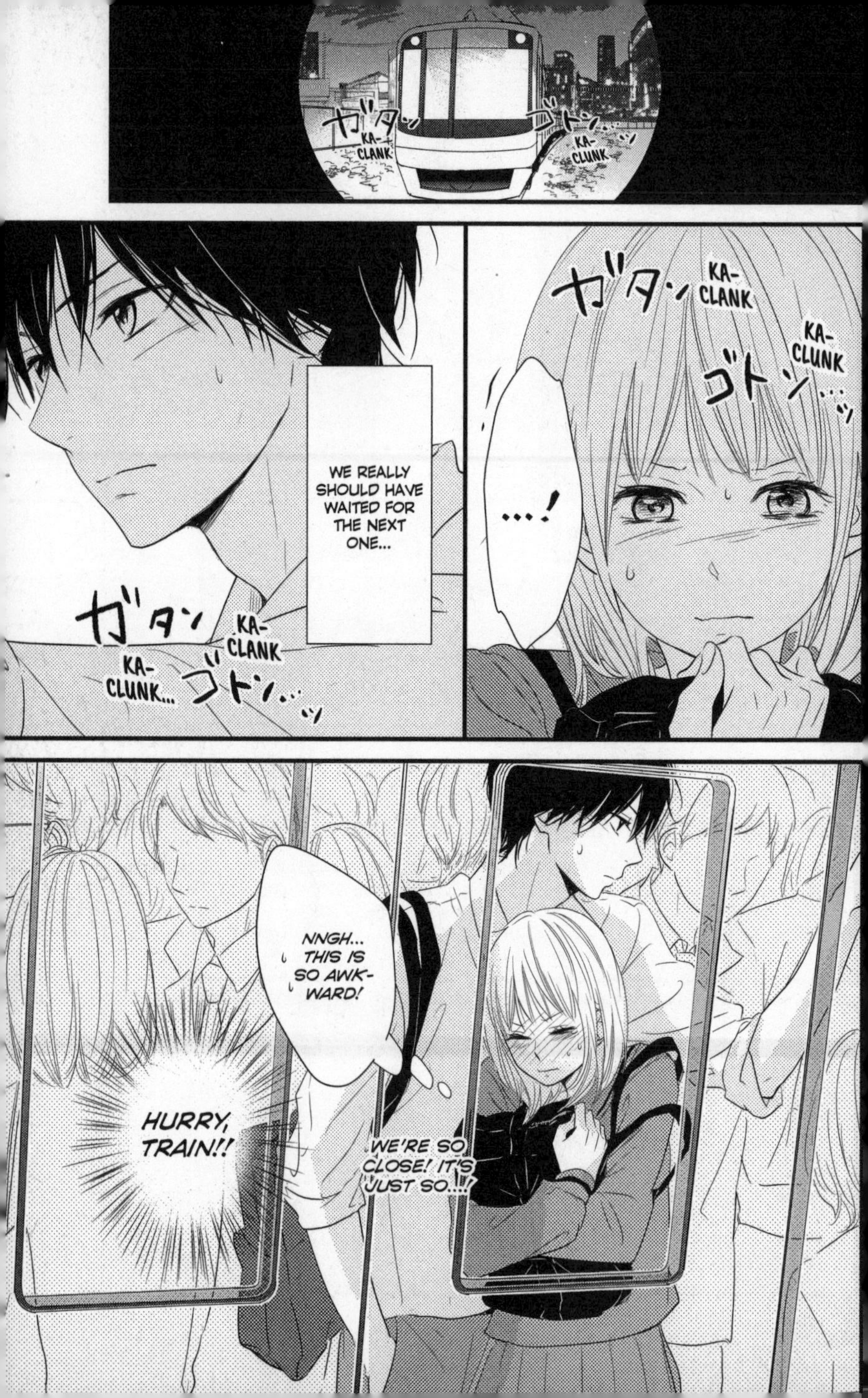
ガタッ
KA-CLANK
ゴトン…ッ
KA-CLUNK
ガタン
KA-CLANK
KA-CLUNK
ゴトン…ッ
…!
WE REALLY SHOULD HAVE WAITED FOR THE NEXT ONE...
ガタン
KA-CLANK
KA-CLUNK...
ゴトン…ッ
WE'RE SO CLOSE! IT'S JUST SO...!!
NNGH... THIS IS SO AWK-WARD!
HURRY, TRAIN!!

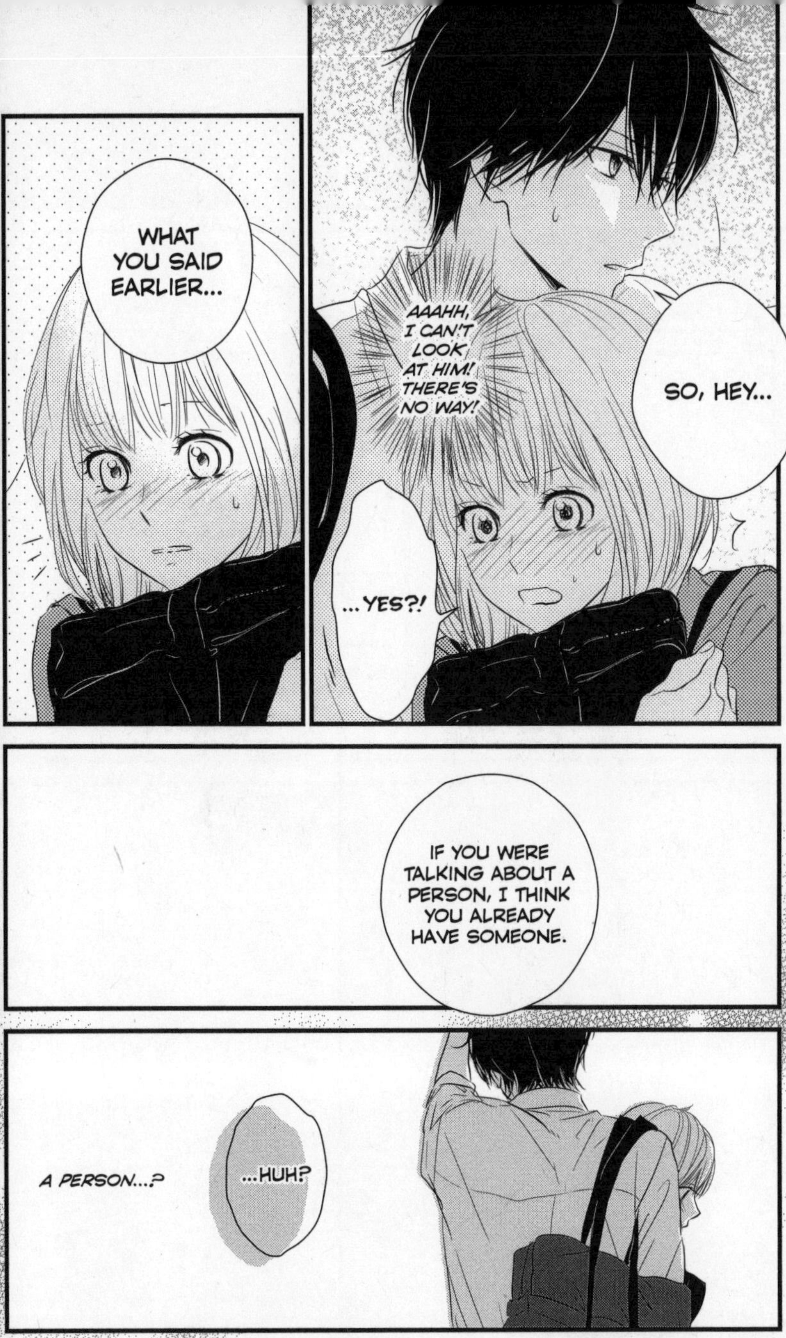
SO, HEY...
AAAHH, I CAN'T LOOK AT HIM! THERE'S NO WAY!
...YES?!
WHAT YOU SAID EARLIER...
IF YOU WERE TALKING ABOUT A PERSON, I THINK YOU ALREADY HAVE SOMEONE.
...HUH?
A PERSON...?

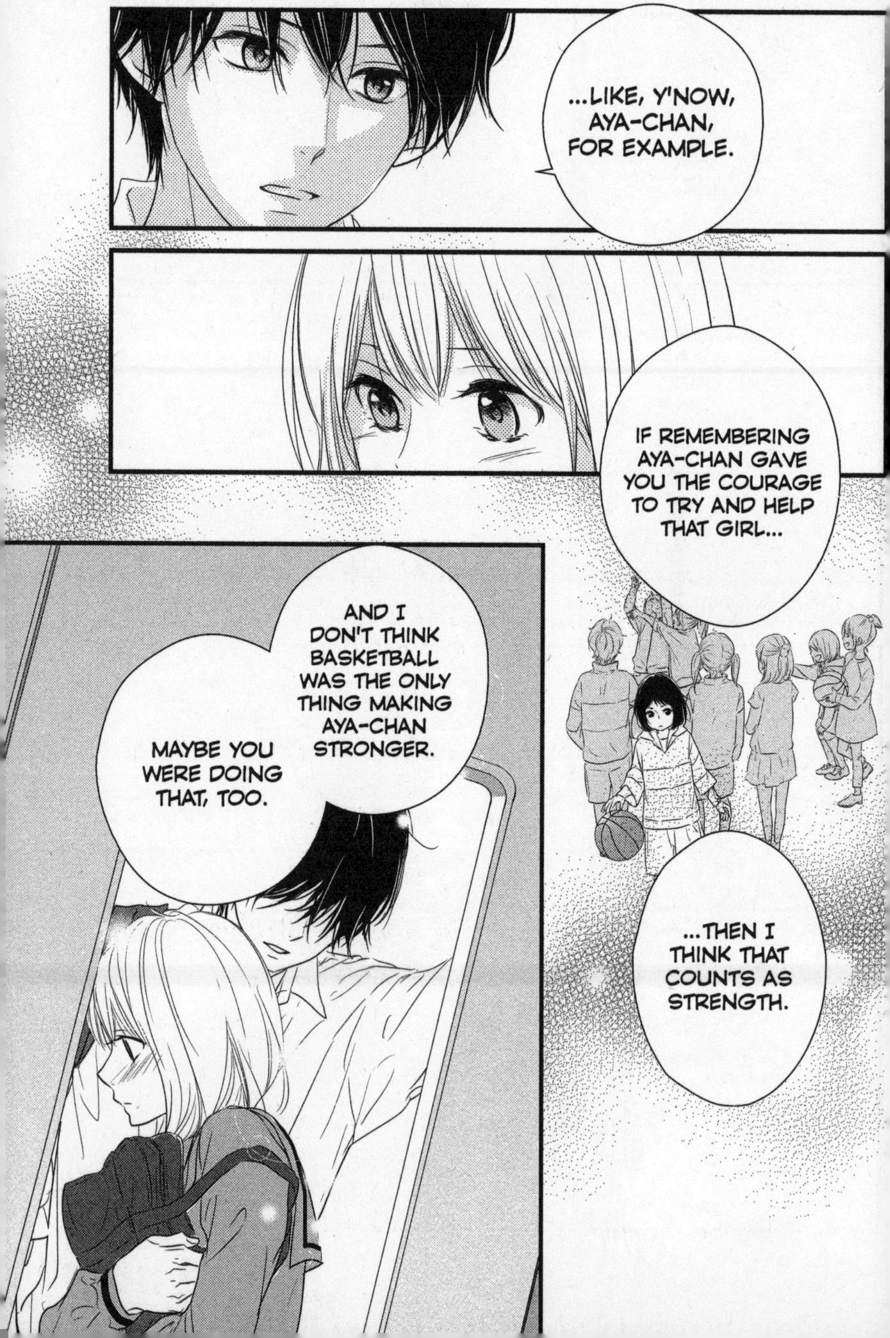
...LIKE, Y'NOW, AYA-CHAN, FOR EXAMPLE.
IF REMEMBERING AYA-CHAN GAVE YOU THE COURAGE TO TRY AND HELP THAT GIRL...
...THEN I THINK THAT COUNTS AS STRENGTH.
AND I DON'T THINK BASKETBALL WAS THE ONLY THING MAKING AYA-CHAN STRONGER.
MAYBE YOU WERE DOING THAT, TOO.

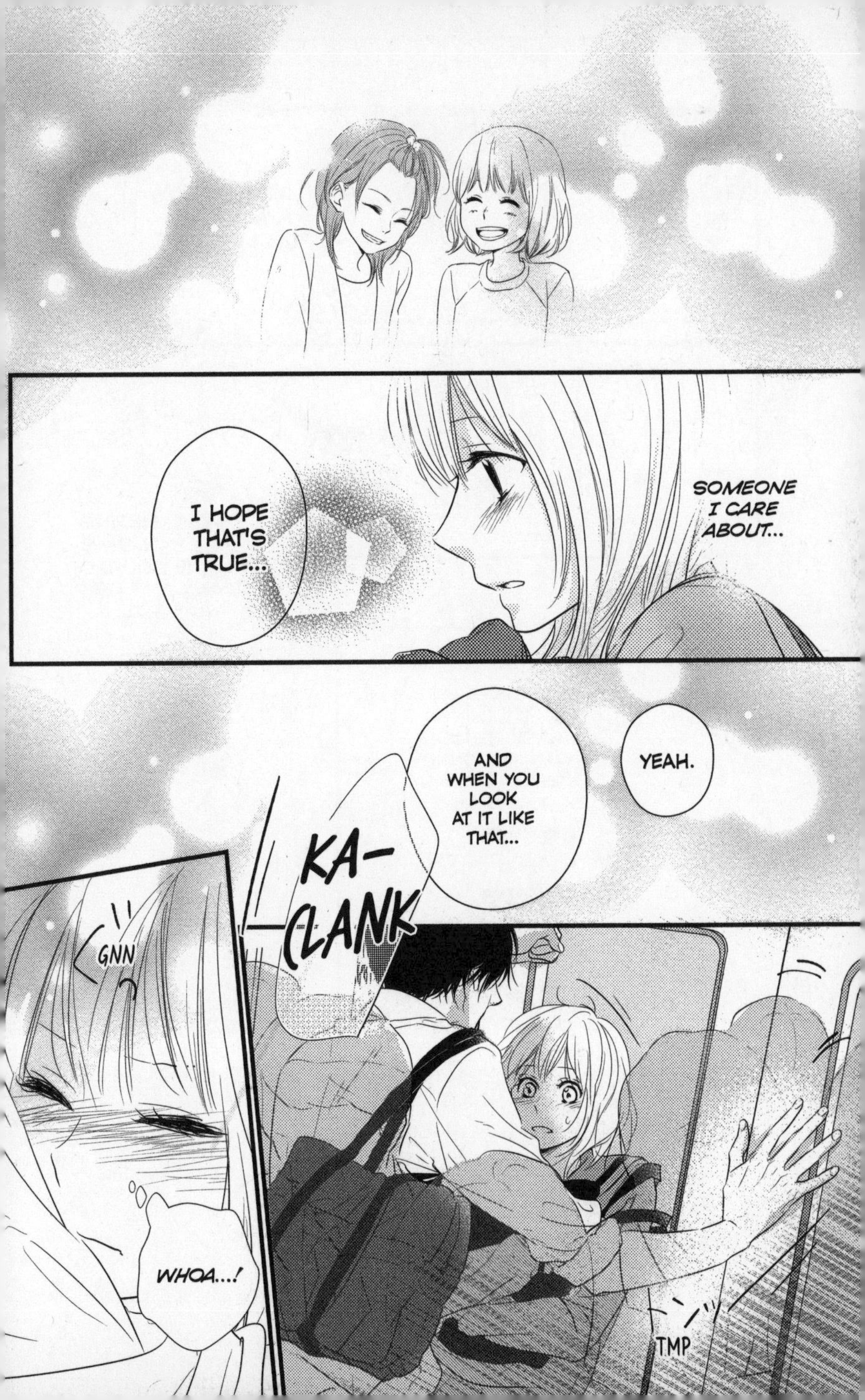
SOMEONE I CARE ABOUT...
I HOPE THAT'S TRUE...
YEAH.
AND WHEN YOU LOOK AT IT LIKE THAT...
KA-CLANK
TMP
GNN
WHOA...!

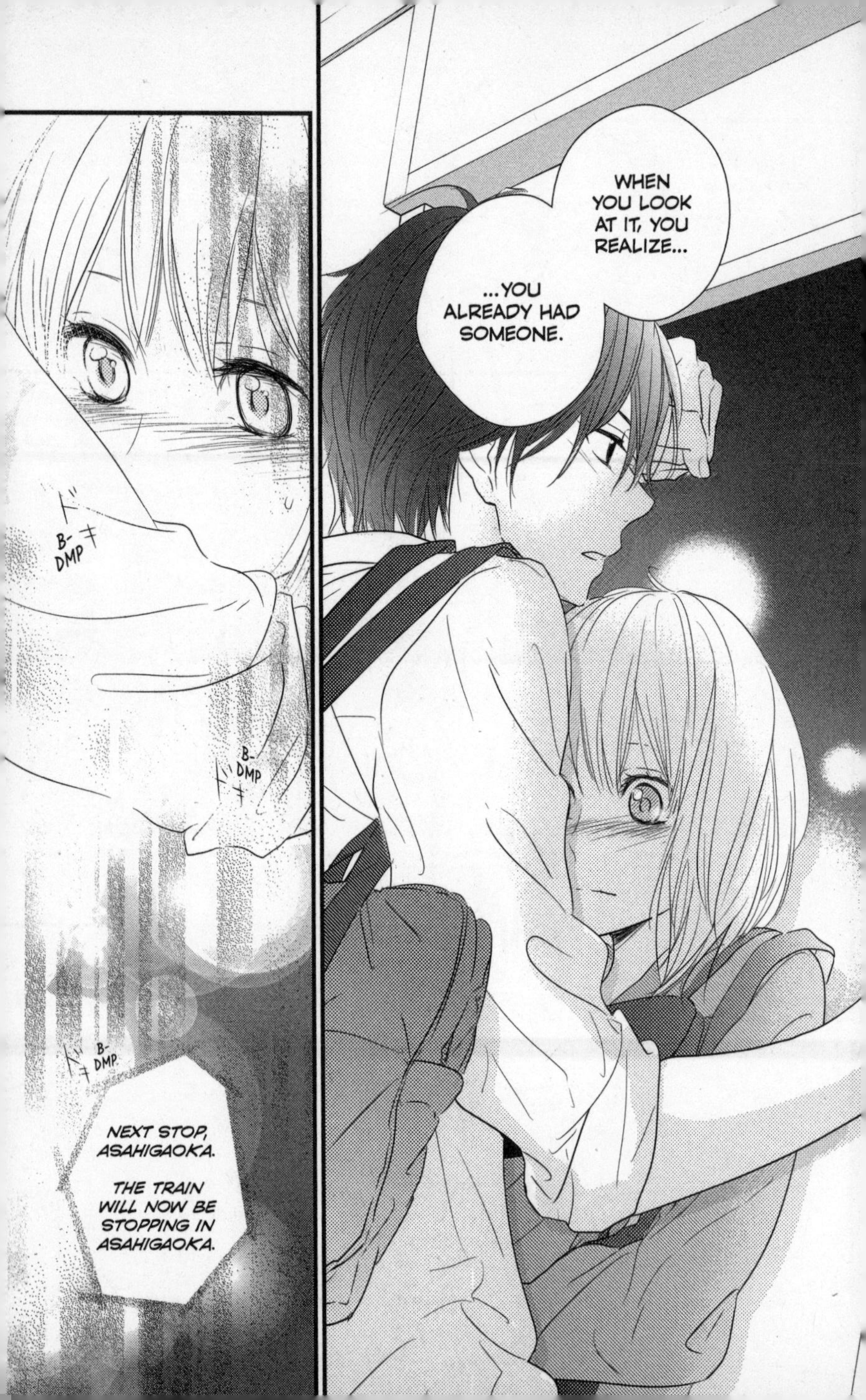
WHEN YOU LOOK AT IT, YOU REALIZE...
...YOU ALREADY HAD SOMEONE.
B-DMP
B-DMP
B-DMP
NEXT STOP, ASAHIGAOKA.
THE TRAIN WILL NOW BE STOPPING IN ASAHIGAOKA.

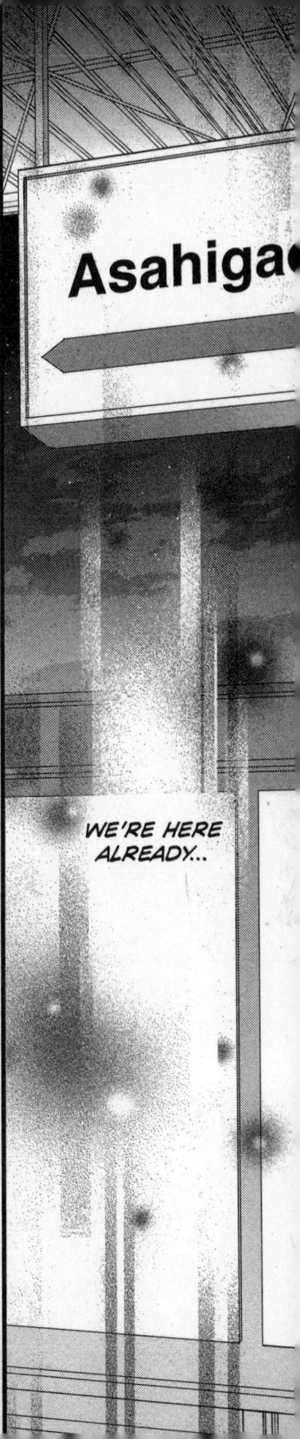
Asahigao
WE'RE HERE ALREADY...
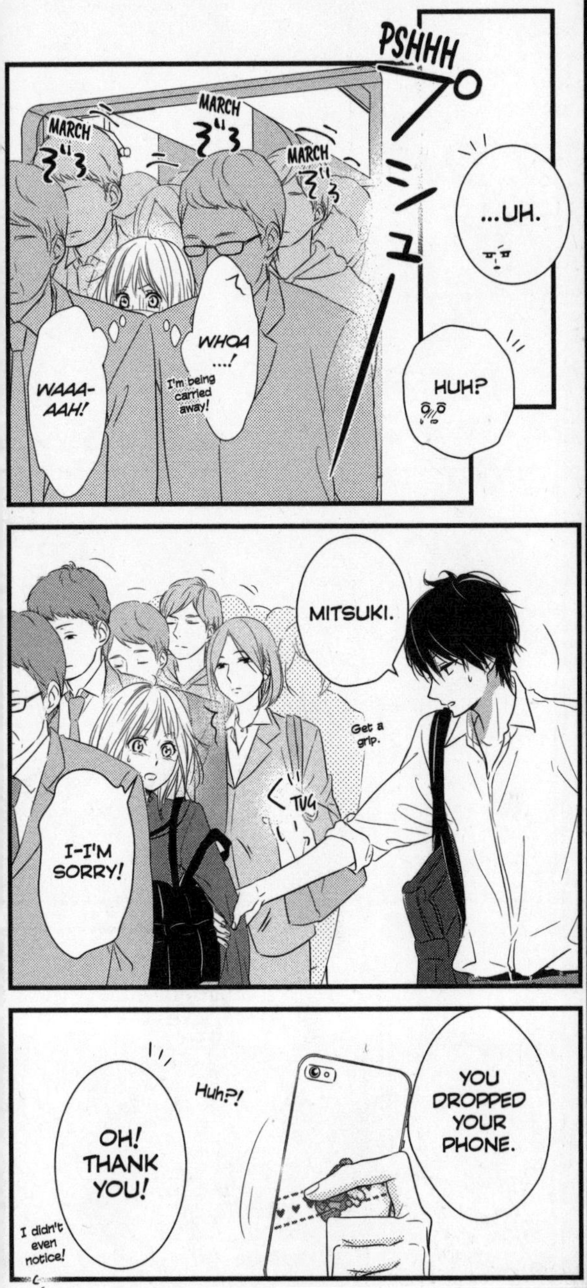
PSHHH
...UH.
HUH?
MARCH
MARCH
MARCH
WHOA ...!
I'm being carried away!
WAAA-AAH!
MITSUKI.
Get a grip.
TUG
I-I'M SORRY!
YOU DROPPED YOUR PHONE.
Huh?!
OH! THANK YOU!
I didn't even notice!

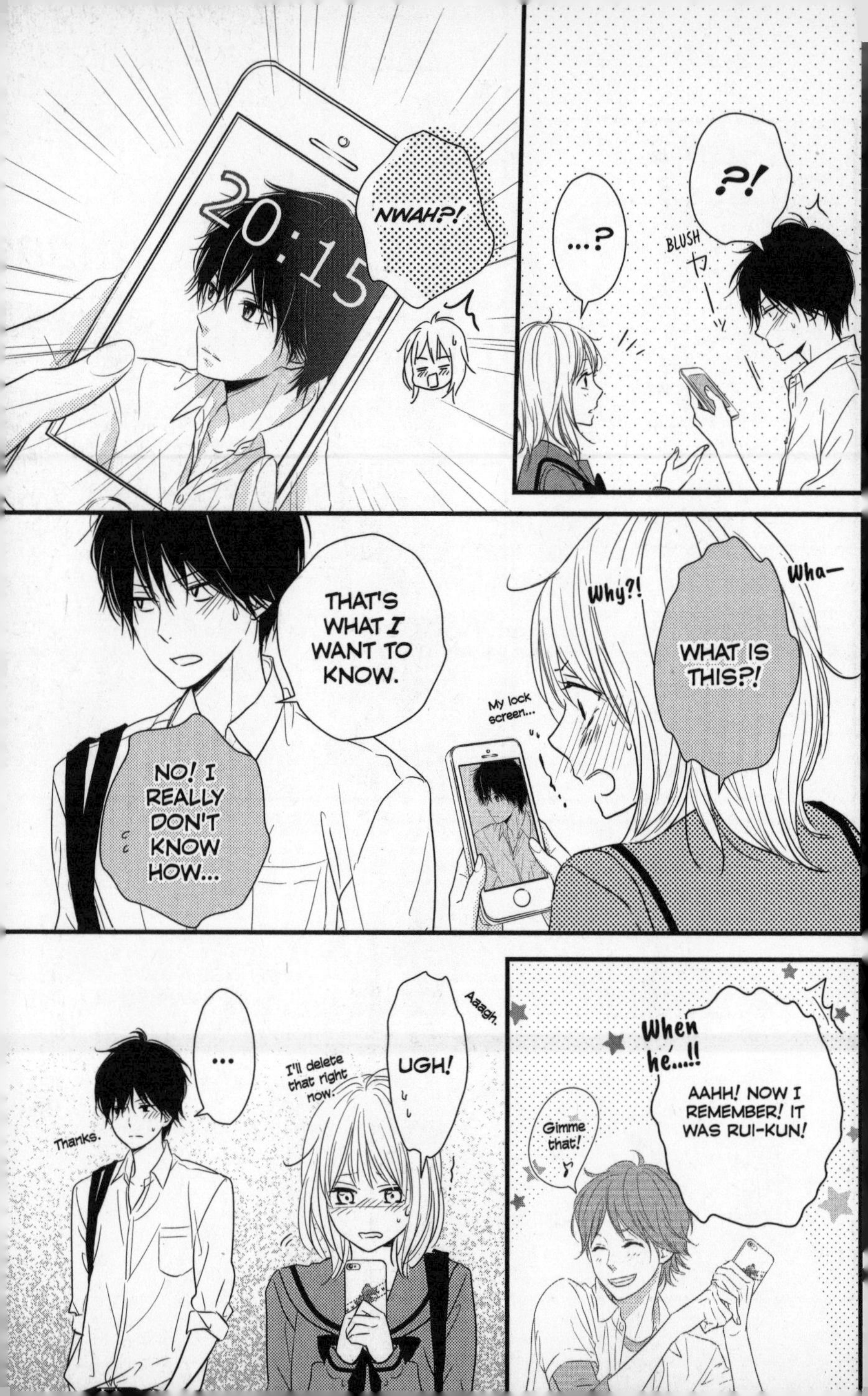
?!
BLUSH
...?
NWAH?!
Wha—
WHAT IS THIS?!
Why?!
My lock screen...
THAT'S WHAT I WANT TO KNOW.
NO! I REALLY DON'T KNOW HOW...
When he...!!
AAHH! NOW I REMEMBER! IT WAS RUI-KUN!
Gimme that!
Aaagh.
UGH!
I'll delete that right now.
...
Thanks.

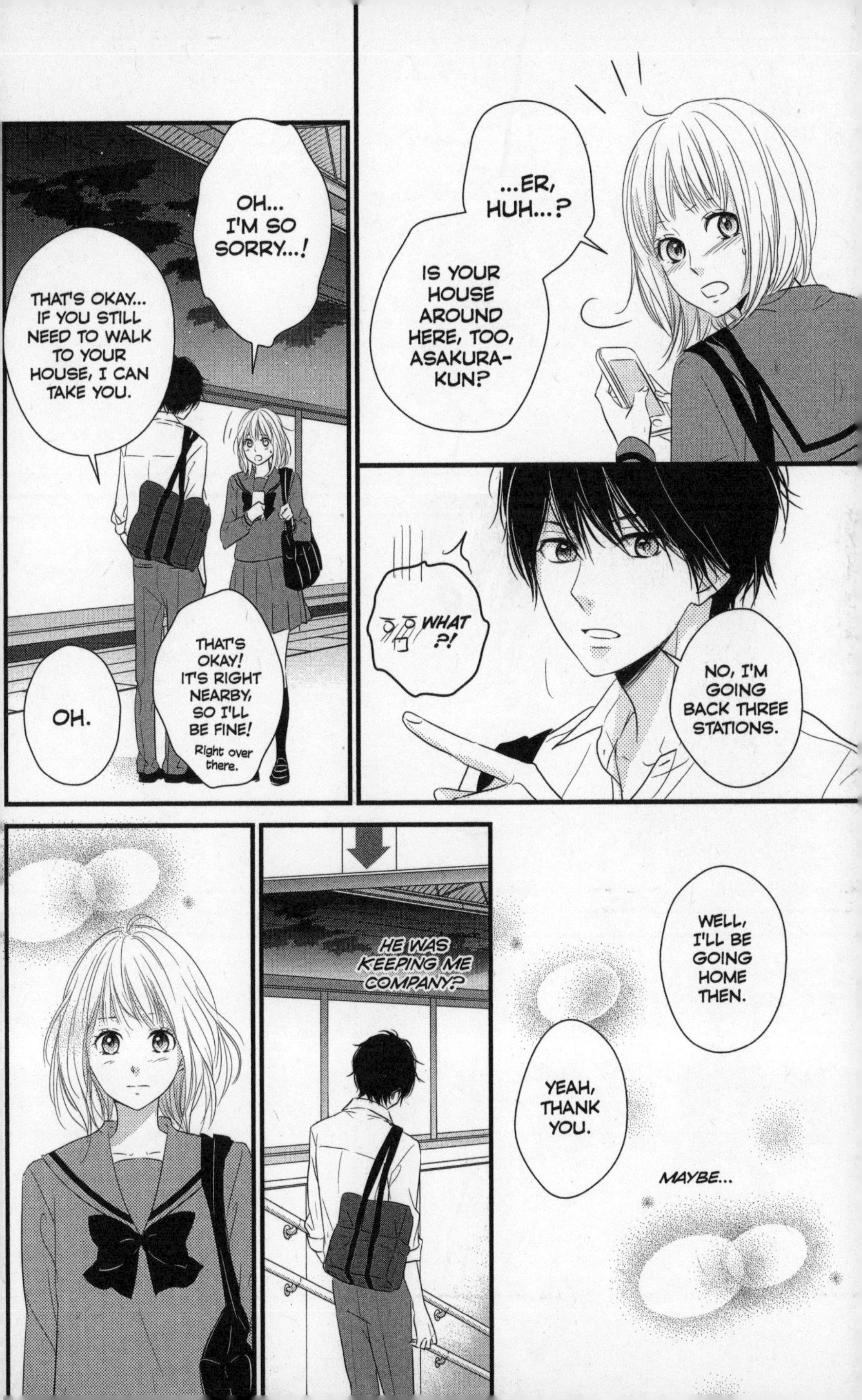
...ER, HUH...?
IS YOUR HOUSE AROUND HERE, TOO, ASAKURA-KUN?
NO, I'M GOING BACK THREE STATIONS.
WHAT ?!
OH... I'M SO SORRY...!
THAT'S OKAY... IF YOU STILL NEED TO WALK TO YOUR HOUSE, I CAN TAKE YOU.
THAT'S OKAY! IT'S RIGHT NEARBY, SO I'LL BE FINE!
Right over there.
OH.
WELL, I'LL BE GOING HOME THEN.
YEAH, THANK YOU.
MAYBE...
HE WAS KEEPING ME COMPANY?

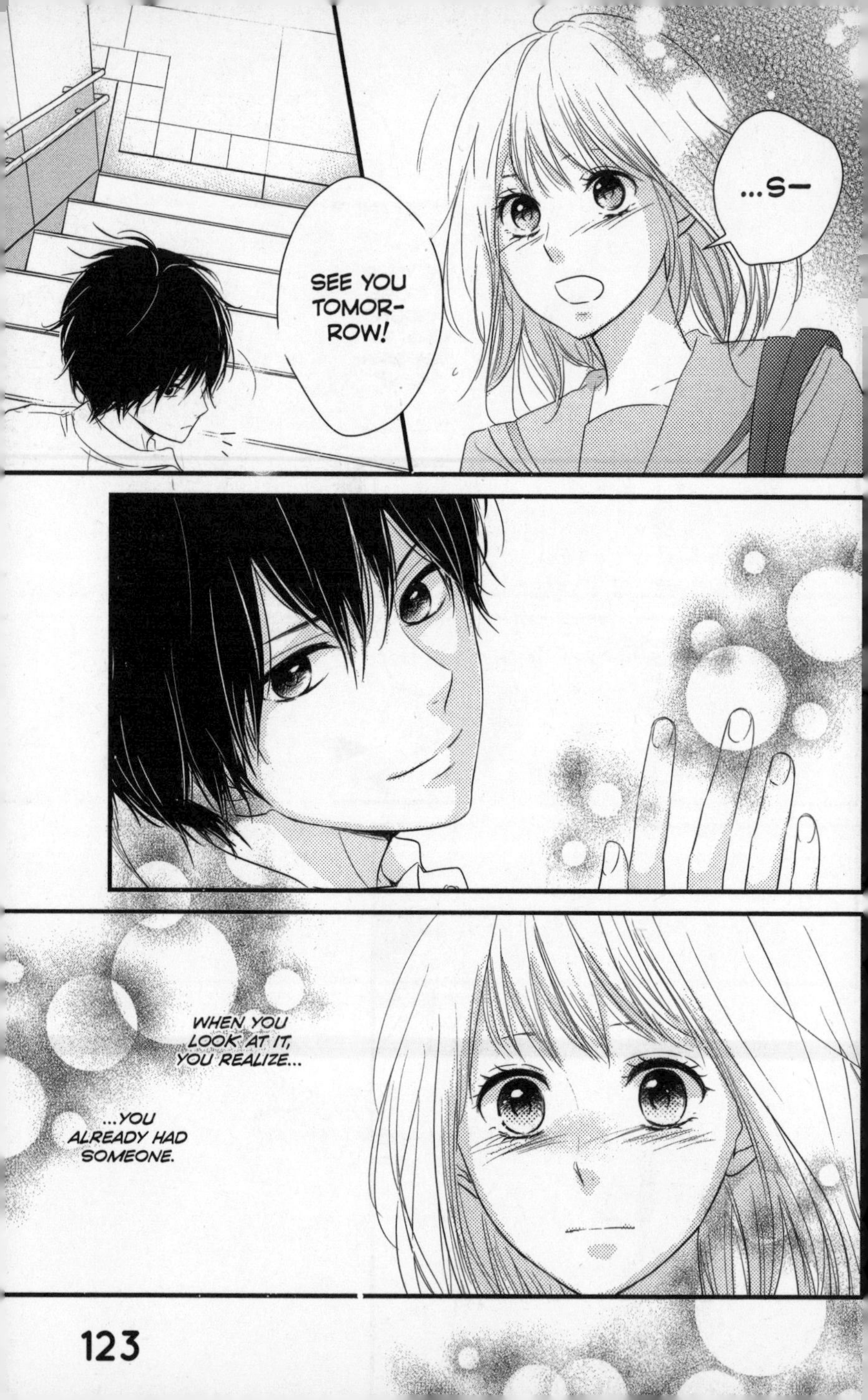
...S—
SEE YOU TOMORROW!
WHEN YOU LOOK AT IT, YOU REALIZE...
...YOU ALREADY HAD SOMEONE.

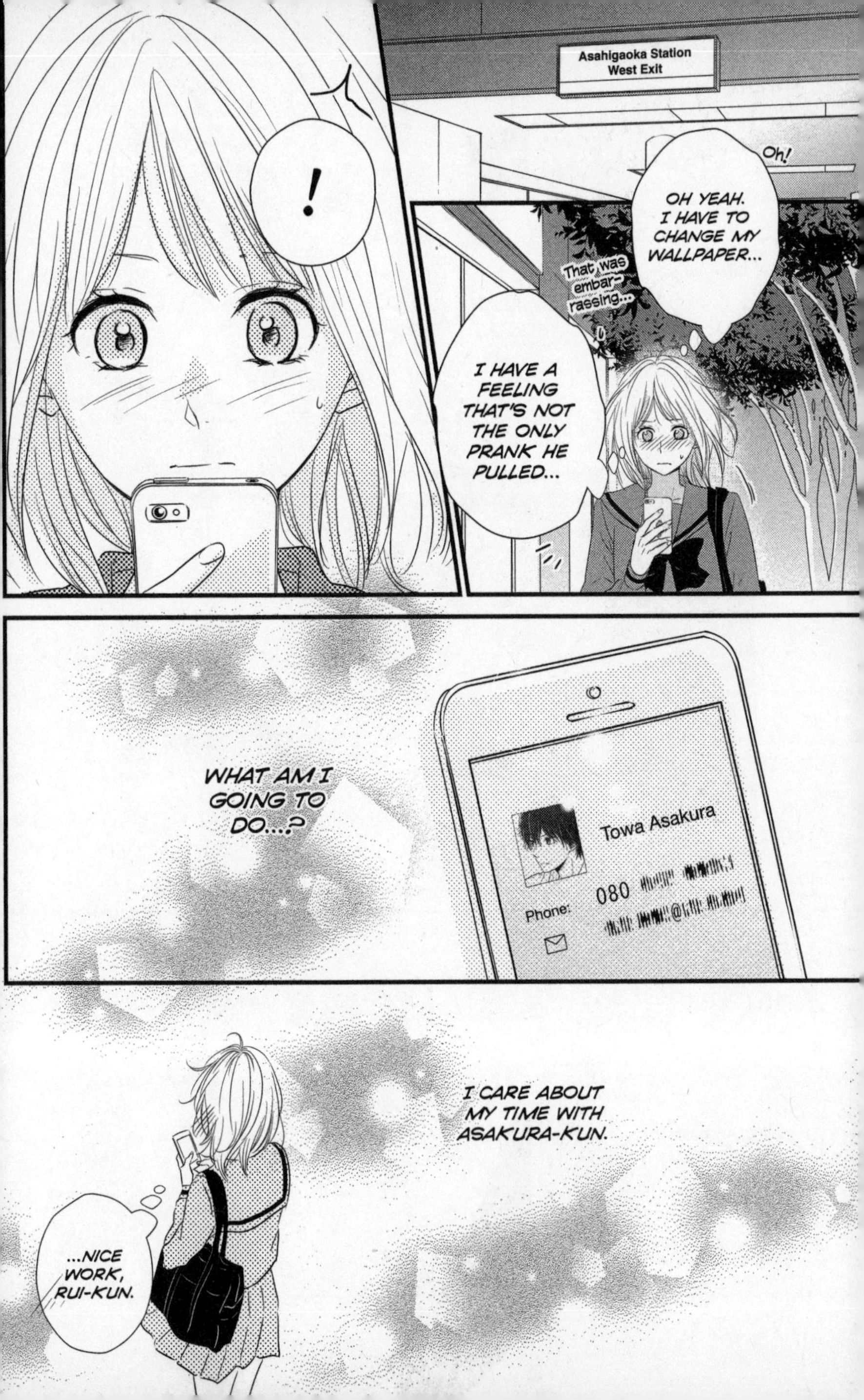
Asahigaoka Station West Exit
Oh!
OH YEAH. I HAVE TO CHANGE MY WALLPAPER...
That was embarrassing...
I HAVE A FEELING THAT'S NOT THE ONLY PRANK HE PULLED...
!
Towa Asakura
080
Phone:
WHAT AM I GOING TO DO...?
I CARE ABOUT MY TIME WITH ASAKURA-KUN.
...NICE WORK, RUI-KUN.

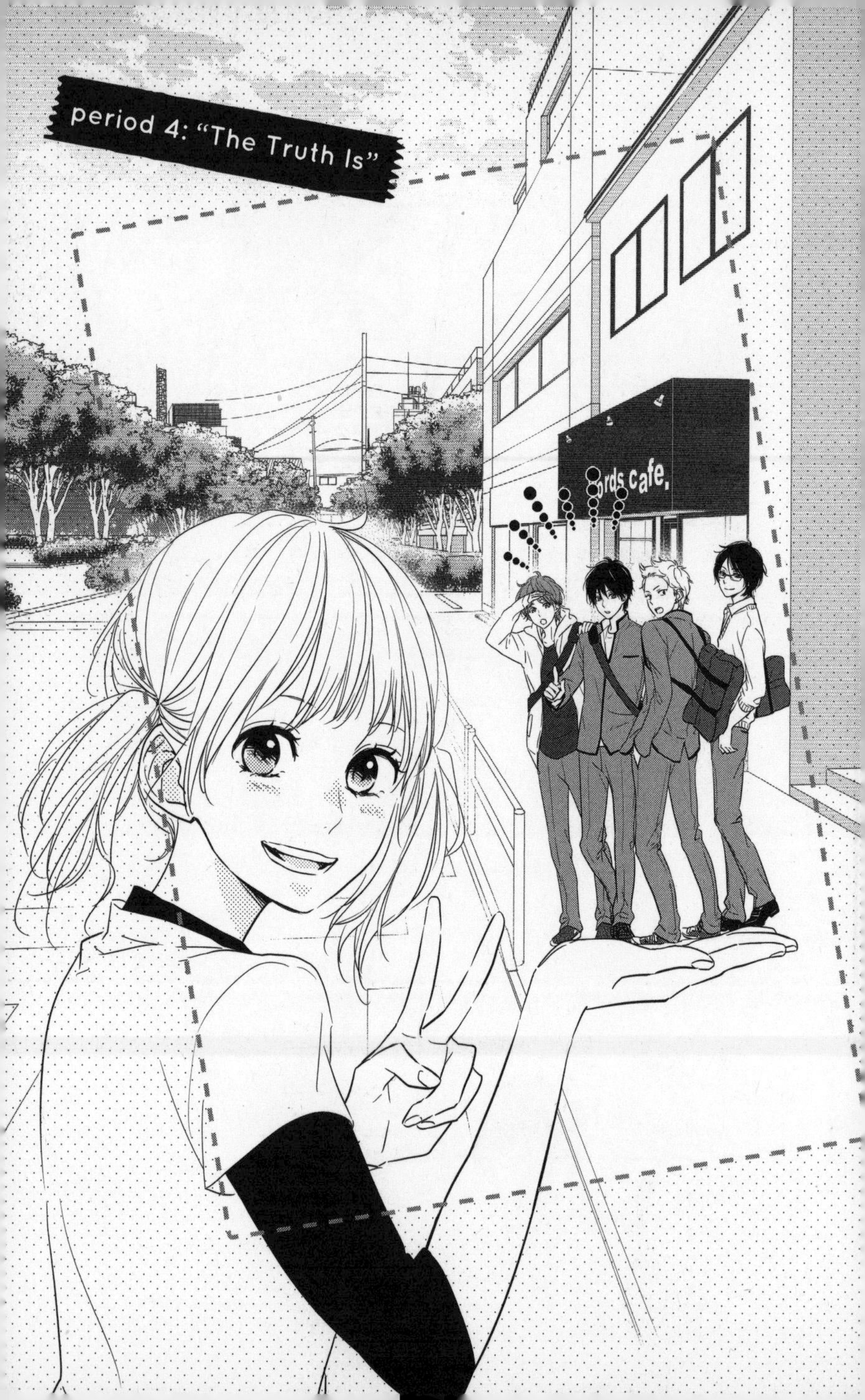
period 4: “The Truth Is”

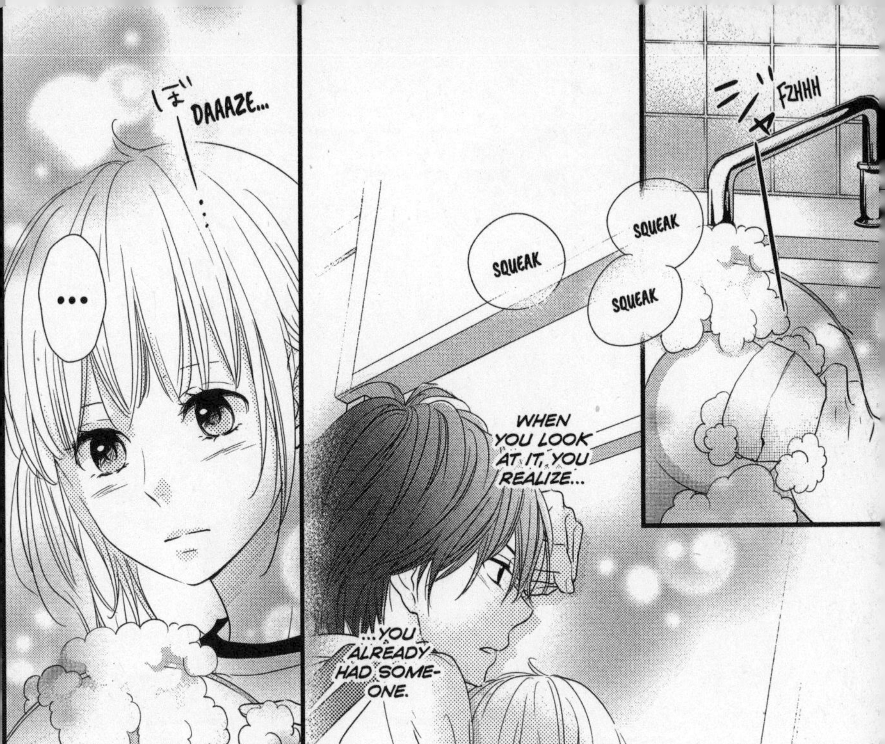
ジャ
FZHHH
SQUEAK
SQUEAK
SQUEAK
WHEN YOU LOOK AT IT, YOU REALIZE...
...YOU ALREADY HAD SOME-ONE.
ぼ
DAAAZE...
...
...CHAN.

Towa Asakura	5'10" cm/143.3 lbs	Blood type A	Born March 14	Favorite food: His grandma's candied sweet potatoes

Current concern:

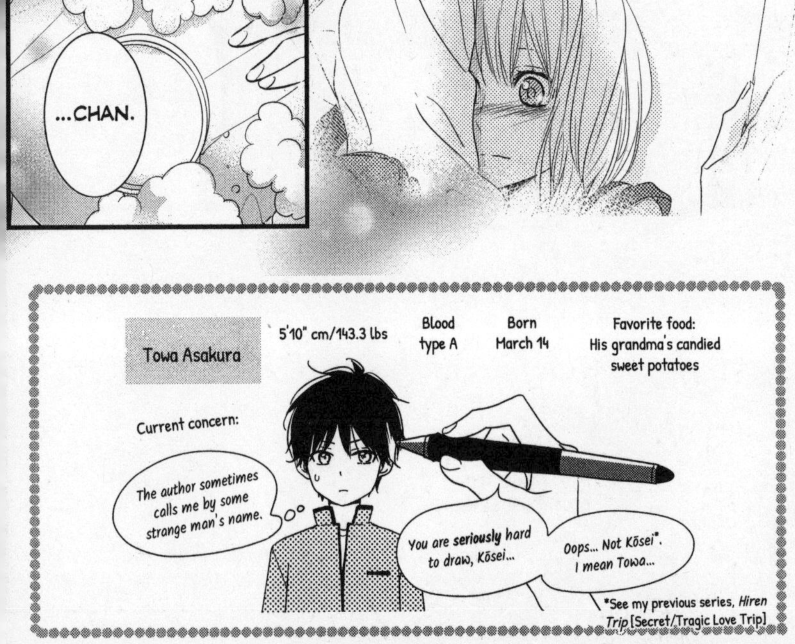
The author sometimes calls me by some strange man's name.
You are **seriously** hard to draw, Kōsei...
Oops... Not Kōsei*. I mean Towa...

*See my previous series, *Hiren Trip* [Secret/Tragic Love Trip]

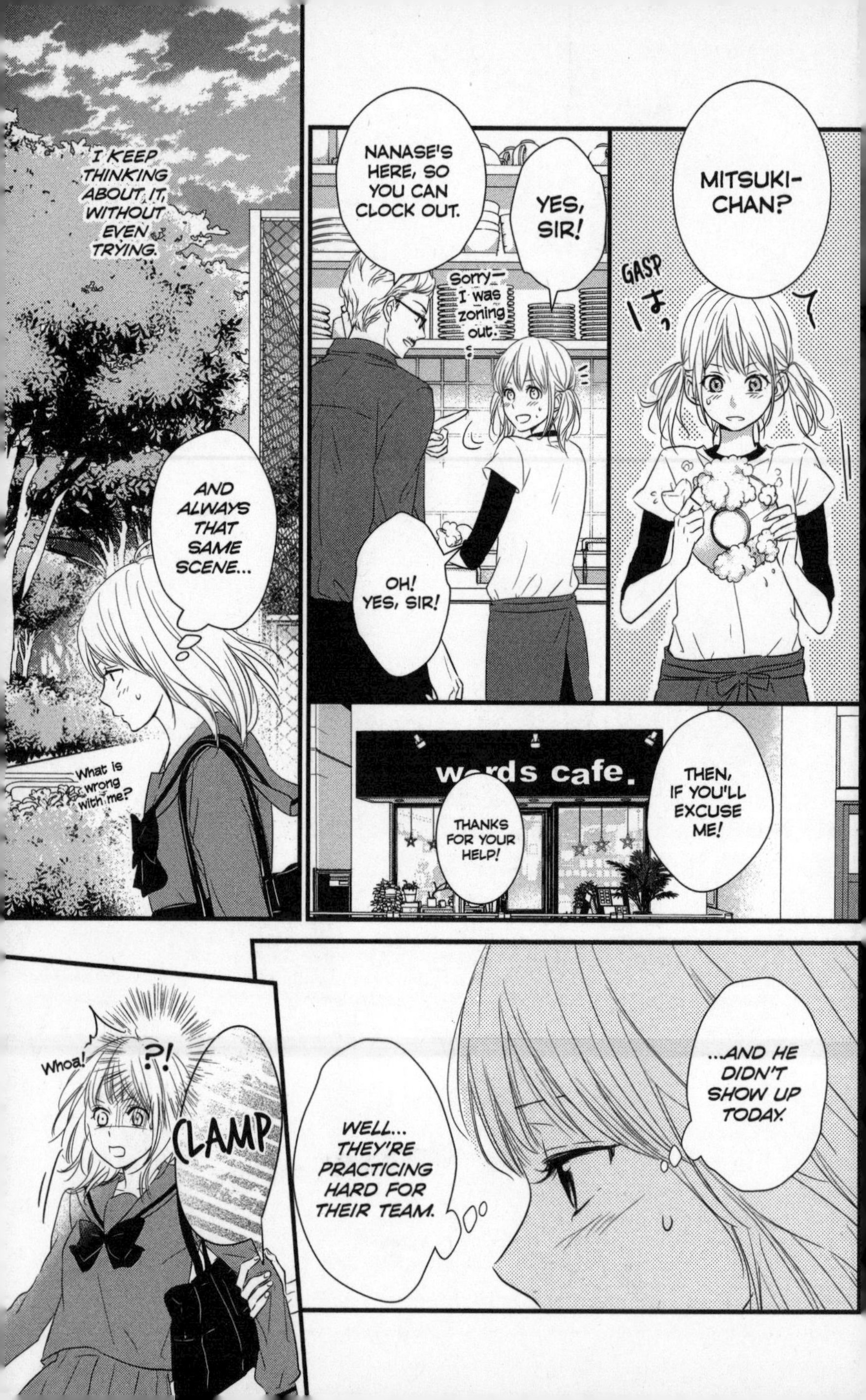
MITSUKI-CHAN?
GASP
YES, SIR!
Sorry— I was zoning out.
NANASE'S HERE, SO YOU CAN CLOCK OUT.
OH! YES, SIR!
THEN, IF YOU'LL EXCUSE ME!
w rds cafe.
THANKS FOR YOUR HELP!
I KEEP THINKING ABOUT IT, WITHOUT EVEN TRYING.
AND ALWAYS THAT SAME SCENE...
What is wrong with me?
...AND HE DIDN'T SHOW UP TODAY.
WELL... THEY'RE PRACTICING HARD FOR THEIR TEAM.
?!
Whoa!
CLAMP

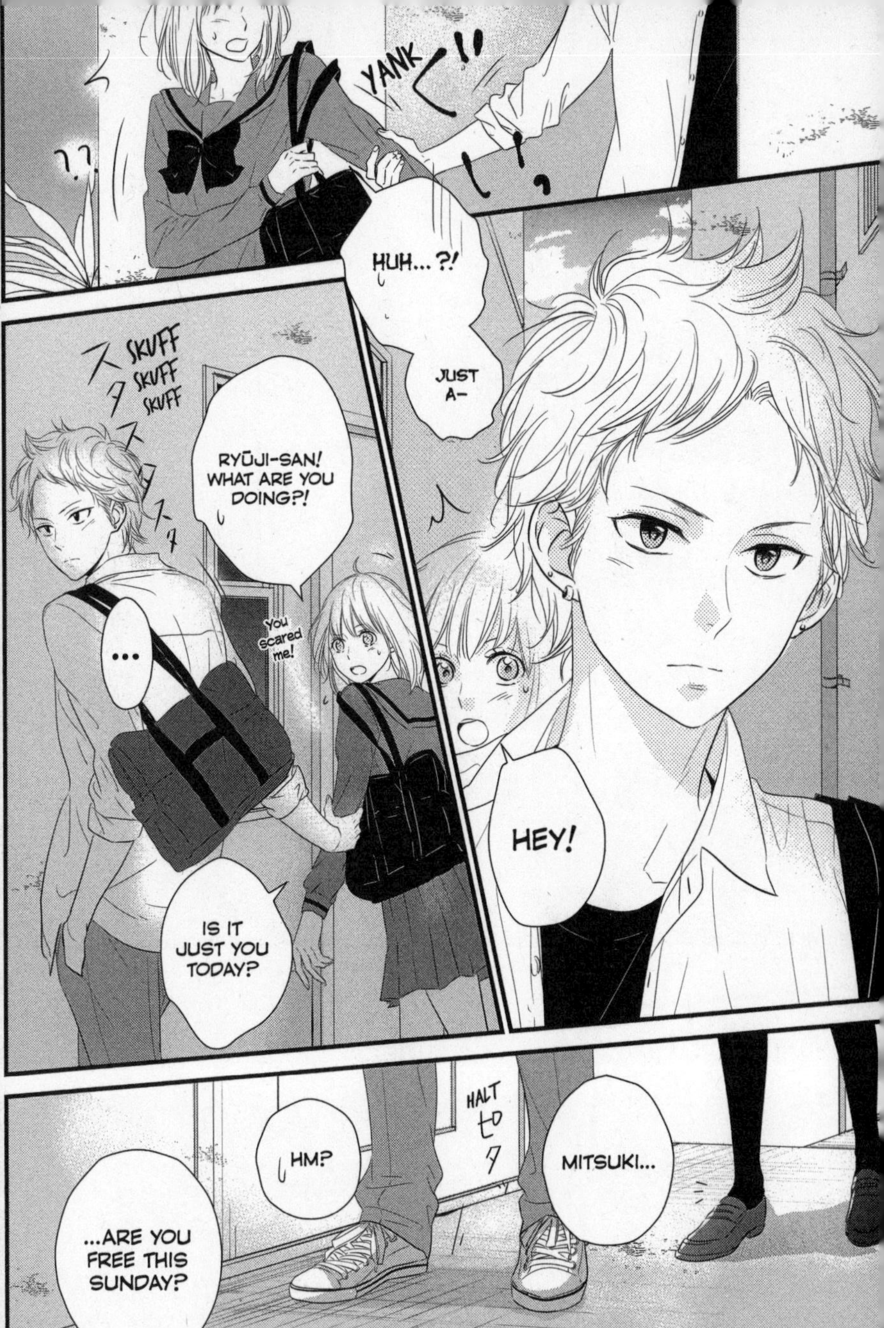
YANK
HUH...?!
JUST A-
HEY!
SKUFF SKUFF SKUFF
スタスタスタ
RYŪJI-SAN! WHAT ARE YOU DOING?!
You scared me!
...
IS IT JUST YOU TODAY?
HALT
ピタ
MITSUKI...
HM?
...ARE YOU FREE THIS SUNDAY?

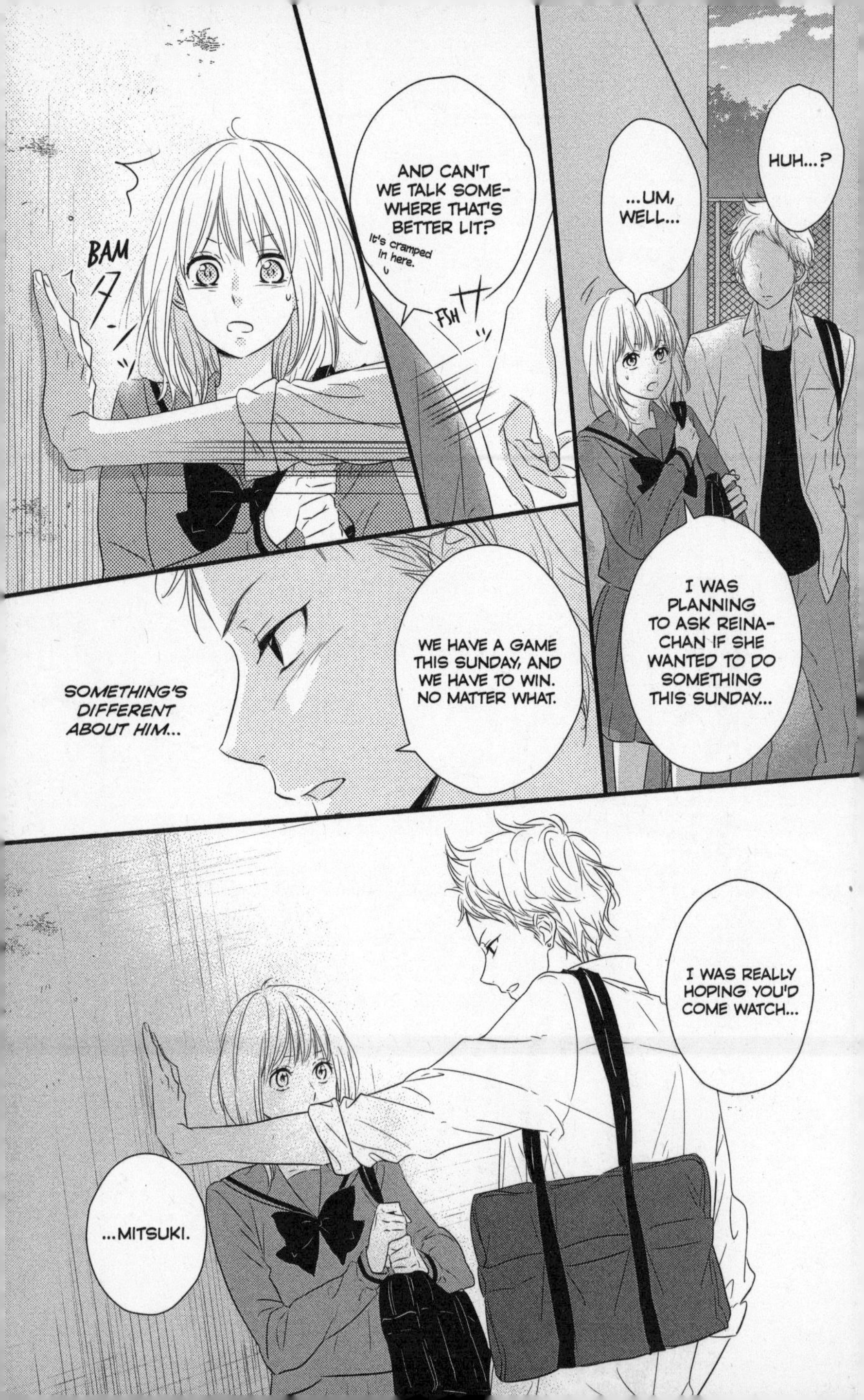
HUH...?
...UM, WELL...
I WAS PLANNING TO ASK REINA-CHAN IF SHE WANTED TO DO SOMETHING THIS SUNDAY...
AND CAN'T WE TALK SOME-WHERE THAT'S BETTER LIT?
It's cramped in here.
FSH
BAM
WE HAVE A GAME THIS SUNDAY, AND WE HAVE TO WIN. NO MATTER WHAT.
SOMETHING'S DIFFERENT ABOUT HIM...
I WAS REALLY HOPING YOU'D COME WATCH...
...MITSUKI.

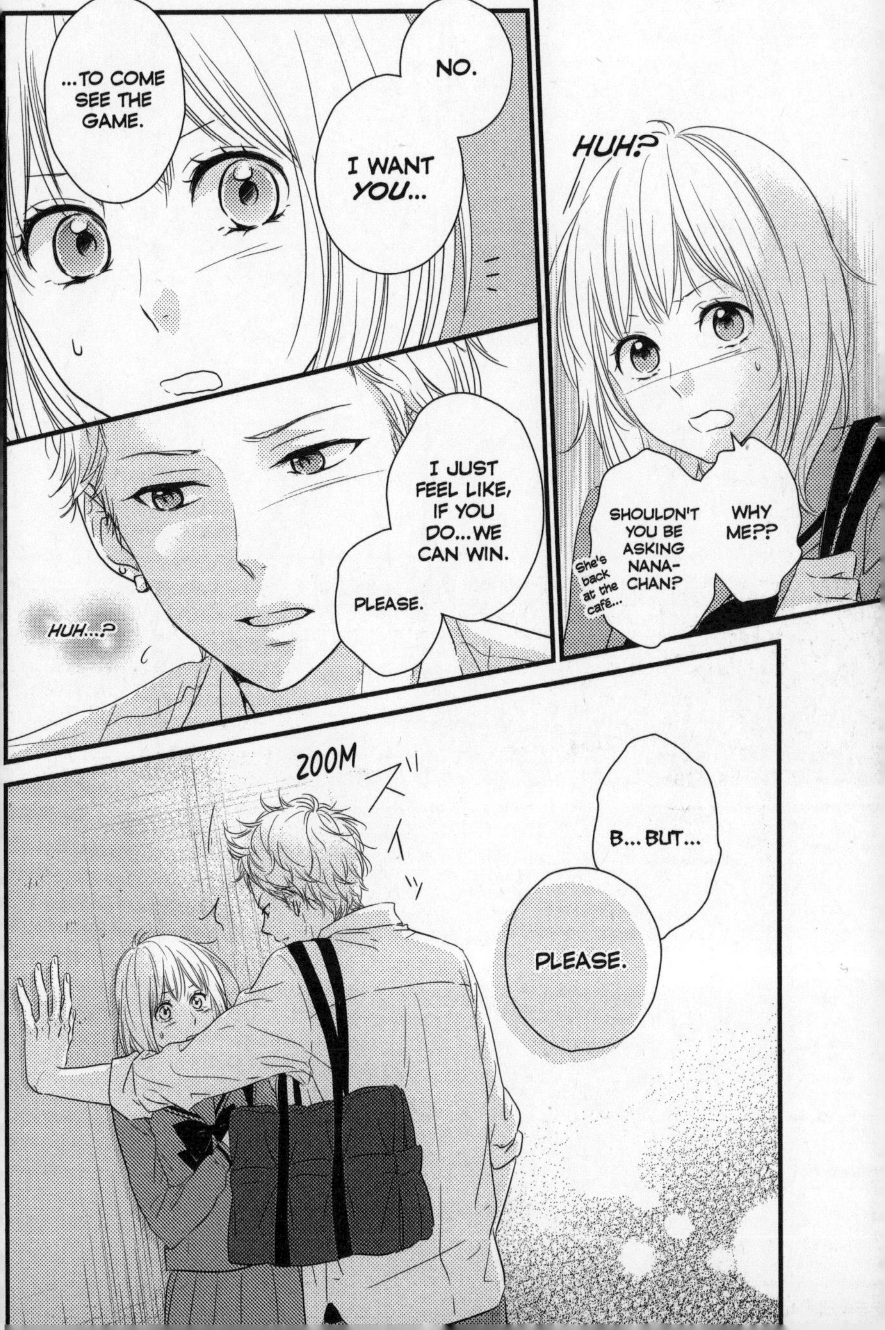
HUH?
WHY ME??
SHOULDN'T YOU BE ASKING NANA-CHAN?
She's back at the café...
NO.
I WANT *YOU*...
...TO COME SEE THE GAME.
I JUST FEEL LIKE, IF YOU DO...WE CAN WIN.
PLEASE.
HUH...?
B... BUT...
ZOOM
PLEASE.

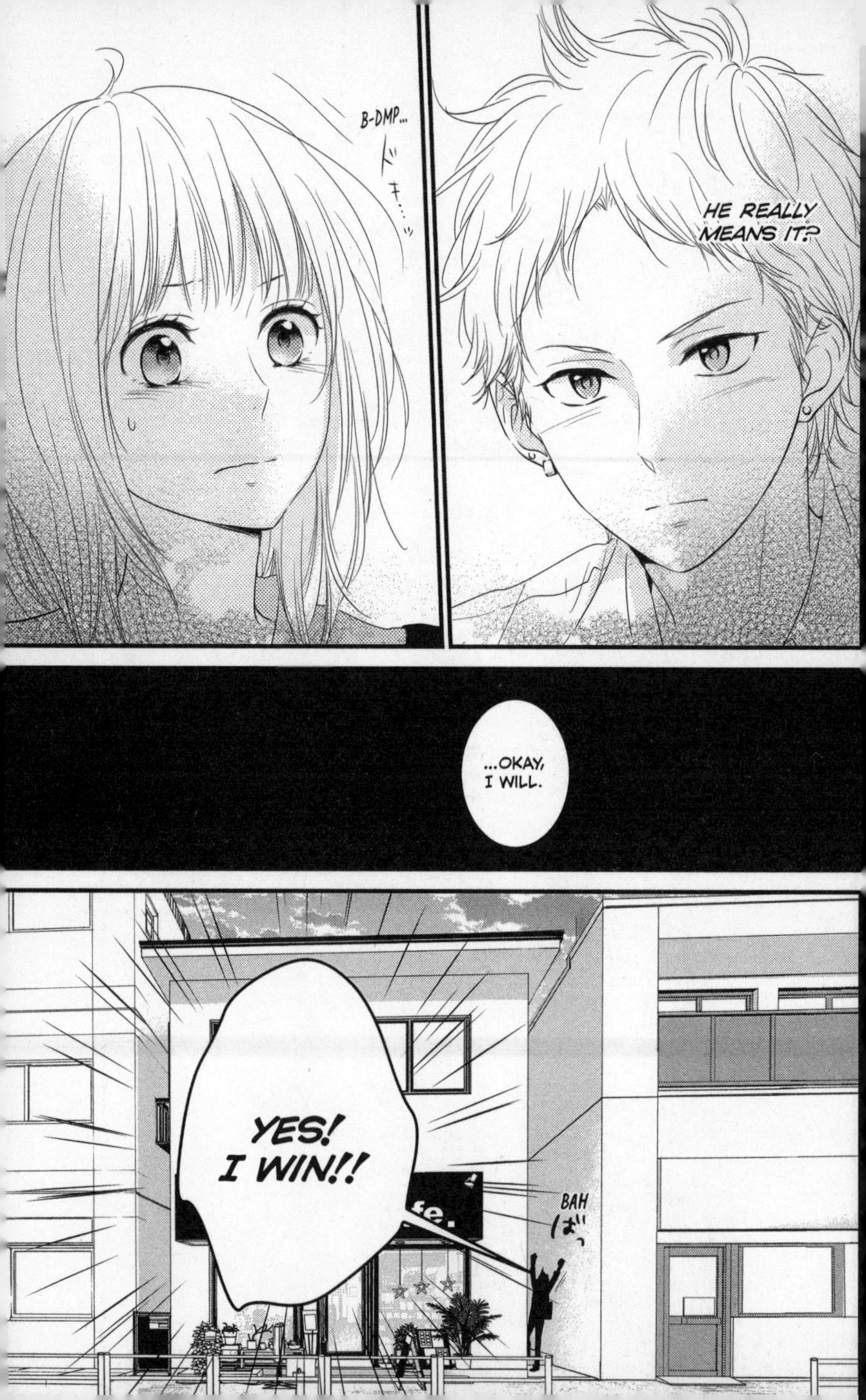
HE REALLY MEANS IT?
B-DMP...
ドキ…ッ
...OKAY, I WILL.
YES! I WIN!!
BAH
ばっ

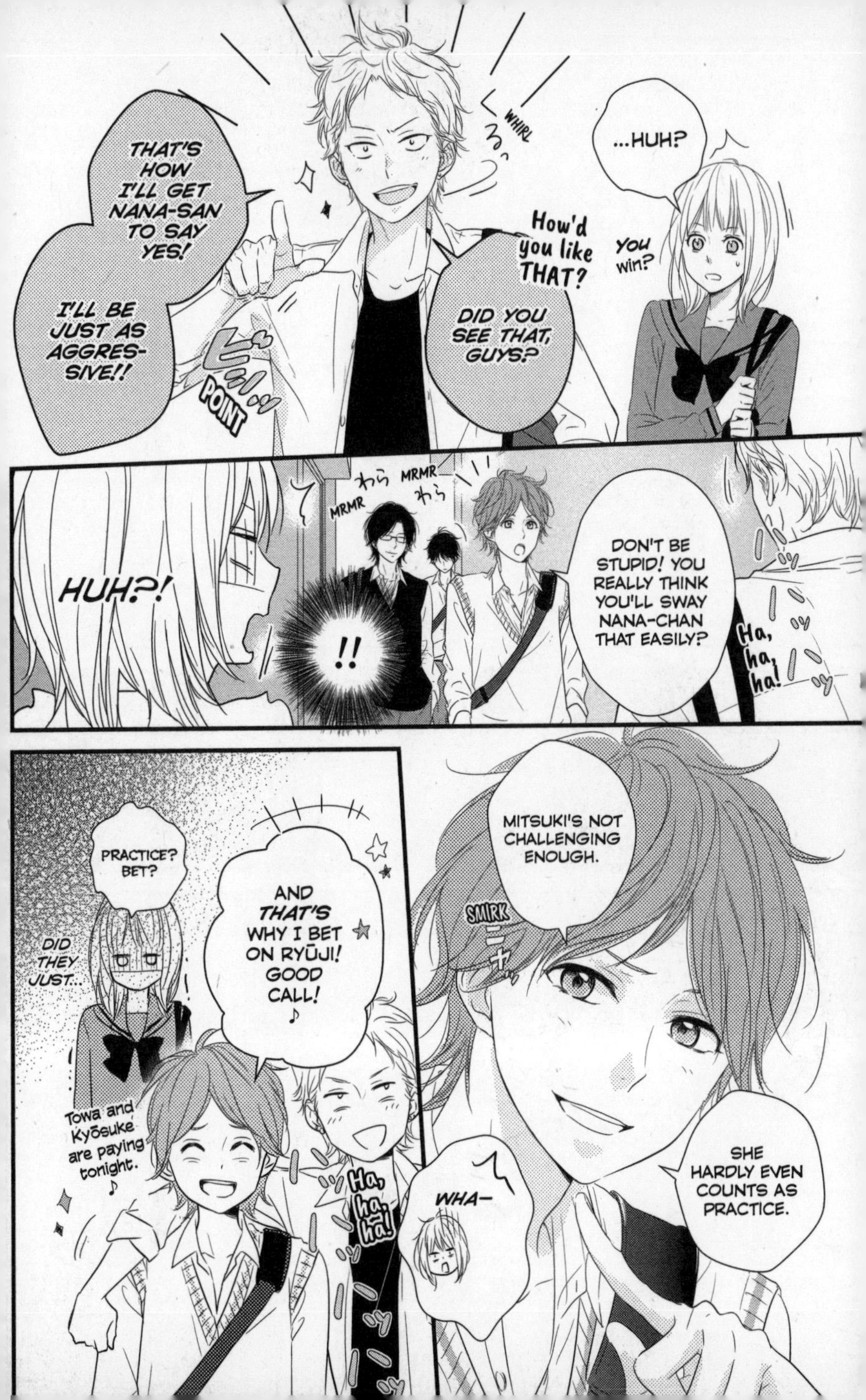
...HUH?
You win?
How'd you like THAT?
WHIRL
DID YOU SEE THAT, GUYS?
THAT'S HOW I'LL GET NANA-SAN TO SAY YES!
I'LL BE JUST AS AGGRES-SIVE!!
POINT
Ha, ha, ha!
DON'T BE STUPID! YOU REALLY THINK YOU'LL SWAY NANA-CHAN THAT EASILY?
わら MRMR
わら MRMR
!!
HUH?!
MITSUKI'S NOT CHALLENGING ENOUGH.
SMIRK
SHE HARDLY EVEN COUNTS AS PRACTICE.
WHA-
AND THAT'S WHY I BET ON RYŪJI! GOOD CALL! ♪
PRACTICE? BET?
DID THEY JUST...
Ha, ha, ha!
Towa and Kyōsuke are paying tonight. ♪

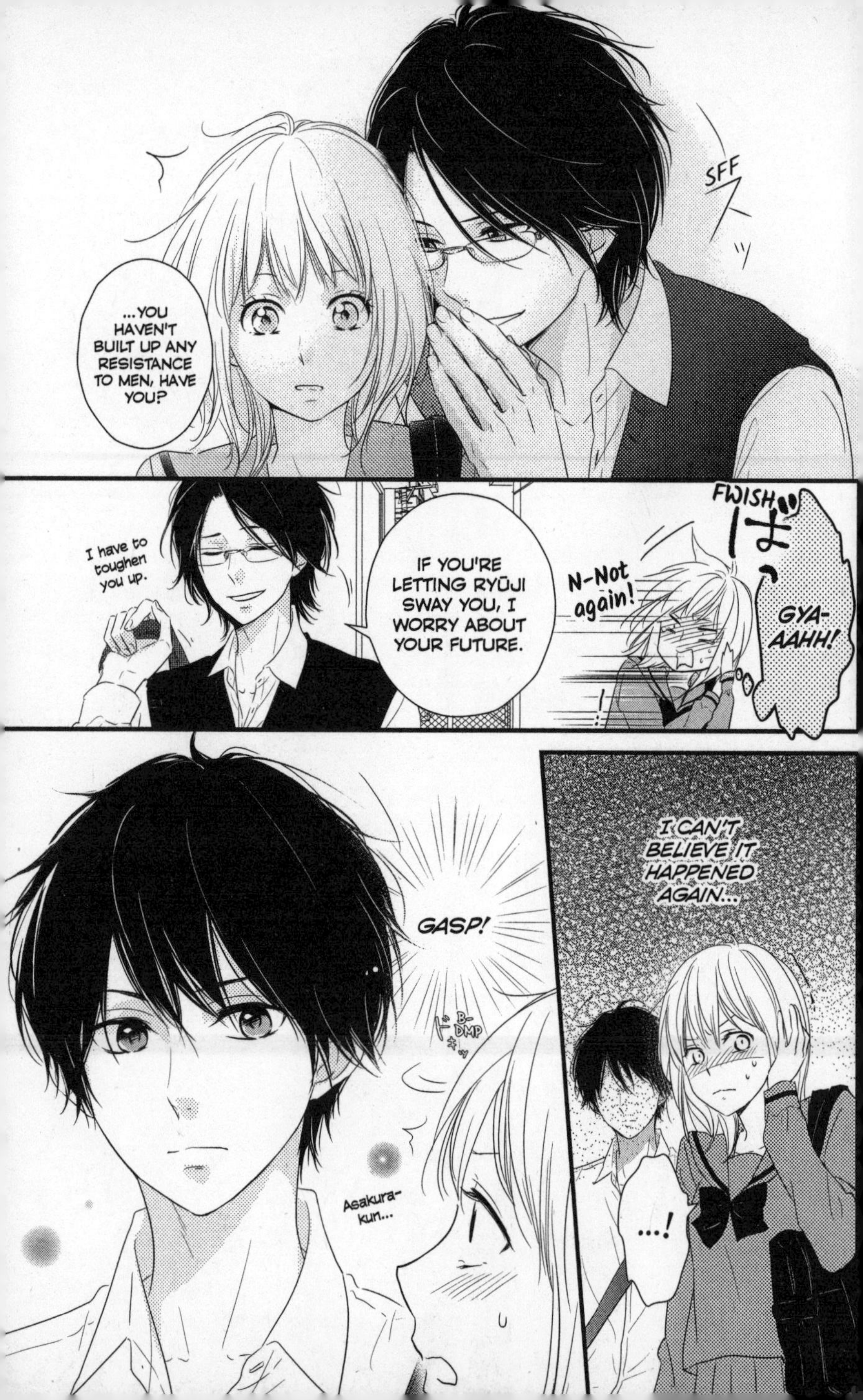
SFF
...YOU HAVEN'T BUILT UP ANY RESISTANCE TO MEN, HAVE YOU?
FWISH
GYA-AAHH!
N-Not again!
IF YOU'RE LETTING RYŪJI SWAY YOU, I WORRY ABOUT YOUR FUTURE.
I have to toughen you up.
I CAN'T BELIEVE IT HAPPENED AGAIN...
...!
GASP!
B-DMP
Asakura-kun...

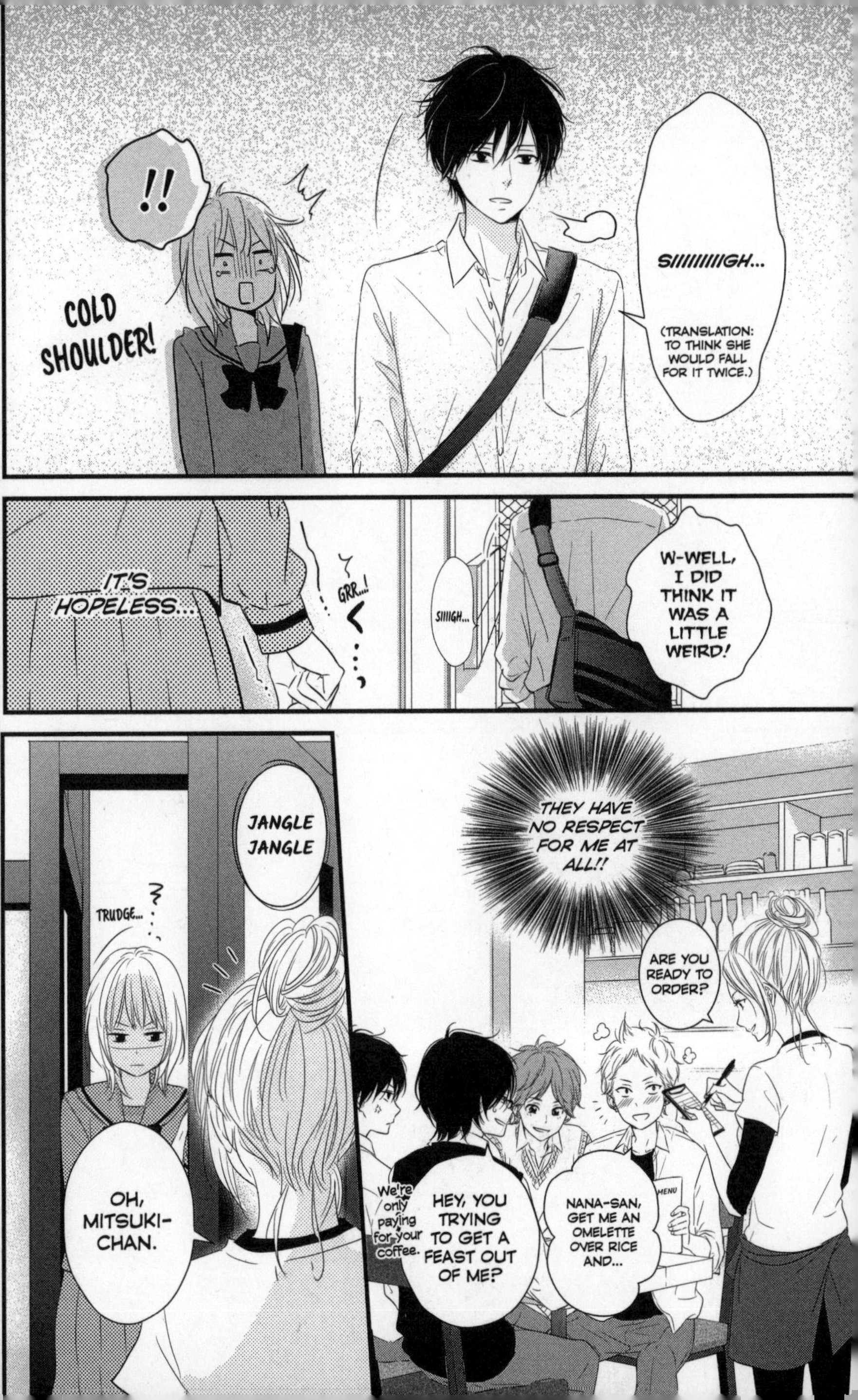
SIIIIIIIIGH...
(TRANSLATION: TO THINK SHE WOULD FALL FOR IT TWICE.)
!!
COLD SHOULDER!
W-WELL, I DID THINK IT WAS A LITTLE WEIRD!
SIIIGH...
GRR...!
IT'S HOPELESS...
THEY HAVE NO RESPECT FOR ME AT ALL!!
ARE YOU READY TO ORDER?
NANA-SAN, GET ME AN OMELETTE OVER RICE AND...
HEY, YOU TRYING TO GET A FEAST OUT OF ME?
We're only paying for your coffee.
JANGLE JANGLE
TRUDGE...
OH, MITSUKI-CHAN.

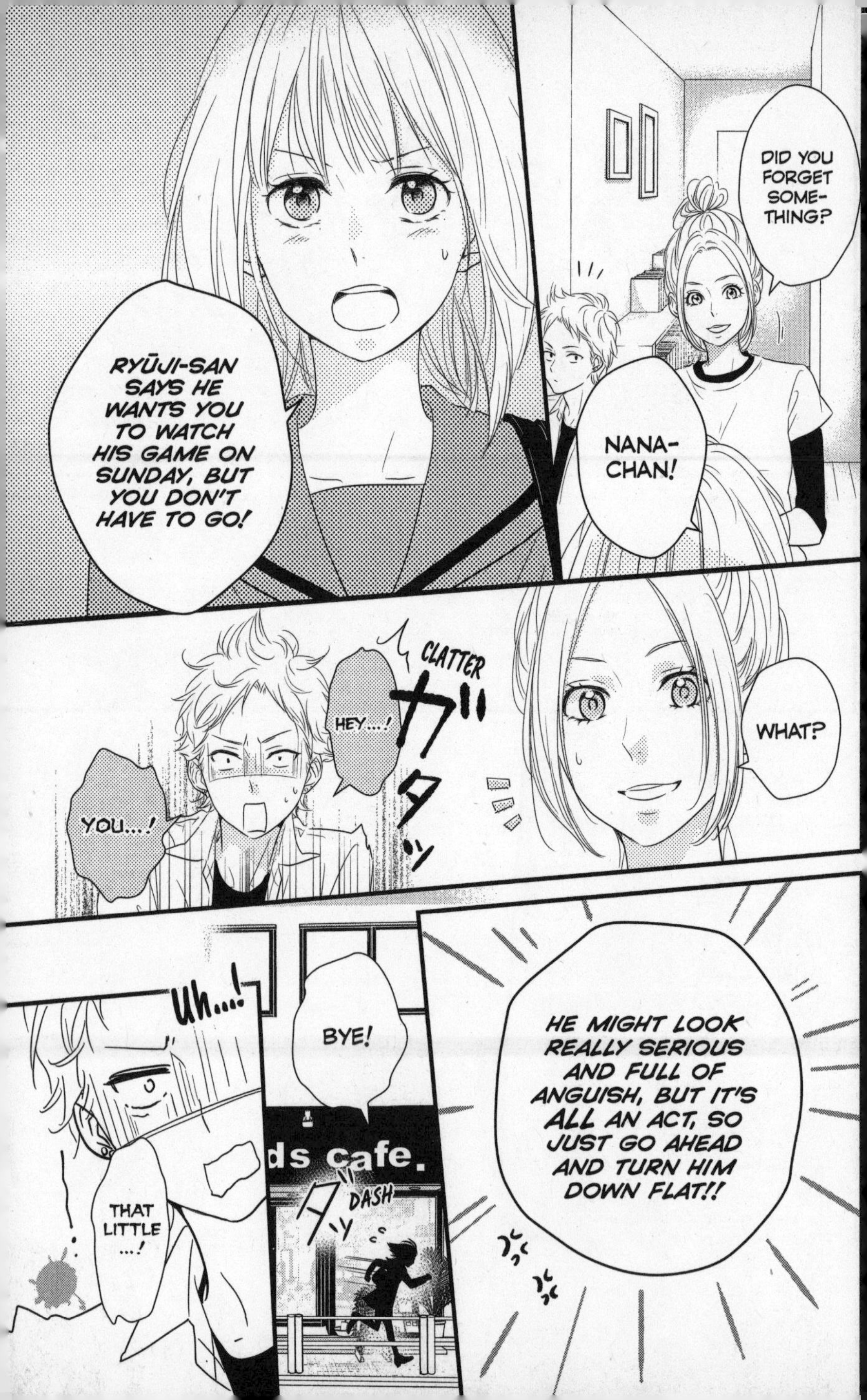
DID YOU FORGET SOME-THING?
NANA-CHAN!
RYŪJI-SAN SAYS HE WANTS YOU TO WATCH HIS GAME ON SUNDAY, BUT YOU DON'T HAVE TO GO!
WHAT?
CLATTER
HEY...!
YOU...!
HE MIGHT LOOK REALLY SERIOUS AND FULL OF ANGUISH, BUT IT'S ALL AN ACT, SO JUST GO AHEAD AND TURN HIM DOWN FLAT!!
BYE!
ds cafe.
DASH
Uh...!
THAT LITTLE ...!

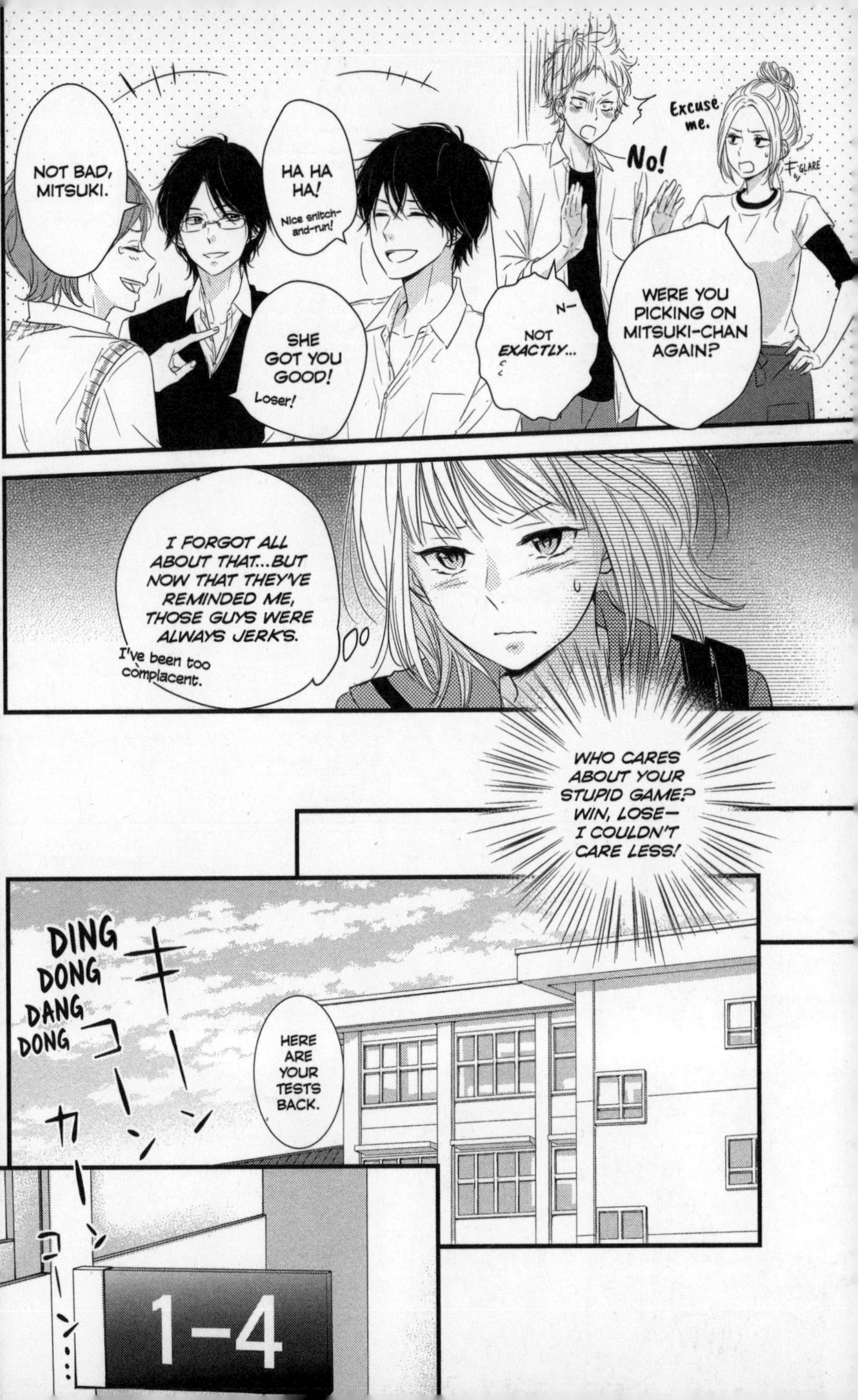
Excuse me.
WERE YOU PICKING ON MITSUKI-CHAN AGAIN?
GLARE
No!
N— NOT EXACTLY...
HA HA HA!
Nice snitch-and-run!
SHE GOT YOU GOOD!
Loser!
NOT BAD, MITSUKI.
I FORGOT ALL ABOUT THAT...BUT NOW THAT THEY'VE REMINDED ME, THOSE GUYS WERE ALWAYS JERKS.
I've been too complacent.
WHO CARES ABOUT YOUR STUPID GAME? WIN, LOSE— I COULDN'T CARE LESS!
DING DONG DANG DONG
HERE ARE YOUR TESTS BACK.
1-4

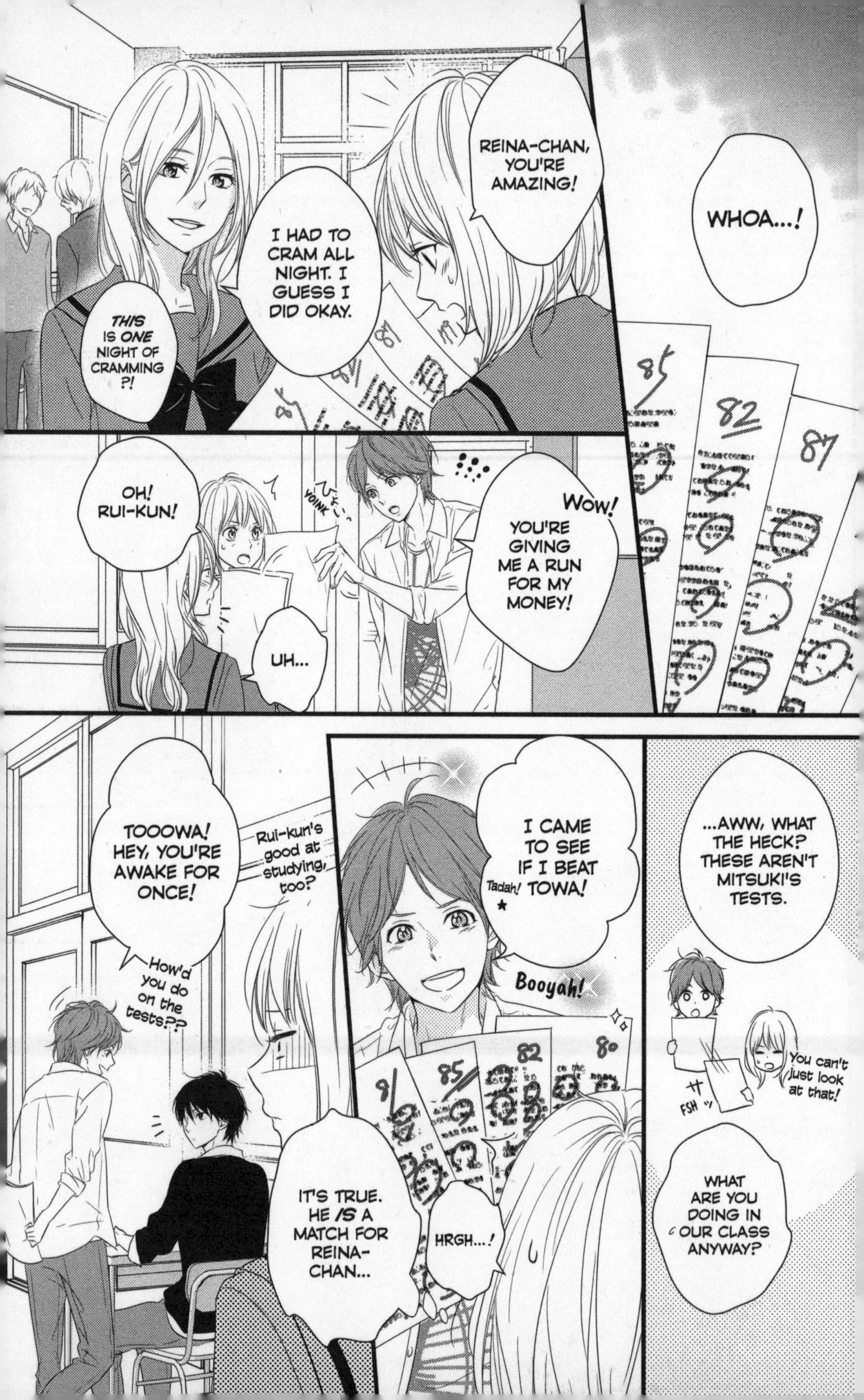
WHOA...!
REINA-CHAN, YOU'RE AMAZING!
I HAD TO CRAM ALL NIGHT. I GUESS I DID OKAY.
THIS IS *ONE* NIGHT OF CRAMMING?!
WOW!
YOU'RE GIVING ME A RUN FOR MY MONEY!
YOINK
OH! RUI-KUN!
UH...
...AWW, WHAT THE HECK? THESE AREN'T MITSUKI'S TESTS.
FSH
You can't just look at that!
WHAT ARE YOU DOING IN OUR CLASS ANYWAY?
I CAME TO SEE IF I BEAT TOWA!
Tadah!
Booyah!
HRGH...!
IT'S TRUE. HE *IS* A MATCH FOR REINA-CHAN...
TOOOWA! HEY, YOU'RE AWAKE FOR ONCE!
Rui-kun's good at studying, too?
How'd you do on the tests??

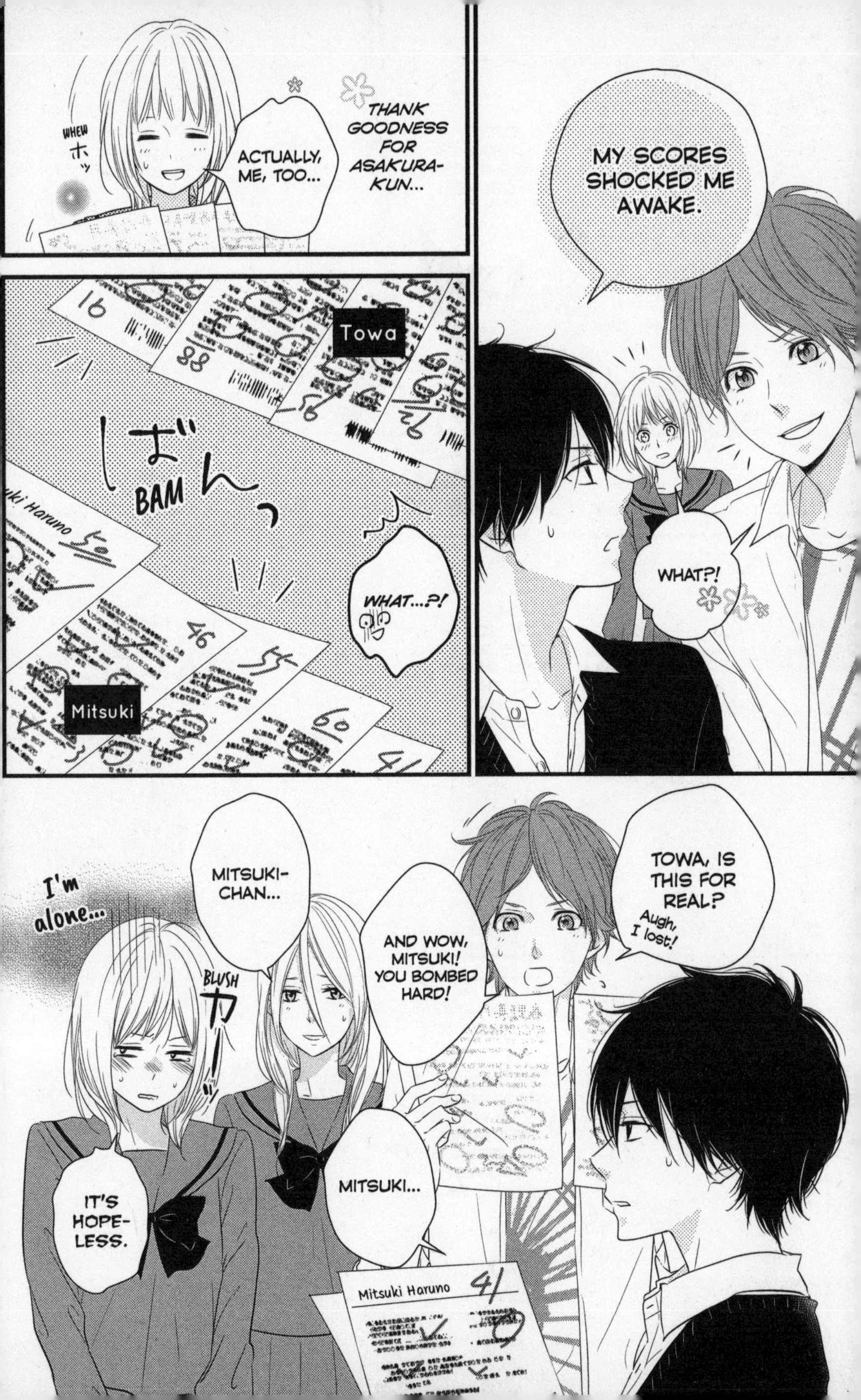
MY SCORES SHOCKED ME AWAKE.
WHAT?!
WHEW
ホッ
ACTUALLY, ME, TOO...
THANK GOODNESS FOR ASAKURA-KUN...
Towa
16
88
ばんっ
BAM
WHAT...?!
Mitsuki
46
60
41
TOWA, IS THIS FOR REAL?
Augh, I lost!
AND WOW, MITSUKI! YOU BOMBED HARD!
MITSUKI-CHAN...
BLUSH
カーッ
I'm alone...
MITSUKI...
IT'S HOPELESS.
Mitsuki Haruno 41

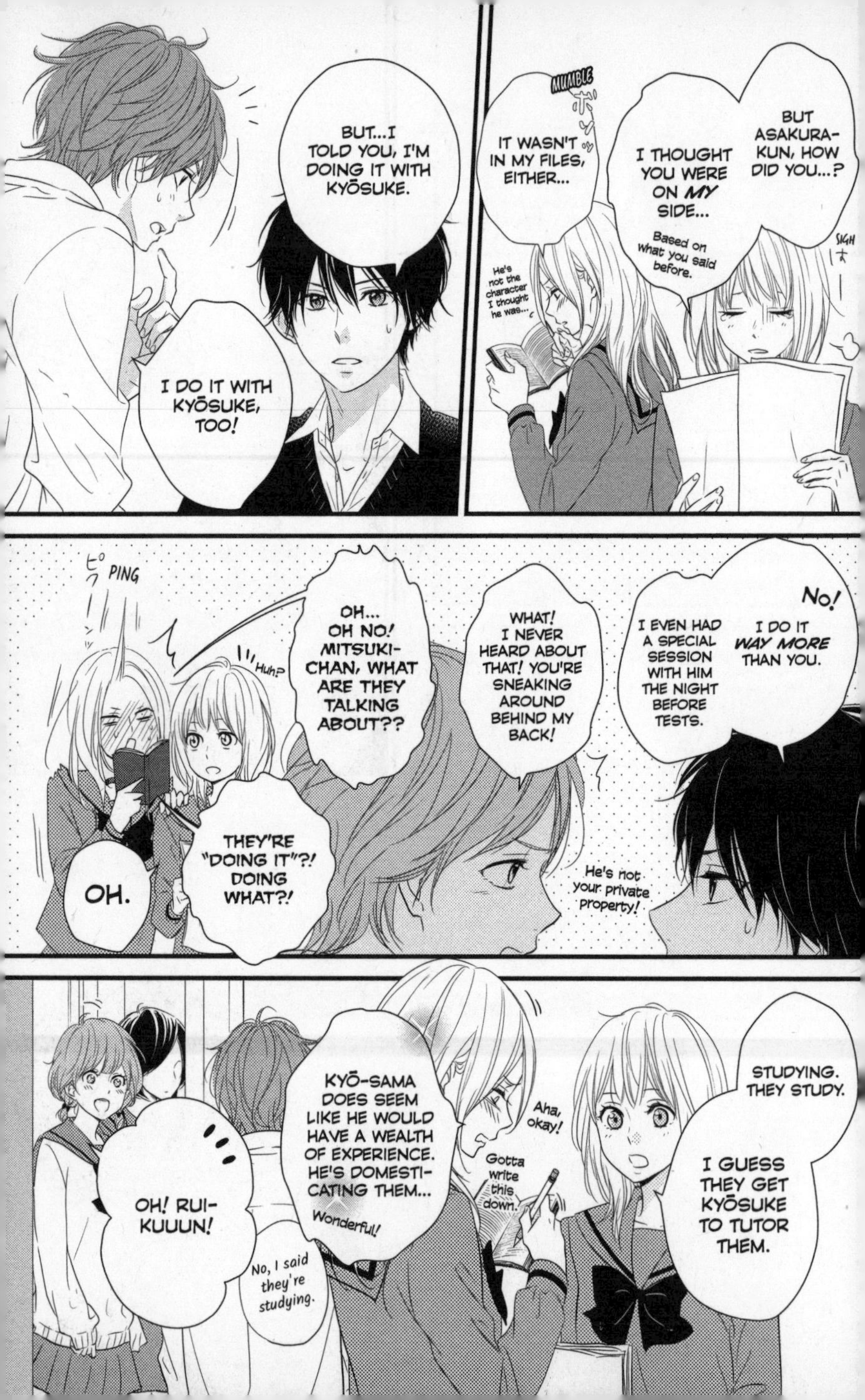
BUT ASAKURA-KUN, HOW DID YOU...?
SIGH
I THOUGHT YOU WERE ON *MY* SIDE...
Based on what you said before.
MUMBLE
IT WASN'T IN MY FILES, EITHER...
He's not the character I thought he was...
BUT...I TOLD YOU, I'M DOING IT WITH KYŌSUKE.
I DO IT WITH KYŌSUKE, TOO!
No!
I DO IT *WAY MORE* THAN YOU.
I EVEN HAD A SPECIAL SESSION WITH HIM THE NIGHT BEFORE TESTS.
He's not your private property!
WHAT! I NEVER HEARD ABOUT THAT! YOU'RE SNEAKING AROUND BEHIND MY BACK!
OH... OH NO! MITSUKI-CHAN, WHAT ARE THEY TALKING ABOUT??
Huh?
PING
THEY'RE "DOING IT"?! DOING WHAT?!
OH.
STUDYING. THEY STUDY.
I GUESS THEY GET KYŌSUKE TO TUTOR THEM.
Aha, okay!
Gotta write this down.
KYŌ-SAMA DOES SEEM LIKE HE WOULD HAVE A WEALTH OF EXPERIENCE. HE'S DOMESTICATING THEM...
Wonderful!
No, I said they're studying.
...
OH! RUI-KUUUN!

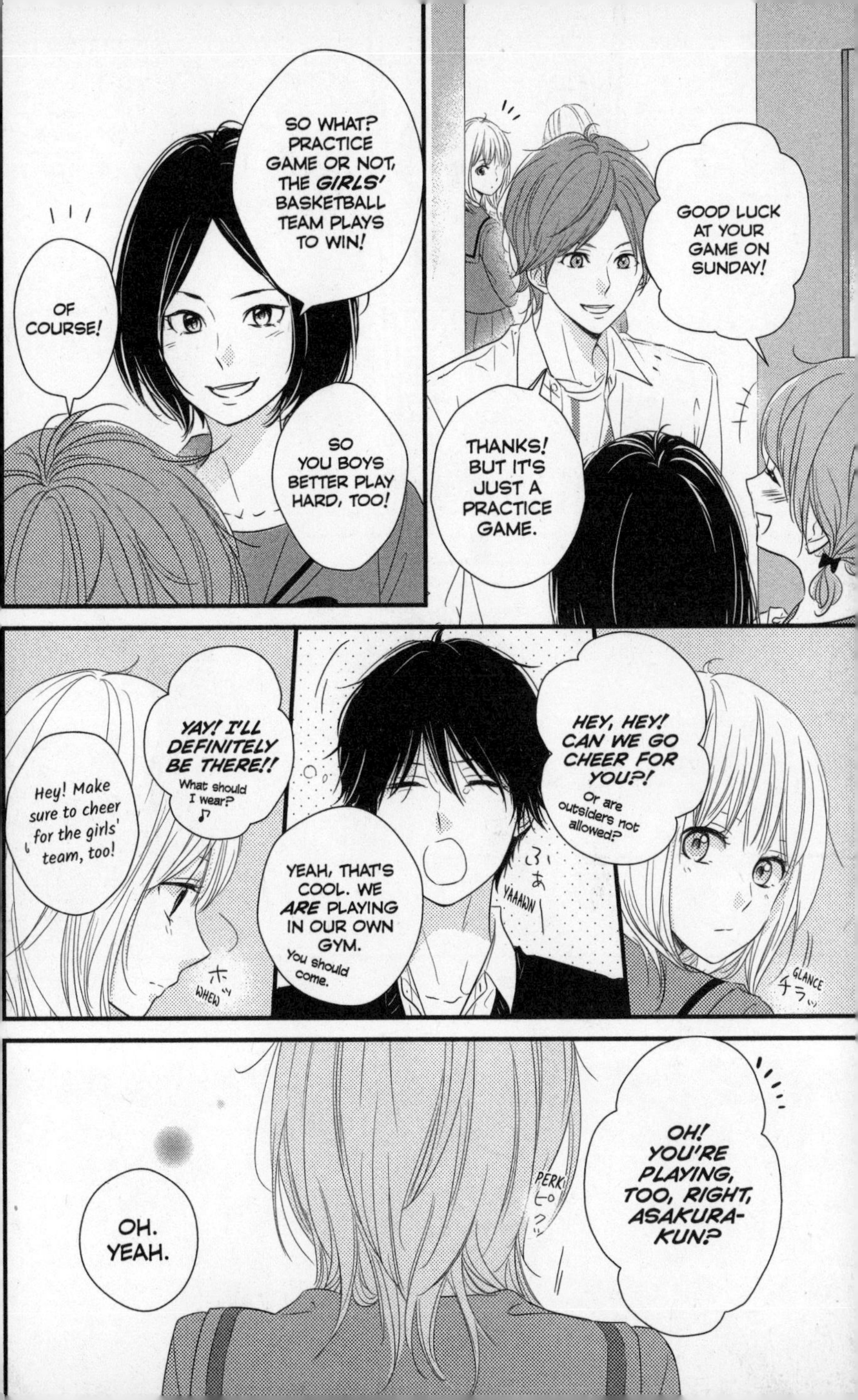
GOOD LUCK AT YOUR GAME ON SUNDAY!
THANKS! BUT IT'S JUST A PRACTICE GAME.
SO WHAT? PRACTICE GAME OR NOT, THE *GIRLS'* BASKETBALL TEAM PLAYS TO WIN!
SO YOU BOYS BETTER PLAY HARD, TOO!
OF COURSE!
HEY, HEY! CAN WE GO CHEER FOR YOU?!
Or are outsiders not allowed?
GLANCE
チラッ
ふぁ
YAAAWN
YEAH, THAT'S COOL. WE *ARE* PLAYING IN OUR OWN GYM.
You should come.
YAY! I'LL DEFINITELY BE THERE!!
What should I wear? ♪
Hey! Make sure to cheer for the girls' team, too!
ホッ
WHEW
OH! YOU'RE PLAYING, TOO, RIGHT, ASAKURA-KUN?
PERK
ピクッ
OH. YEAH.

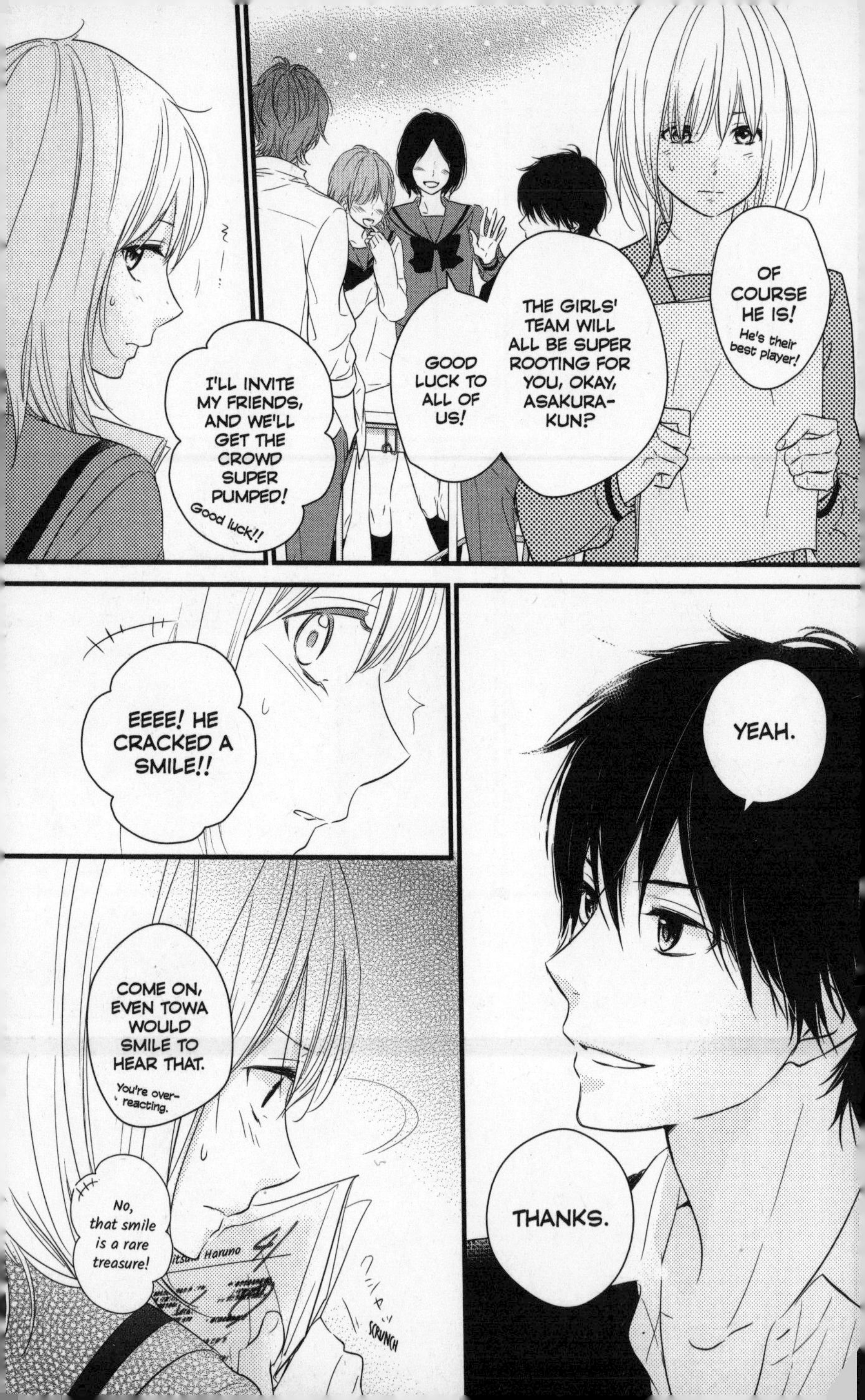
OF COURSE HE IS!
He's their best player!
THE GIRLS' TEAM WILL ALL BE SUPER ROOTING FOR YOU, OKAY, ASAKURA-KUN?
GOOD LUCK TO ALL OF US!
I'LL INVITE MY FRIENDS, AND WE'LL GET THE CROWD SUPER PUMPED!
Good luck!!
YEAH.
THANKS.
EEEE! HE CRACKED A SMILE!!
COME ON, EVEN TOWA WOULD SMILE TO HEAR THAT.
You're over-reacting.
No, that smile is a rare treasure!
SCRUNCH

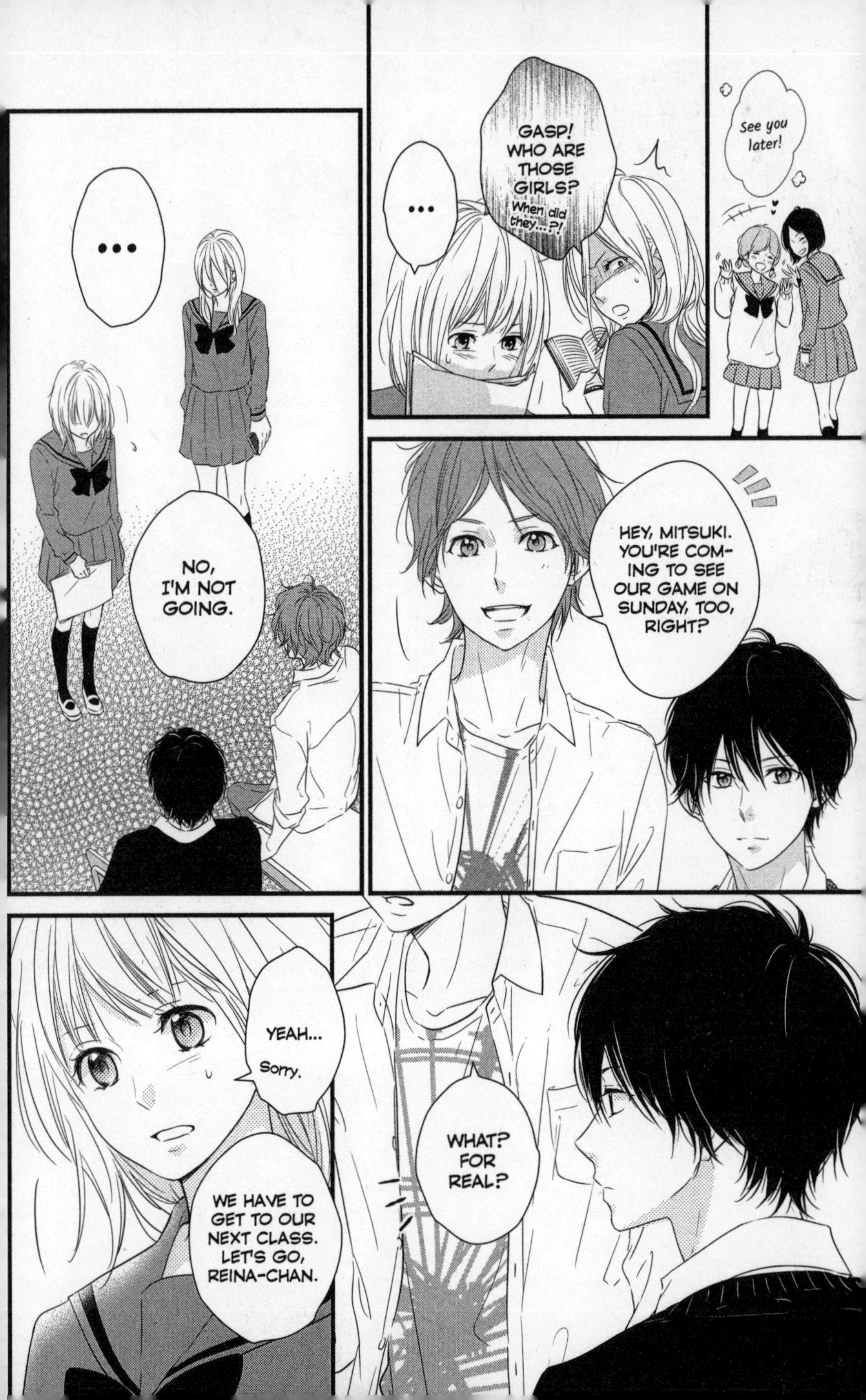
See you later!
GASP! WHO ARE THOSE GIRLS?
When did they...?!
...
HEY, MITSUKI. YOU'RE COMING TO SEE OUR GAME ON SUNDAY, TOO, RIGHT?
...
NO, I'M NOT GOING.
WHAT? FOR REAL?
YEAH...
Sorry.
WE HAVE TO GET TO OUR NEXT CLASS. LET'S GO, REINA-CHAN.

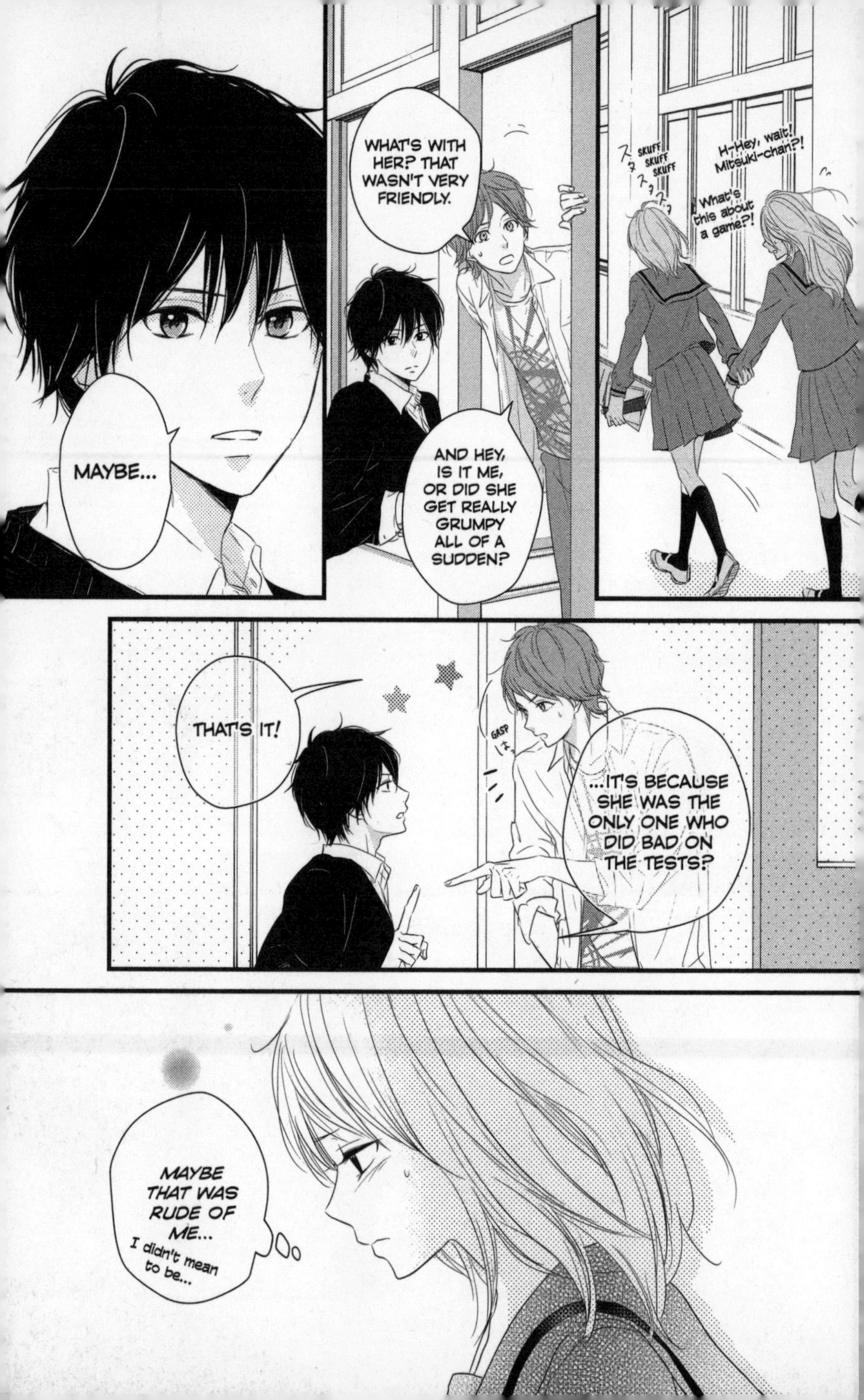
SKUFF SKUFF SKUFF
H-Hey, wait! Mitsuki-chan?!
What's this about a game?!
WHAT'S WITH HER? THAT WASN'T VERY FRIENDLY.
AND HEY, IS IT ME, OR DID SHE GET REALLY GRUMPY ALL OF A SUDDEN?
MAYBE...
GASP
...IT'S BECAUSE SHE WAS THE ONLY ONE WHO DID BAD ON THE TESTS?
THAT'S IT!
MAYBE THAT WAS RUDE OF ME...
I didn't mean to be...

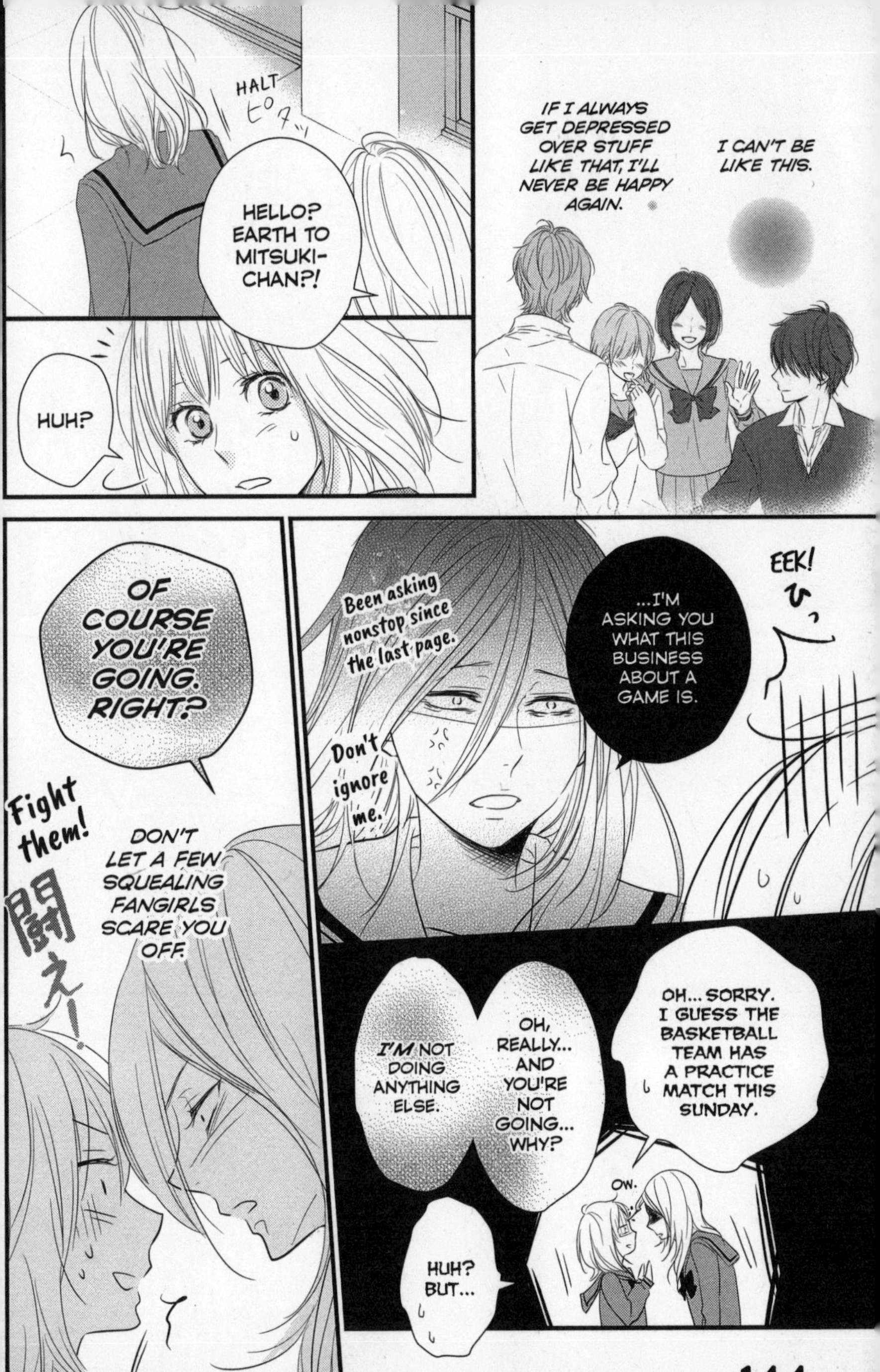
I CAN'T BE LIKE THIS.
IF I ALWAYS GET DEPRESSED OVER STUFF LIKE THAT, I'LL NEVER BE HAPPY AGAIN.
HALT
ピクッ
HELLO? EARTH TO MITSUKI-CHAN?!
HUH?
EEK!
ひっ
...I'M ASKING YOU WHAT THIS BUSINESS ABOUT A GAME IS.
Been asking nonstop since the last page.
Don't ignore me.
OH... SORRY. I GUESS THE BASKETBALL TEAM HAS A PRACTICE MATCH THIS SUNDAY.
OH, REALLY... AND YOU'RE NOT GOING... WHY?
I'M NOT DOING ANYTHING ELSE.
OW.
HUH? BUT...
OF COURSE YOU'RE GOING. RIGHT?
Fight them!
闘え!
DON'T LET A FEW SQUEALING FANGIRLS SCARE YOU OFF.

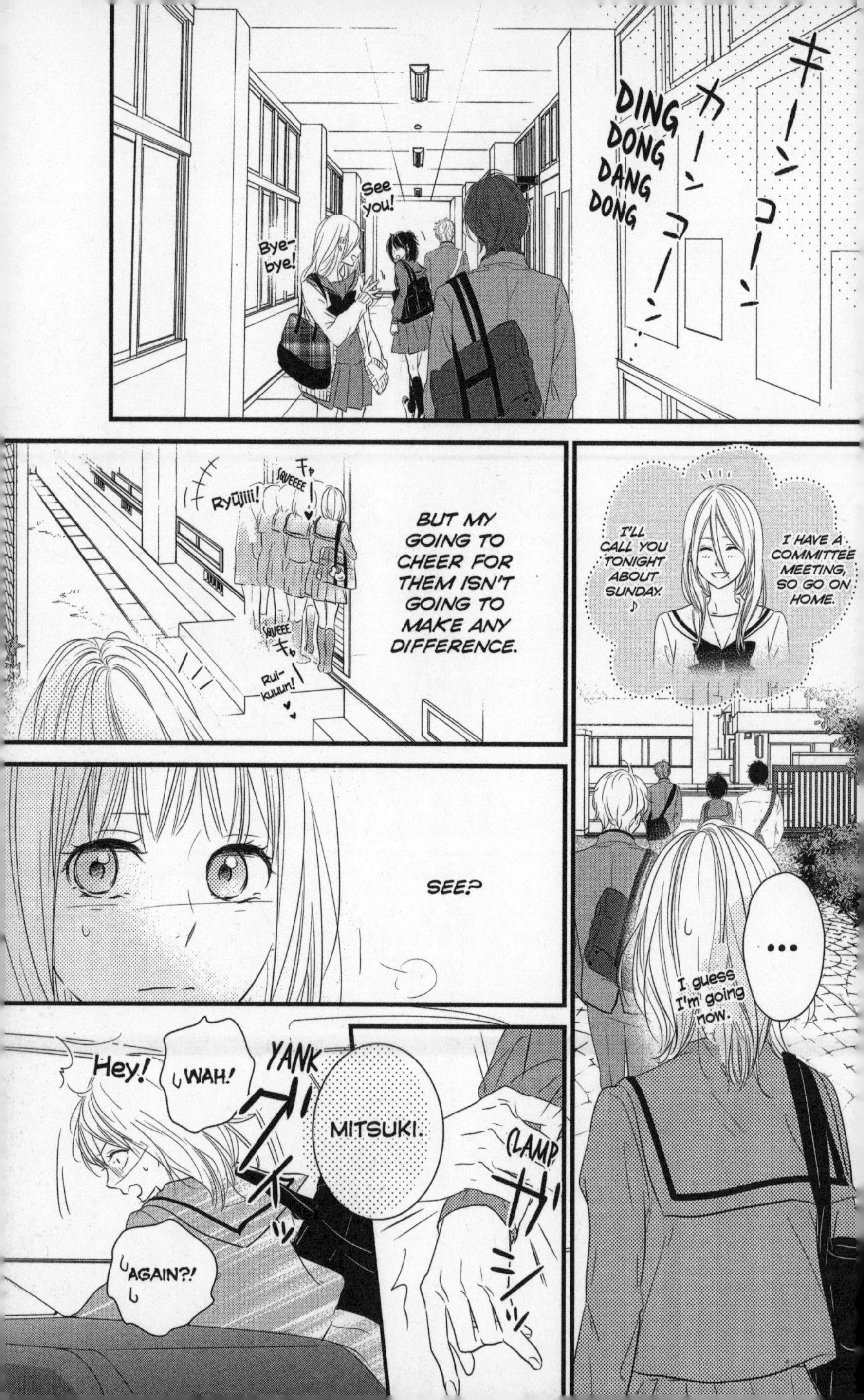
DING DONG DANG DONG
See you!
Bye-bye!
I HAVE A COMMITTEE MEETING, SO GO ON HOME.
I'LL CALL YOU TONIGHT ABOUT SUNDAY. ♪
...
I guess I'm going now.
BUT MY GOING TO CHEER FOR THEM ISN'T GOING TO MAKE ANY DIFFERENCE.
SQUEEEE
Ryūjiii!
SQUEEE
Rui-kuuun!
SEE?
CLAMP
MITSUKI.
YANK
WAH!
Hey!
AGAIN?!

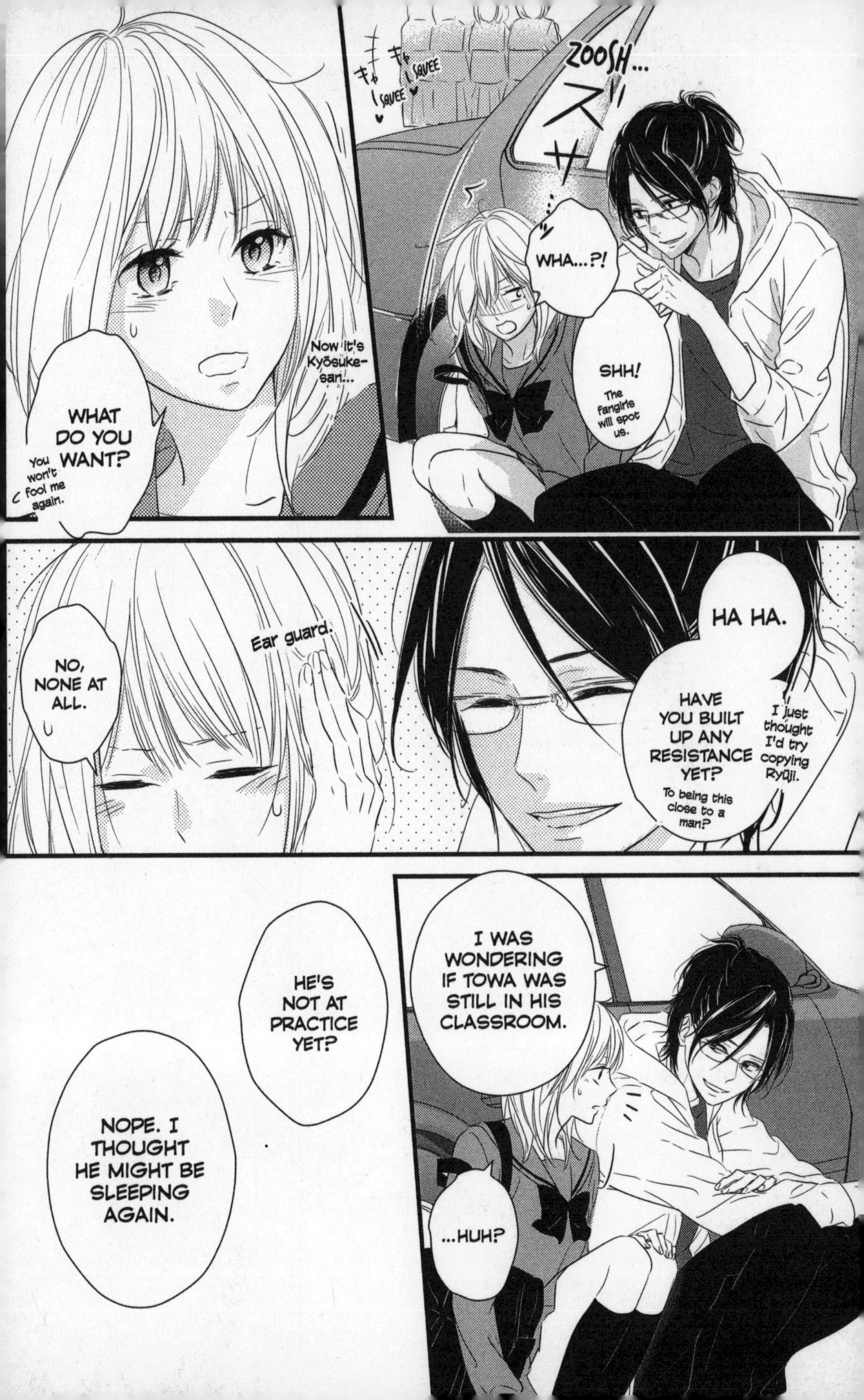
ZOOSH...
スッ
キャ キャ
SQUEE SQUEE
WHA...?!
SHH!
The fangirls will spot us.
Now it's Kyōsuke-san...
WHAT DO YOU WANT?
You won't fool me again.
HA HA.
HAVE YOU BUILT UP ANY RESISTANCE YET?
To being this close to a man?
I just thought I'd try copying Ryūji.
Ear guard.
NO, NONE AT ALL.
I WAS WONDERING IF TOWA WAS STILL IN HIS CLASSROOM.
...HUH?
HE'S NOT AT PRACTICE YET?
NOPE. I THOUGHT HE MIGHT BE SLEEPING AGAIN.

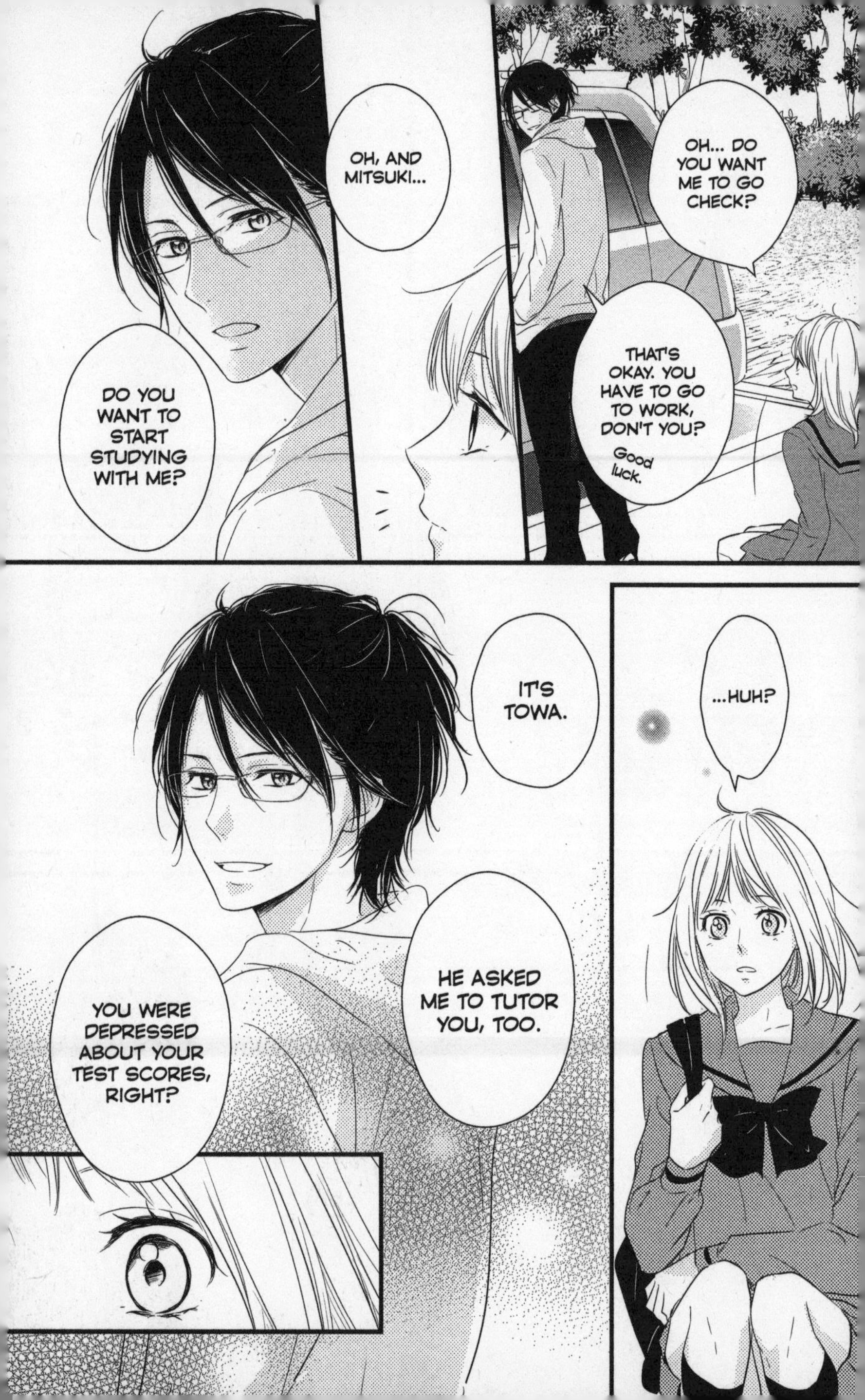
OH... DO YOU WANT ME TO GO CHECK?
THAT'S OKAY. YOU HAVE TO GO TO WORK, DON'T YOU?
Good luck.
OH, AND MITSUKI...
DO YOU WANT TO START STUDYING WITH ME?
...HUH?
IT'S TOWA.
HE ASKED ME TO TUTOR YOU, TOO.
YOU WERE DEPRESSED ABOUT YOUR TEST SCORES, RIGHT?

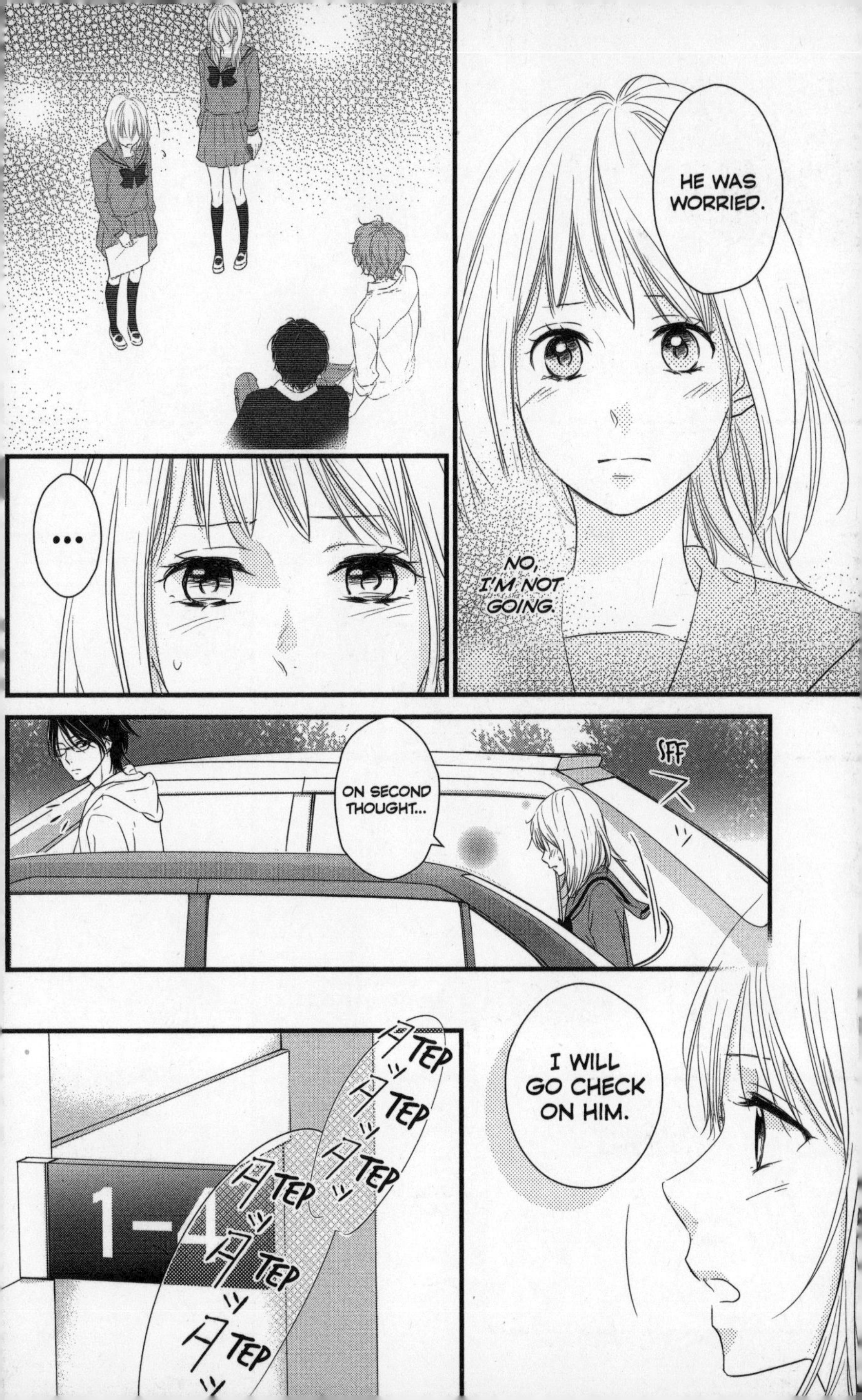
HE WAS WORRIED.
NO, I'M NOT GOING.
...
SFF
ON SECOND THOUGHT...
I WILL GO CHECK ON HIM.
TEP TEP TEP TEP TEP TEP
1-4

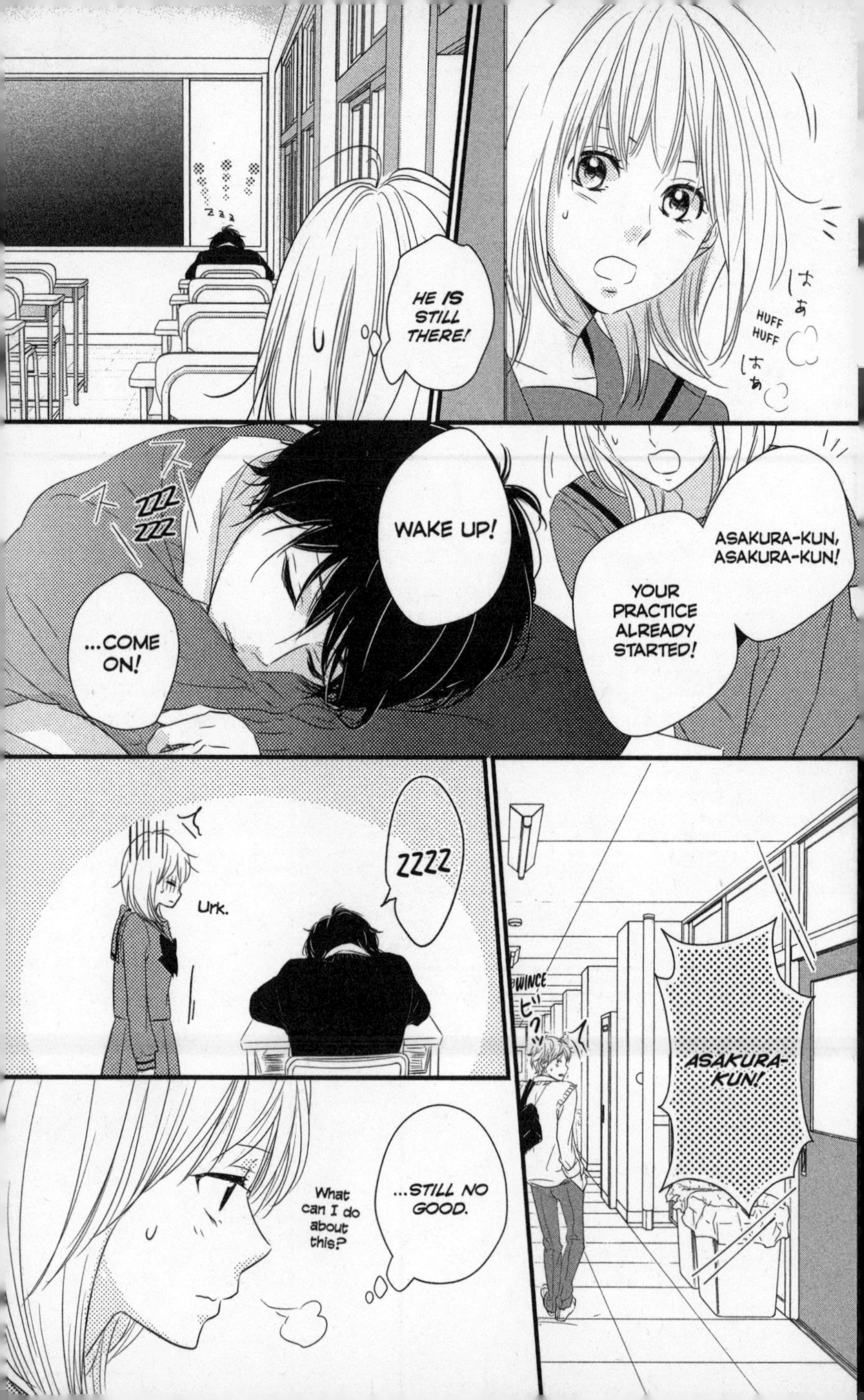
はあ
HUFF HUFF
はあ
HE IS STILL THERE!
Z z z
ASAKURA-KUN, ASAKURA-KUN!
YOUR PRACTICE ALREADY STARTED!
WAKE UP!
ZZZ ZZZ
...COME ON!
ASAKURA-KUN!
WINCE
ビクッ
ZZZZ
Urk.
...STILL NO GOOD.
What can I do about this?

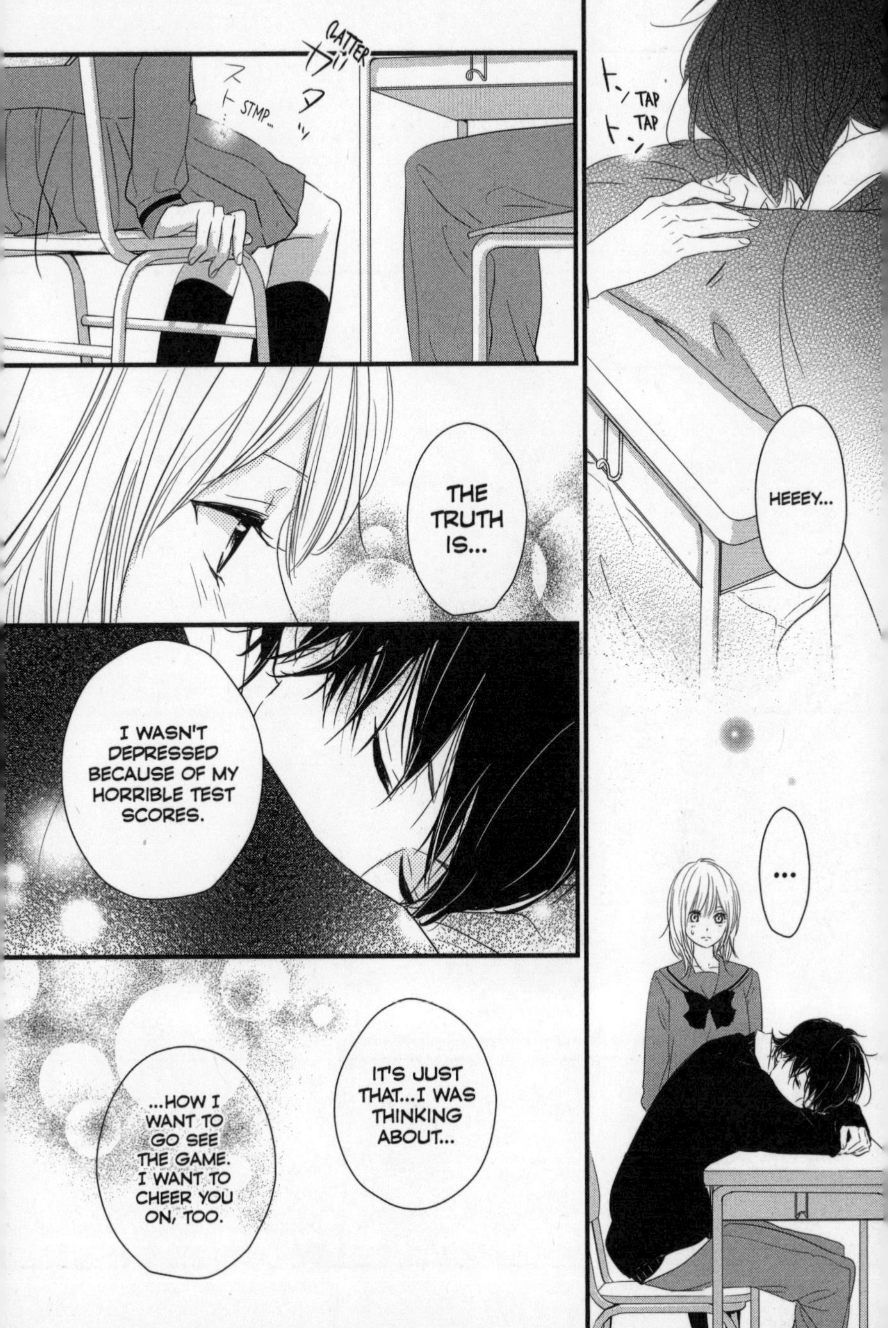
TAP
TAP
HEEEY...
...
CLATTER
STMP...
THE TRUTH IS...
I WASN'T DEPRESSED BECAUSE OF MY HORRIBLE TEST SCORES.
IT'S JUST THAT...I WAS THINKING ABOUT...
...HOW I WANT TO GO SEE THE GAME. I WANT TO CHEER YOU ON, TOO.

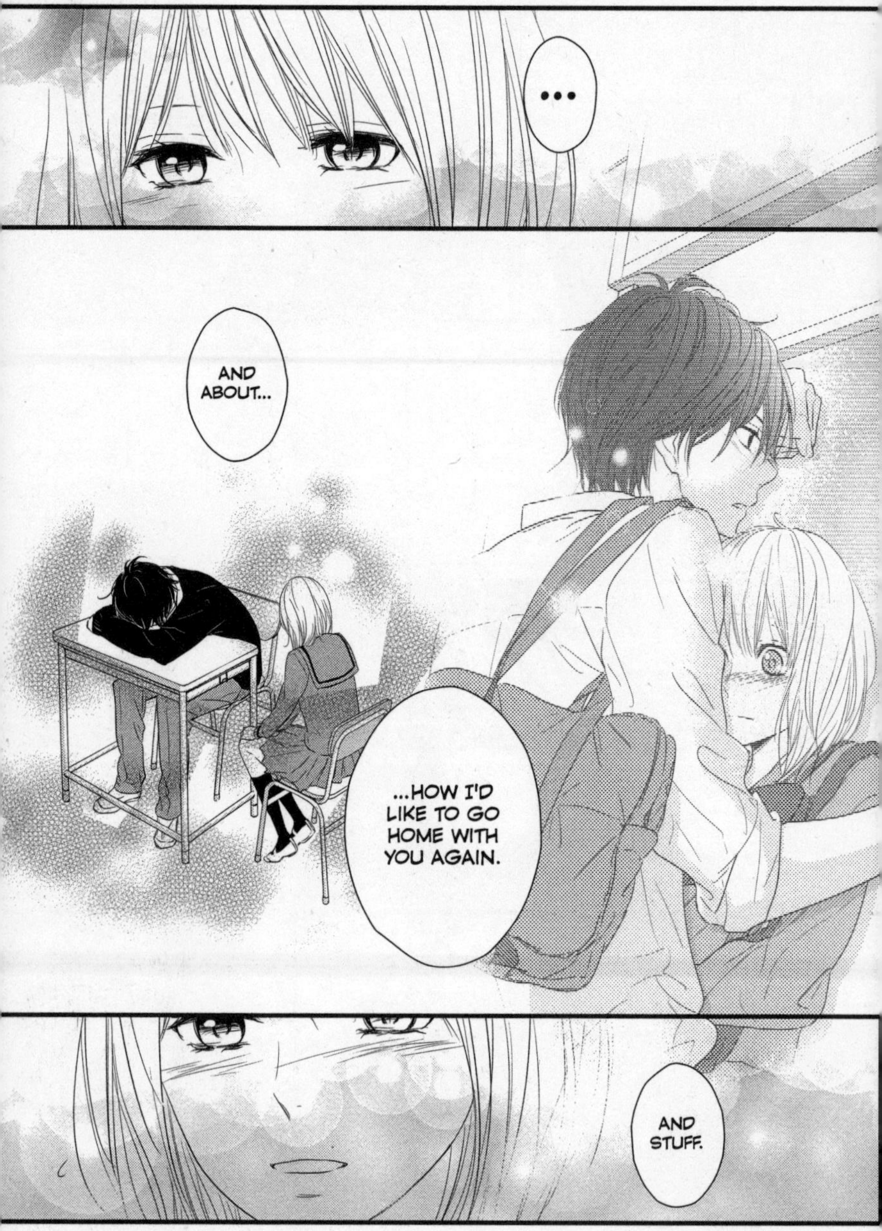
...
AND ABOUT...
...HOW I'D LIKE TO GO HOME WITH YOU AGAIN.
AND STUFF.

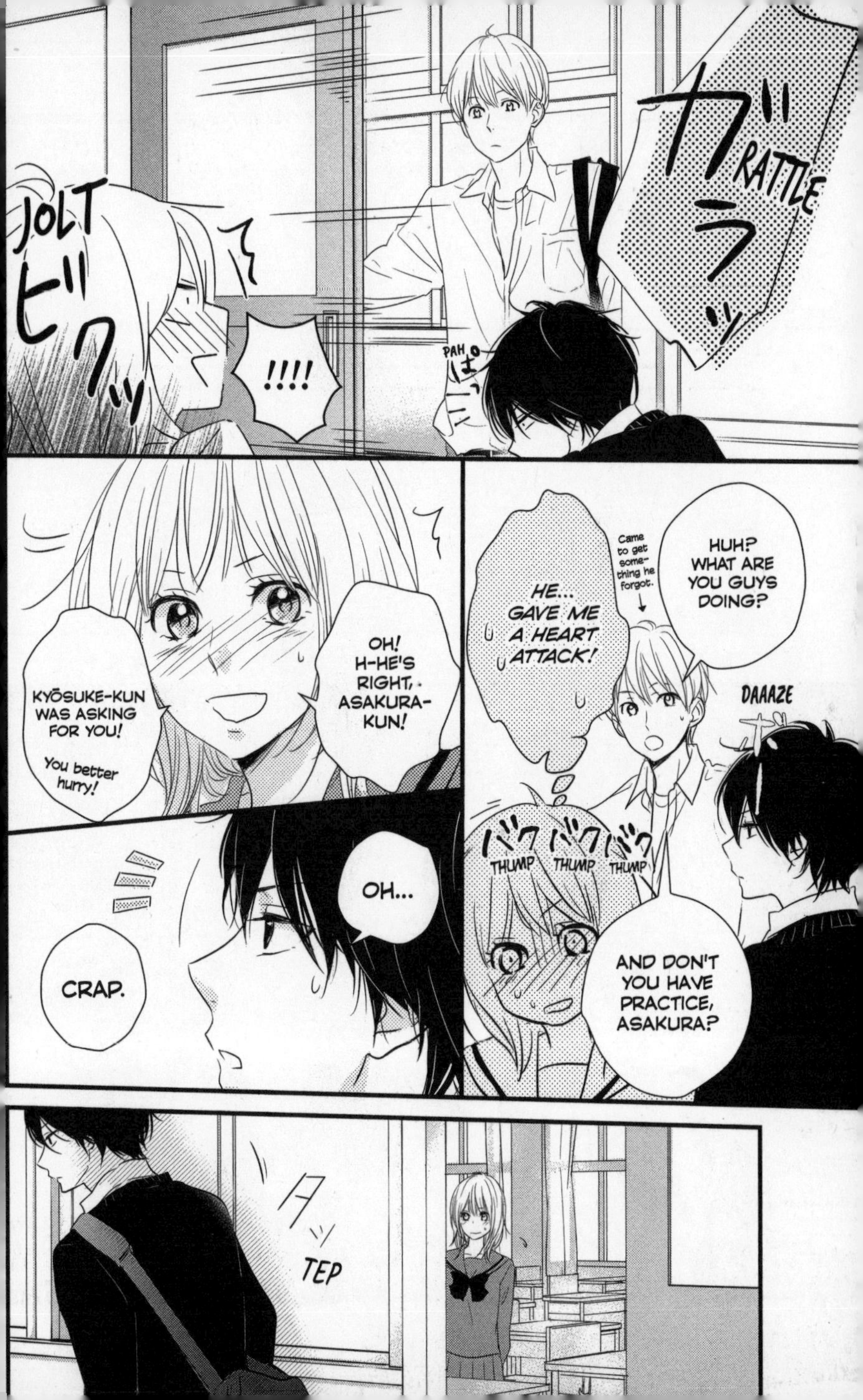
RATTLE
PAH
!!!!
JOLT
HUH? WHAT ARE YOU GUYS DOING?
Came to get something he forgot.
HE... GAVE ME A HEART ATTACK!
DAAAZE
THUMP THUMP THUMP
AND DON'T YOU HAVE PRACTICE, ASAKURA?
OH! H-HE'S RIGHT, ASAKURA-KUN!
KYŌSUKE-KUN WAS ASKING FOR YOU!
You better hurry!
OH...
CRAP.
TEP

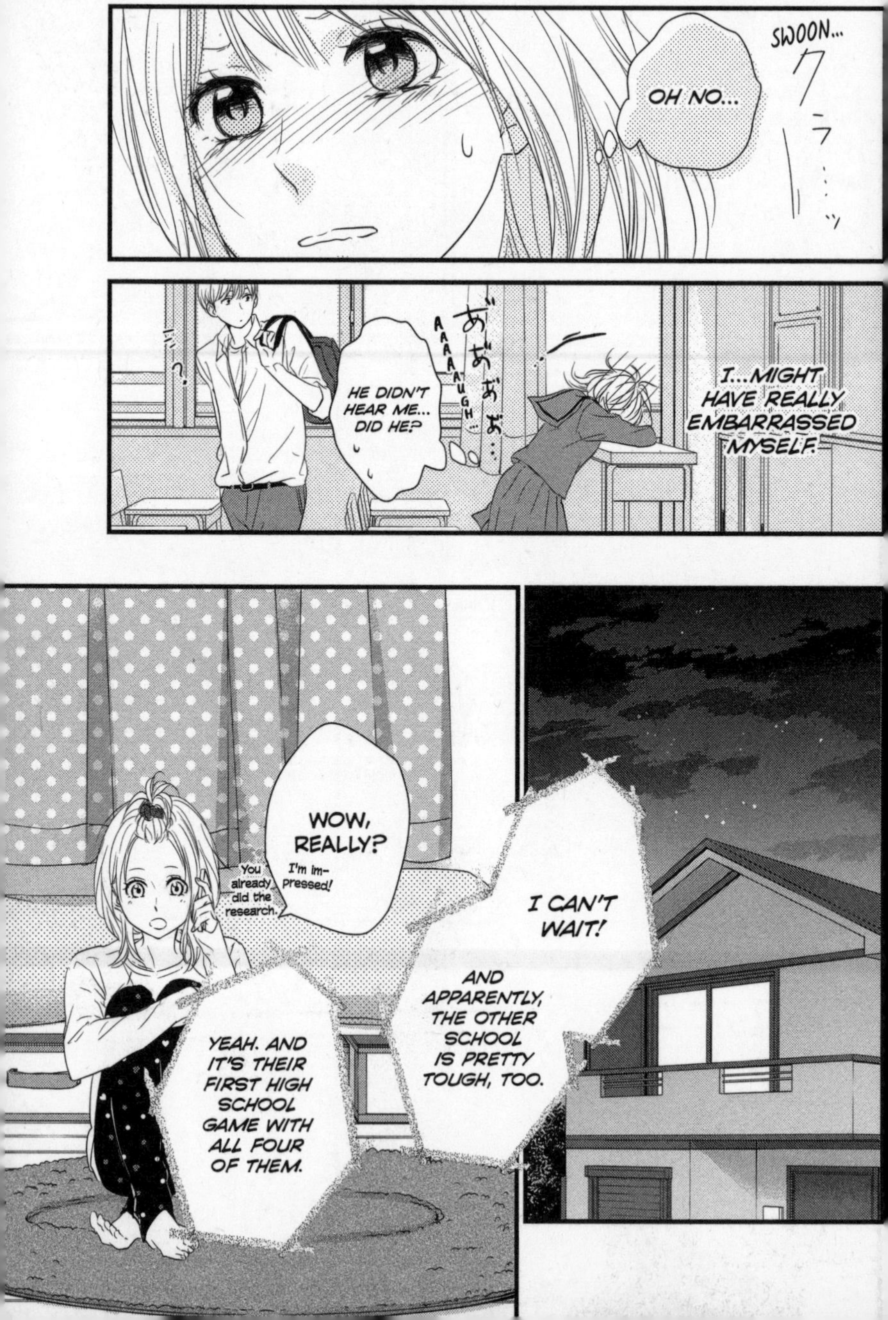
SWOON...
クラ…ッ
OH NO...
I...MIGHT HAVE REALLY EMBARRASSED MYSELF.
あぁぁ…
AAAAAUGH...
HE DIDN'T HEAR ME... DID HE?
?
I CAN'T WAIT!
AND APPARENTLY, THE OTHER SCHOOL IS PRETTY TOUGH, TOO.
YEAH. AND IT'S THEIR FIRST HIGH SCHOOL GAME WITH ALL FOUR OF THEM.
WOW, REALLY?
I'm impressed!
You already did the research.

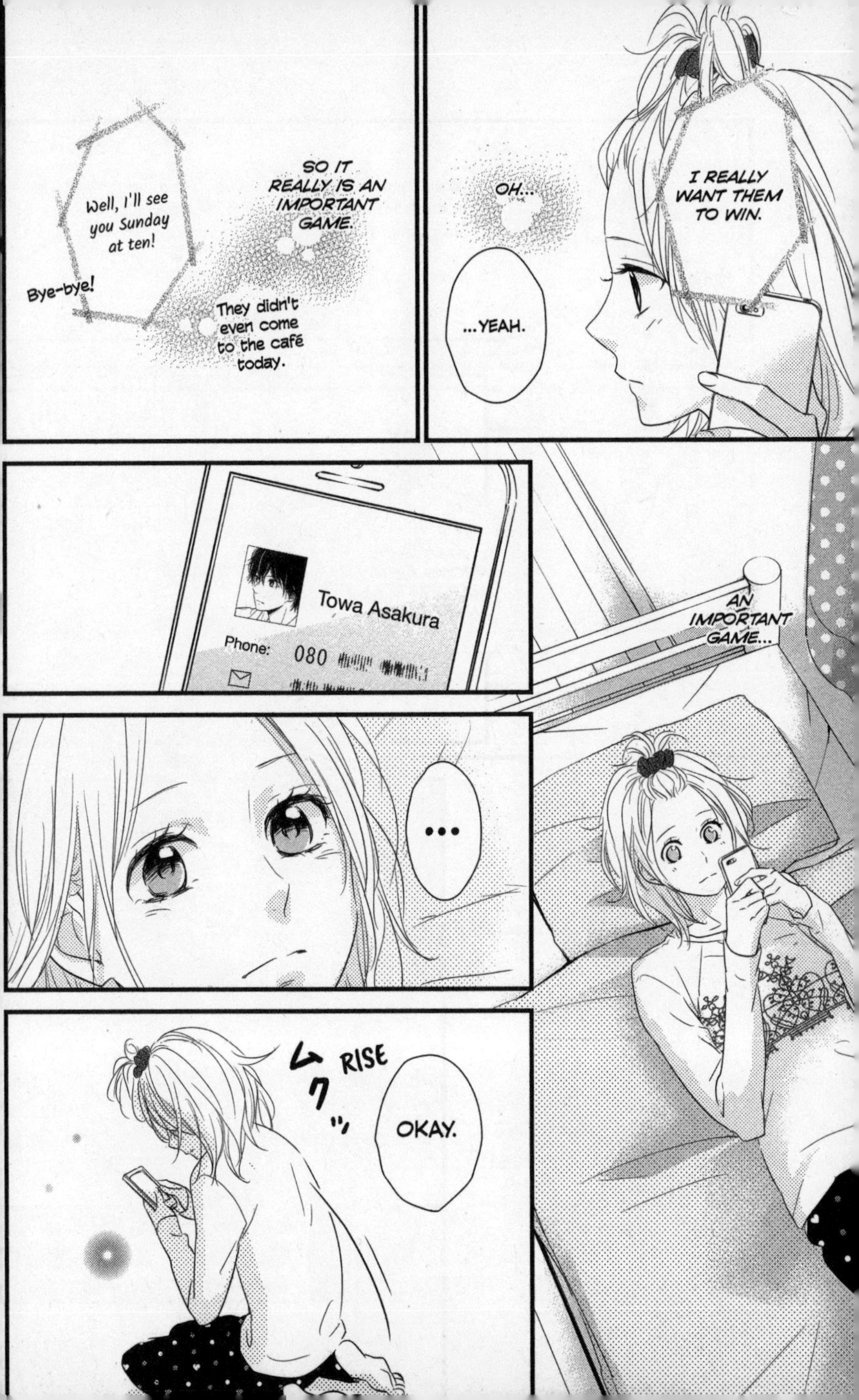
I REALLY WANT THEM TO WIN.
OH...
...YEAH.
SO IT REALLY IS AN IMPORTANT GAME.
Well, I'll see you Sunday at ten!
They didn't even come to the café today.
Bye-bye!
AN IMPORTANT GAME...
Towa Asakura
Phone: 080
...
RISE
OKAY.

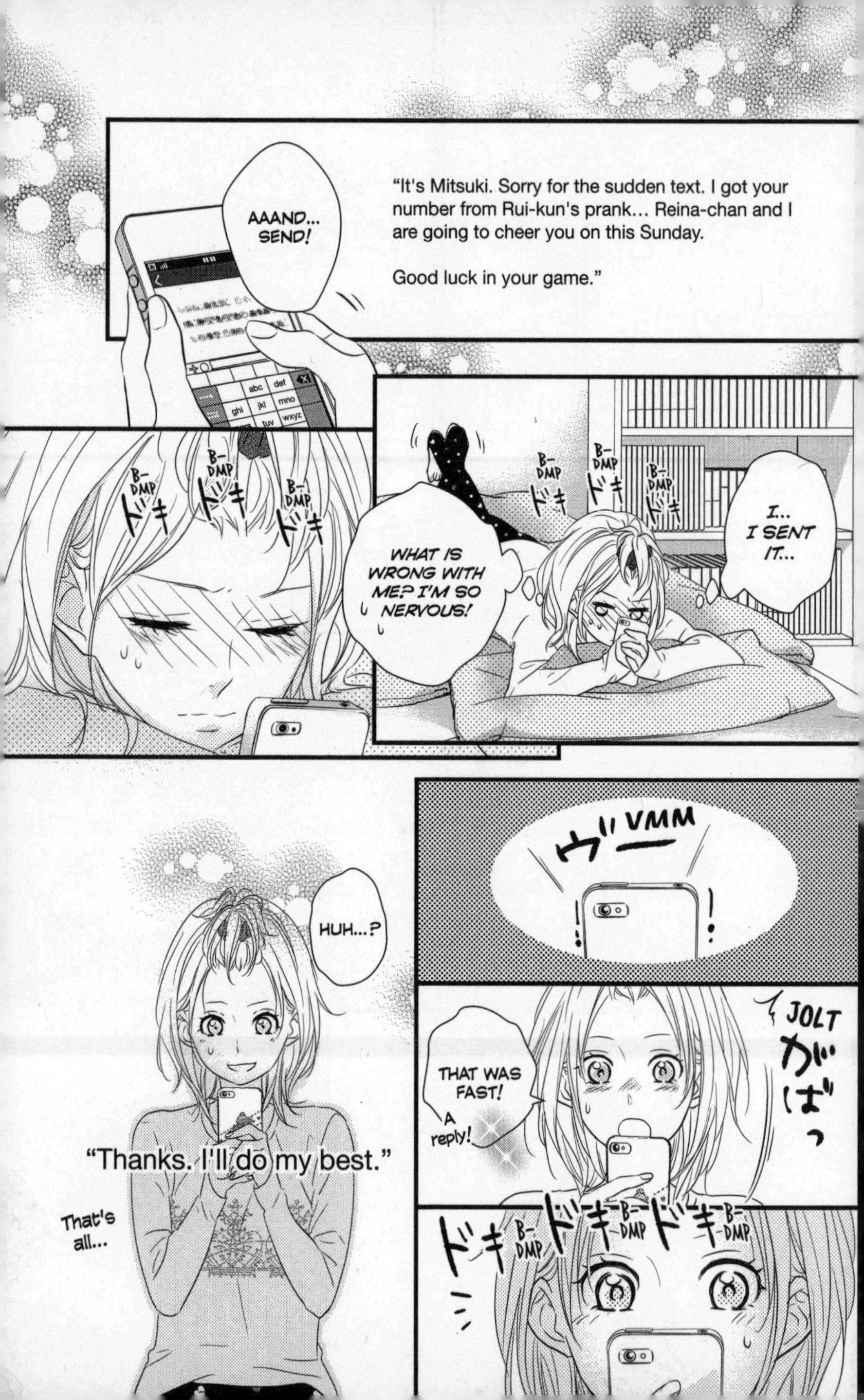
"It's Mitsuki. Sorry for the sudden text. I got your number from Rui-kun's prank... Reina-chan and I are going to cheer you on this Sunday.
Good luck in your game."
AAAND... SEND!
abc def ghi jkl mno tuv wxyz
B-DMP ドキ
B-DMP ドキ
B-DMP ドキ
I... I SENT IT...
WHAT IS WRONG WITH ME? I'M SO NERVOUS!
B-DMP ドキ
B-DMP ドキ
B-DMP ドキ
ヴー VMM
JOLT がばっ
THAT WAS FAST!
A reply!
B-DMP ドキ
B-DMP ドキ
B-DMP ドキ
HUH...?
"Thanks. I'll do my best."
That's all...

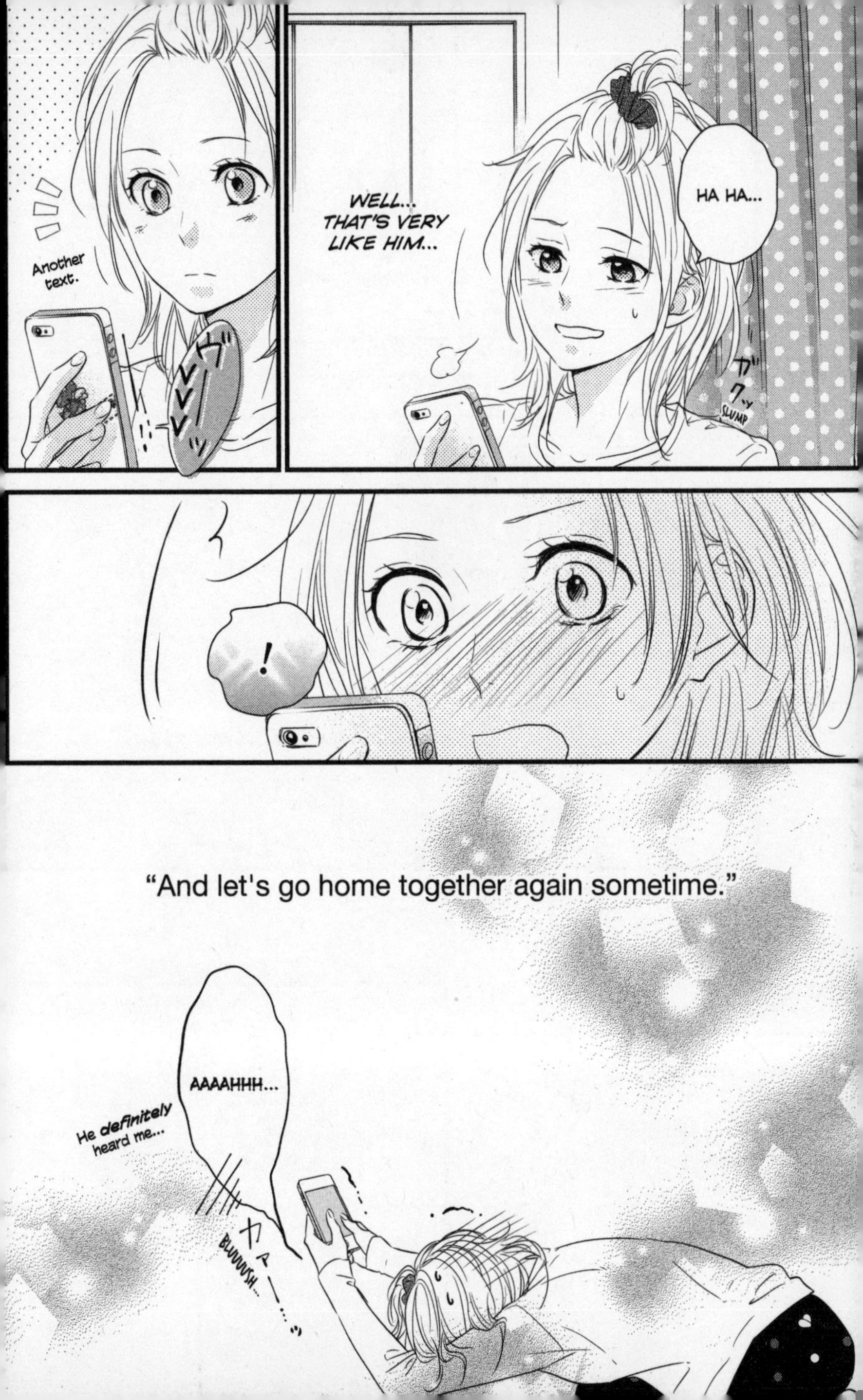
HA HA...
WELL... THAT'S VERY LIKE HIM...
SLUMP
Another text.
!
"And let's go home together again sometime."
AAAAHHH...
He definitely heard me...
BLUUUSH...

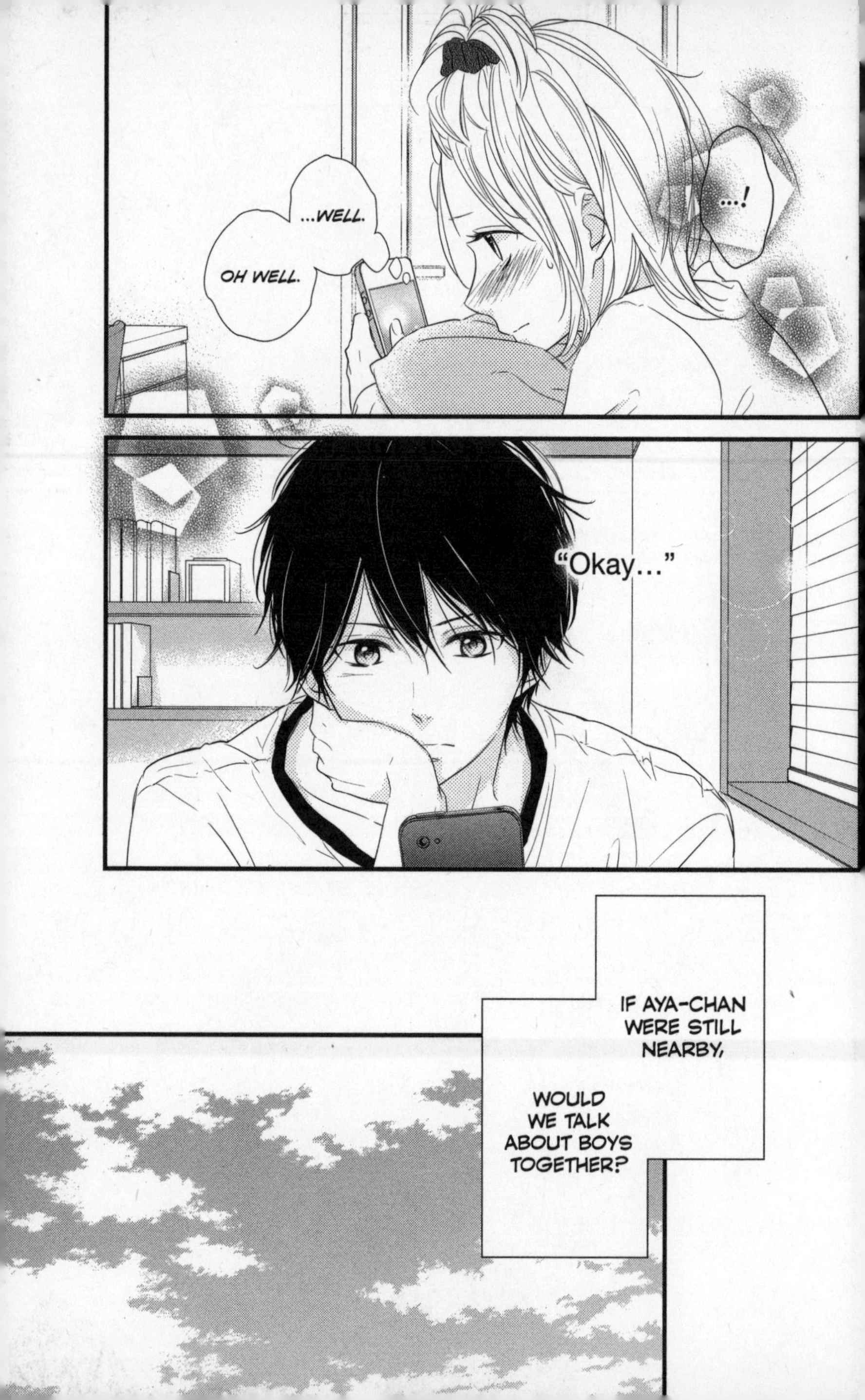
...!
...WELL.
OH WELL.
"Okay..."
IF AYA-CHAN WERE STILL NEARBY,
WOULD WE TALK ABOUT BOYS TOGETHER?

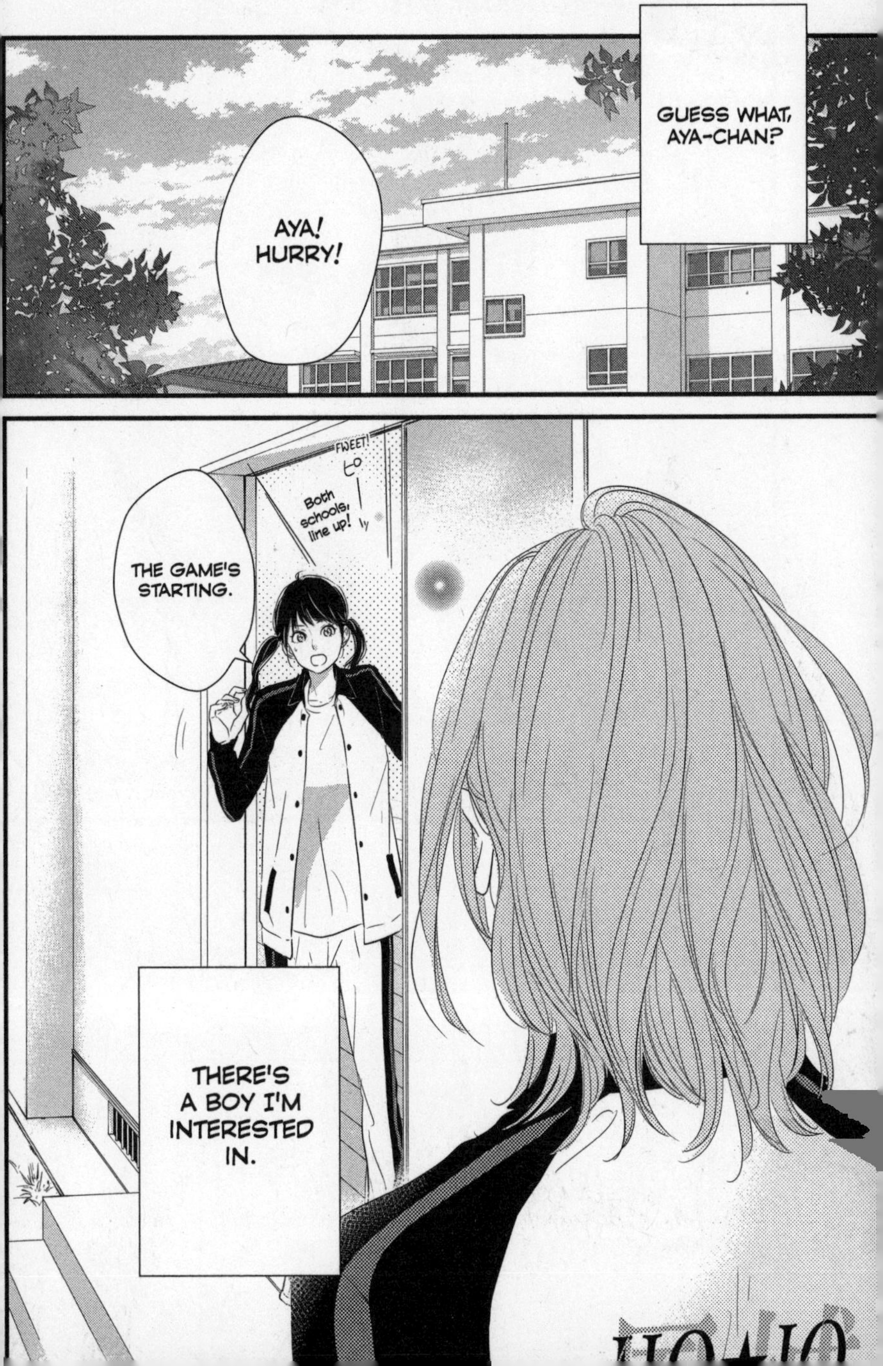
GUESS WHAT, AYA-CHAN?
AYA! HURRY!
FWEET!
Both schools, line up!
THE GAME'S STARTING.
THERE'S A BOY I'M INTERESTED IN.

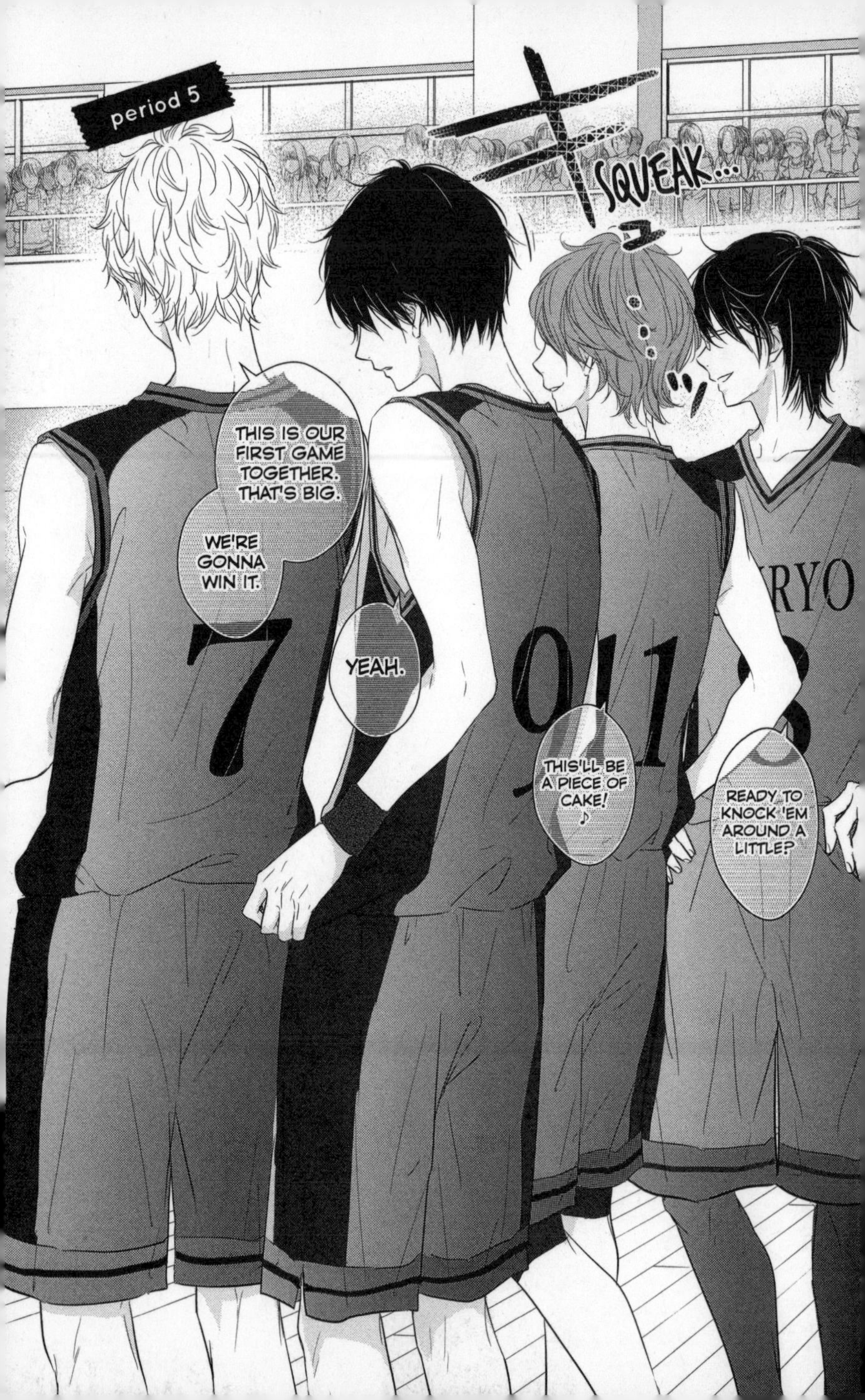
period 5
SQUEAK...
THIS IS OUR FIRST GAME TOGETHER. THAT'S BIG.
WE'RE GONNA WIN IT.
YEAH.
THIS'LL BE A PIECE OF CAKE! ♪
READY TO KNOCK 'EM AROUND A LITTLE?

period 5: "The Big Game"

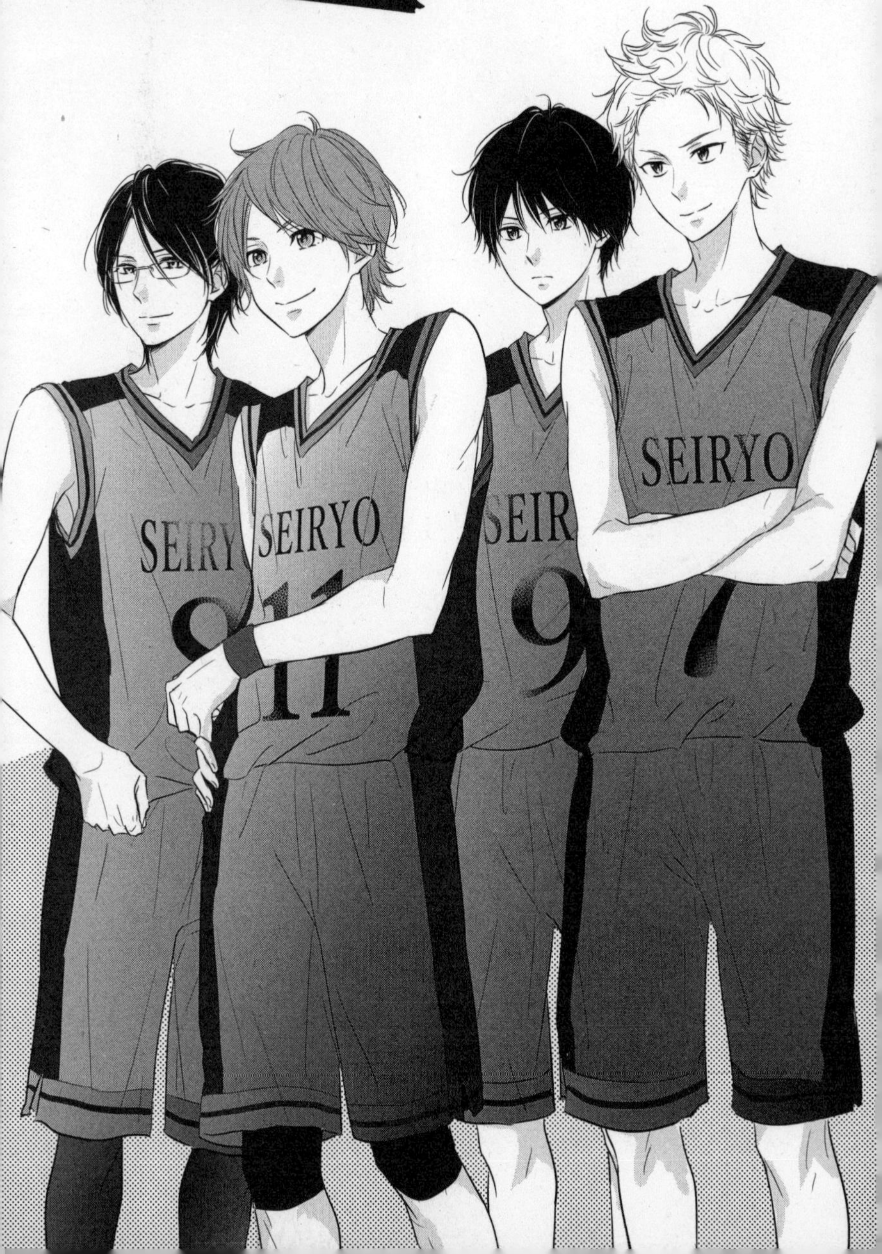
SEIRYO
7
SEIR
9
SEIRYO
11
SEIRY
8

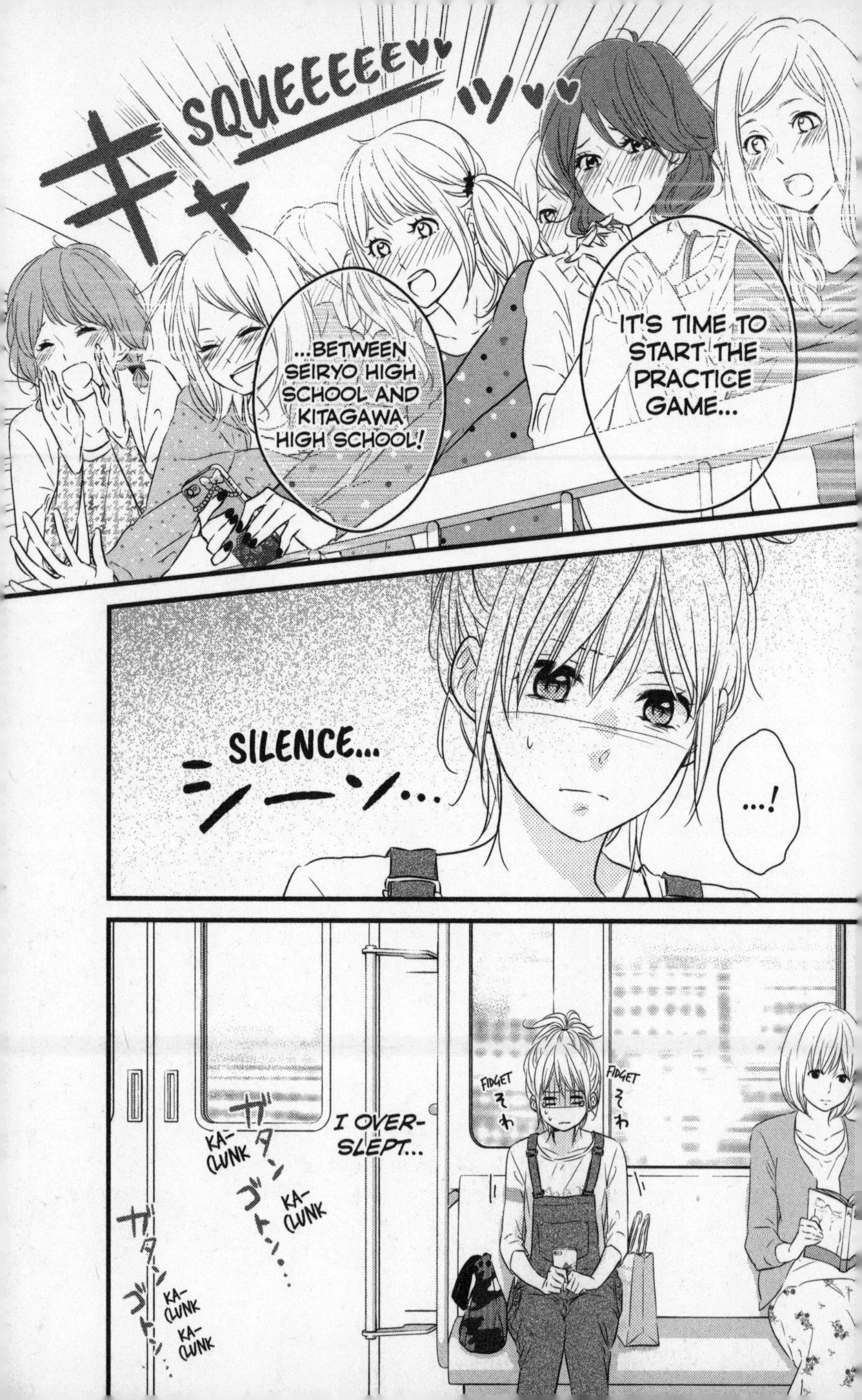
SQUEEEEEE
キャーッ
IT'S TIME TO START THE PRACTICE GAME...
...BETWEEN SEIRYO HIGH SCHOOL AND KITAGAWA HIGH SCHOOL!
...!
SILENCE...
シーン...
FIDGET
そわ
FIDGET
そわ
I OVER-SLEPT...
KA-CLUNK
ガタン
KA-CLUNK
ゴトン...
ガタン
ゴトン...
KA-CLUNK
KA-CLUNK

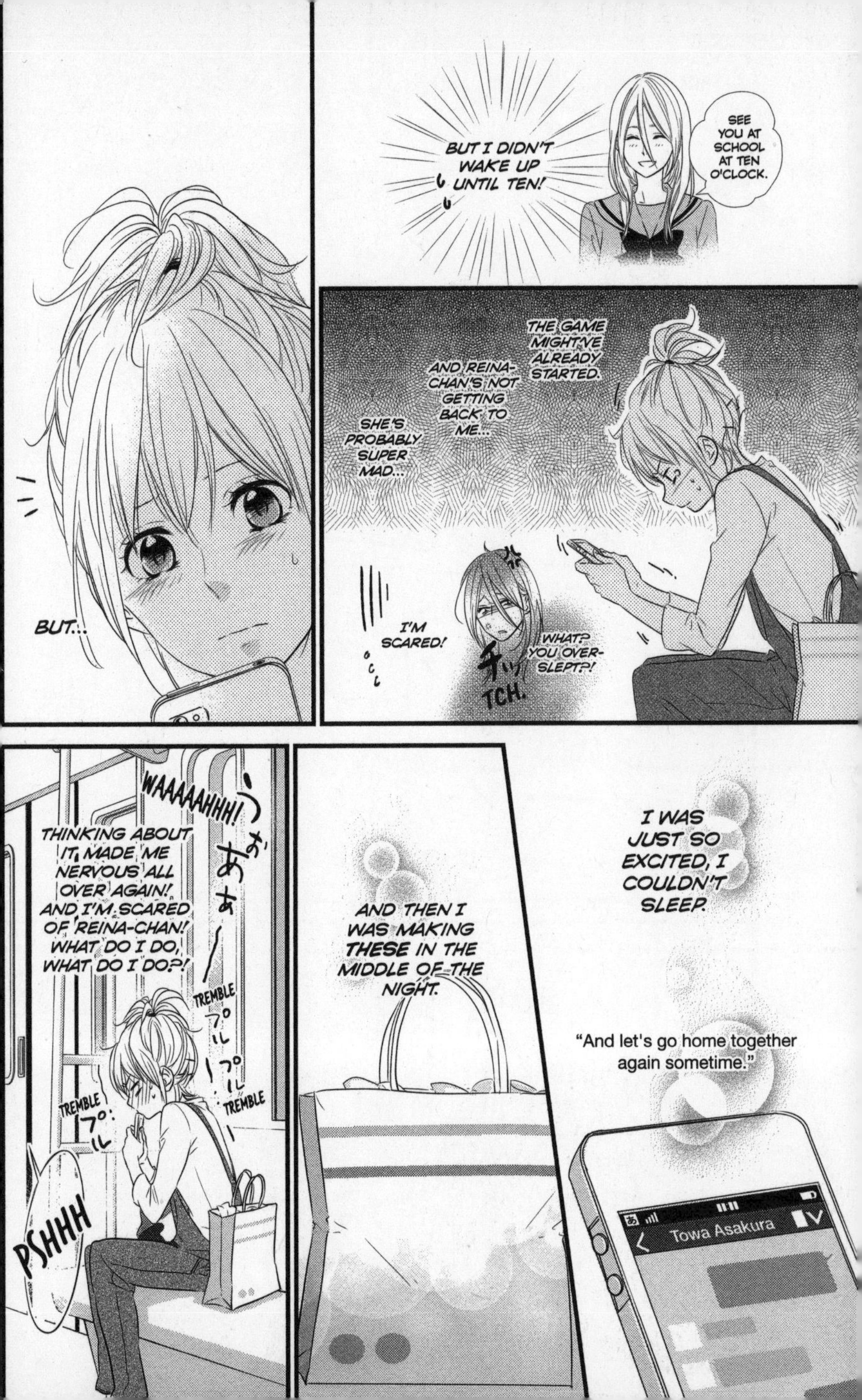
SEE YOU AT SCHOOL AT TEN O'CLOCK.
BUT I DIDN'T WAKE UP UNTIL TEN!
THE GAME MIGHT'VE ALREADY STARTED.
AND REINA-CHAN'S NOT GETTING BACK TO ME...
SHE'S PROBABLY SUPER MAD...
WHAT? YOU OVER-SLEPT?!
チッ
TCH.
I'M SCARED!
BUT...
I WAS JUST SO EXCITED, I COULDN'T SLEEP.
“And let's go home together again sometime.”
Towa Asakura
AND THEN I WAS MAKING THESE IN THE MIDDLE OF THE NIGHT.
うおあぁ
WAAAAAHHH!
THINKING ABOUT IT, MADE ME NERVOUS ALL OVER AGAIN! AND I'M SCARED OF REINA-CHAN! WHAT DO I DO, WHAT DO I DO?!
プルプル
TREMBLE
TREMBLE
プル
TREMBLE
PSHHH

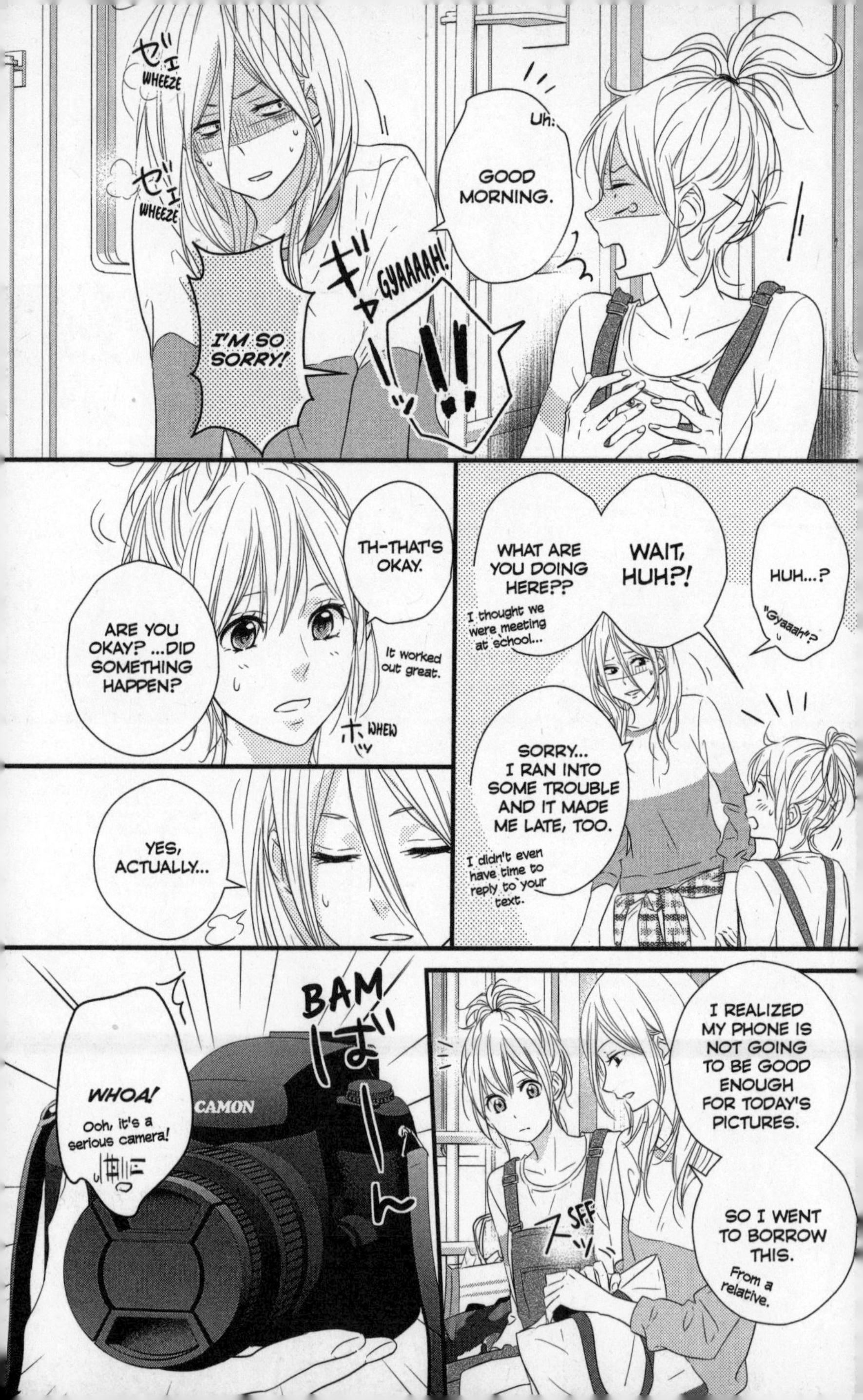

Uh:
GOOD MORNING.
GYAAAAH!
I'M SO SORRY!
WHEEZE
WHEEZE
HUH...?
"Gyaaah"?
WAIT, HUH?!
WHAT ARE YOU DOING HERE??
I thought we were meeting at school...
SORRY... I RAN INTO SOME TROUBLE AND IT MADE ME LATE, TOO.
I didn't even have time to reply to your text.
TH-THAT'S OKAY.
ARE YOU OKAY? ...DID SOMETHING HAPPEN?
It worked out great.
WHEW
YES, ACTUALLY...
I REALIZED MY PHONE IS NOT GOING TO BE GOOD ENOUGH FOR TODAY'S PICTURES.
SO I WENT TO BORROW THIS.
From a relative.
SFF
BAM
WHOA!
Ooh, it's a serious camera!
CAMON

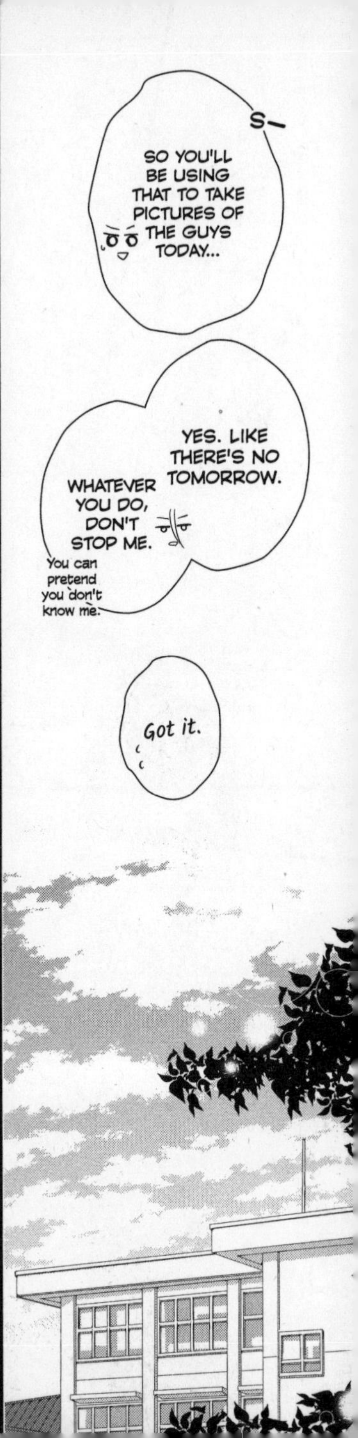
S—
SO YOU'LL BE USING THAT TO TAKE PICTURES OF THE GUYS TODAY...
YES. LIKE THERE'S NO TOMORROW.
WHATEVER YOU DO, DON'T STOP ME.
You can pretend you don't know me.
Got it.
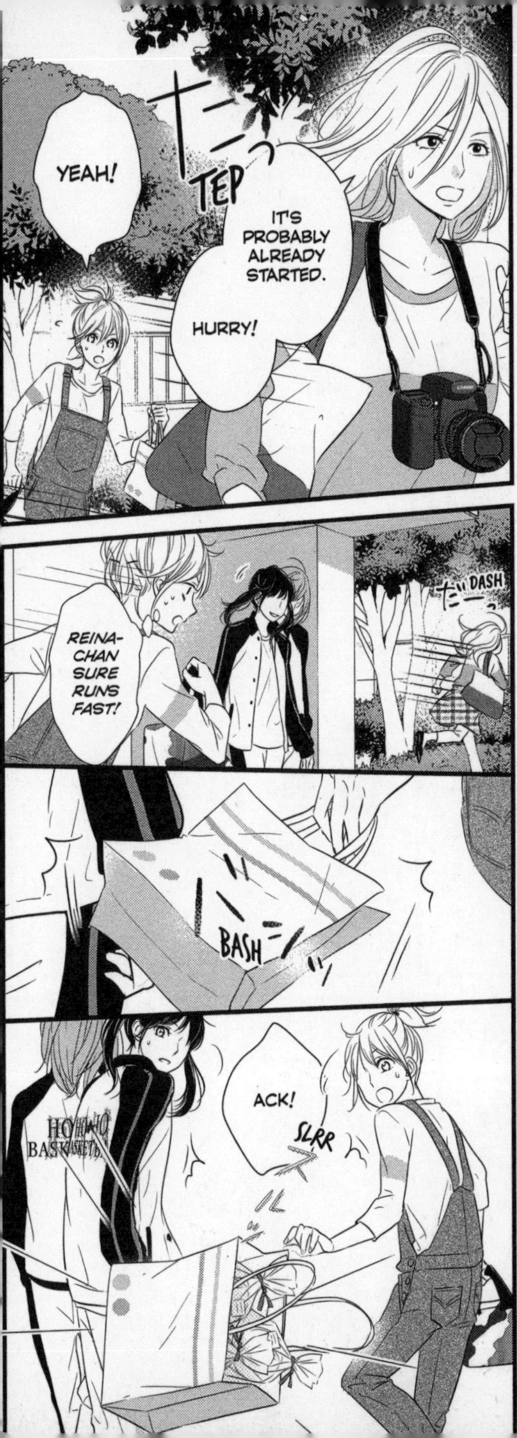
TEP
IT'S PROBABLY ALREADY STARTED.
HURRY!
YEAH!
DASH
REINA-CHAN SURE RUNS FAST!
BASH
ACK!
SLRR

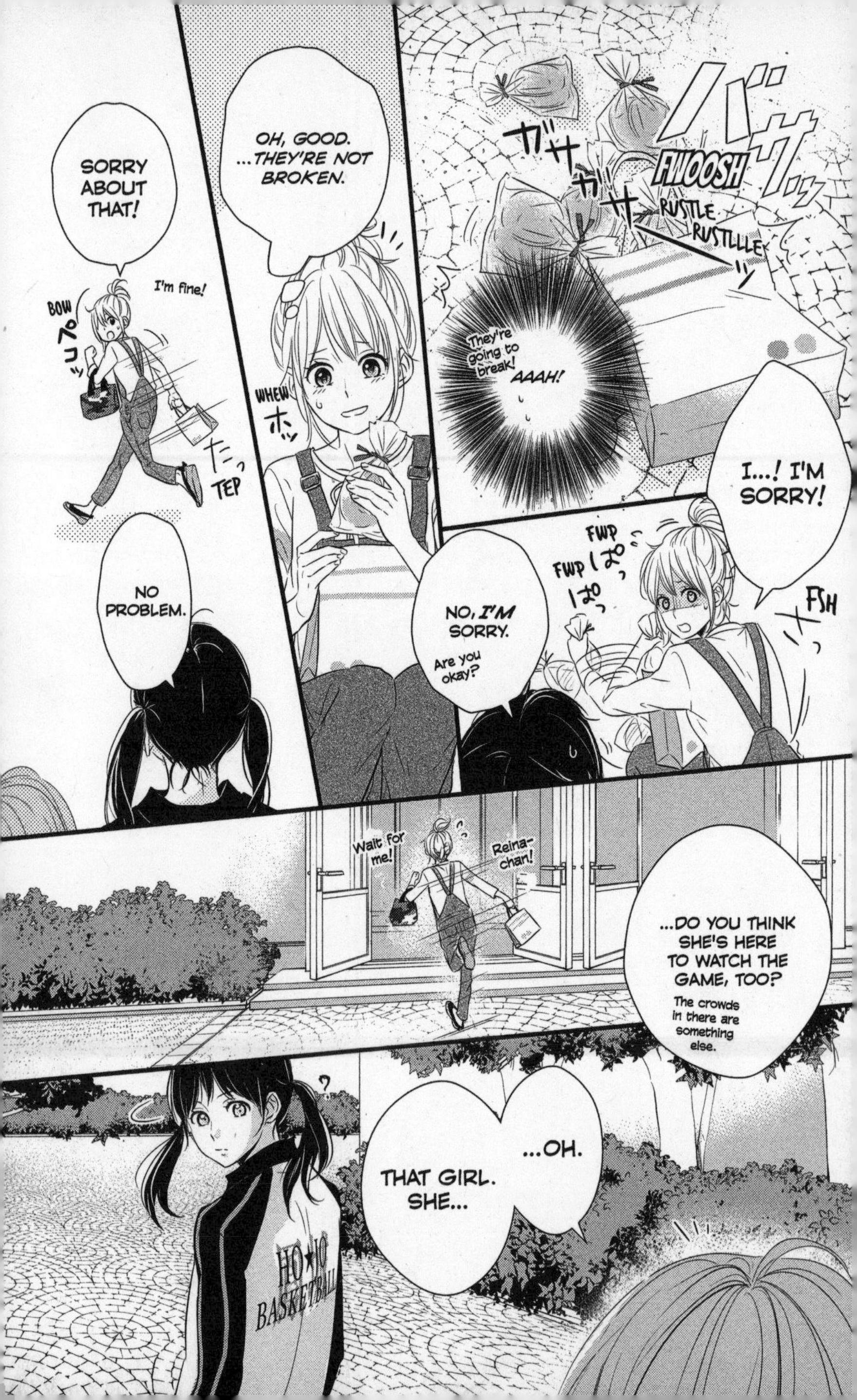
FWOOSH
RUSTLE
RUSTLLLE
They're going to break!
AAAH!
I...! I'M SORRY!
FSH
FWP
FWP
NO, I'M SORRY.
Are you okay?
OH, GOOD. ...THEY'RE NOT BROKEN.
WHEW
SORRY ABOUT THAT!
I'm fine!
BOW
TEP
NO PROBLEM.
...DO YOU THINK SHE'S HERE TO WATCH THE GAME, TOO?
The crowds in there are something else.
Reina-chan!
Wait for me!
...OH.
THAT GIRL. SHE...
HO★JO BASKETBALL

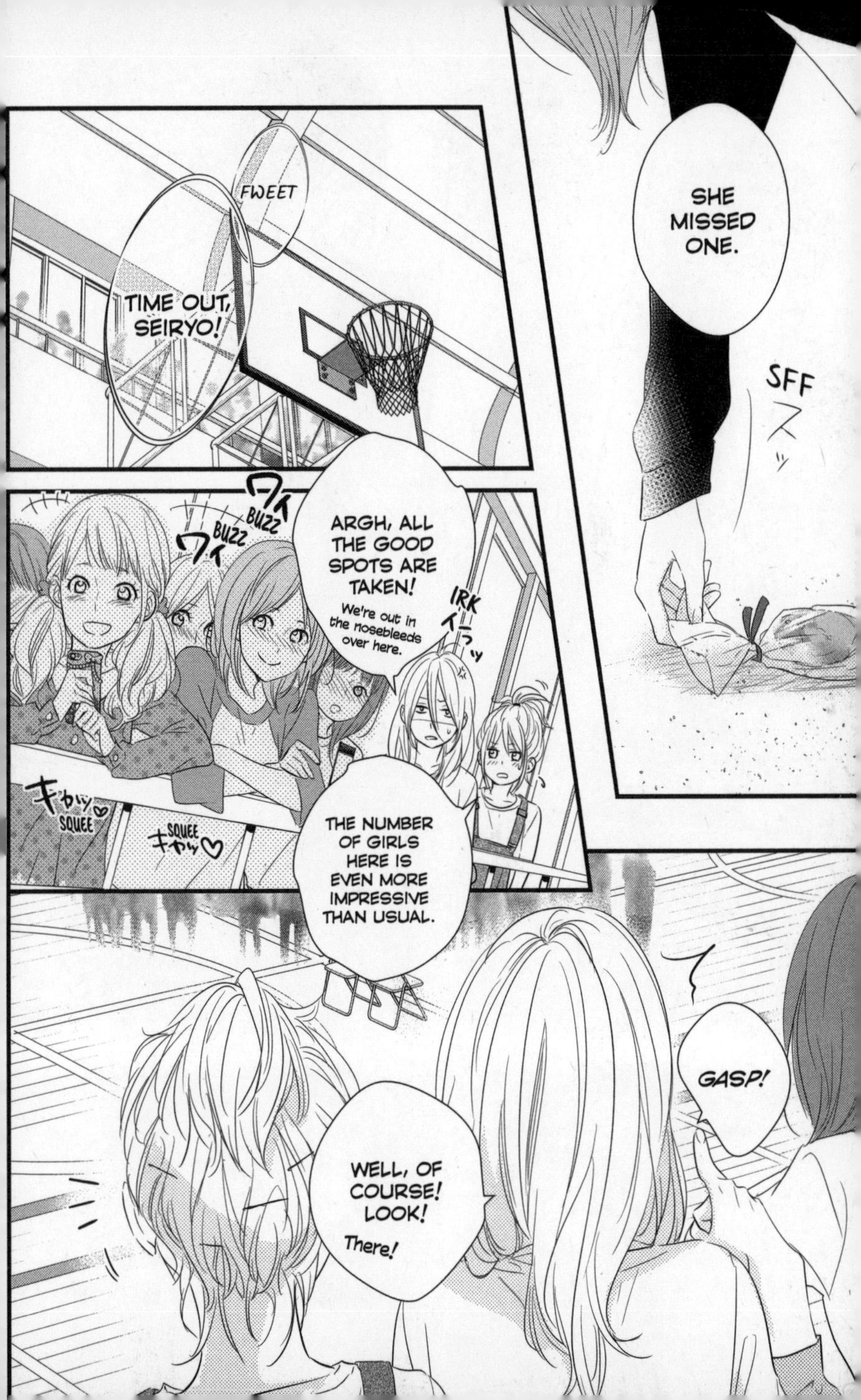
SHE MISSED ONE.
SFF
スッ
FWEET
TIME OUT, SEIRYO!
ARGH, ALL THE GOOD SPOTS ARE TAKEN!
We're out in the nosebleeds over here.
IRK
イラッ
ワイ
BUZZ
BUZZ
ワイ
THE NUMBER OF GIRLS HERE IS EVEN MORE IMPRESSIVE THAN USUAL.
SQUEE
キャッ♡
キャッ♡
SQUEE
GASP!
WELL, OF COURSE! LOOK!
There!

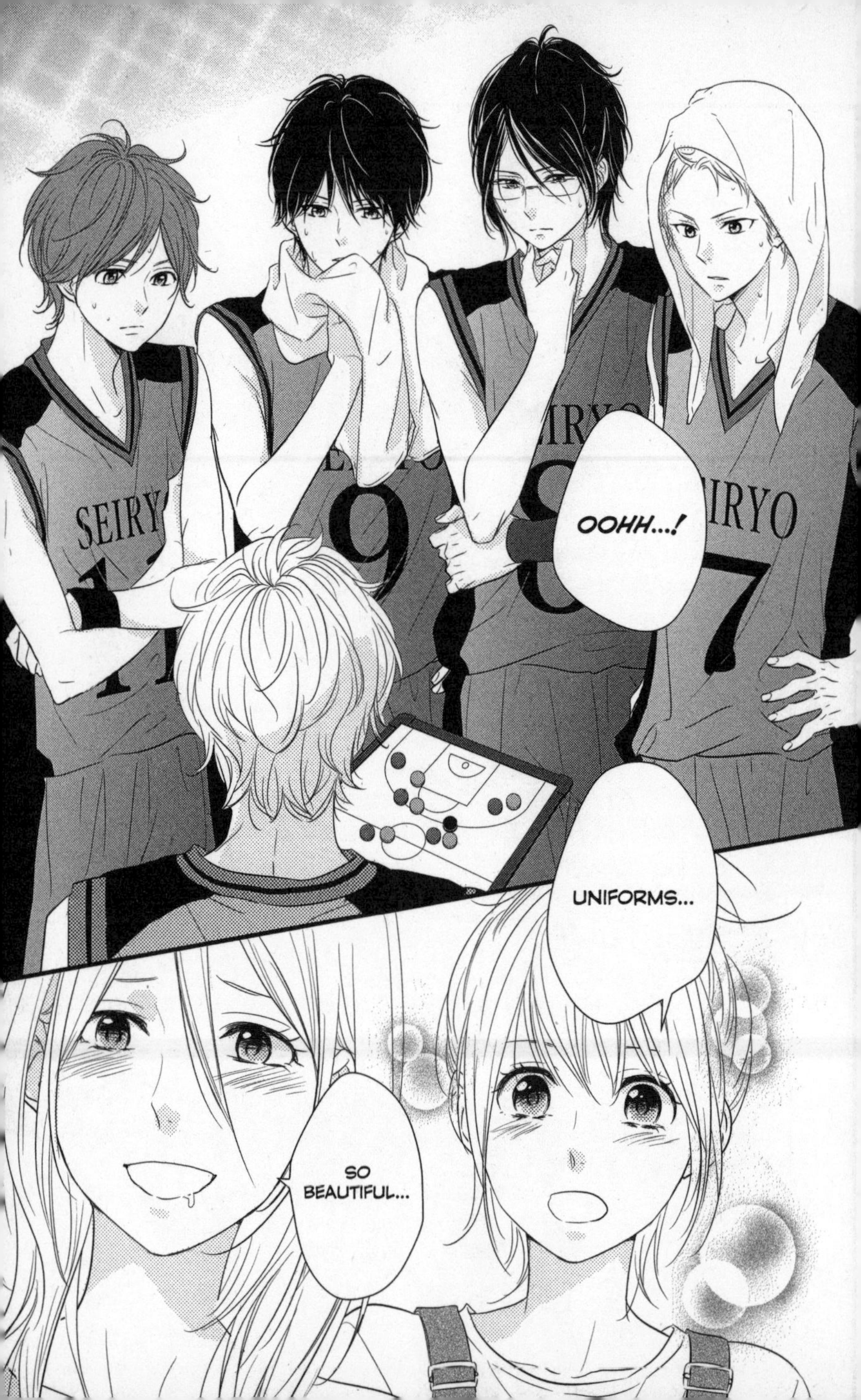
OOHH...!
UNIFORMS...
SO BEAUTIFUL...

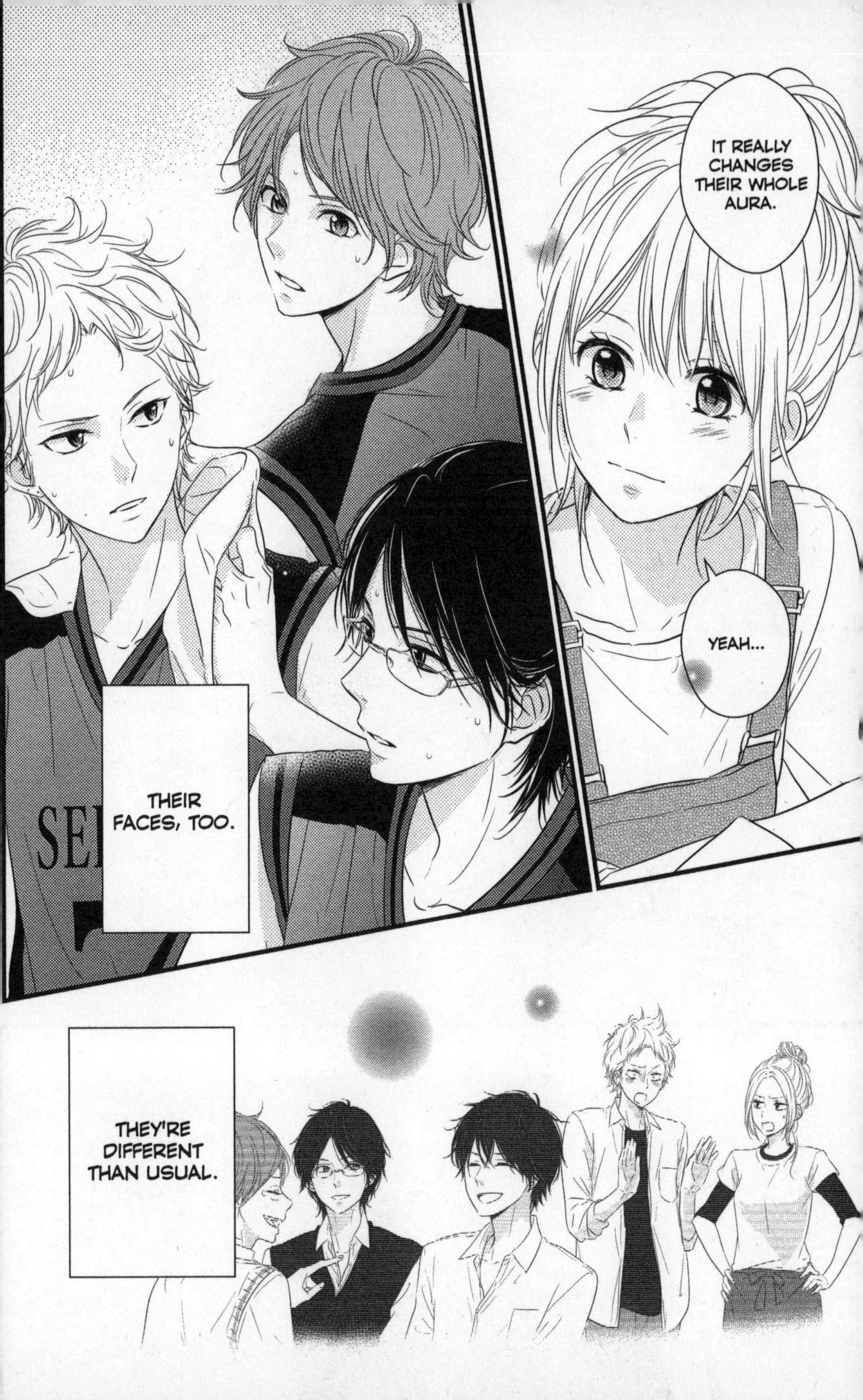
IT REALLY CHANGES THEIR WHOLE AURA.
YEAH...
THEIR FACES, TOO.
THEY'RE DIFFERENT THAN USUAL.

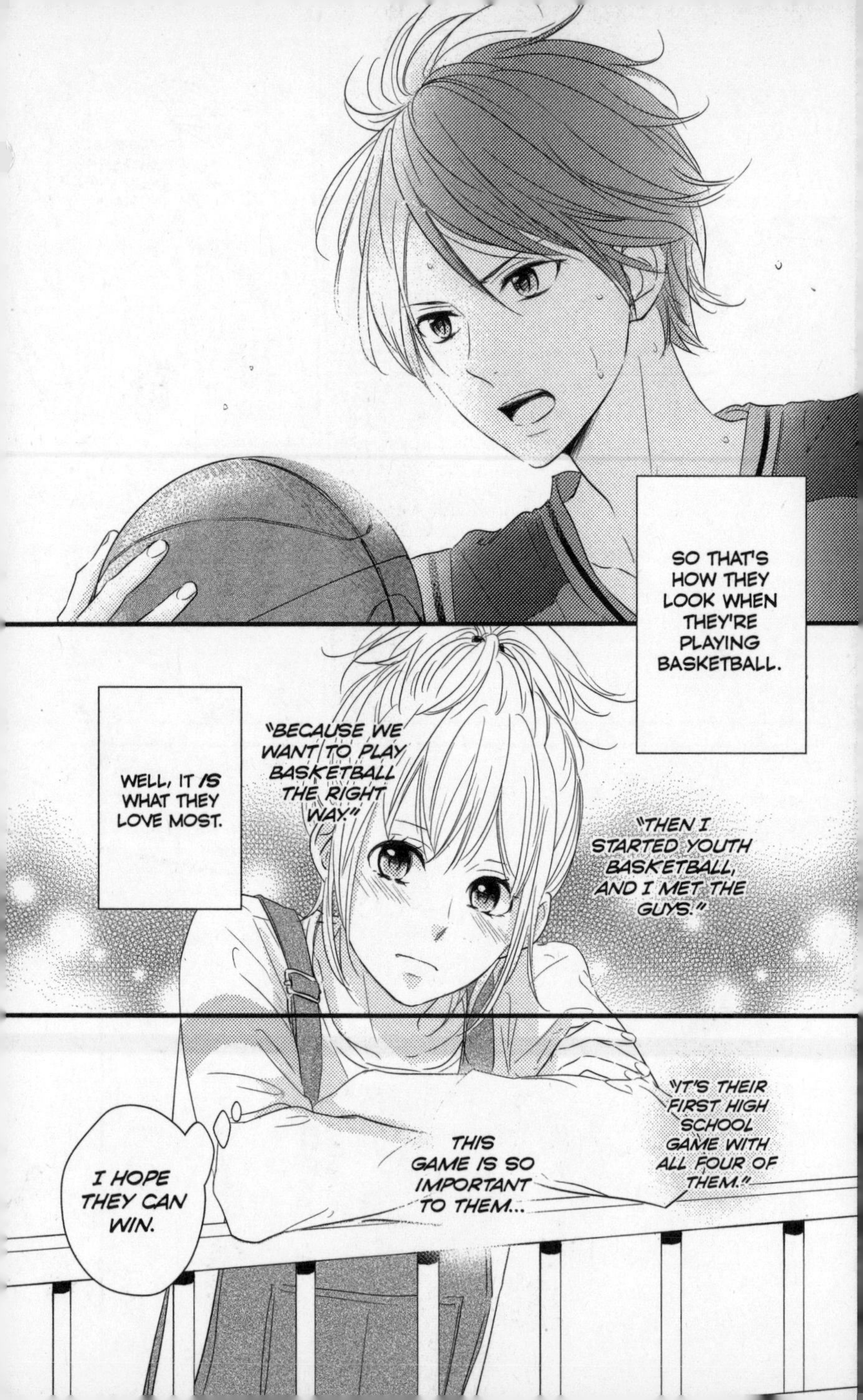
SO THAT'S HOW THEY LOOK WHEN THEY'RE PLAYING BASKETBALL.
"THEN I STARTED YOUTH BASKETBALL, AND I MET THE GUYS."
"BECAUSE WE WANT TO PLAY BASKETBALL THE RIGHT WAY."
WELL, IT *IS* WHAT THEY LOVE MOST.
"IT'S THEIR FIRST HIGH SCHOOL GAME WITH ALL FOUR OF THEM."
THIS GAME IS SO IMPORTANT TO THEM...
I HOPE THEY CAN WIN.

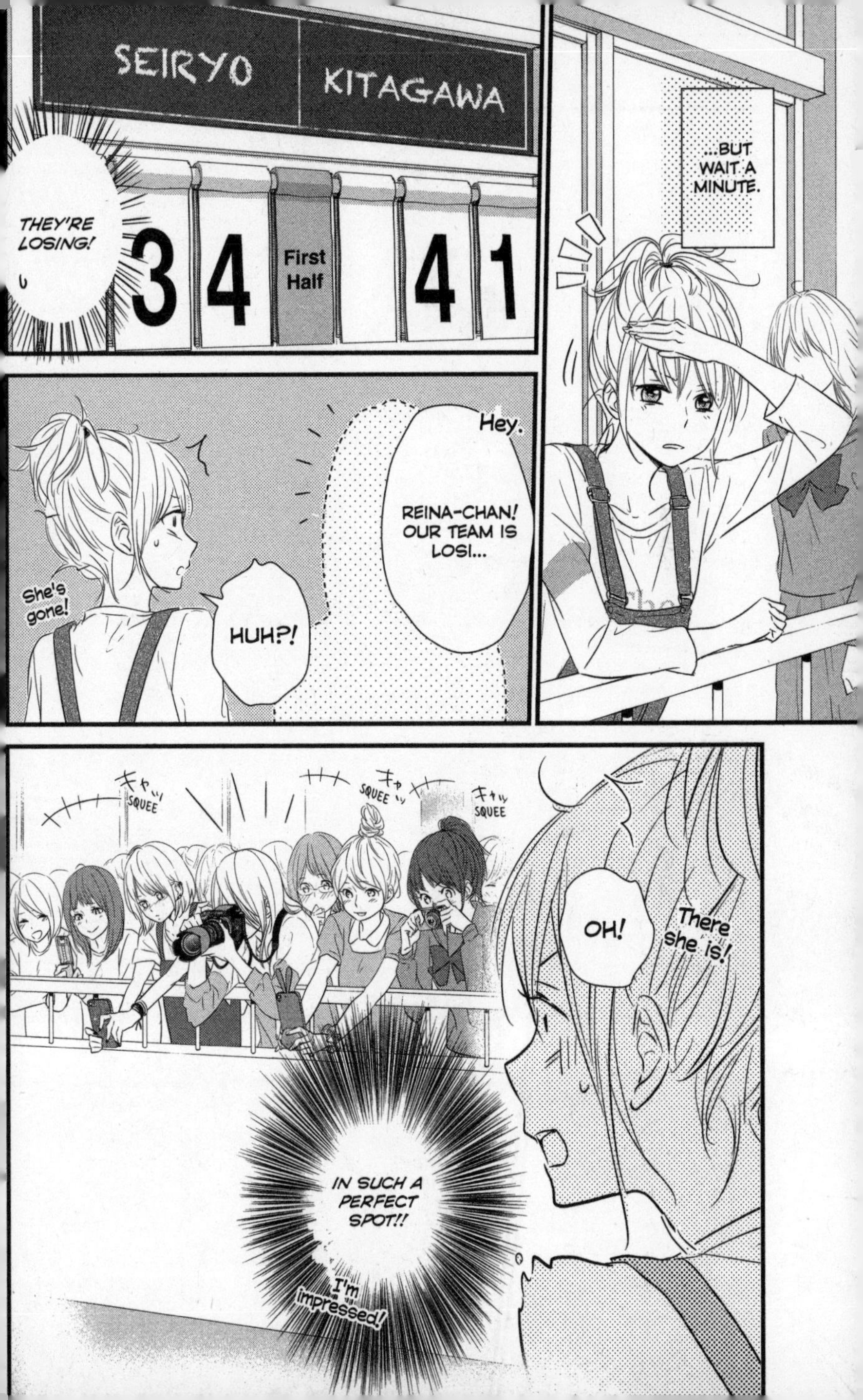
...BUT WAIT A MINUTE.
SEIRYO
KITAGAWA
34
First Half
41
THEY'RE LOSING!
Hey.
REINA-CHAN! OUR TEAM IS LOSI...
HUH?!
She's gone!
OH!
There she is!
キャッ SQUEE
キャッ SQUEE
キャッ SQUEE
IN SUCH A PERFECT SPOT!!
I'm impressed!

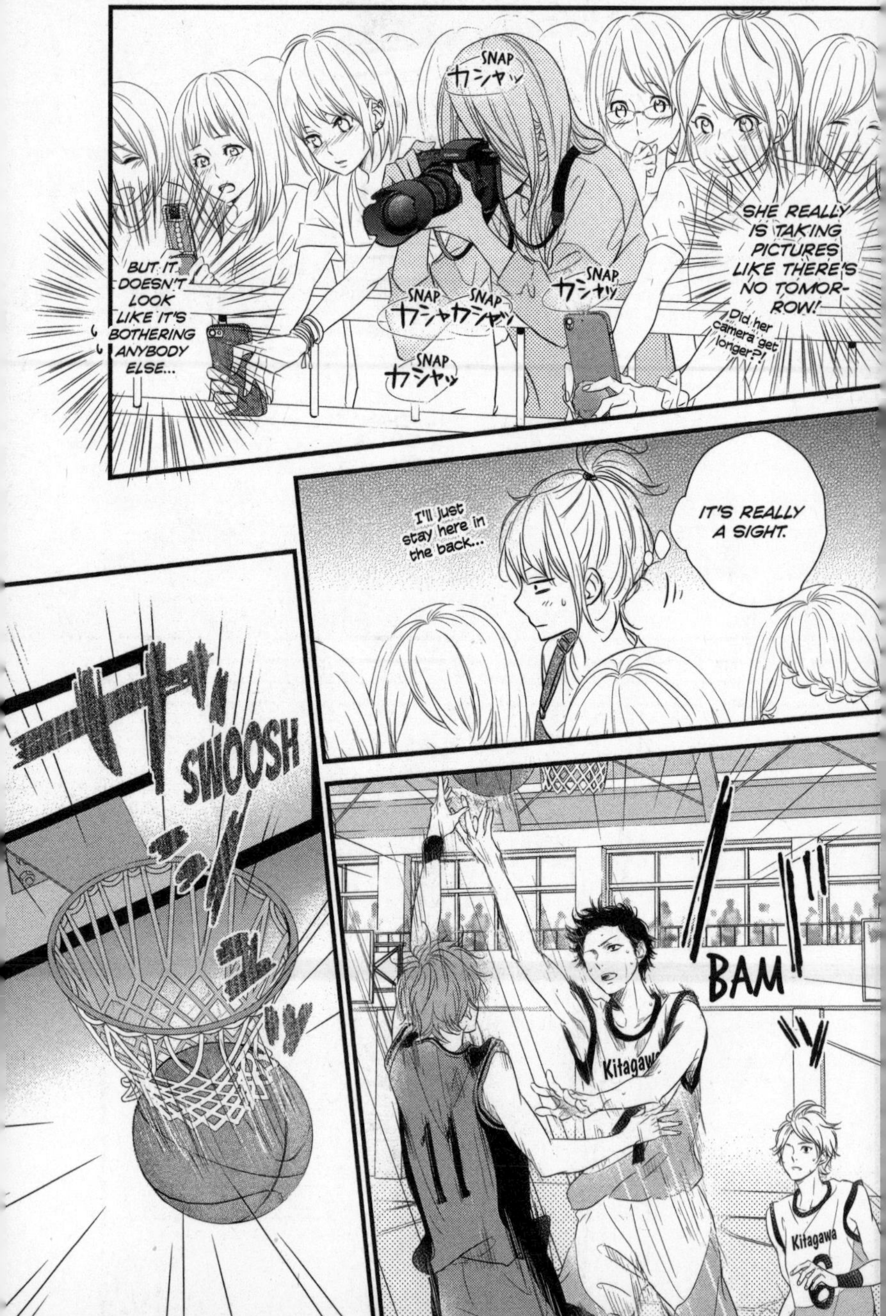
SHE REALLY IS TAKING PICTURES LIKE THERE'S NO TOMORROW!
Did her camera get longer?!
SNAP カシャッ
SNAP カシャッ
SNAP SNAP カシャカシャッ
SNAP カシャッ
BUT IT DOESN'T LOOK LIKE IT'S BOTHERING ANYBODY ELSE...
IT'S REALLY A SIGHT.
I'll just stay here in the back...
BAM
Kitagawa
Kitagawa
SWOOSH

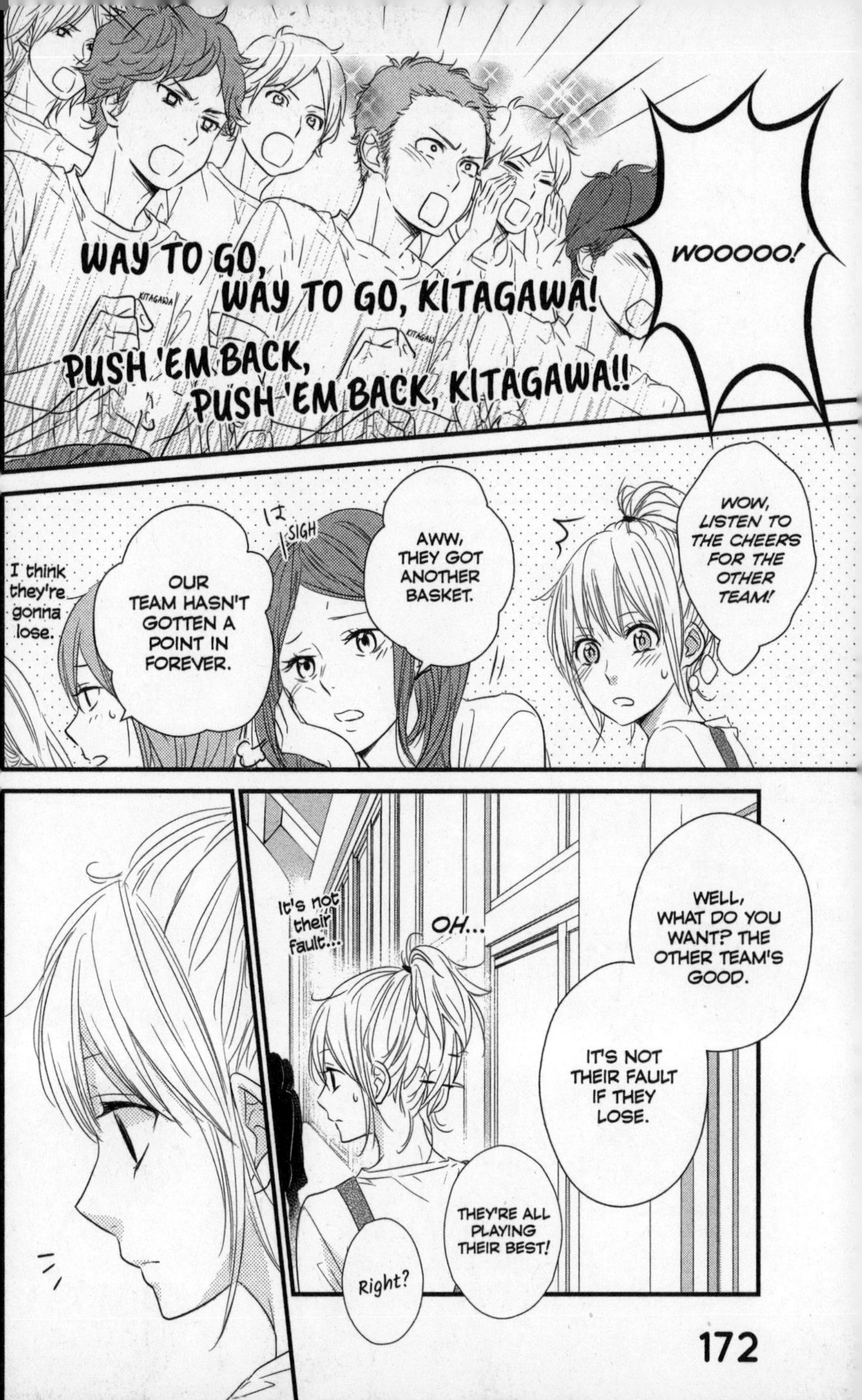
WOOOOO!
WAY TO GO, WAY TO GO, KITAGAWA!
PUSH 'EM BACK, PUSH 'EM BACK, KITAGAWA!!
WOW, LISTEN TO THE CHEERS FOR THE OTHER TEAM!
AWW, THEY GOT ANOTHER BASKET.
は SIGH
OUR TEAM HASN'T GOTTEN A POINT IN FOREVER.
I think they're gonna lose.
WELL, WHAT DO YOU WANT? THE OTHER TEAM'S GOOD.
IT'S NOT THEIR FAULT IF THEY LOSE.
OH...
It's not their fault...
THEY'RE ALL PLAYING THEIR BEST!
Right?

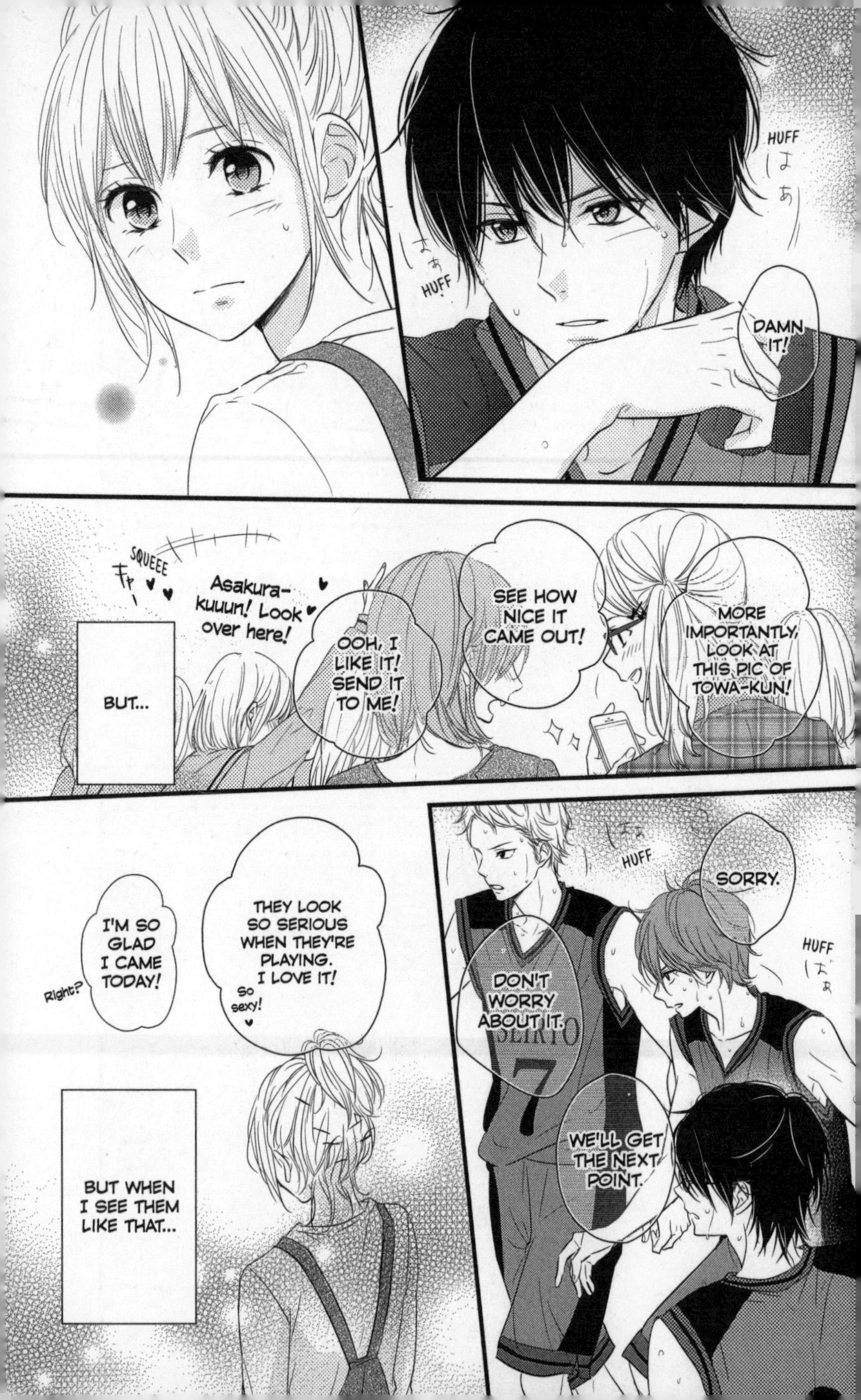

HUFF
はあ
DAMN IT!
HUFF
MORE IMPORTANTLY, LOOK AT THIS PIC OF TOWA-KUN!
SEE HOW NICE IT CAME OUT!
OOH, I LIKE IT! SEND IT TO ME!
Asakura-kuuun! Look over here!
SQUEEE
BUT...
SORRY.
HUFF
HUFF
DON'T WORRY ABOUT IT.
WE'LL GET THE NEXT POINT.
THEY LOOK SO SERIOUS WHEN THEY'RE PLAYING. I LOVE IT!
So sexy!
I'M SO GLAD I CAME TODAY!
Right?
BUT WHEN I SEE THEM LIKE THAT...

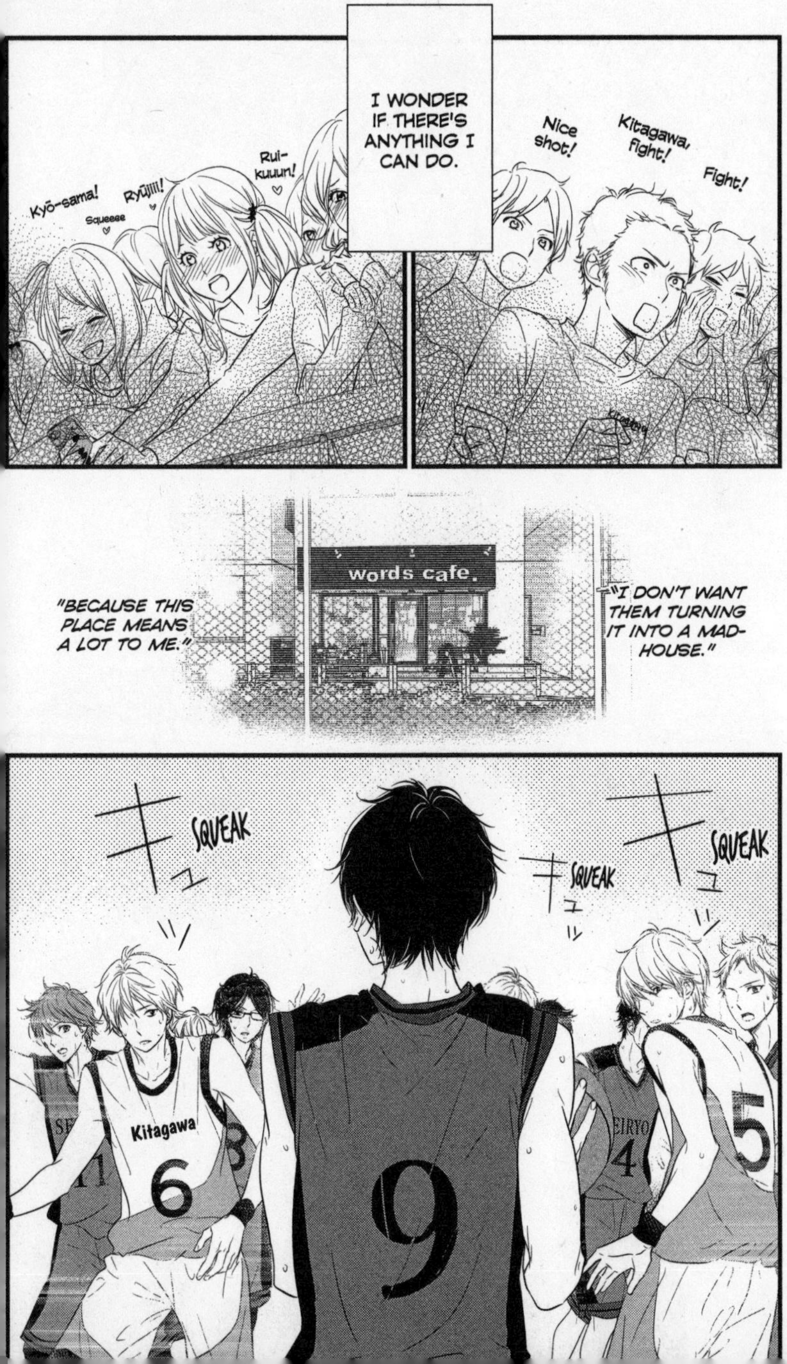
Fight!
Kitagawa, fight!
Nice shot!
I WONDER IF THERE'S ANYTHING I CAN DO.
Rui-kuuun!
Ryūjiii!
Kyō-sama!
Squeeee
"I DON'T WANT THEM TURNING IT INTO A MAD-HOUSE."
words cafe.
"BECAUSE THIS PLACE MEANS A LOT TO ME."
SQUEAK
SQUEAK
SQUEAK
Kitagawa

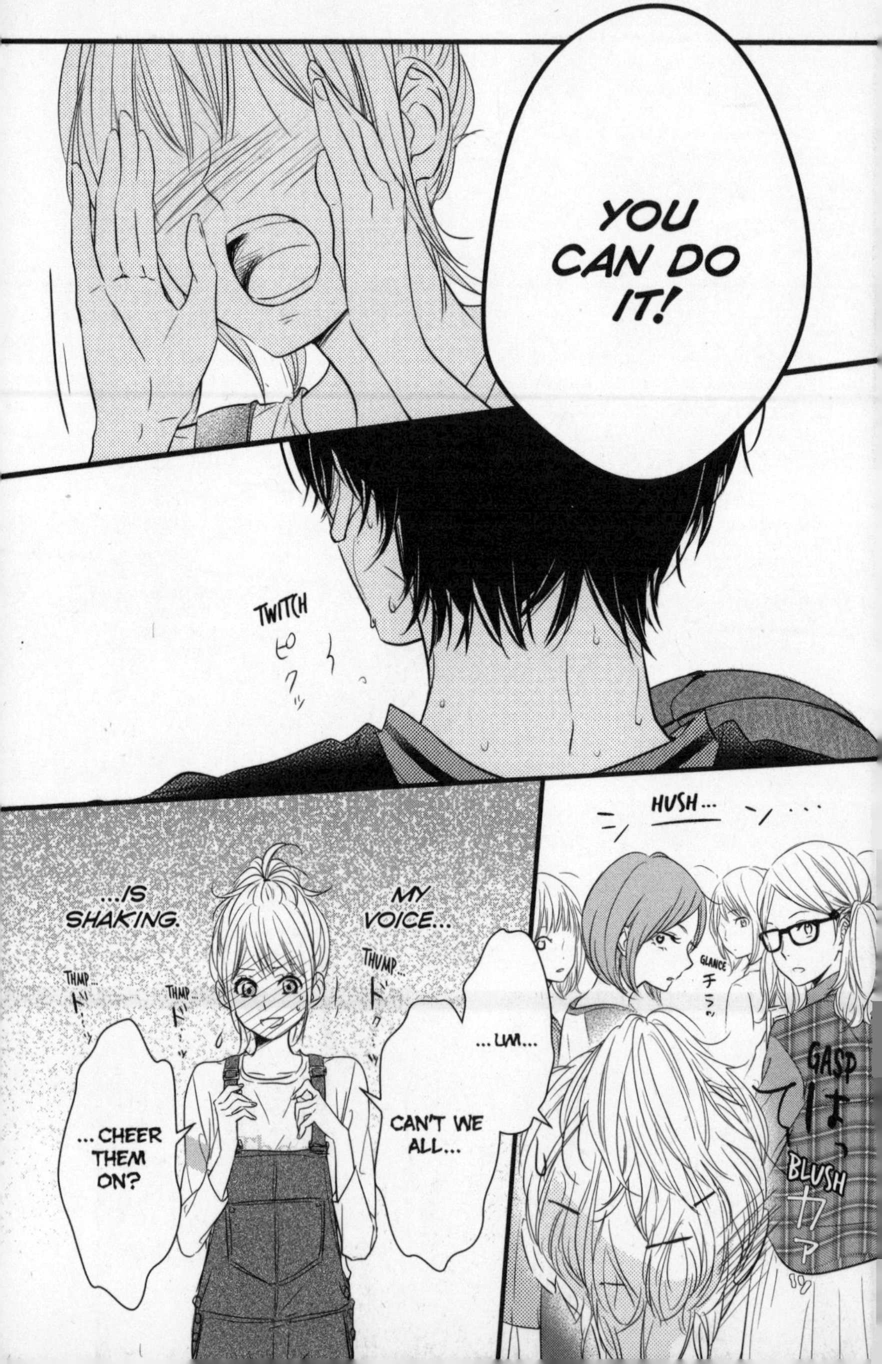

YOU CAN DO IT!
TWITCH
ピクッ
HUSH...
GLANCE
チラッ
GASP
はっ
BLUSH
カァッ
MY VOICE...
THUMP...
...IS SHAKING.
THMP...
THMP...
...UM...
CAN'T WE ALL...
...CHEER THEM ON?

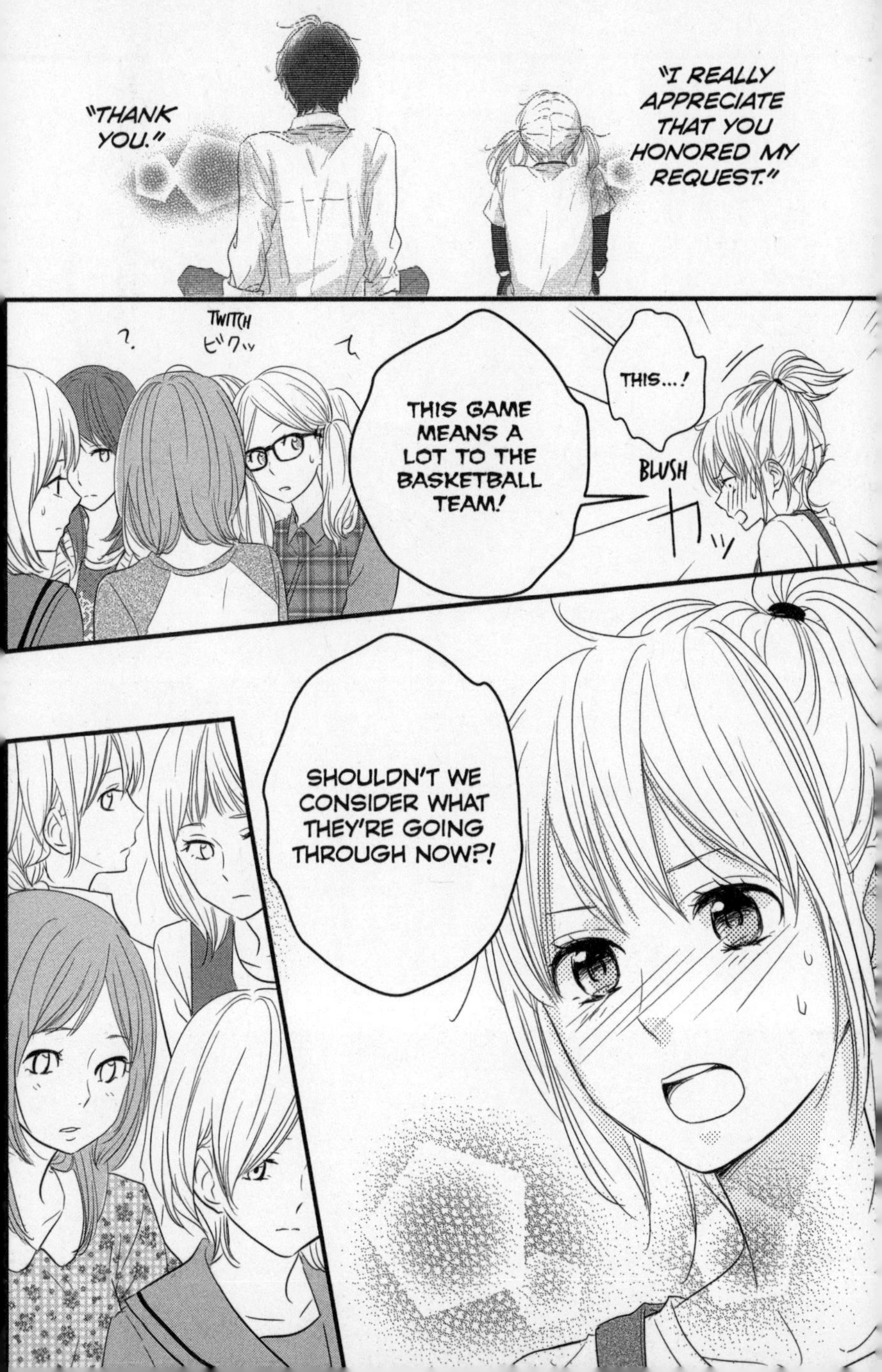
"I REALLY APPRECIATE THAT YOU HONORED MY REQUEST."
"THANK YOU."
THIS...!
BLUSH
カッ
THIS GAME MEANS A LOT TO THE BASKETBALL TEAM!
TWITCH
ビクッ
SHOULDN'T WE CONSIDER WHAT THEY'RE GOING THROUGH NOW?!

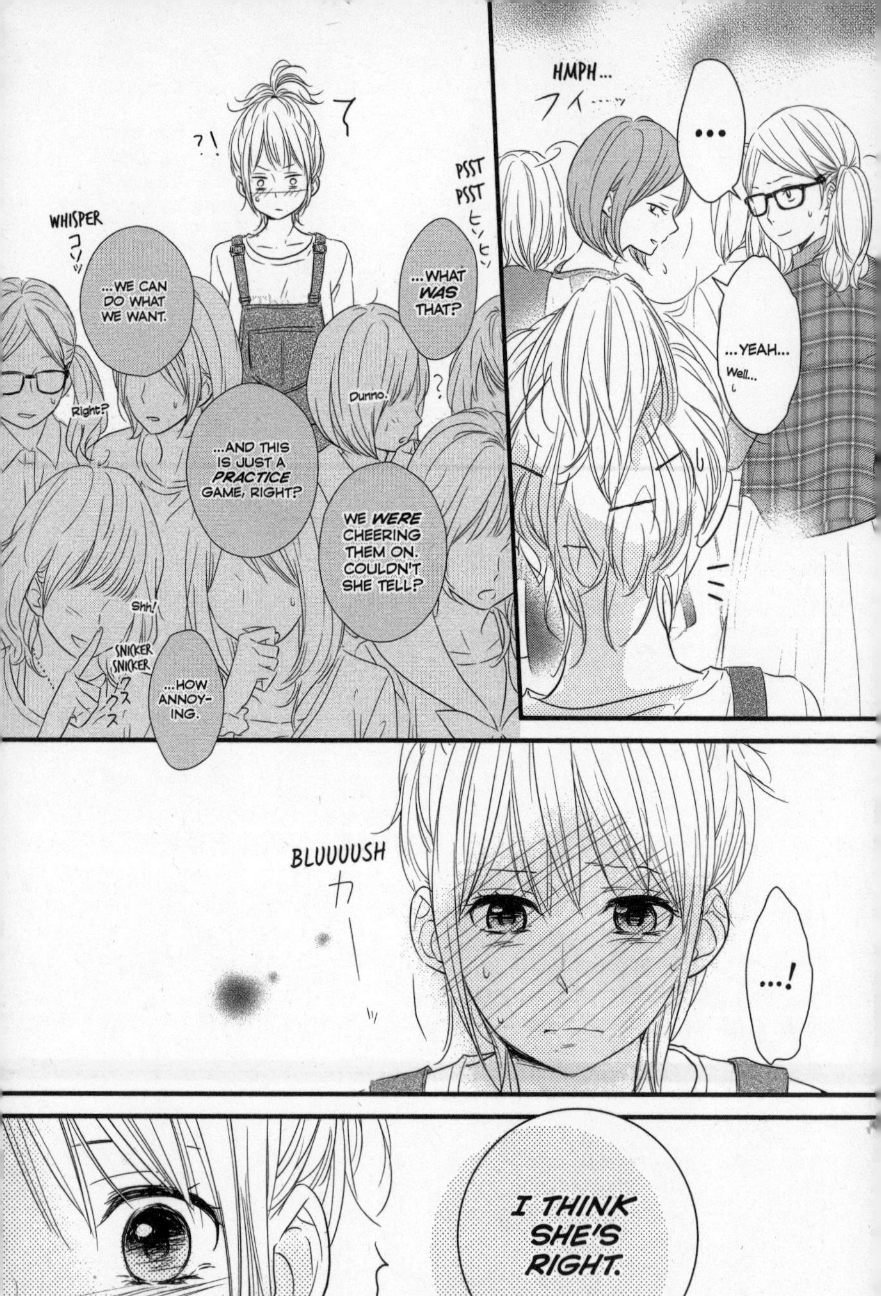
HMPH...
フイ…ッ
...
...YEAH...
Well...
?!
PSST PSST
ヒソヒソ
...WHAT WAS THAT?
Dunno.
?
WHISPER
コソッ
...WE CAN DO WHAT WE WANT.
Right?
...AND THIS IS JUST A PRACTICE GAME, RIGHT?
WE WERE CHEERING THEM ON. COULDN'T SHE TELL?
Shh!
SNICKER SNICKER
クスクス
...HOW ANNOY-ING.
...!
BLUUUUSH
カーッ
I THINK SHE'S RIGHT.

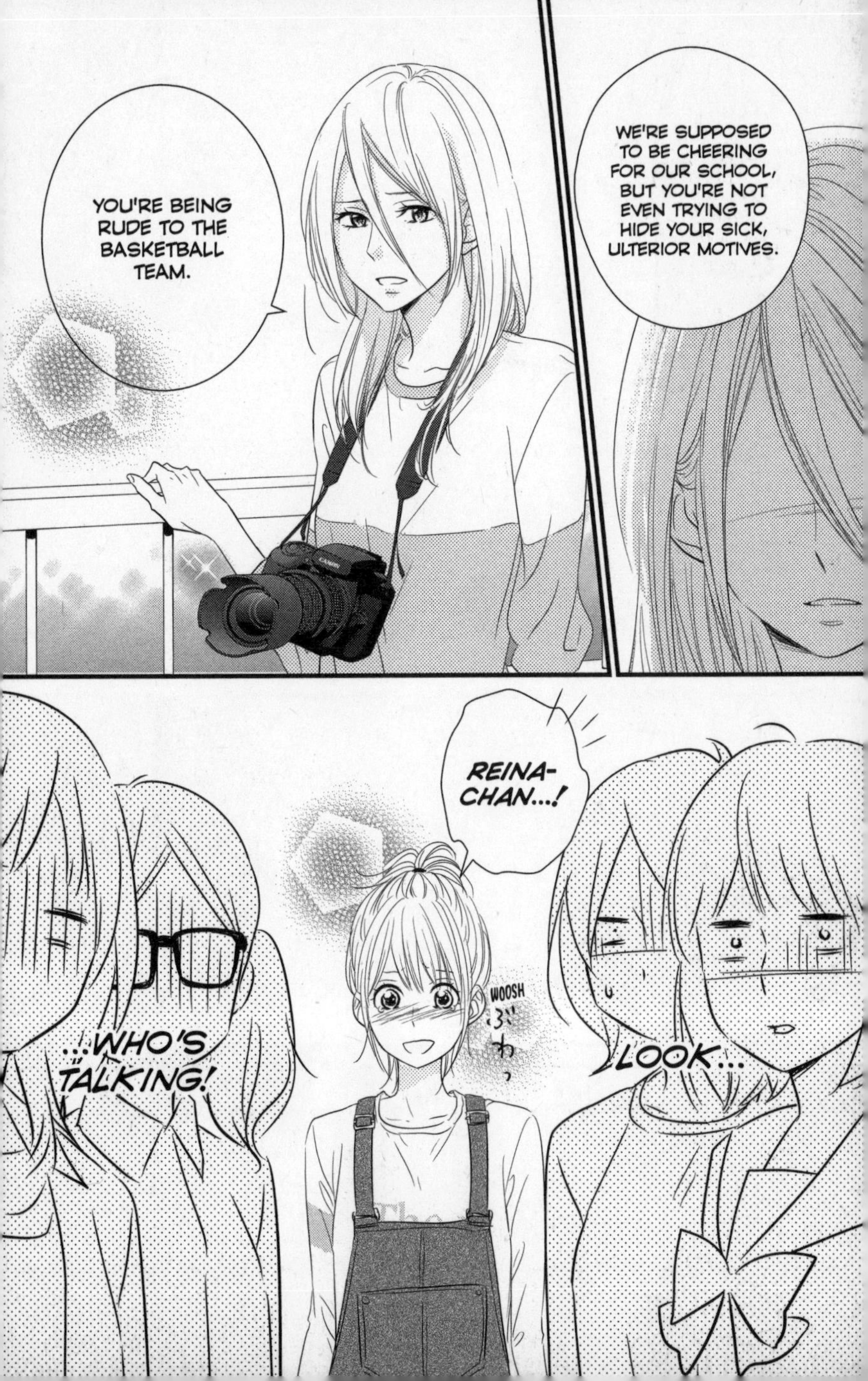
WE'RE SUPPOSED TO BE CHEERING FOR OUR SCHOOL, BUT YOU'RE NOT EVEN TRYING TO HIDE YOUR SICK, ULTERIOR MOTIVES.
YOU'RE BEING RUDE TO THE BASKETBALL TEAM.
REINA-CHAN...!
LOOK...
WOOSH
ぶわっ
...WHO'S TALKING!

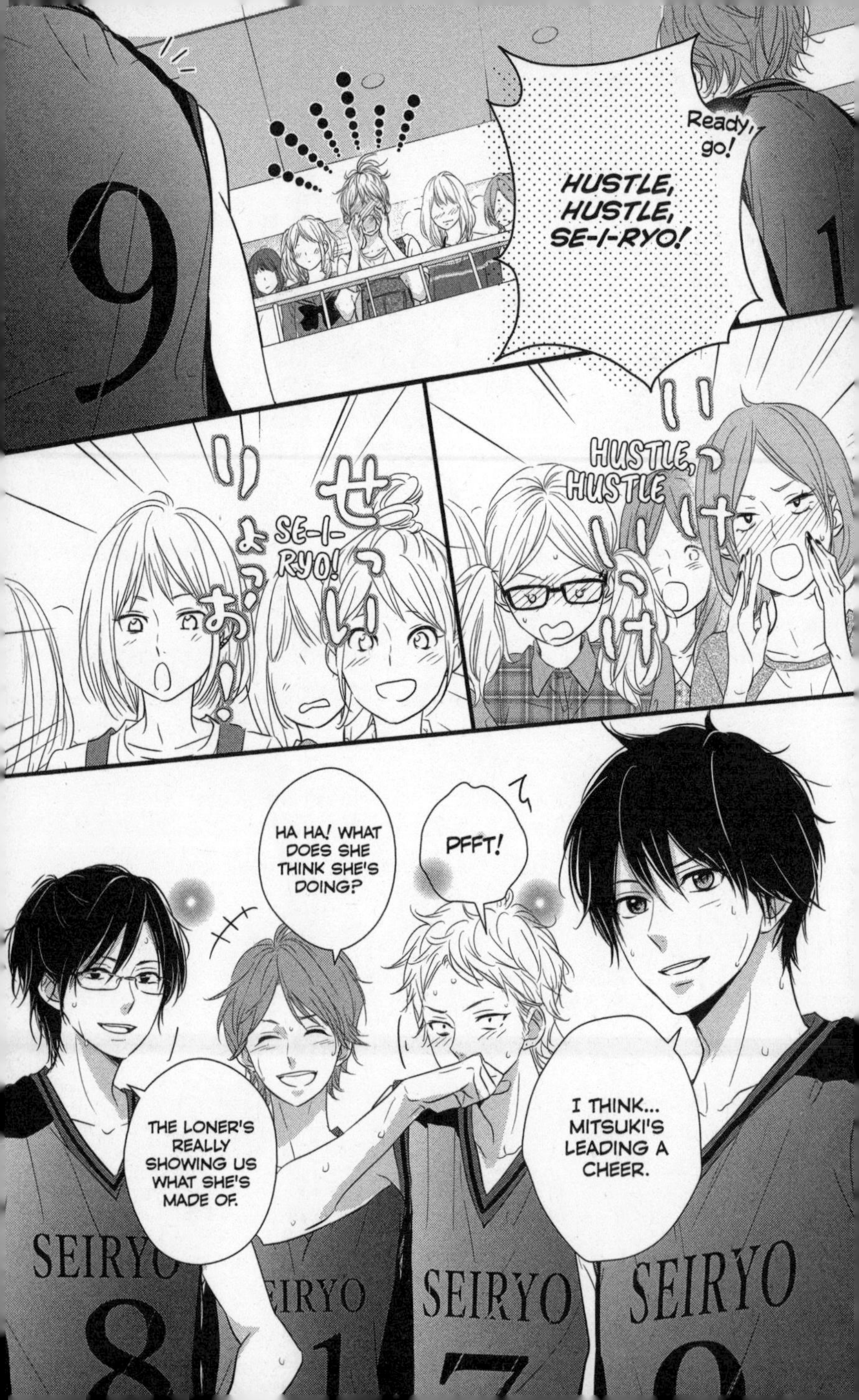

Ready, go!
HUSTLE, HUSTLE, SE-I-RYO!
HUSTLE, HUSTLE
SE-I-RYO!
PFFT!
HA HA! WHAT DOES SHE THINK SHE'S DOING?
I THINK... MITSUKI'S LEADING A CHEER.
THE LONER'S REALLY SHOWING US WHAT SHE'S MADE OF.

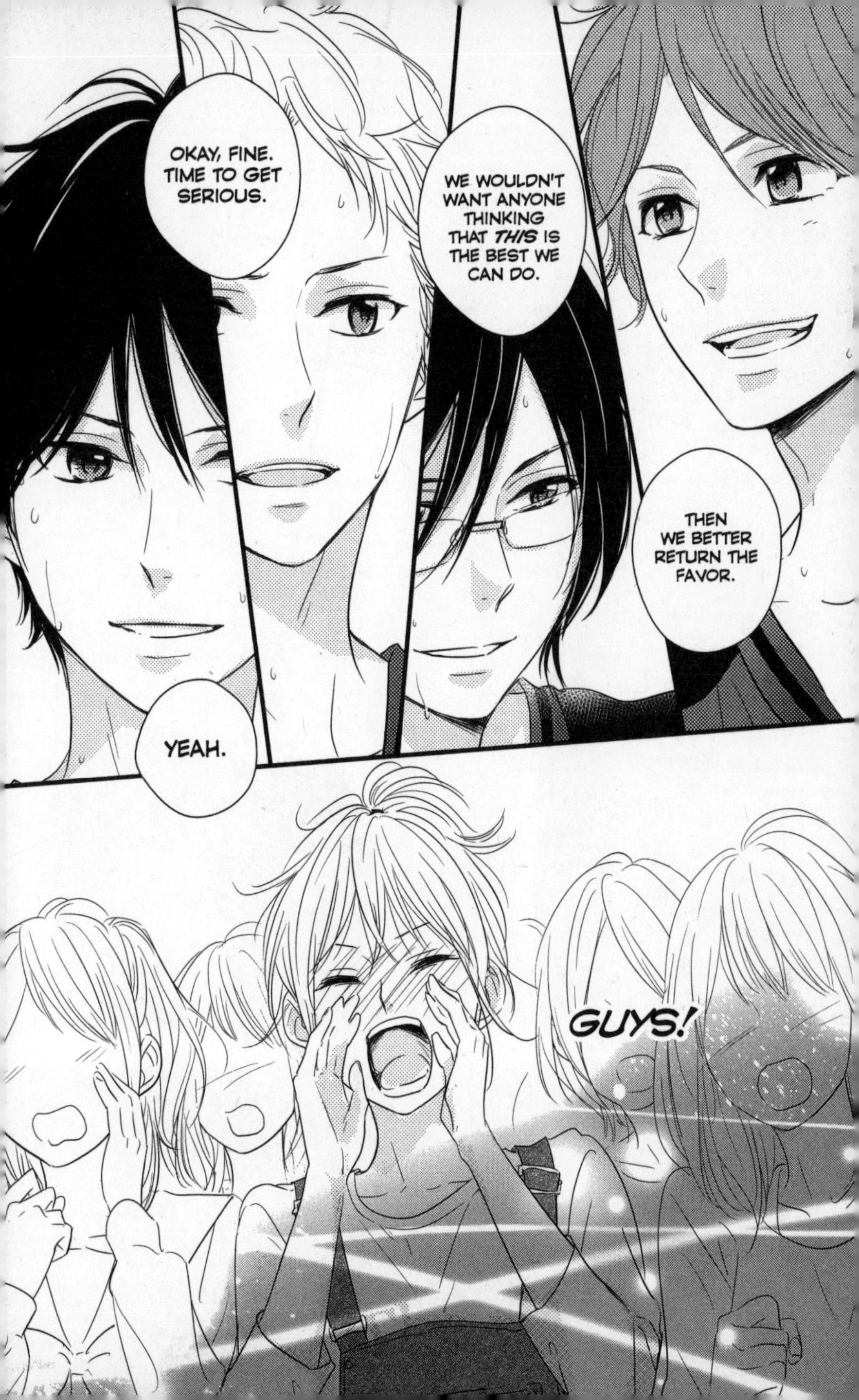
WE WOULDN'T WANT ANYONE THINKING THAT *THIS* IS THE BEST WE CAN DO.
THEN WE BETTER RETURN THE FAVOR.
OKAY, FINE. TIME TO GET SERIOUS.
YEAH.
GUYS!

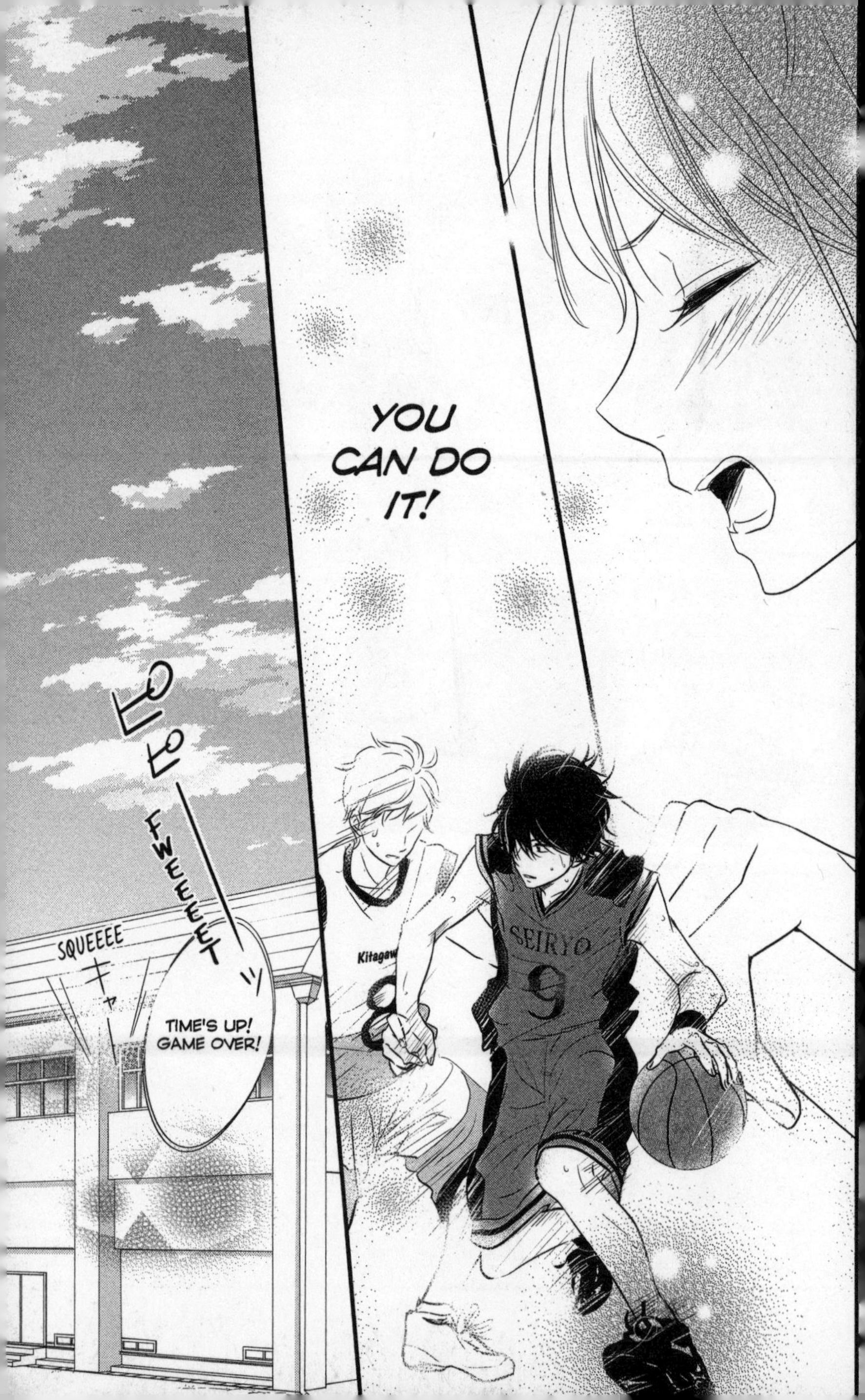
SEIRYO
YOU CAN DO IT!
ピピーッ
FWEEEEET
TIME'S UP! GAME OVER!
キャー
SQUEEEE

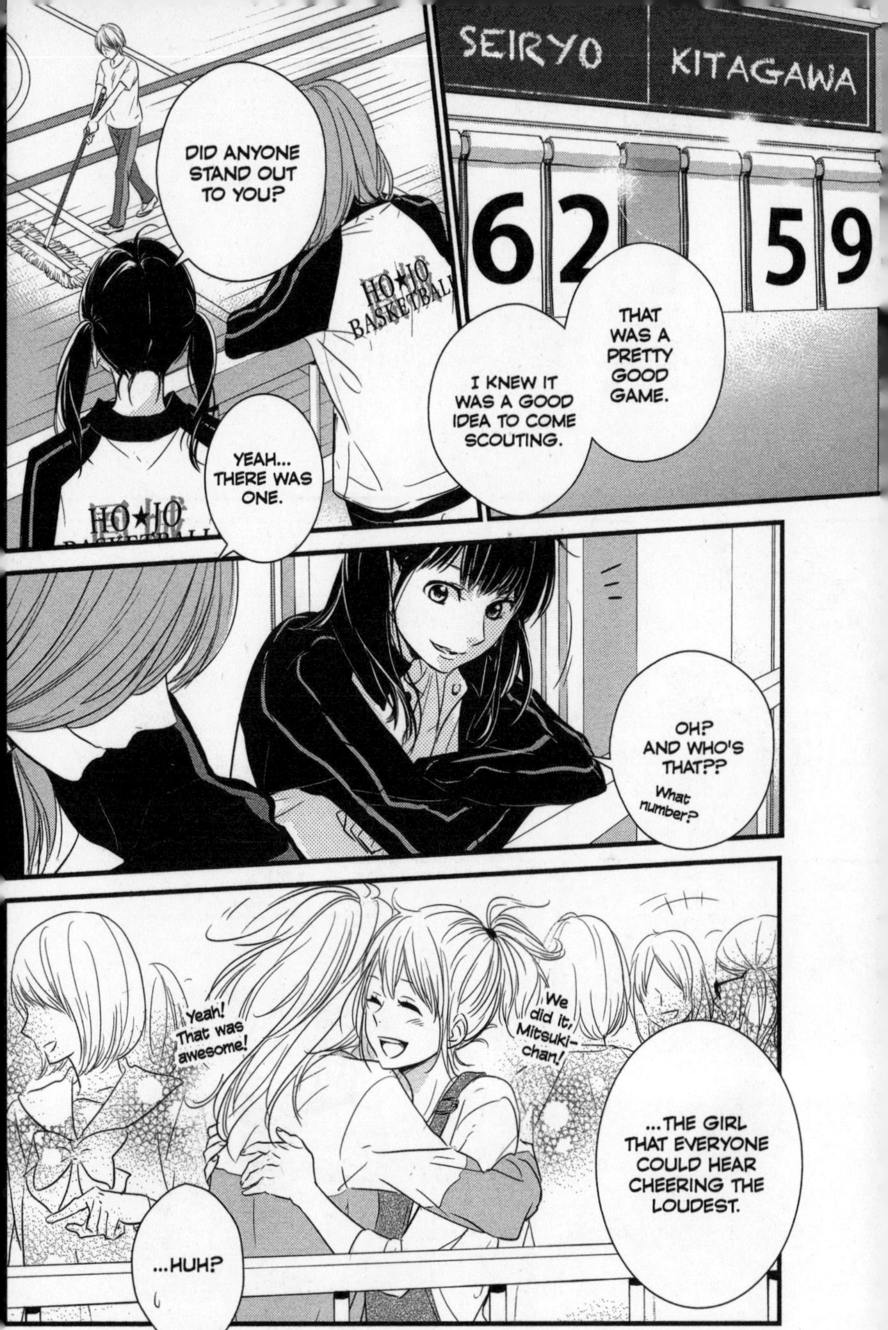
SEIRYO
KITAGAWA
62
59
THAT WAS A PRETTY GOOD GAME.
I KNEW IT WAS A GOOD IDEA TO COME SCOUTING.
DID ANYONE STAND OUT TO YOU?
YEAH... THERE WAS ONE.
OH? AND WHO'S THAT??
What number?
...THE GIRL THAT EVERYONE COULD HEAR CHEERING THE LOUDEST.
We did it, Mitsuki-chan!
Yeah! That was awesome!
...HUH?

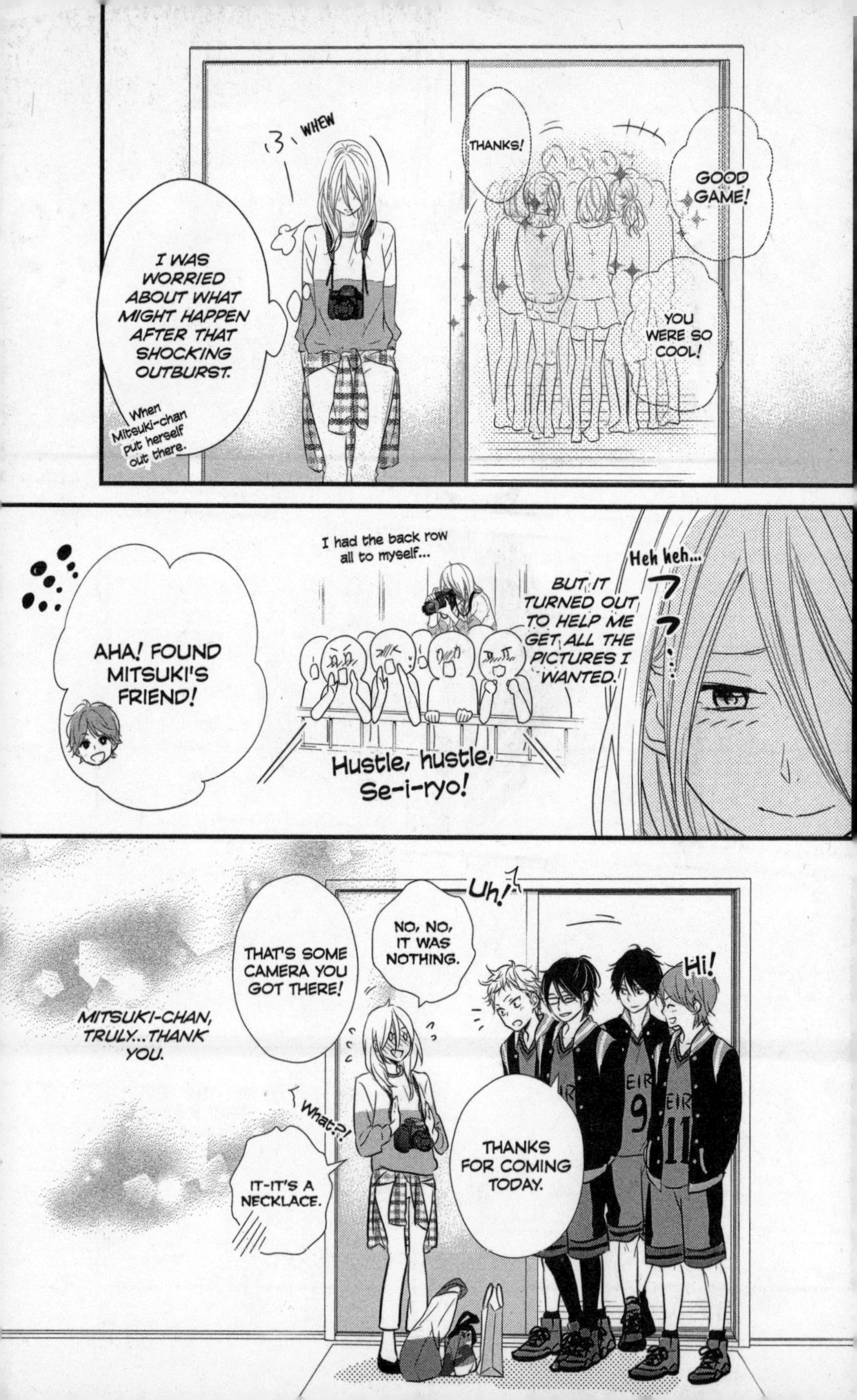
GOOD GAME!
YOU WERE SO COOL!
THANKS!
WHEW
I WAS WORRIED ABOUT WHAT MIGHT HAPPEN AFTER THAT SHOCKING OUTBURST.
When Mitsuki-chan put herself out there.
Heh heh...
BUT IT TURNED OUT TO HELP ME GET ALL THE PICTURES I WANTED.
I had the back row all to myself...
Hustle, hustle, Se-i-ryo!
AHA! FOUND MITSUKI'S FRIEND!
Hi!
THANKS FOR COMING TODAY.
Uh!
NO, NO, IT WAS NOTHING.
THAT'S SOME CAMERA YOU GOT THERE!
What?!
IT-IT'S A NECKLACE.
MITSUKI-CHAN, TRULY...THANK YOU.

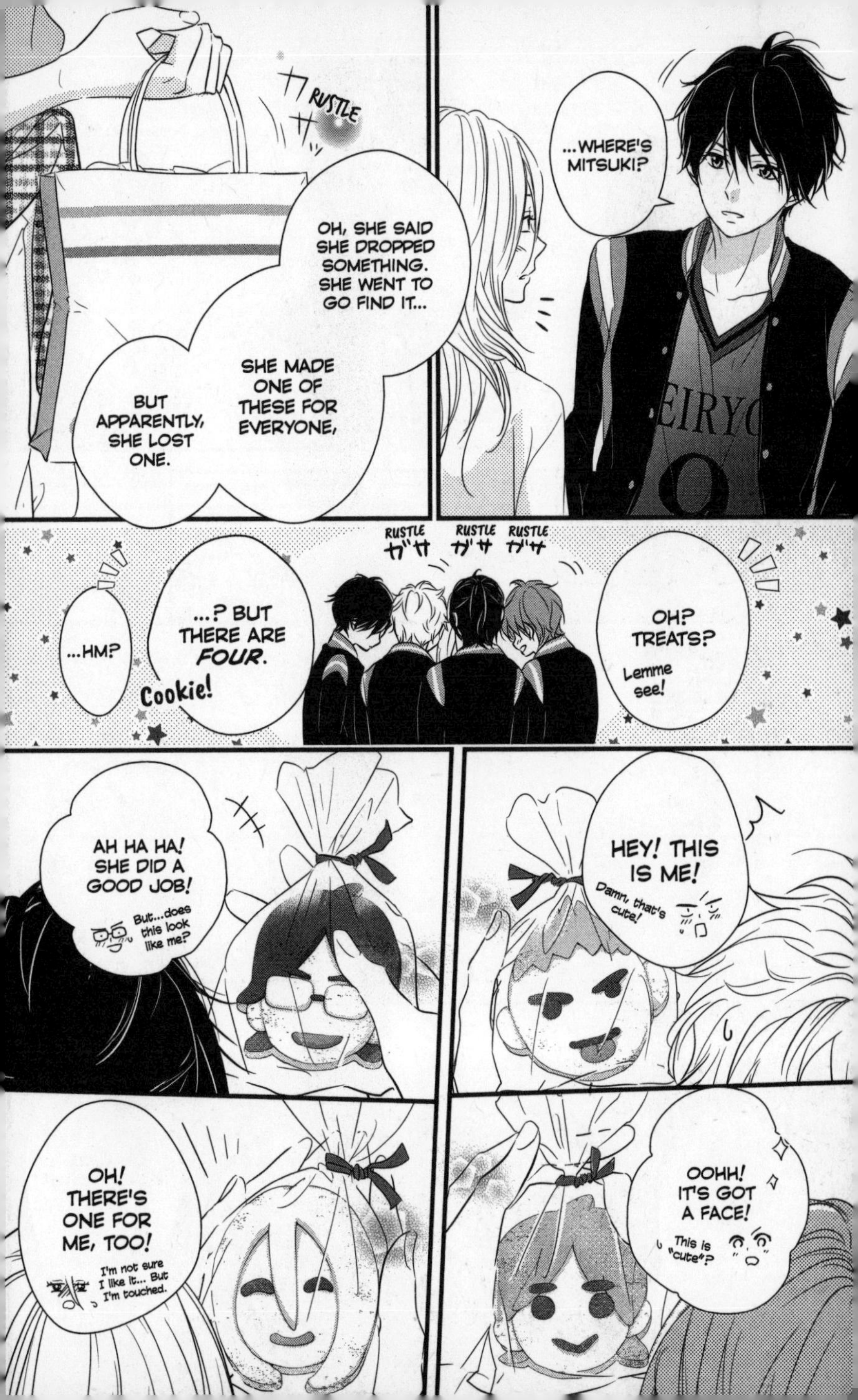
...WHERE'S MITSUKI?
RUSTLE
OH, SHE SAID SHE DROPPED SOMETHING. SHE WENT TO GO FIND IT...
SHE MADE ONE OF THESE FOR EVERYONE,
BUT APPARENTLY, SHE LOST ONE.
OH? TREATS?
Lemme see!
RUSTLE ガサ
RUSTLE ガサ
RUSTLE ガサ
...? BUT THERE ARE FOUR.
Cookie!
...HM?
HEY! THIS IS ME!
Damn, that's cute!
AH HA HA! SHE DID A GOOD JOB!
But...does this look like me?
OOHH! IT'S GOT A FACE!
This is "cute"?
OH! THERE'S ONE FOR ME, TOO!
I'm not sure I like it... But I'm touched.

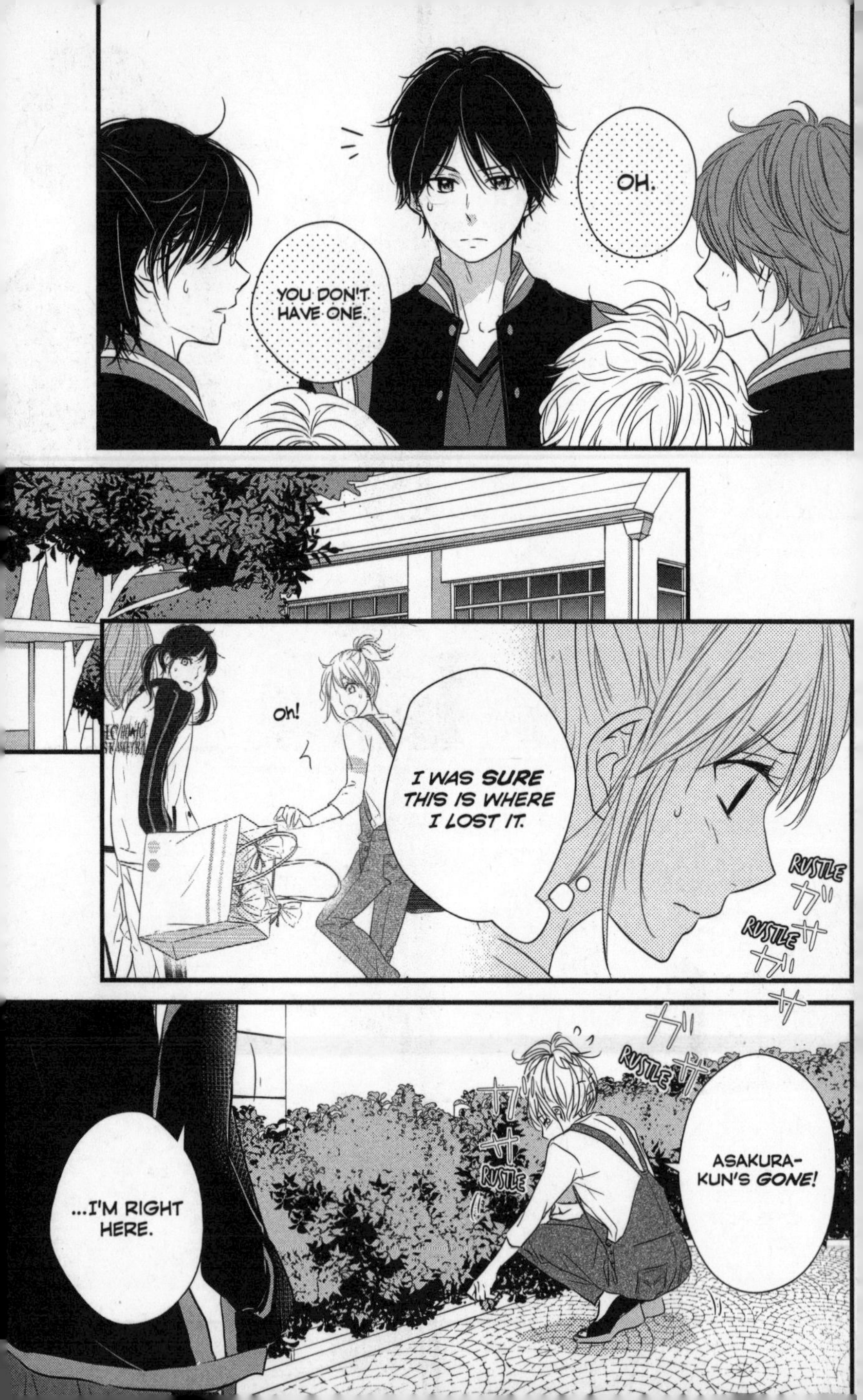
OH.
YOU DON'T HAVE ONE.
RUSTLE
RUSTLE
I WAS SURE THIS IS WHERE I LOST IT.
Oh!
RUSTLE
ASAKURA-KUN'S GONE!
RUSTLE
...I'M RIGHT HERE.

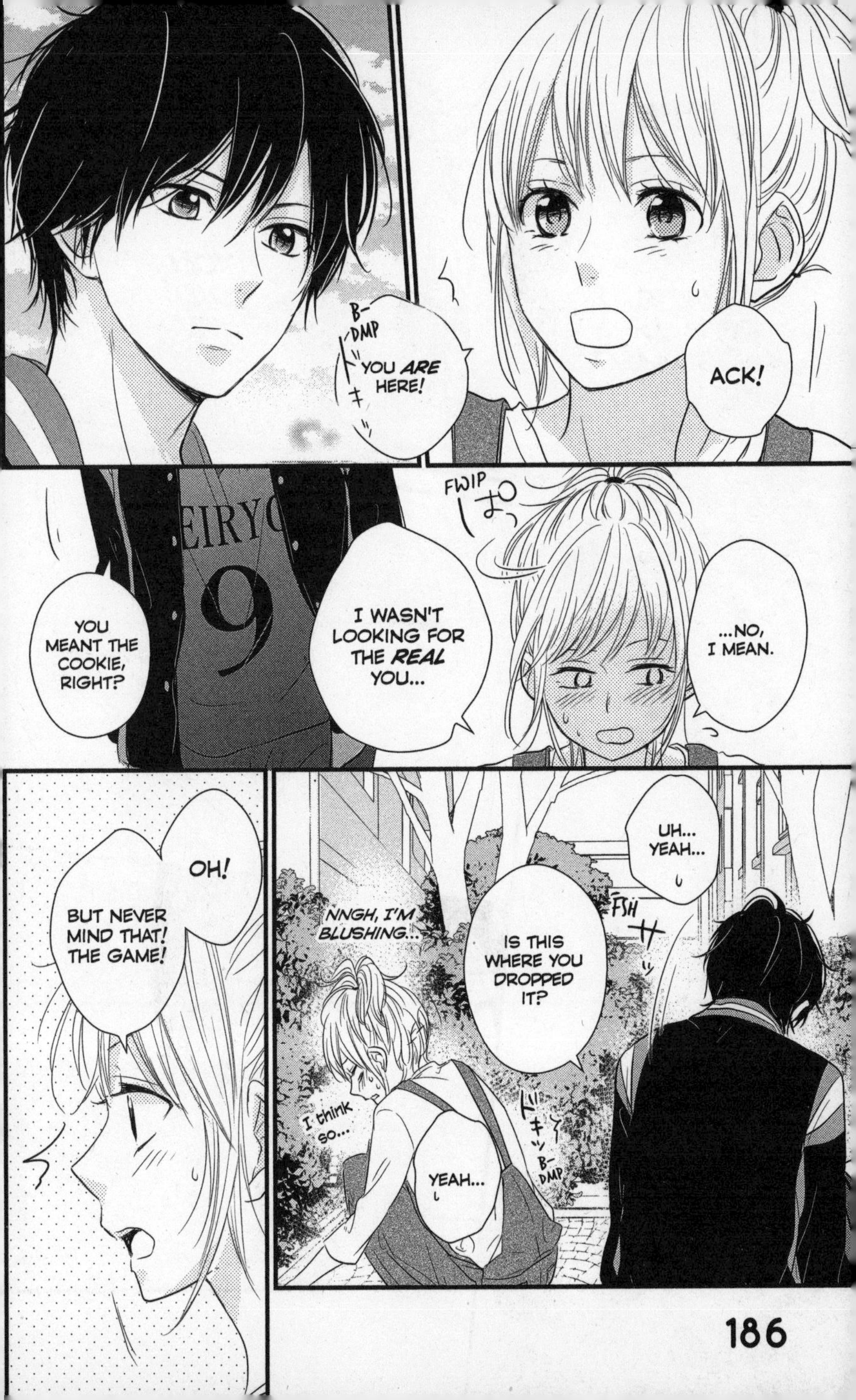
ACK!
B-DMP
YOU ARE HERE!
...NO, I MEAN.
FWIP
I WASN'T LOOKING FOR THE REAL YOU...
YOU MEANT THE COOKIE, RIGHT?
UH... YEAH...
FSH
IS THIS WHERE YOU DROPPED IT?
NNGH, I'M BLUSHING...
B-DMP
YEAH...
I think so...
OH!
BUT NEVER MIND THAT! THE GAME!

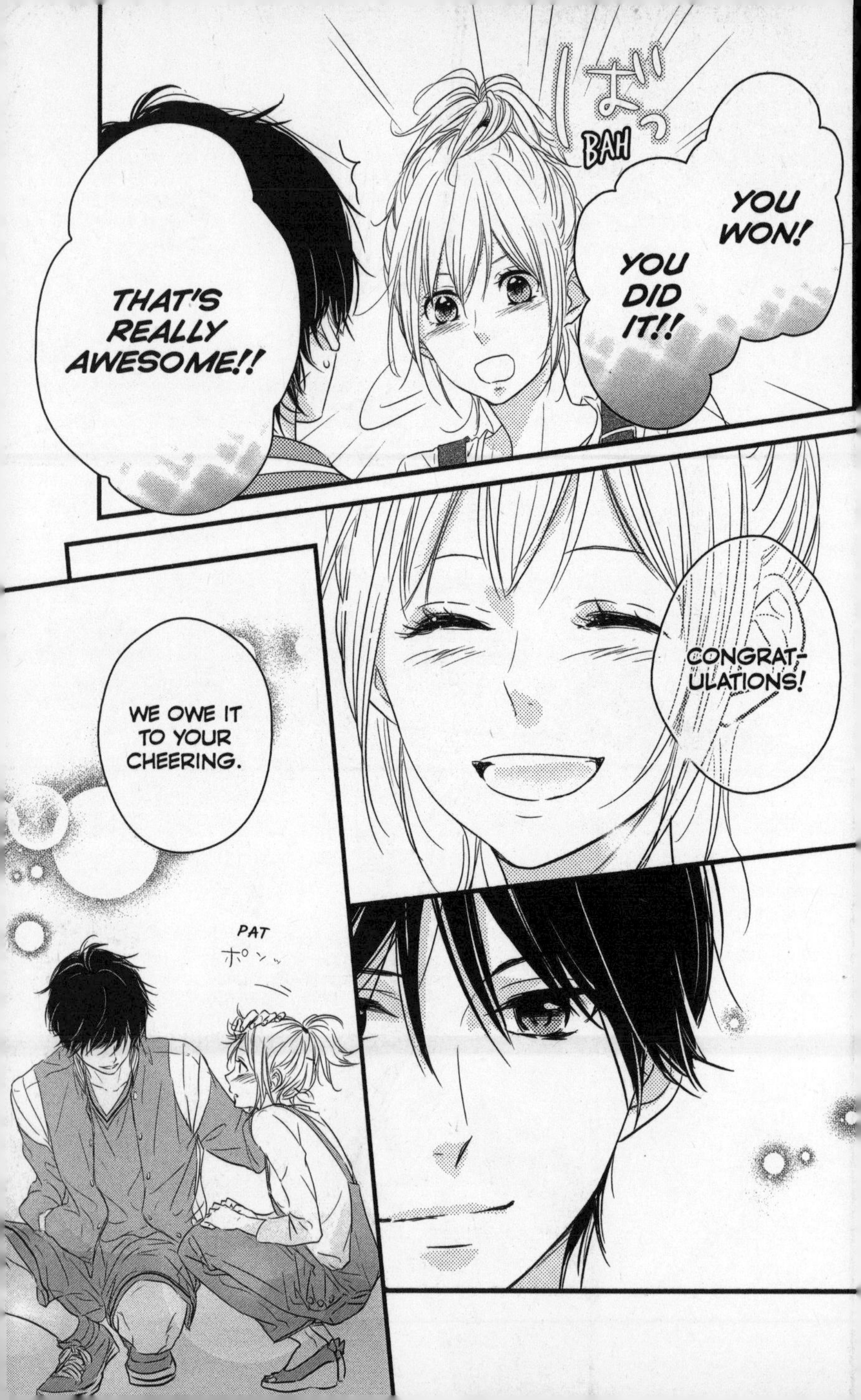
ぱっ
BAH
YOU WON!
YOU DID IT!!
THAT'S REALLY AWESOME!!
CONGRAT-ULATIONS!
WE OWE IT TO YOUR CHEERING.
PAT
ポンッ

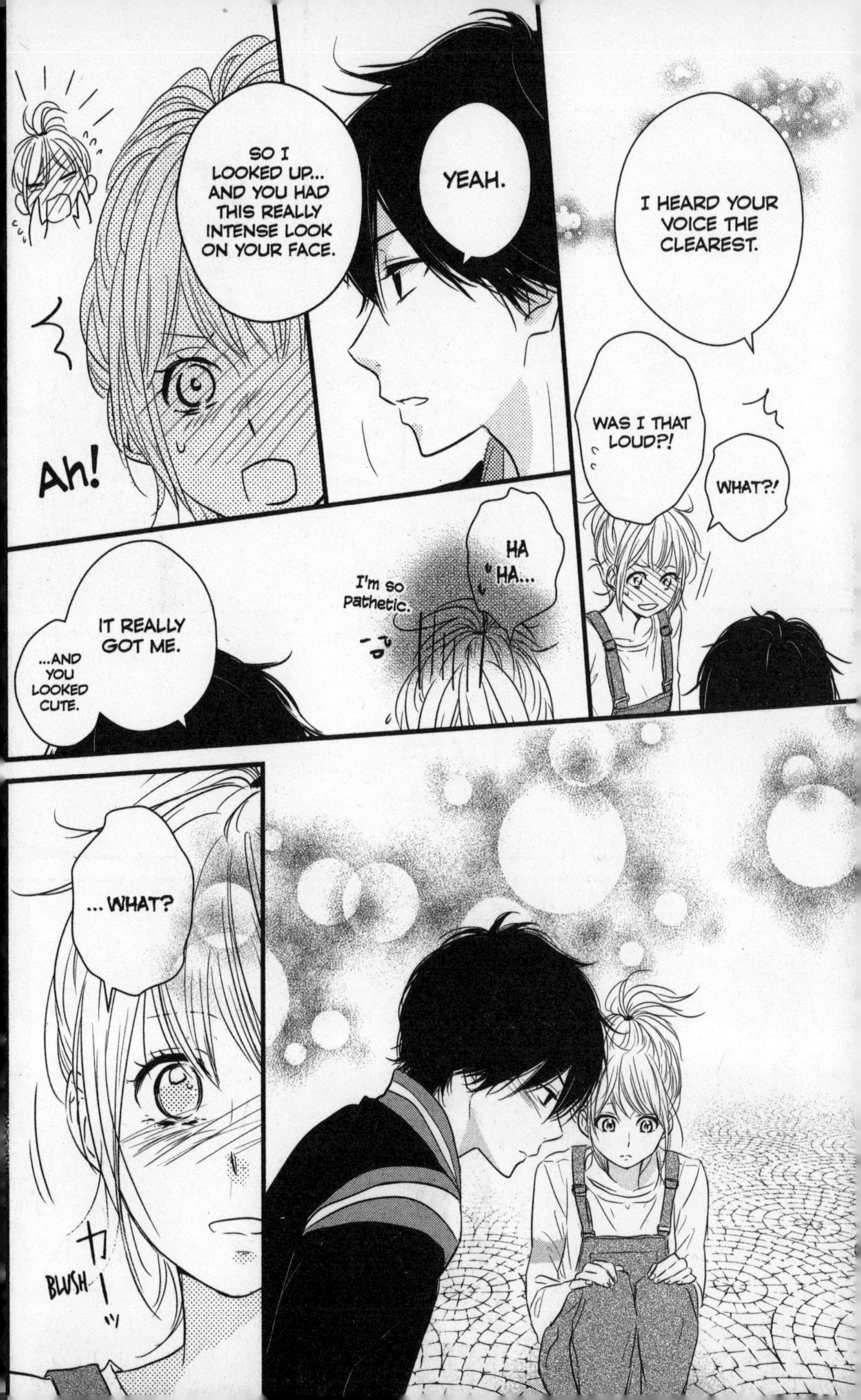
I HEARD YOUR VOICE THE CLEAREST.
WHAT?!
WAS I THAT LOUD?!
YEAH.
SO I LOOKED UP... AND YOU HAD THIS REALLY INTENSE LOOK ON YOUR FACE.
Ah!
HA HA...
I'm so pathetic.
IT REALLY GOT ME.
...AND YOU LOOKED CUTE.
...WHAT?
BLUSH

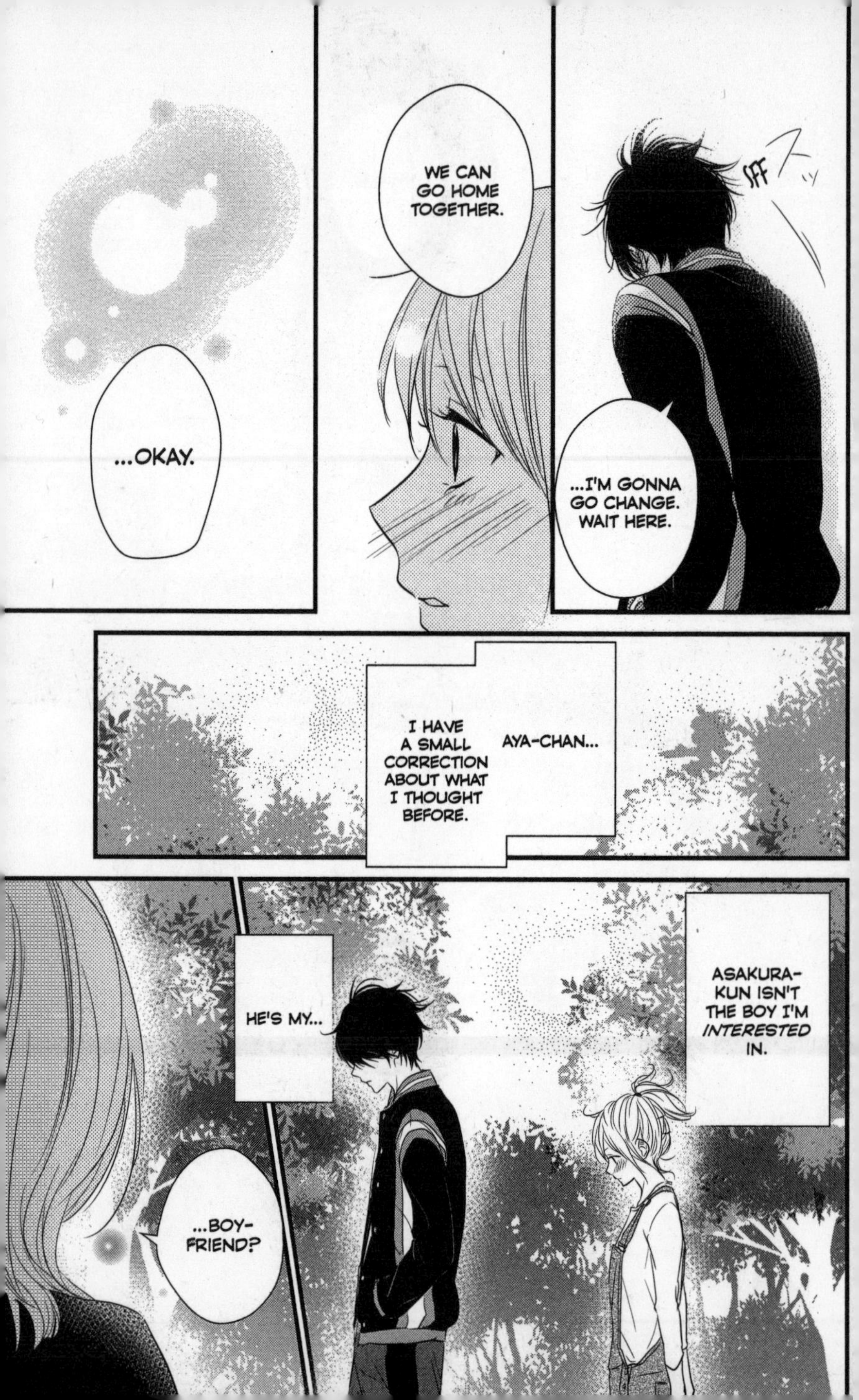
SFF
...I'M GONNA GO CHANGE. WAIT HERE.
WE CAN GO HOME TOGETHER.
...OKAY.
AYA-CHAN...
I HAVE A SMALL CORRECTION ABOUT WHAT I THOUGHT BEFORE.
ASAKURA-KUN ISN'T THE BOY I'M *INTERESTED* IN.
HE'S MY...
...BOY-FRIEND?

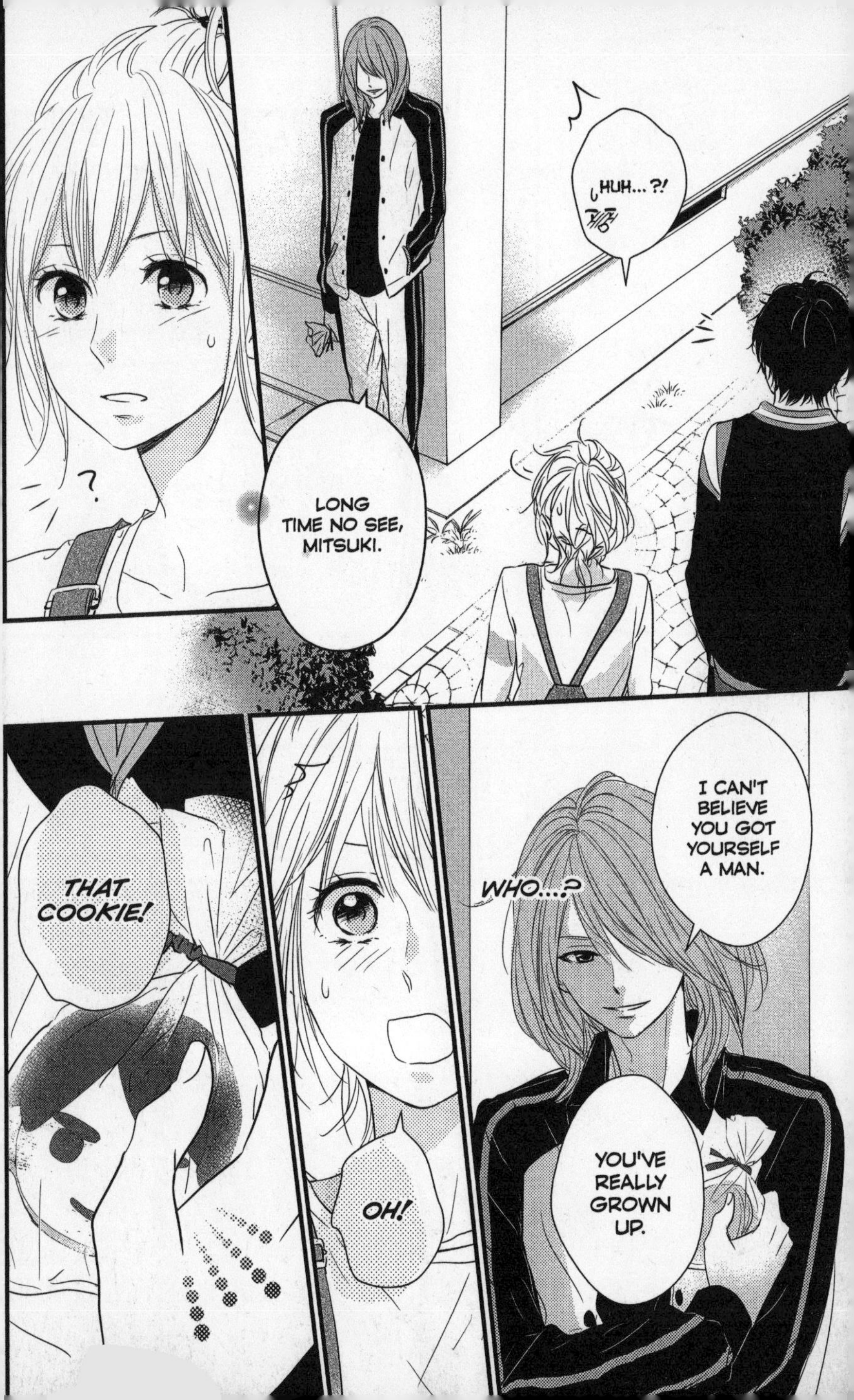
HUH...?!
LONG TIME NO SEE, MITSUKI.
I CAN'T BELIEVE YOU GOT YOURSELF A MAN.
WHO...?
YOU'VE REALLY GROWN UP.
OH!
THAT COOKIE!

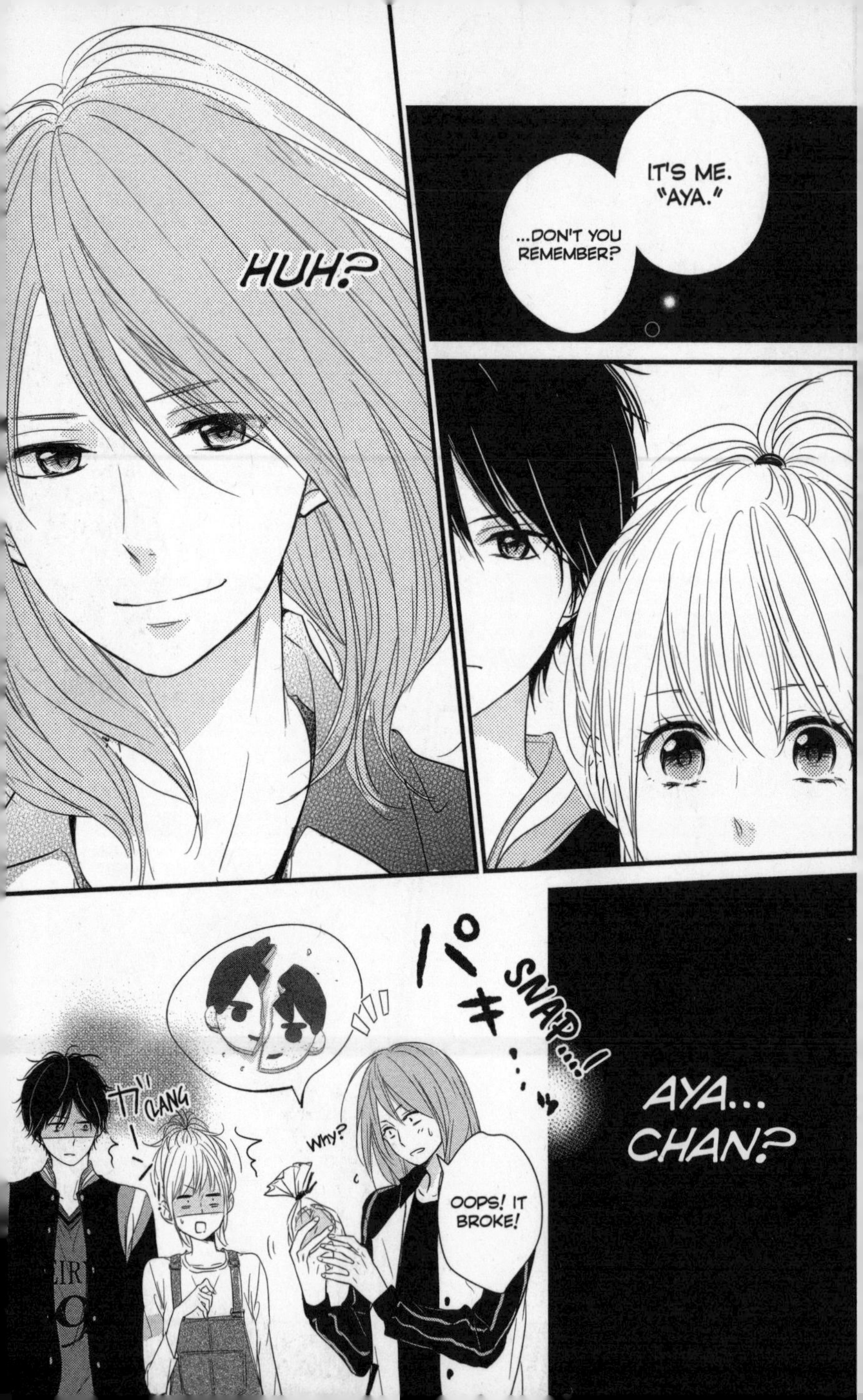
IT'S ME. "AYA."
...DON'T YOU REMEMBER?
HUH?
AYA... CHAN?
パキ
SNAP...!
OOPS! IT BROKE!
Why?
ガ
CLANG

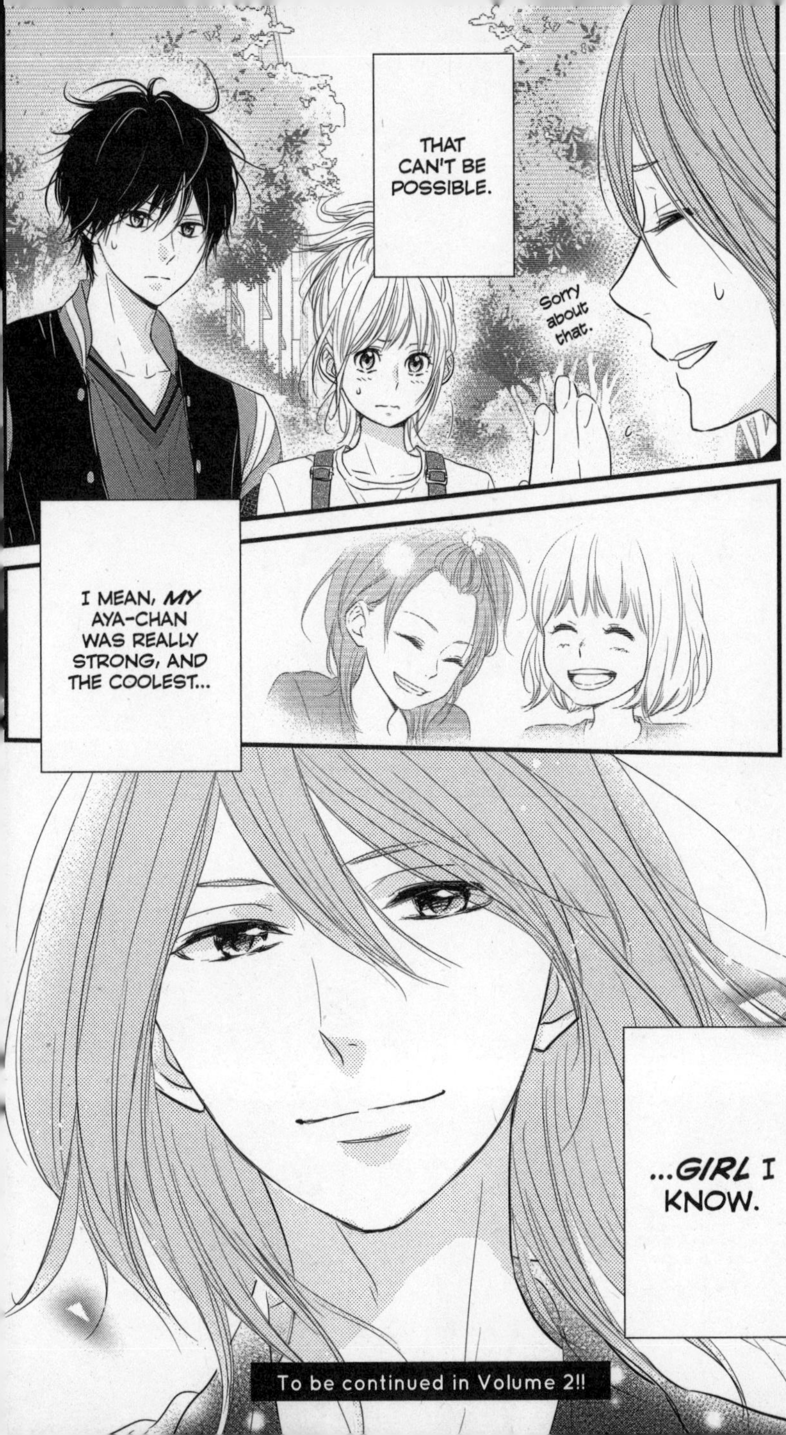
Sorry about that.
THAT CAN'T BE POSSIBLE.
I MEAN, *MY* AYA-CHAN WAS REALLY STRONG, AND THE COOLEST...
...*GIRL* I KNOW.
To be continued in Volume 2!!

Actually Super Sadistic

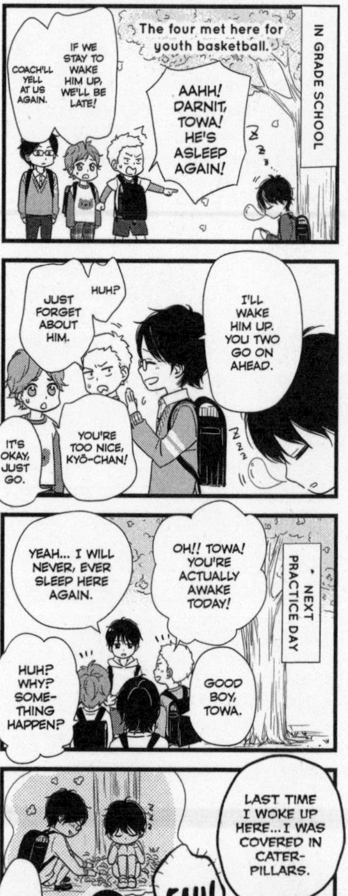
IN GRADE SCHOOL
The four met here for youth basketball.
AAHH! DARNIT, TOWA! HE'S ASLEEP AGAIN!
IF WE STAY TO WAKE HIM UP, WE'LL BE LATE!
COACH'LL YELL AT US AGAIN.
I'LL WAKE HIM UP. YOU TWO GO ON AHEAD.
HUH?
JUST FORGET ABOUT HIM.
YOU'RE TOO NICE, KYŌ-CHAN!
IT'S OKAY, JUST GO.
NEXT PRACTICE DAY
OH!! TOWA! YOU'RE ACTUALLY AWAKE TODAY!
YEAH... I WILL NEVER, EVER SLEEP HERE AGAIN.
GOOD BOY, TOWA.
HUH? WHY? SOMETHING HAPPEN?
LAST TIME I WOKE UP HERE... I WAS COVERED IN CATERPILLARS.
EW!
Heh heh heh...
HE'S LAUGHING...

Something That Happens on Every Basketball Team?

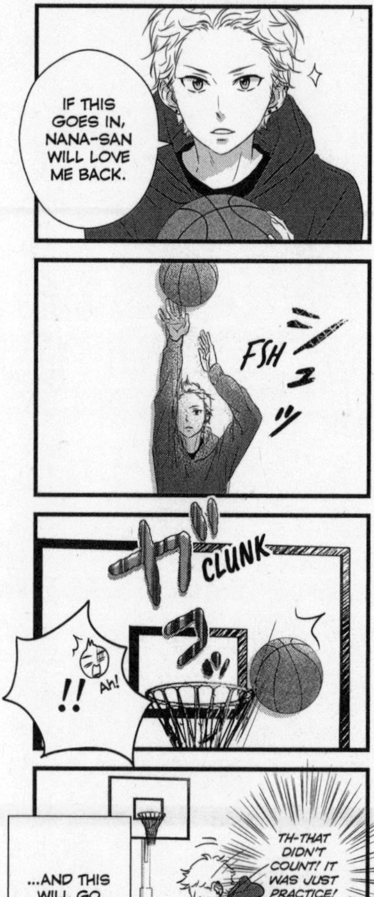
IF THIS GOES IN, NANA-SAN WILL LOVE ME BACK.
FSH
CLUNK
!!
AH!
TH-THAT DIDN'T COUNT! IT WAS JUST PRACTICE!
...AND THIS WILL GO ON UNTIL IT GOES IN.

I did it all the time...

Afterword.

Thank you, everyone who read *Waiting for Spring* 1. Did you enjoy it?
I'm always hyperventilating about deadlines as I draw this series, but when all is said and done, I really do enjoy it. It reminds me of my days on the basketball team, and I shout, "I wanna go to basketball practice!" and weep, "I wish I had had friends like them!" and I really feel how wonderful adolescence is.
And so, I'm going to work hard to make this manga one that will give the readers all the emotions it gives me, in addition to the general enjoyment they'll get from reading this.
I will continue to draw each and every chapter with care, so I hope you'll give it a chance.

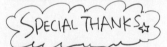
SPECIAL THANKS☆

My editor, everyone on the *Dessert* editorial team, Designer-sama, everyone who was involved in the creation of this work.
My assistants (main assistant Masuda-san, Aki-chan, Bō-chan)
My family, friends, and everyone else who always supports me.

Words Cafe-sama

(A wonderful café in Kita Ward, Osaka)

To everyone who picked up this volume, with my sincerest gratitude,

June 24, 2014   Anashin

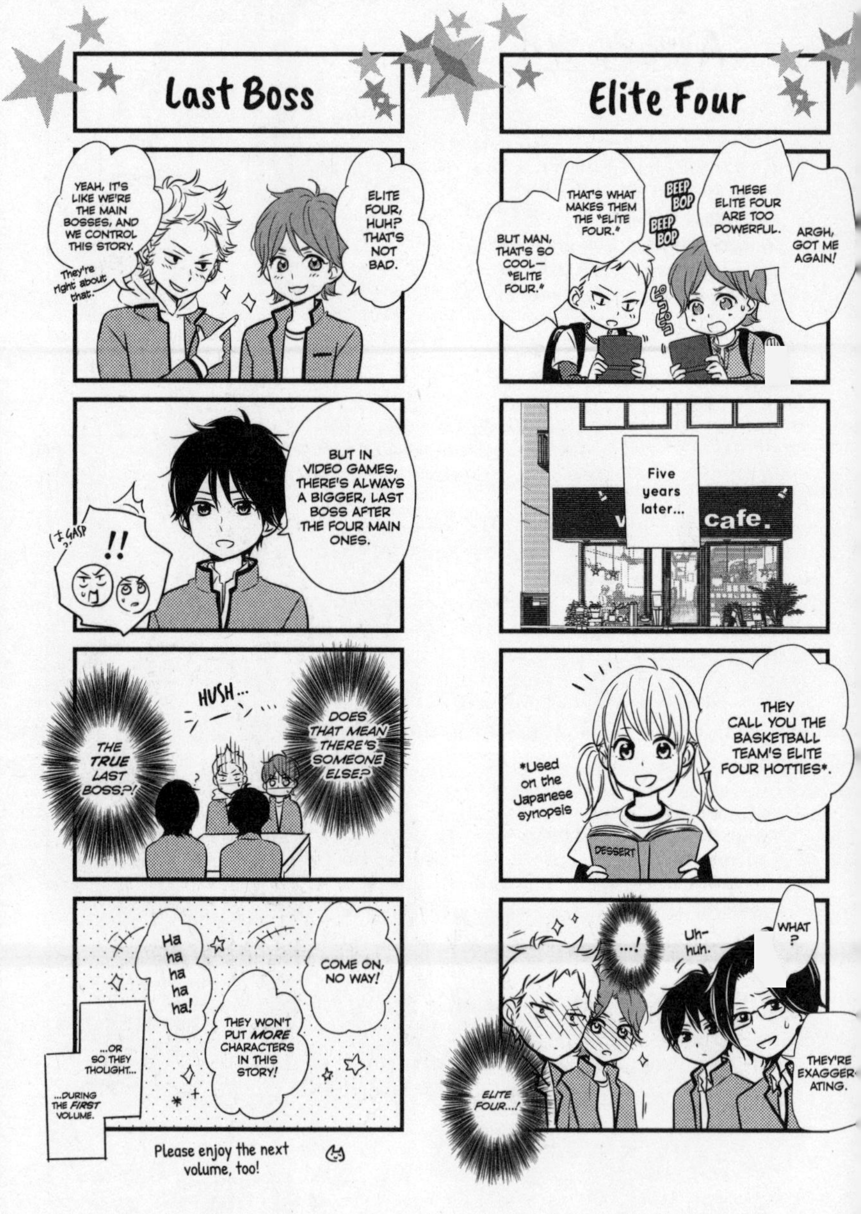
Elite Four
ARGH, GOT ME AGAIN!
THESE ELITE FOUR ARE TOO POWERFUL.
BEEP BOP
BEEP BOP
THAT'S WHAT MAKES THEM THE "ELITE FOUR."
BUT MAN, THAT'S SO COOL—"ELITE FOUR."
cafe.
Five years later...
THEY CALL YOU THE BASKETBALL TEAM'S ELITE FOUR HOTTIES*.
*Used on the Japanese synopsis
DESSERT
WHAT?
THEY'RE EXAGGERATING.
Uh-huh.
...!
ELITE FOUR...!
Last Boss
ELITE FOUR, HUH? THAT'S NOT BAD.
YEAH, IT'S LIKE WE'RE THE MAIN BOSSES, AND WE CONTROL THIS STORY.
They're right about that.
BUT IN VIDEO GAMES, THERE'S ALWAYS A BIGGER, LAST BOSS AFTER THE FOUR MAIN ONES.
!!
は GASP
DOES THAT MEAN THERE'S SOMEONE ELSE?
HUSH...
THE TRUE LAST BOSS?!
COME ON, NO WAY!
THEY WON'T PUT MORE CHARACTERS IN THIS STORY!
Ha ha ha ha ha!
...OR SO THEY THOUGHT...
...DURING THE FIRST VOLUME.
Please enjoy the next volume, too!

Translation Notes

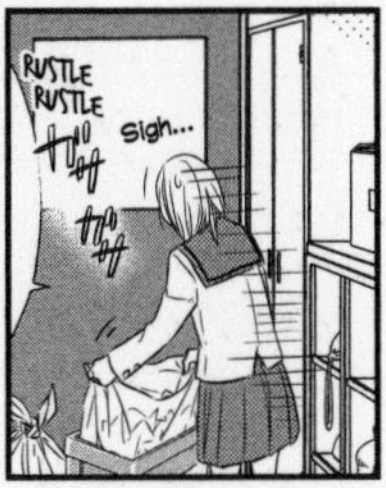
RUSTLE
RUSTLE
Sigh...

I chose a high school, page 8
In Japan, kids don't just go to the school they live closest to. To an extent, they have a choice of what school to attend, and if they're accepted, they're in. There are all kinds of factors that go into choosing a school—prestige, cutest uniforms, convenience, etc. Presumably, Mitsuki chose a high school where there wouldn't be anyone who knew her from her previous schools, thus giving her the chance to start with a clean slate.

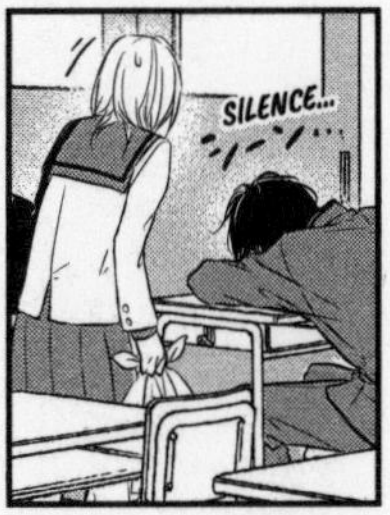
SILENCE...

I know his given name, page 9
In Japan, when you're just getting to know someone, it can be very rude to address them by their given name. Sometimes it's appropriate to ask someone how they prefer to be addressed, but that's not feasible when the addressee is asleep. Mitsuki's safest bet would be to call him by his surname and add the honorific -kun (similar to the English "Mr.", but used in this case for boys the speaker's age or younger), but she doesn't know his surname, and so is at a loss as to how to address him. It is unclear what makes the girls think they can get away with calling them by his first name—he may have given them permission, or they might just be shameless fangirls talking about their favorite celebrity. Either way, Mitsuki doesn't want to be rude, so she would prefer to use his surname.

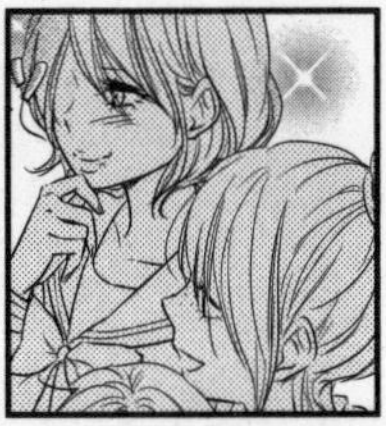

If you could see him blush, page 12
More specifically, this girl wants to see Ryūji act *dere-dere*, which is a state in which a person cannot hide feelings of love and affection, and usually involves blushing. The acts of a person in such a state are especially endearing when that person has a normally unsentimental personality.

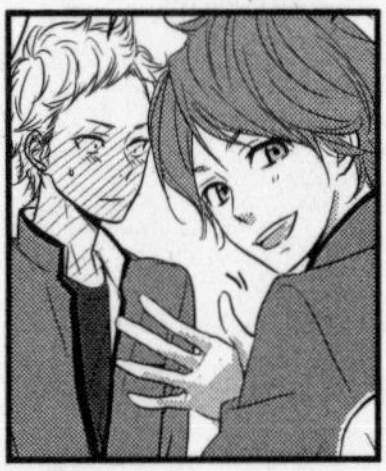

Nanase-nēsan, page 24
Nēsan (pronounced nay-sahn) is an honorific used to address young women. It means "older sister," and so expresses a little more familiarity than a simple -san.

Roll up our sleeves, page 88
There is a saying in Japanese used in reference to helping people that translates as "to strip a layer of skin," but of course it's not meant literally. It comes from the days when everyone wore kimono, and the "skin" in question actually refers to the kimono. When helping with physical tasks, the sleeves of the kimono would get in the way, so in order to get more involved, the helper would take his arm out of one sleeve of the kimono, thus bearing his arm and shoulder. Here, Towa uses a much shorter version of the saying and asks, "Want me to strip?"

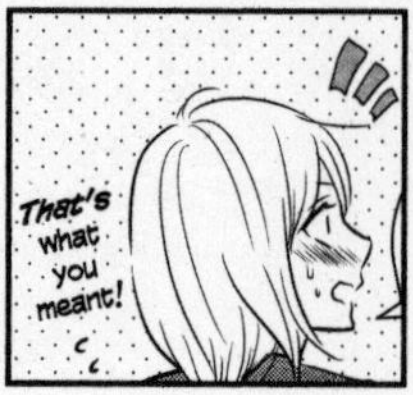
That's what you meant!

Chocolates and birthday gifts, page 108
Rui's birthday happens to fall on Valentine's Day, which is a little different in Japan than it is in North America. Traditionally in Japan, Valentine's Day is the day girls give chocolate to the men and boys in their lives, often to show appreciation for their friendship or help at work or school, but also to show a particular boy that she is interested in him romantically. Rui is popular enough that he is sure to get chocolates from several girls with whom he may or may not already be acquainted, but it's still presumptuous of him to assume that one of those girls will be Mitsuki.

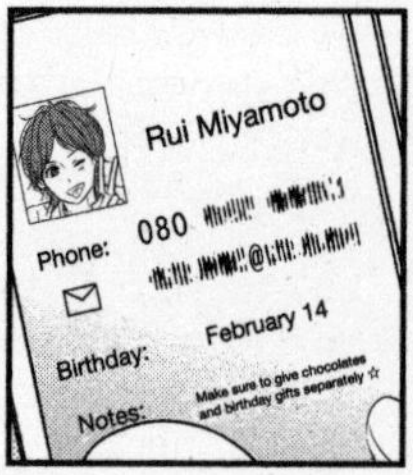
Rui Miyamoto
Phone:
080
Birthday:
February 14
Notes:
Make sure to give chocolates and birthday gifts separately ☆

We have to get to our next class, page 142
More accurately, Mitsuki says, "We're moving next," or in other words, "Our next class is in a different room." In Japanese high schools, the students stay in one classroom most of the day, while the teachers move around each period to teach the various subjects. The exceptions to this include P.E. and other classes that require special equipment such as a science class, which would be held in the science lab. Since she didn't specify that they're going to the gym, they're probably going to a science, cooking, or other such class.

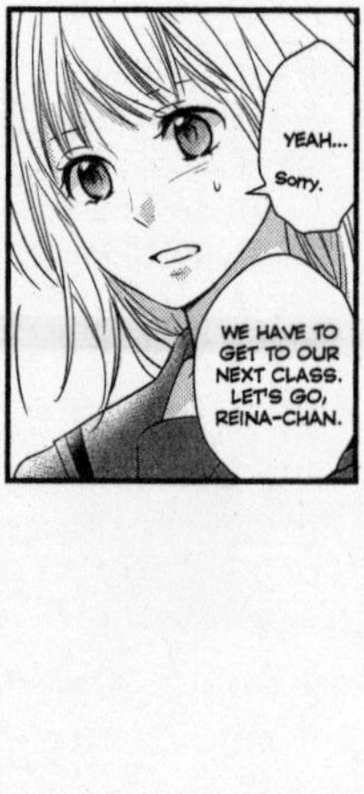
YEAH... Sorry.
WE HAVE TO GET TO OUR NEXT CLASS. LET'S GO, REINA-CHAN.

A new series from the creator of *Soul Eater*, the megahit manga and anime seen on Toonami!

"Fun and lively... a great start!"
-Adventures in Poor Taste

FIRE FORCE

By Atsushi Ohkubo

The city of Tokyo is plagued by a deadly phenomenon: spontaneous human combustion! Luckily, a special team is there to quench the inferno: The Fire Force! The fire soldiers at Special Fire Cathedral 8 are about to get a unique addition. Enter Shinra, a boy who possesses the power to run at the speed of a rocket, leaving behind the famous "devil's footprints" (and destroying his shoes in the process). Can Shinra and his colleagues discover the source of this strange epidemic before the city burns to ashes?

The Black Museum The Ghost and the Lady

By Kazuhiro Fujita

Deep in Scotland Yard in London sits an evidence room dedicated to the greatest mysteries of British history. In this "Black Museum" sits a misshapen hunk of lead—two bullets fused together—the key to a wartime encounter between Florence Nightingale, the mother of modern nursing, and a supernatural Man in Grey. This story is unknown to most scholars of history, but a special guest of the museum will tell the tale of *The Ghost and the Lady...*

Praise for Kazuhiro Fujita's *Ushio and Tora*

"A charming revival that combines a classic look with modern depth and pacing... **Essential viewing both for curmudgeons and new fans alike.**" — Anime News Network

"**GREAT!** The first episode of *Ushio and Tora* captures the essence of '90s anime." — IGN

HAPPINESS

ハピネス

By Shuzo Oshimi

From the creator of *The Flowers of Evil*

Nothing interesting is happening in Makoto Ozaki's first year of high school. HIs life is a series of quiet humiliations: low-grade bullies, unreliable friends, and the constant frustration of his adolescent lust. But one night, a pale, thin girl knocks him to the ground in an alley and offers him a choice.

Now everything is different. Daylight is searingly bright. Food tastes awful. And worse than anything is the terrible, consuming thirst...

Praise for Shuzo Oshimi's *The Flowers of Evil*

"A shockingly readable story that vividly—one might even say queasily—evokes the fear and confusion of discovering one's own sexuality. Recommended." —The Manga Critic

"A page-turning tale of sordid middle school blackmail." —Otaku USA Magazine

"A stunning new horror manga." —Third Eye Comics

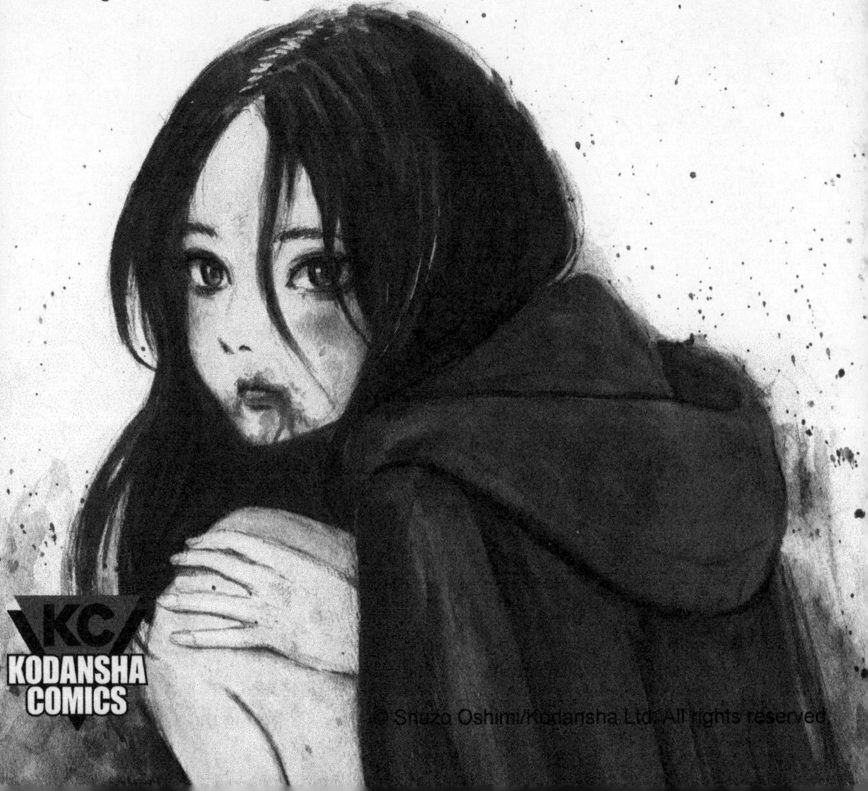

KODANSHA COMICS

KC
KODANSHA
COMICS

Japan's most powerful spirit medium delves into the ghost world's greatest mysteries!

Story by Kyo Shirodaira, famed author of mystery fiction and creator of *Spiral*, *Blast of Tempest*, and *The Record of a Fallen Vampire*.

Both touched by spirits called yôkai, Kotoko and Kurô have gained unique superhuman powers. But to gain her powers Kotoko has given up an eye and a leg, and Kurô's personal life is in shambles. So when Kotoko suggests they team up to deal with renegades from the spirit world, Kurô doesn't have many other choices, but Kotoko might just have a few ulterior motives...

IN/SPECTRE

STORY BY **KYO SHIRODAIRA**
ART BY **CHASHIBA KATASE**

KC
KODANSHA
COMICS

New action series from Hiroyuki Takei, creator of the classic shonen franchise Shaman King!

In medieval Japan, a bell hanging on the collar is a sign that a cat has a master. Norachiyo's bell hangs from his katana sheath, but he is nonetheless a stray — a ronin. This one-eyed cat samurai travels across a dishonest world, cutting through pretense and deception with his blade.

NEKOGAHARA

STRAY CAT SAMURAI

By
Hiroyuki Takei

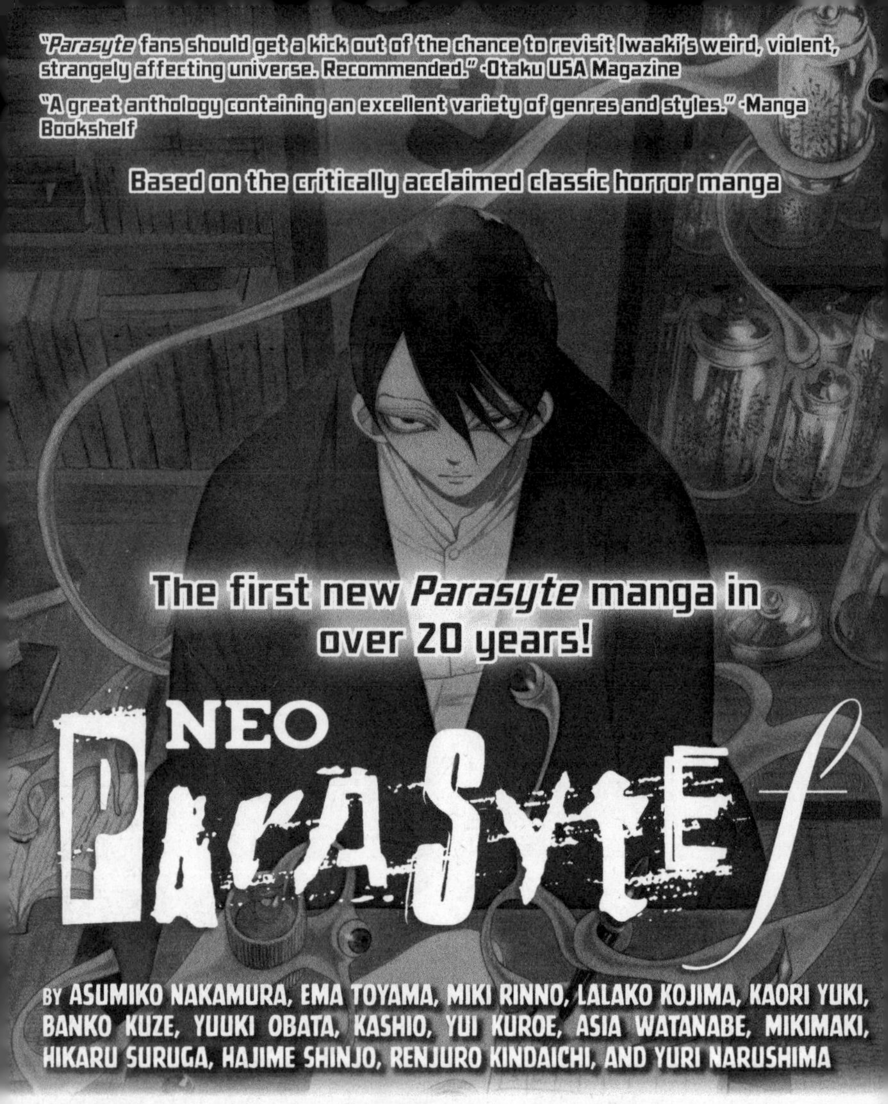

Based on the critically acclaimed classic horror manga

The first new *Parasyte* manga in over 20 years!

NEO Parasyte f

BY ASUMIKO NAKAMURA, EMA TOYAMA, MIKI RINNO, LALAKO KOJIMA, KAORI YUKI, BANKO KUZE, YUUKI OBATA, KASHIO, YUI KUROE, ASIA WATANABE, MIKIMAKI, HIKARU SURUGA, HAJIME SHINJO, RENJURO KINDAICHI, AND YURI NARUSHIMA

A collection of chilling new *Parasyte* stories from Japan's top shojo artists!

Parasites: shape-shifting aliens whose only purpose is to assimilate with and consume the human race... but do these monsters have a different side? A parasite becomes a prince to save his romance-obsessed female host from a dangerous stalker. Another hosts a cooking show, in which the real monsters are revealed. These and 13 more stories, from some of the greatest shojo manga artists alive today, together make up a chilling, funny, and entertaining tribute to one of manga's horror classics!

KC KODANSHA COMICS

KC
KODANSHA
COMICS

"I'm pleasantly surprised to find modern shojo using cross-dressing as a dramatic device to deliver social commentary... Recommended."

-Otaku USA Magazine

The prince in his dark days

By **Hico Yamanaka**

A drunkard for a father, a household of poverty... For 17-year-old Atsuko, misfortune is all she knows and believes in. Until one day, a chance encounter with Itaru–the wealthy heir of a huge corporation–changes everything. The two look identical, uncannily so. When Itaru curiously goes missing, Atsuko is roped into being his stand-in. There, in his shoes, Atsuko must parade like a prince in a palace. She encounters many new experiences, but at what cost…?

Having lost his wife, high school teacher Kōhei Inuzuka is doing his best to raise his young daughter Tsumugi as a single father. He's pretty bad at cooking and doesn't have a huge appetite to begin with, but chance brings his little family together with one of his students, the lonely Kotori. The three of them are anything but comfortable in the kitchen, but the healing power of home cooking might just work on their grieving hearts.

"This season's number-one feel-good anime!" —Anime News Network

"A beautifully-drawn story about comfort food and family and grief. Recommended." —Otaku USA Magazine

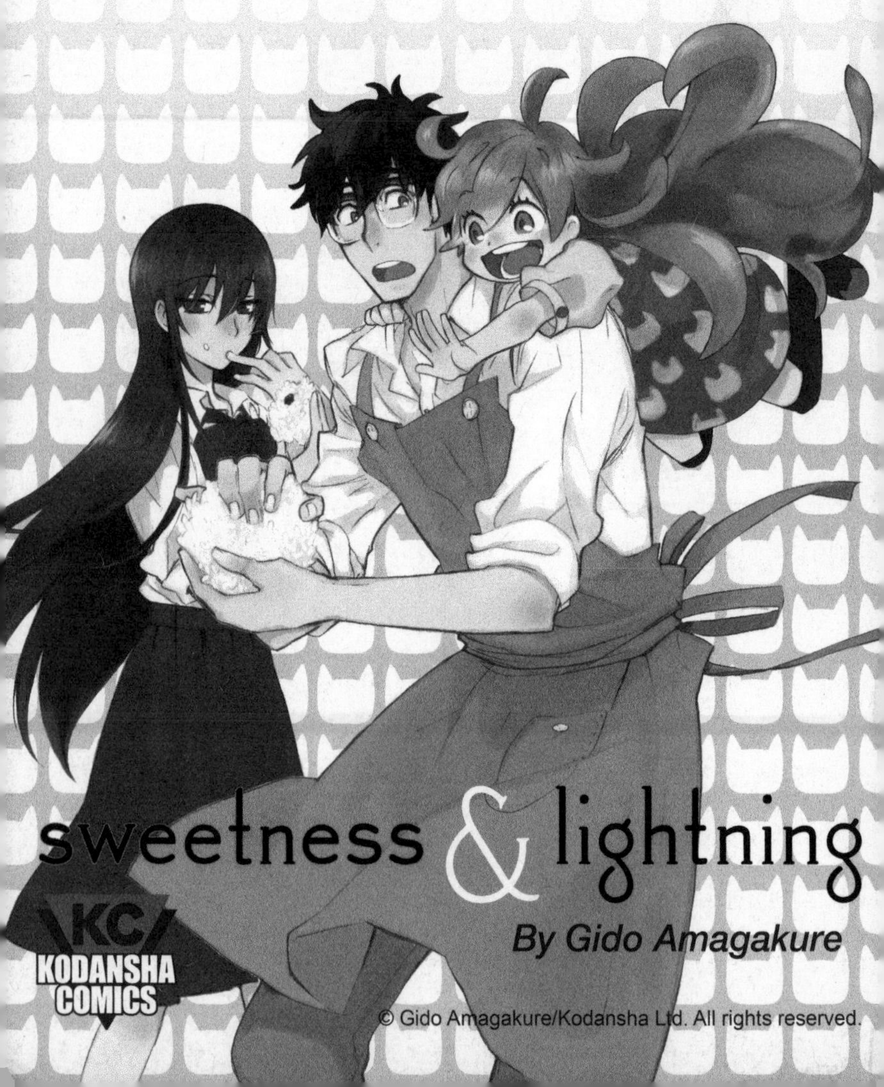
sweetness & lightning
By Gido Amagakure
KC
KODANSHA
COMICS
© Gido Amagakure/Kodansha Ltd. All rights reserved.

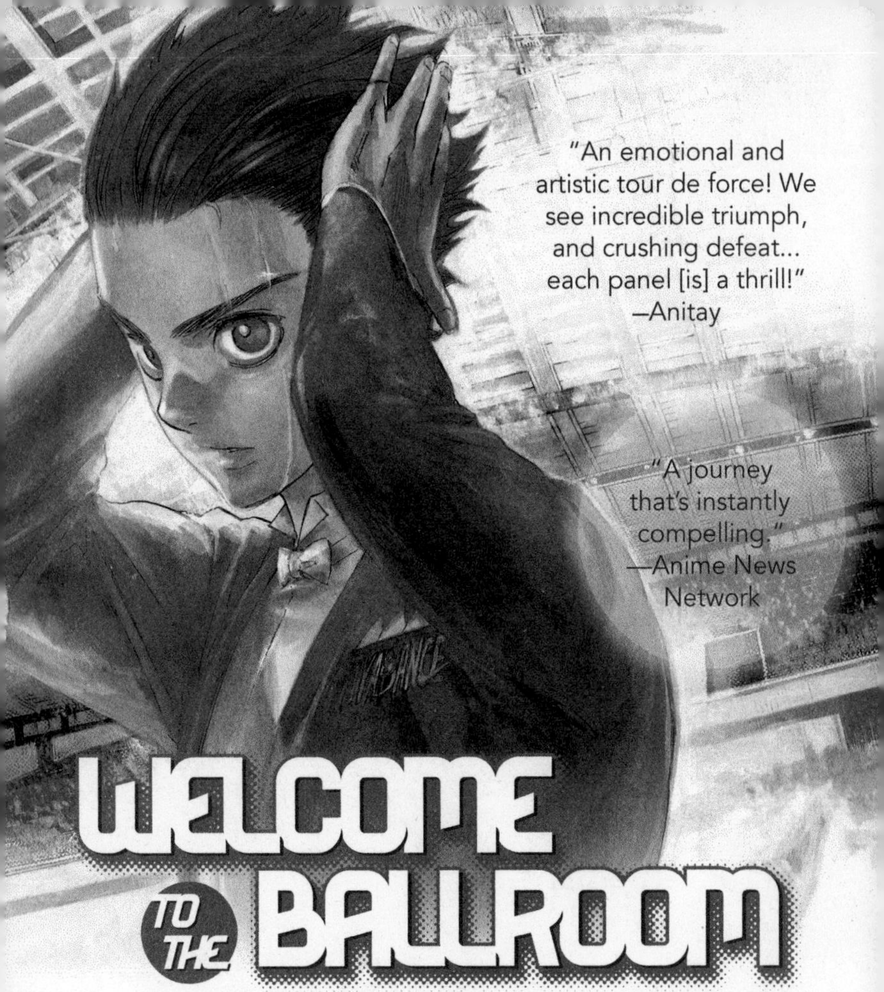

"An emotional and artistic tour de force! We see incredible triumph, and crushing defeat... each panel [is] a thrill!"
—Anitay

"A journey that's instantly compelling."
—Anime News Network

WELCOME TO THE BALLROOM

By Tomo Takeuchi

Feckless high school student Tatara Fujita wants to be good at something—anything. Unfortunately, he's about as average as a slouchy teen can be. The local bullies know this, and make it a habit to hit him up for cash, but all that changes when the debonair Kaname Sengoku sends them packing. Sengoku's not the neighborhood watch, though. He's a professional ballroom dancer. And once Tatara Fujita gets pulled into the world of ballroom, his life will never be the same.

KC KODANSHA COMICS

The award-winning manga about what happens inside you!

"Far more entertaining than it ought to be... what kid doesn't want to think that every time they sneeze a torpedo shoots out their nose?"
–Anime News Network

Strep throat! Hay fever! Influenza! The world is a dangerous place for a red blood cell just trying to get her deliveries finished. Fortunately, she's not alone...she's got a whole human body's worth of cells ready to help out! The mysterious white blood cells, the buff and brash killer T cells, even the cute little platelets—everyone's got to come together if they want to keep you healthy!

Cells at Work!

はたらく細胞

By Akane Shimizu

Waiting for Spring volume 1 is a work of fiction. Names, characters, places, and incidents are the products of the author's imagination or are used fictitiously. Any resemblance to actual events, locales, or persons, living or dead, is entirely coincidental.

A Kodansha Comics Trade Paperback Original

Published in the United States by Kodansha Comics, an imprint of Kodansha USA Publishing, LLC, New York.

Publication rights for this English edition arranged through Kodansha Ltd, Tokyo.

ISBN 978-1-63236-516-3

Printed in the United States of America.

www.kodanshacomics.com

9 8 7 6 5 4 3 2 1
Translation: Alethea and Athena Nibley
Lettering: Sara Linsley
Editing: Ajani Oloye
Kodansha Comics edition cover design by Phil Balsman